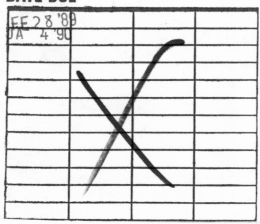

Fear
No
Evil

Natan
Sharansky

Fear No Evil

Translated by Stefani Hoffman

 Random House New York

Copyright© 1988 by Random House, Inc. All rights reserved under International and Pan-American Copyright Conventions. Published in the United States by Random House, Inc., New York and simultaneously in Canada by Random House of Canada Limited, Toronto.

Library of Congress Cataloging-in-Publication Data
Shcharansky, Anatoly.
    Fear no evil / by Natan Sharansky; translated from the Russian by Stefani Hoffman.
        p. cm.
    Includes index.
    ISBN 0-394-55878-2
    1. Shcharanksky, Anatoly—Imprisonment, 1977-1986. 2. Jews—Soviet
Union—Biography. 3. Refuseniks—Biography. 4. Political
prisoners—Soviet Union—Biography. 5. Civil rights—Soviet Union.
I. Title.
DS135.R95S497   1988
323.4′092′4—dc19
[B]   87-43228
        CIP

Manufactured in the United States of America
98765432
First Edition

Book design by Bernard Klein

To my mother and my Avital

Contents

Preface

SHORTLY after six o'clock on the evening of March 15, 1977, I was abducted by the KGB outside an apartment on Gorky Street in downtown Moscow and brought to Lefortovo Prison. There the KGB charged me with espionage and treason against the Soviet Union, crimes punishable by death. I spent the next nine years in prison and labor camp, mainly on a special disciplinary regime, including more than four hundred days in punishment cells, and more than two hundred days on hunger strikes. During the long months of interrogation and isolation before my trial, and for all the years that followed, my captors were determined to break me, to make me confess to crimes I had never committed, and then to parade me before the world. They wanted to use me to destroy the two groups I worked for—Jews who hoped to leave for Israel and dissidents who spoke out on behalf of human rights. This book is about what happened to me during nearly a decade as a prisoner of the KGB. It is the story of a charade the Soviets call their system of law. It is the story of how I survived.

But first, a little of my background. I was only five when Stalin died, but the memory of that day in 1953 is still clear in my mind. Solemn music filled the streets from the radio loudspeakers, and the people of Stalino, as the Ukrainian city of Donetsk was known in those days, wore black armbands. Enormous portraits of Stalin hung everywhere. "No laughing or rowdiness today," explained our kindergarten teacher. "This is a very sad day. Joseph Vissarionovich Stalin, our leader and teacher, is dead."

To me Stalin was merely a symbol, a word from a verse we

repeated like an oath in kindergarten—"Thank you, Comrade Stalin, for our happy childhood"—or from the song we marched to: "Moscow and Peking, Moscow and Peking, Russians and Chinese are brothers forever; Stalin and Mao are watching over us." But the announcement that kindergarten would be closed for several days of mourning—that was very real, and on my way home it was hard not to smile.

Mama was crying when I came in, and only later did I learn the real reason for her tears: she was afraid of pogroms. During Stalin's final days his revived campaign of anti-Semitism, which was especially virulent in the Ukraine, had grown even more heated. Who knew what terrible events might follow in the wake of his death?

Earlier that day, Mama had been in the town square, where people gathered to listen to the news. As Mama watched in horror a man walked up to an old Jewish woman and slapped her in the face. "Damn kikes," he shouted. "You killed our Stalin and now you're crying?" Nobody came to her defense, and my brother and I weren't allowed to leave the apartment for days.

My father was a journalist, with his own views on educating children. Whether the topic was sex or politics, he wanted us to learn the facts from him, rather than in the streets. He told me and my brother, Leonid, who was seven, that Stalin had killed many innocent people, that in his final years he had begun persecuting Jews, and that we were very fortunate that this terrible butcher was dead. Papa warned us not to repeat these comments to anyone.

This was when I first learned that in order to survive in Soviet society you had to function on two levels at once: what you really thought and what you allowed yourself to tell other people. I lived with this dual reality until 1973, when I joined the *aliyah* movement of Jews who were struggling for their right to emigrate to Israel. (*Aliyah* is Hebrew for "ascent," and refers to the process of moving to Israel.) Now, for the first time in my life, I was no longer afraid to say what I really believed—about my fellow citizens, the country I lived in, and the values I adhered to. At the age of twenty-five I finally learned what a joy it was to be free.

Papa was born in Odessa in 1904, which made him thirteen at the time of the Revolution. His father was a religious Zionist who had dreamed of moving to Palestine, and Papa's older brother had fulfilled this dream and changed his name from Sharansky to Sharon. But, like most of his generation, Papa had believed that the Revolution would solve the Jewish problem, and that the destiny of the Jews was to work together with other peoples to create an earthly paradise.

But it didn't work out that way.

When I was young, Papa taught me that being Jewish was nothing to be ashamed of, which was an important lesson in a society where well-bred people considered it vulgar to use the word "Jew" in the presence of a Jew. Like most of my generation, I grew up completely unaware of the religion, language, culture, and history of my people. Words like Torah, Passover, Yom Kippur, and even Shabbat meant nothing to us. But Papa was a storyteller, and he sometimes told us tales from the Bible—about Joseph and his brothers, or Samson and Delilah. Did these stories leave a special imprint on my soul? Did I feel that this was *my* history, that those were *my* ancestors who went down to Egypt to escape the famine in their own land, and ended up in slavery? If so, those feelings lay dormant for years.

No, in those days my conscious association with the word "Jew" was limited to the bureaucratic phrase "fifth line." In the identity papers of my parents and most of our acquaintances, the word *Yevrei,* Jew, was filled in under "Nationality" in the fifth line of the document. Above all, it meant that your opportunities in Soviet society were severely limited.

Officially, of course, there were no barriers for Jews. But I grew up hearing constant references to the fifth line, which explained why X didn't get a certain job or Y wasn't accepted into an outstanding institute despite his qualifications, or why there was no point in applying to this school or that hospital because they already had a Jew there "and the director doesn't want to be accused of turning the place into a synagogue." This phrase, incidentally, was the only context where I ever heard the word "synagogue" as a child. There were approximately fifty thousand Jews in Donetsk, but no synagogues. Nor were there any Jewish schools—not in Donetsk or anywhere else in the country. No Hebrew books were published in the Soviet Union, and there were no opportunities to study Hebrew or Jewish history.

Not that I felt any pull in these directions. In those days the beginning and the end of my Jewishness was an awareness of anti-Semitism. As an adolescent I had come across some lines of Julian Tuwim, a Polish-Jewish poet who wrote after the Holocaust that he felt himself Polish by virtue of the blood flowing in his veins (by which he meant Polish culture and literature), and Jewish by virtue of the blood that flowed *out* of his veins. In other words, when Jews were attacked he felt a solidarity with them. I felt that Tuwim was speaking for me. I loved Russian culture, and it was from Tolstoy and Dostoevsky, Chekhov and Bulgakov, that I derived all my dissident passion—or so I thought. But I was a Jew because of anti-Semitism. If it had ever disappeared, I would have been happy to declare myself a Russian.

Because Jews of my generation had no desire to live a double life, or to be handicapped by a Jewish affiliation that meant little to us, we constantly looked for a means of escape. For many of us the scientific-technological revolution arrived at precisely the right time, with the world of science as a kind of castle where you could protect yourself from the shifting winds of official ideology. But first you had to be accepted into one of these castles, which was far from being a routine procedure. I applied to the Moscow Institute of Physics and Technology, the leading school of its kind, which liked to compare itself with M.I.T. Although officially there were no restrictions, it was well known that Jewish applicants had to score especially high to be admitted. (Two years later, in the aftermath of the Six-Day War, the institute became completely closed to Jews.)

I was euphoric when they accepted me, for now nothing could prevent me from delving into the eternal mysteries of life. But the self-congratulatory fanfare ringing in my ears could not entirely jam the soft but insistent voice from deep within me, a voice that wondered whether I wasn't trying to separate myself from my people and my fate.

Twenty years before Gorbachev, our institute was a bastion of *glasnost.* Having apparently decided that we were *Wunderkinder* who could not be brainwashed with official propaganda, the authorities didn't even try. As a result, our restrictions were not as clearly drawn as they were for most Soviet citizens. Even so, the message was clear: All this talk about rights, freedom, justice—it's only talk. What do these words really mean when compared with the laws of Newton, Galileo, and Einstein? Like regimes, ideologies come and go, and moral values are relative. But here at the institute you have the opportunity to discover *eternal* values.

A handful of students were determined to express their own eternal values: they spoke their minds, and tried to do what was just. Occasionally such people were expelled from the institute, and some who went too far were even arrested. Although most of us sympathized with our courageous colleagues, we were quick to retreat into the castle of science.

One day in 1970 I was on a train to the institute, reading the *Morning Star*, a daily newspaper published by the Communist Party in England. I loved reading the *Morning Star*, and the *Daily Worker* out of New York—no other English newspapers were available to Soviet citizens—because I had a passion for English and was constantly striving to improve my reading skills. Despite their orientation, these publications were also a way to learn a little more about the outside world.

On this particular morning I came across a story on Andrei Sakharov and his newly formed Committee for Human Rights. Although the article was critical of Sakharov, it provided information about his group. I had read Sakharov's famous letter to the Soviet leadership, which was circulated by our student samizdat, and had heard about his Committee for Human Rights on a Voice of America broadcast. I decided to translate the article into Russian, and left it on the bulletin board in our dormitory.

Several weeks later I was summoned to the office of the KGB representative in the institute. This was my first meeting with the KGB, and I was terrified. The subject was Sakharov. What was my connection to him? What literature had I received from him and was now distributing? I had never even met Sakharov, so I couldn't understand why they were asking me these questions. I learned later that one of my fellow students had seen me translating the article and had informed the authorities.

In later years, when meetings with the KGB became a regular part of my life, I looked back in shame at this first encounter. While

I made no attempt to betray anyone or to criticize my fellow students, I did try to defend myself. I was eager to show the agent that I was a loyal Soviet citizen just like him, although I already knew in my heart that this wasn't true.

Three years earlier, the Six-Day War had made an indelible impression on me as it did on most Soviet Jews, for, in addition to fighting for her life, Israel was defending our dignity. On the eve of the war, when Israel's destruction seemed almost inevitable, Soviet anti-Semites were jubilant. But a few days later even anti-Jewish jokes started to change, and throughout the country, in spite of pro-Arab propaganda, you could now see a grudging respect for Israel and for Jews. A basic, eternal truth was returning to the Jews of Russia—that personal freedom wasn't something you could achieve through assimilation. It was available only by reclaiming your historical roots.

The following year brought another important milestone in my life. When the Soviets invaded Czechoslovakia, I felt ashamed of being a Soviet citizen. I was also struck by the reaction of many of my fellow students. "During the war we sacrificed one hundred fifty thousand boys in Czechoslovakia to save the Czechs from the Germans," they said. "And now they want to disown us?" These people had no doubts as to the Soviet Union's right to control the fate of the Czechs.

In the hot discussions of those days, which quickly went beyond the events of Czechoslovakia, I discovered a fundamental difference between my own mentality and that of the loyal Soviet citizen. His self-respect derived from being part of the Soviet system, and the more powerful the system, the stronger he felt. Law was a concept belonging to the authorities, so the idea that the authorities could *violate* the law was seen as a logical contradiction. The authorities *were* the law, and the system knew best. And if, in this framework, the individual was left with some fragments of freedom, he ought to be grateful to the leaders of the land and not make further demands.

I soon came to understand that this mentality constituted the real power of the regime. The state was maintained not by tanks and missiles, or even by camps and prisons. These were necessary, of course, but only for strengthening the *real* base of the regime—the consciousness of the slave who looks for guidance to the good czar, the leader, the teacher.

By now the appeal of Zionism was growing stronger, and the authorities responded with a virulent anti-Israel campaign. The regime arranged press conferences, where tamed Jews declared that Soviet Jews wanted nothing to do with "fascist" Israel. But the louder they shouted, the more obvious it was that the Zionist movement was growing, especially when television brought the issue into every Jewish household. I was close with several families who started on the road to Zionism, and friends began giving me books about Israel, including the novel *Exodus*, which was circulated in samizdat form and had an enormous influence on Jews of my generation. By the time I graduated, I was ready to go on aliyah.

In the spring of 1973 I applied for my exit visa. As part of the process, I had to write a letter of resignation to the Komsomol (the Communist youth organization) at the Institute for Oil and Gas, where I was working as a computer specialist. In response, the Komsomol convened a public meeting to condemn me. Hundreds of people turned out, for instead of the standard bureaucratic agenda there was the promise of real drama.

After several anti-Israel speeches, the head of the group asked, "Does anyone have a question for Sharansky, who has betrayed us all?" The questions were predictable: Why does Israel persist in occupying Arab lands? How can you forsake the Soviet Union, which saved your own people from Hitler?

But the organizers of the meeting had not anticipated that I would actually respond to these questions. After a brief lecture on modern Jewish history and the founding of Israel, I explained the real background of the Six-Day War, and how despite all the propaganda they had heard, Israel was not the aggressor. I described how Nasser had closed the Straits of Tiran, expelled the UN peacekeeping force, and amassed one hundred thousand troops on Israel's border while threatening to annihilate the Jews. That, I pointed out, was the context for Israel's surprise "aggression" against Egyptian air bases on June 5, 1967.

The longer I spoke, the better I felt; it was as if the tension that had built up within me for years was finally being released. With every passing minute I became more free, more myself. Moreover, the audience was growing interested and the atmosphere less hostile.

"But you're leaving the Soviet Union and going over to our enemies," protested one of the Komsomol officers. "You pledged to defend the Soviet motherland and this makes you a traitor." This was the first time I was ever called a traitor, but I would hear that word many times in the future, until it became part of the charge against me.

But now I simply replied, "Why a traitor? To apply for an exit visa is not a violation of Soviet law." Even this simplistic response surprised many of those present. How could the authorities permit people to leave? Why, in Stalin's time they'd know what to do with someone like him!

A young woman I knew jumped up and said, "If you go to Israel and my husband is sent to Egypt, you'll be shooting at him."

"Galina," I replied, "why will your husband be in Egypt? If he's there to fight against Israel, I'll have even more reason to go." After this, Galina didn't speak to me for months. The official record of the meeting noted that "Sharansky stated he would go to Israel to kill Soviet soldiers who were fulfilling their international duty." The first piece of evidence for my future criminal case was already in hand.

The Komsomol meeting was a thrilling and liberating experience, for it marked the first time in my life that I publicly said what I believed. From the authorities' perspective, however, it was a disaster. That a parasite like me was allowed to spew his poison at a public forum was an unforgivable offense that couldn't go unpunished. A few days later the head of the group was dismissed.

Normally, a Jew who applies for an exit visa is fired immediately. But as a graduate of the Institute of Physics and Technology, I was considered a "young specialist" who, under the law, is required to stay on for three years and can be fired only for certain very specific reasons. And so I remained at my job until March of 1975, when they finally dismissed me.

My real life was elsewhere, however, and at the center of that life were the regular Saturday gatherings of Jewish activists who met on the street across from the Moscow synagogue on Arkhipova Street. The authorities kept a close eye on us and occasionally dispersed the crowd, but mostly they left us alone. On one of my first visits, someone distributed tickets for the World University Games, which were being held in Moscow in August 1973. Israel was sending a small delegation, and having never seen a real Israeli, I was tremendously excited.

We attended the opening ceremonies, where Yassir Arafat was the guest of honor and the Israeli team was booed by the crowd. We returned the following night to watch the Israeli basketball team, and during the intermission we actually spoke with the players. The third night, when the Israelis played Puerto Rico, the hall was packed with soldiers, and many refuseniks who arrived with tickets were told that no seats were available. (Refuseniks are Soviet Jews whose application for an exit visa has been refused.) When the Israelis appeared, there was shouting and whistling, and calls of *"Zhid"*—kikes. And when a woman in our group unfolded a big banner in Hebrew, MAZAL TOV L'YISRAEL, Good Luck to Israel, a group of soldiers immediately jumped over spectators in order to tear it down. It was a real battle; the Israelis stopped the game and demanded that our safety be guaranteed.

After the game, which the Israelis won, several of us were punched and kicked on the way out. Despite the temptation to fight back, we knew that any attempt to defend ourselves would result in our arrest and imprisonment. It was a frightening moment. Thus far my struggle to emigrate had been purely bureaucratic, but now, suddenly, I felt like a soldier in battle. I was familiar with state anti-Semitism, but it was shocking to see this same phenomenon in its raw form.

We were able to leave safely only because a crowd of foreign correspondents had gathered outside the arena. Dozens of policemen and plainclothes officers glared at us, but they left us alone. This was when I began to understand that we could use the foreign press to protect us.

Later that week, following a volleyball match, a group of us stood beside the bus that would carry the Israeli team back to their dormitory. Several rows of KGB and police were there to prevent any contact between us as the athletes left the locker room. "What songs do you know?" the Israelis on the bus called to us through the windows. We started singing together across the border of KGB men, and because we didn't know many Hebrew songs, we sang the same ones again and again, especially "Heveinu Shalom Aleichem" (We Bring You Peaceful Greetings). Today, whenever I hear this song it reminds me of my brief Zionist youth.

For me these few days were like an entire youth movement compressed into a single week, and from then on I was permanently involved in aliyah activities. The driving force of the movement were approximately a hundred Jewish activists from Moscow, Leningrad, Riga, Kiev, and other cities. We created underground seminars for learning Hebrew, maintained contacts with Jews abroad, and organized demonstrations. Among my fellow activists I became known as Natan, the name of my great-grandfather, which my parents had felt was too Jewish for the Stalin era.

I started out as a demonstrator. After discreetly informing the foreign press, a handful of us would stand in a central square in Moscow and raise signs with slogans such as "We Want to Live in Israel"; "Visas to Israel Instead of Prisons"; and "Freedom for Prisoners of Zion."

A successful demonstration would continue for a minute or two until the KGB or the police arrested us. (Often, through informers, the authorities knew about our demonstrations in advance.) Nobody could predict what would happen next. There might be a fine of fifteen or twenty rubles, a fifteen-day jail sentence, or a far more serious penalty. After our demonstration in front of the Lenin Library, two of my friends, Mark Nashpitz and Boris Tsitlyonok, were sentenced to five years of exile in distant Siberia.

In the midst of these demonstrations I met Avital and we fell in love. We were married on July 4, 1974; on the following day she left for Israel. Avital's spirit is on every page of this book, even when her name does not appear. She was like the air I breathed; from the moment we met she was with me always.

Demonstrations were important to remind the world of our struggle, but demonstrations alone were not enough. I soon became acquainted with Sasha Lunts, a fifty-year-old mathematician and one of the leaders of our movement. His apartment reminded me of a doctor's office, with people coming to see him from all parts of the country. Lunts had a sincere interest in the fate of every Soviet Jew, whether he was a shoemaker from Derbent or a carpenter from

Bobruisk who had applied for a visa and was helplessly fighting the cruel and idiotic bureaucratic machine.

Lunts drew up lists of refuseniks, and maintained records on who had been refused, on what grounds, whether the family needed material help, and so on. He also organized several fact-finding trips to other communities to collect additional information about refuseniks. The world had to know about these people; it was a necessary condition not only for saving them but for ensuring that thousands of others (and in good years, tens of thousands) would be able to emigrate.

It was in Sasha Lunts's apartment that I came to know some of the foreign correspondents who were stationed in Moscow, and soon the activity for which my friends jokingly called me "spokesman" took up most of my time. Because I spoke English with some fluency, I began to organize press conferences and meet with a steady stream of correspondents, diplomats, politicians, and Jewish activists from the West.

The more intense my activity, the more closely I was watched by the KGB. I was often detained in the streets and brought in for talks with their bosses. They argued with me, warned me, and threatened me, but their harassment was merely an annoyance that inspired me to become even more active.

For years I was under constant surveillance, as my tails changed shifts every eight hours and followed me day and night. I grew accustomed to the sound of their car engines under my window—they ran the engine all night to keep the heater going—just as in my student days I got used to the sound of my neighbor playing his tape recorder in the next room. In time the surveillance became more overt, and before long the tails were breathing down my neck, running behind me on the stairs of the subway, joining me on buses and in elevators, and sometimes even in taxis—in which case I insisted that we split the fare.

Among the many Jewish activists with whom I was associated, a smaller group crystallized who became my comrades-in-arms. After Sasha Lunts left for Israel, the responsibility for maintaining lists of refuseniks passed to Dina Beilin. No detail was too trivial for Dina, who worked with refuseniks day and night, giving them advice, looking over their documents, and helping them struggle against the KGB.

Dina was tough on herself, and no less demanding of her friends. While I actually enjoyed our struggle, for her it was more like a noble duty, which is why there were sometimes conflicts between us. Why hadn't I taken care of this? Why had I missed that meeting? She took everything personally. We would quarrel, but the next day our common struggle with the KGB would unite us again. I always knew she was a true friend.

Information about Prisoners of Zion—refuseniks who were jailed for their efforts to live in Israel—came from Ida Nudel. Ida knew everything: where A was being held, and under what conditions; when B's birthday was; how many days C was kept in the punishment cell; when D's family would be allowed to visit him. She was in regular contact with the prisoners and their families, with the Soviet authorities, and with our friends in the West. Ida did everything possible to break down the barriers between Jewish activists in Moscow and in prison.

Volodia Slepak was a veteran of our movement. His name was widely known in the West, and his apartment in the center of Moscow was always full of guests from abroad. He would slowly smoke his pipe, displaying tremendous patience as the same discussions with our foreign guests dragged on year after year.

"But he falls asleep during meetings," said those who were envious of his fame.

"That's his business," I would reply. We had no shortage of people who could speak elegantly and write statements, but Slepak was courageous and reliable, and he stood up to the authorities like a rock. Even the police near the synagogue and the KGB tails seemed to sense his inner strength and treated him with a cautious respect.

Alexander Lerner was an internationally known specialist in cybernetics, and the authorities felt betrayed when he became one of the first high-ranking scientists to apply for an exit visa. He organized a seminar in applied mathematics for refusenik scientists, and I was one of the participants. But even more useful from my perspective were the opportunities to talk with him about strategic and tactical questions in our struggle. Even if you didn't agree with everything Lerner said, even if he sometimes seemed too cautious, it was important to hear the views of a man who knew the system intimately. And if you had time between meetings, you'd go to his apartment, where his wife, Judith, would always give you a good meal and a piece of cake to keep you going.

I also enjoyed visiting Vitaly and Ina Rubin. Vitaly was a renowned specialist in ancient Chinese philosophy, and his inability to leave the Soviet Union led to great indignation and protests by his fellow Sinologists in the West. As a refusenik, Rubin organized an eclectic seminar on Israel, Judaism, philosophy, history, and related topics. His broad erudition, his easygoing nature, and his openness to different views drew people to his apartment, where you could meet refuseniks, dissidents, foreign correspondents, and diplomats.

But it was his childlike excitement that won me over. Once we were followed by four tails, two for each of us. When I pointed out that I wasn't the only one being followed, Vitaly jumped like a little boy. "Look," he said, "they take me as seriously as they take you!"

In 1975 I volunteered to help Andrei Dmitrievich Sakharov in his contacts with the foreign press and with visitors from abroad. I was full of respect for this outstanding man. Sakharov was a true scientist who tried to see all sides of a question, which wasn't always the case with those who quoted him. And although his tiny apartment was always full of visitors, he seemed surprisingly alone in his historical confrontation.

We all tend to play roles in this world, but when I translated for Sakharov at his press conferences I saw no gap between his inner thoughts and his public statements—no pretense, no show whatsoever. When I called to congratulate him for winning the Nobel Prize, he said, "It belongs to all of us." Coming from Sakharov it didn't sound banal, and I knew that he really meant it.

Later, I met Yuri Orlov, the outstanding physicist and longtime dissident. A few months after the approval of the Helsinki Final Act, which included provisions on human rights, I proposed to Orlov and the dissident writer Andrei Amalrik that we ought to make it as difficult as possible for the Soviet Union to ignore those accords. As a result of our discussions, which continued for months, Orlov proposed the idea of a public group to monitor compliance with human rights agreements, and I became one of the founding members. While my own focus was on Jewish emigration, I was also active on behalf of people from many national and religious groups whose rights were brutally violated by the Soviet regime, including Pentecostals and Catholics, Ukrainians, and Crimean Tatars. The Helsinki Watch Group also produced documents about human rights violations in Soviet prisons, labor camps, and psychiatric hospitals. My interest in helping other persecuted peoples was an important part of my own freedom—a freedom that became real only after I returned to my Jewish roots.

For the activist Jews of my generation, our movement represented the exact opposite of what our parents had gone through when they were young. But we saw what had happened to their dreams, and we understood that the path to liberation could not be found in denying our own roots while pursuing universal goals. On the contrary: we had to deepen our commitment, because only he who understands his own identity and has already become a free person can work effectively for the human rights of others.

In Israel, while I was writing this book, I came upon an image by the American writer Cynthia Ozick that captures this idea perfectly. The shofar, the ram's horn that is sounded in the synagogue on the High Holidays, is narrow at one end and wide at the other. Nothing happens if you blow into the wide end. But if you blow into the narrow end, the call of the shofar rings loud and true.

Treason, that is, an act intentionally committed by a citizen of the USSR to the detriment of the independence of the state, the territorial inviolability, or the military might of the USSR—going over to the side of the enemy, espionage, transmission of a state or military secret to a foreign state, flight abroad or refusal to return from abroad to the USSR, rendering aid to a foreign state in carrying on hostile activity against the USSR, or a conspiracy for the purpose of seizing power—shall be punished by deprivation of freedom for a term of ten to fifteen years with confiscation of property with or without additional exile for a term of two to five years, or by death with confiscation of property.

—Article 64-A of the Soviet Criminal Code

Though I walk through the valley of the shadow of death
I will fear no evil
For thou art with me.

   —PSALM 23

Book One

March 15, 1977—July 15, 1978

"So at last they've done it."

The words kept pounding at my brain and repeating themselves over and over, like words on a broken record. I was in the back of a light-gray Volga sedan. On either side of me a KGB agent held my hand on his knee. In the front, beside the driver, another agent reported over the radio that the operation had been successfully completed.

Behind us, a fifth man was crammed into the tiny space along the rear window. Perhaps he was guarding me from that unlikely position, but more likely he was there to block the view of the two foreign correspondents who had just witnessed my abduction. Only a moment ago I had been seized by half a dozen men and pushed into the car. I sat there feeling depleted, but also relieved. Now that they had finally done it, the agonizing eleven-day death watch was over.

On March 4, 1977, a full-page article in *Izvestia* had accused me and several other Jewish activists of working for the CIA and carrying out espionage against the Soviet Union. As soon as the article appeared, foreign correspondents came to see me for a final interview, and friends stopped by to offer their support. But everyone knew that the real purpose of these visits was to say good-bye. I felt like a man with a terminal illness. His family and friends do their best to convince him that everything will be fine, and they try to believe it themselves.

"They'll never do it, Tolya. It would be the trial of the century." I had heard this assurance only hours ago and desperately wanted to believe it. Even now, in the car, I still clung to that hope. And yet—"So at last they've done it."

But perhaps this wasn't really happening. It was still possible, wasn't it? In the past few days I had imagined my own arrest so often that perhaps this was just one more bad dream. Perhaps in another moment I would wake up and this whole scene would fade away.

The car jerked as it veered left onto Gorky Street, jolting me back to reality. As we turned, my hand slipped off the knee of the agent on my right. Swiftly, professionally, he grabbed me tightly by the wrist. He was no stranger, this skinny blond kid with the dumb grin on his face; he had been one of my tails for well over a year. Today, however, he looked nervous and severe.

The agent next to the driver was calling in for instructions: should they go through the center of town, or along the Yauza River? Better take a good look, I told myself, you're seeing Moscow for the last time. I stared out the window, but nothing registered. By tomorrow I wouldn't even remember which route we had taken.

As we drove up to Lefortovo Prison, the heavy iron doors—the first of two pairs, which never open simultaneously—began to separate. Suddenly, I was seized by an absurd and idiotic fear that they would ask me to breathe into one of those tubes and would discover I was drunk. As if I were being brought in for a mere traffic violation!

Half an hour earlier I had tossed down a few drops of cognac, which was a lot for me, as I normally can't tolerate anything stronger than a light wine. A group of us were meeting in Vladimir Slepak's apartment for our weekly Hebrew lesson, doing our best to maintain a reasonably normal existence in spite of the drastic accusations in *Izvestia* and the increasingly brazen behavior of our tails. Whenever I went out I was followed by two cars and eight men, who formed a human cage around me on the street. Instead of lurking in the shadows, they now came right up to me, as if the KGB wanted to remind me that my days were numbered and resistance was senseless.

At six o'clock, as the class was ending, David Satter of the London *Financial Times* and Hal Piper of the Baltimore *Sun* rushed in with the sensational news that Mikhail Stern had been freed. Stern, a

Jewish physician from the Ukraine who had applied for an exit visa, was arrested back in 1974 on several trumped-up charges and sentenced to eight years in a labor camp. Even by Soviet standards, this was a crude and cynical attempt to intimidate other Jews who were contemplating aliyah. Eleven days ago, only hours before the *Izvestia* article changed my life forever, I had organized another press conference for Stern's wife.

The news of his release called for a celebration. The only liquor in Slepak's apartment was a little cognac, but that was all we needed to drink a toast to Mikhail Stern's freedom. "As you can see," I told the two reporters, who had come for our reaction, "we're delighted that Stern has been freed. But nobody will be fooled by the official statement that he was released for reasons of health. I suspect the regime took this step to distract world opinion from the recent accusations in *Izvestia* against Jewish activists. There could be new arrests at any moment."

"They drove away!" cried the Beard—our nickname for Slepak—who was standing at the window.

"And they're no longer in the hall," said Masha Slepak, who had opened the door to check.

"They," of course, were the KGB, who had been stationed in and around the building for days. All of this was in my honor, as I had been staying with the Slepaks ever since the *Izvestia* article appeared.

I ran to the window and, sure enough, the car that was parked downstairs had disappeared. A good sign, but what about the second car? I climbed up on the ledge to get a better view. Damn it, the other one was still there—only, now it was closer to the front door. And it soon became clear that the tails just outside Slepak's apartment hadn't left, after all, but had merely gone up to the attic for some kind of meeting.

"What does all this mean?" the correspondents asked.

"Let's check it experimentally," I replied, grabbing my coat and a handful of two-kopek coins for the public phone. "I'm going out to call the other correspondents with a statement about Stern's release." Slepak's own phone had long ago been disconnected by the authorities.

Piper and Satter came with me. So did the Beard. Ever since the article appeared, he kept hold of my hand whenever we left the building. "If they arrest you," he said, "at least I'll be your witness." Slepak knew that I might well be accused of provoking my own arrest. If they came to take me, he would tell the real story to the foreign press and, through them, to the world.

Between the cognac and the excitement, I forgot to grab my satchel, where I had packed a sweater, long underwear, a scarf, warm socks, and a book. After all, a man accused of espionage could find himself in prison at any moment, which is not a place you want to go without warm clothing.

As we approached the elevator two KGB men rushed down the stairs to join us. "Ride with us!" they shouted. Only three passengers at a time were permitted to ride in this elevator, although you could squeeze in five if you had to. But with Slepak and me, the two correspondents, and the tails, there were six of us.

"I'll take the stairs," said the Beard. "Hal and David can go with you."

For the first time in days, Slepak let go of my hand and hurried down the stairs from the seventh floor. That was the last time I saw my friend until 1987, when after seventeen years of waiting, including five years in Siberia, he was finally given an exit visa.

With five of us packed into the elevator, my nose was squashed against the walkie-talkie of one of the tails, which bulged out from under his coat. This was the same towheaded kid who would soon be sitting on my right in the car. I noticed that his arm was shaking violently. "They're nervous," I told the correspondents in English. "Something's about to happen."

The elevator door opened and I headed for the street. Suddenly I was grabbed by a sea of hands, and the next thing I knew I was plunging through the door and straight into a car—a prisoner of the KGB.

At Lefortovo, the KGB interrogation prison, I was brought to Lieutenant Colonel Galkin, a small, elderly man in glasses who introduced himself with an ingratiating smile: "Deputy head of the investigative division of the KGB for Moscow and Moscow Province." And just as solicitously and with a touch of embarrassment, he handed me a sheet of paper: "Here," he said. "We shall be working together."

The document was an arrest warrant "on suspicion of committing a crime under Article 64-A, treason in the form of aid to capitalist states in carrying out hostile activity against the USSR." I quickly put the paper on the table so that Galkin wouldn't notice my trembling hands. My heart sank and my throat tightened. I understood that despite the clear warning of the *Izvestia* article and all my mental preparations, I was still harboring the hope of being charged under Article 70 and not 64-A.

Article 70, the standard charge against dissidents, was defined by the Criminal Code as "agitation or propaganda carried on for the purpose of subverting or weakening the Soviet regime." It carried a maximum sentence of seven years' imprisonment plus five more of internal exile.

Article 64 was much more serious, and included such crimes as engaging in espionage and rendering aid to enemy states. The maximum sentence under Article 64-A was death, and the only other Jewish activists charged under this article had been accused of planning to hijack an airplane.

"You probably weren't prepared for 64-A," said Galkin, as if reading my thoughts. "You expected 70."

"No," I replied. "After all, your people already warned me in *Izvestia* that I was a spy. That was very kind of you." I tried to smirk, but my voice betrayed me: it came out hoarse and my smile was forced.

Galkin's own smile quickly disappeared as he seemed disappointed by my response. "Ah, yes, *Izvestia*, " he said with a sigh. Then he turned to one of the guards: "Proceed with the search."

Three sergeants were already in the room, along with an elderly female paramedic. Politely but firmly, they ordered me to undress. They began a personal search, looking over my things and carefully examining my body as if it, too, were just another object.

After Galkin's initial welcome, the search came as a rude reminder of my new status. From now on, nothing belonged to me— not my clothes, not my watch, not my wedding ring, not even my own body. I was a prisoner. At any moment they could empty my pockets, tear off my clothes, and poke their fingers into my mouth or up my rectum.

During my nine years in captivity, I met men who had survived years in the Gulag and had been searched hundreds of times. But in spite of all they went through, they could never get used to the searches. With each new search they felt humiliated all over again.

This was fine with the KGB, of course. They knew very well that a prisoner who felt humiliated and had lost his self-respect could never become spiritually uncompromising. He might turn vengeful and cunning, but in that case they could channel his hatred and direct it against his fellow prisoners, which only hastened his demise.

But I didn't understand any of this until much later. In those first few days in Lefortovo, I could only rely on my experience from previous fifteen-day incarcerations in local jails. The first time was in June 1974, when the authorities rounded up a group of Jewish activists to prevent us from staging any public protests during President Nixon's visit to the Soviet Union. On that occasion, when I was stripped and searched, I decided it was best to treat my captors like the weather. A storm can cause you problems, and sometimes those problems can be humiliating. But the storm itself doesn't humiliate you.

Once I understood this, I realized that nothing they did could humiliate me. I could only humiliate myself—by doing something I might later be ashamed of. During my first few days in Lefortovo I repeated this principle over and over until it was part of me: *Nothing they do can humiliate me. I alone can humiliate myself.* Once I had absorbed that idea, nothing—not searches, not punishments, and, five years later, not even several attempts to force-feed me through the rectum during an extended hunger strike—could deprive me of my self-respect.

But just an hour after my arrest, as I stood there naked in front of the three officers and the old woman, I felt dazed, exposed, and embarrassed. While the paramedic and one of the officers studied my body, the others felt every fold of my clothing. At a nearby desk, Galkin drew up the Protocol of Confiscation, which listed the various personal items found in my pockets, including a pen, some notepaper, my identity papers, several rubles, and a handful of change.

When Galkin came to the photograph of my wife, he broke into another friendly smile. (I already knew that KGB officers could be very sweet when it suited their purposes.) "So this is Natasha," he said, setting the picture aside. Turning to me, he felt compelled to explain: "I prepared for this meeting, and I recognize your wife from the pictures."

Several days earlier my apartment had been ransacked, and my wife's letters and all my photographs of her, along with my papers, had disappeared into the belly of the KGB. The picture Galkin was looking at was taken by Papa in June 1974, just a few weeks before our wedding on July 4. Avital—she took her new name in Israel—had left the Soviet Union the next day. At the time, we both expected that my own visa would be approved within a few months. That was almost three years ago.

That photograph was so important to me that I carried it everywhere. When Galkin took it away, I felt utterly alone. The last door was closing, and the circle was growing tighter. Now I was terrified.

"Can I keep the picture?" I said. I preferred not to ask any favors, but I couldn't help myself.

"It will be stored with your personal belongings," he replied. Then, with the studied sincerity of a salesman, he added, "If you reach an agreement with the prison management, you'll get it back." At Lefortovo, as I would be assured repeatedly in the days ahead, the prison and the KGB investigative division functioned separately.

The prison management didn't keep us waiting, for just then a beefy colonel strode into the room. He was around sixty, wearing his uniform and carrying the March 4 issue of *Izvestia*, with the infamous back-page article about Jewish espionage.

"Whom did they bring us?" he asked Galkin. Then he turned to me: "What crimes brought you here?" The colonel spoke coarsely and assertively, and in sharp contrast to the studied formality and politeness of the modern KGB he addressed me with the familiar *ty*, the pronoun normally reserved for close friends and small children.

As I stood there, waiting for them to give back my clothing, I felt myself growing stronger. The colonel's aggressive tone bucked me up a little.

"Don't get familiar with me," I replied. "If there's a criminal here, it's not I. And you know full well who I am. You're even carrying that newspaper!"

The room was silent for several seconds. Then the colonel went to the desk and read the arrest warrant.

"Oh, yes," he said, "you are the traitor." But this time, instead of *ty*, he used the more appropriate *vy*.

"Put him over there," he said, pointing to the far corner of the room. The colonel scrutinized me at length, while I stared back as brazenly as possible.

"What's the matter?" I finally asked. "Haven't you ever seen a naked man before?"

The colonel harrumphed, and turned to the sergeant: "Have you finished examining him? Then give him back his clothes. Don't let him freeze. He'll be able to freeze in the punishment cell."

Turning to me, he finally introduced himself: "Petrenko, Alexander Mitrofanovich, head of the investigative prison of the KGB of the USSR. I'll come to the point: Don't try anything, or it's straight to the punishment cell. It's cold there, and there's hot food only every other day. You'll be crying for your dear mother soon enough."

Galkin interrupted, as if frightened by Petrenko's overly harsh tone: "Anatoly Borisovich, keep in mind that the administration of the prison has no relation to us in the investigative department. We function independently, and neither side is subordinate to the other."

As I put my clothes on I could feel my strength returning. Petrenko's aggressive approach, together with the primitive way that he and Galkin assumed the familiar roles of good guy and bad guy, reminded me that I was among enemies. This was no time for weakness.

Petrenko would not let up: "How did you turn out this way?" he said. "You grew up eating Russian bread, you received an education paid for by the Russian people, and now you betray your motherland? For you and your whole people I fought at the front for four years."

This quick shot of anti-Semitism reminded me exactly whom I was dealing with. It also calmed me down.

"My father also fought at the front," I said. "He spent four years there as a volunteer. Perhaps he did that for your son and your people?"

"Your father?" said Petrenko. "In the army? What division was he in?"

"Artillery."

"Artillery?" He seemed genuinely amazed. "I also fought in the artillery, but I didn't see *your* sort there. What front was he on?"

I practically burst out laughing. Although Petrenko and Galkin started out playing their respective roles, Petrenko had already reverted to his true character, both in his bigotry and in his desire to talk about the war. I suddenly recalled the O. Henry story about the thief who breaks into an apartment. The owner wakes up and confronts him, whereupon the two men quickly embark on an extended discussion of their common ailments and become friends.

But my talk with Petrenko had gone on long enough. "I don't think we have anything more to talk about," I said. "Your attitude toward me is clear."

"So, you don't even want to talk? Clever. I'll talk to your father when he comes to see me. But just remember—don't try anything, or it's straight to the punishment cell." And with that, Petrenko left the room.

Galkin made a few polite remarks that I either didn't take in or don't remember. "We'll see you later on at an interrogation," he said before he left, like a man consoling his friend that they wouldn't be apart for too long.

I sat for another hour or so with the sergeants. The officers were making phone calls, and people were coming in and out, but I noticed almost nothing. Once again I had the sense that none of this was real.

Finally the guards came to bring me to Galkin. We walked for a long time down a long and narrow corridor, stopping here and there and waiting for some sort of signal to proceed. Then we climbed a long and narrow staircase.

Galkin's office was enormous. On the wall behind his desk hung the hammer and sickle. At that moment it resembled a bloodsucking spider. I sat down at a small table at the other end of the room. In front of me were two books—the Criminal Code and the Criminal Procedure Code. Galkin suggested that I look through the Criminal Procedure Code and read about my rights and obligations. I tried, but I just couldn't concentrate. I was overwhelmed by all the legal terminology: suspect, defendant, right to defense, criminal intent, admissible evidence, substantive proof—all these words and phrases that now constituted my new world.

"Now have a look at Article 64-A of the Criminal Code," said Galkin. The book was on the table in front of me, and someone had even left a bookmark at the appropriate page. I read it, although there was really no need to, for during the past few days I had committed the language to memory.

"You have been accused," said Galkin, "—well, in the meantime suspected of, but you will be charged within ten days as provided for in the law—of treason in the form of aid to capitalist states in carrying out hostile activity against the Soviet Union. What do you say about the essence of the charge?"

"I committed no crime," I replied. "My public work as an activist in the Jewish emigration movement and as a member of the Helsinki Watch Group was directed exclusively at informing international public opinion and the appropriate Soviet organizations about crude violations by the Soviet authorities of the rights of citizens striving to emigrate from the USSR. These activities were in complete conformity . . ."

I was speaking automatically, and could hear my own voice reaching me from some far-off place. After the *Izvestia* article appeared, so many foreign journalists had asked me about the meaning and goals of my activities that I had memorized the script. But those were only dress rehearsals, whereas this was opening night.

"Enough!" shouted Galkin, interrupting my response. I was shocked by his tone, which was completely different from that of the kind and mild-mannered gentleman I had encountered only an hour earlier. Although I knew he had been playing a role, this abrupt change in his personality came as a shock. Suddenly, this seemingly affable man was yelling and banging his fist on the table. "This isn't one of your so-called press conferences," he bellowed. "You have slandered us, and the time has come to answer for your crimes. If you transmitted information, then say so—where, when, and to whom. It seems that you don't yet understand your situation. Read it again, the part of the article"—and here he used a legal term I didn't recognize.

I knew what he had in mind, but I asked anyway, "Which part of the article?"

Galkin gave a malicious laugh. The speed with which he switched from that benevolent smile to this disparaging and satanic cackle was simply breathtaking. "Read the part about punishment. You are threatened with capital punishment. *Rasstrel:* death by gunfire."

Rasstrel. I knew it was a possibility, but I had been hoping not to hear this terrible word. Again my heart sank, and again I felt a tightening in my chest and a dry mouth. I should have been prepared for this moment, but in all the discussions I had had with my friends in the past few days about the possibility of my being arrested under Article 64-A, we had tried to avoid any thought of capital punishment. In all my conversations, and even in my last letter to Avital, which I handed to Robert Toth of the *Los Angeles Times* just yesterday, I had spoken only of the possibility of a ten-year sentence. I knew that theoretically one could be shot for human rights activities, but Stalin had been dead for twenty-four years and it was difficult to imagine that any of us would be put to death.

I wasn't sure whether Galkin noticed my reaction, but in any event he continued with great fervor: "Yes, yes, *rasstrel!* And you are the only one who can prevent this, by your frank and sincere repentance. You can't count on your American friends now."

He rambled on, but I had stopped paying attention. Instead, I was desperately trying to convince myself that I shouldn't feel this way. There had been plenty of warning, and none of this should have come as a surprise.

But it did, and I squeezed my trembling hands between my knees, hoping Galkin wouldn't notice. Meanwhile, his voice rose to an even higher pitch: "We warned you. We tried to persuade you. But you continued your criminal activity. And now neither Israel nor America will help you!"

Prior to my arrest I had been summoned to numerous meetings with the KGB, where I was continually warned to stop meeting foreign correspondents and other representatives of Western countries to transmit "slanderous" information. But Galkin was the first representative of the KGB who ever raised his voice at me.

Later, from other prisoners, I would learn that Galkin's outburst was a standard part of the first interrogation, the "moment of truth" when they try to show the newly seized "criminal" just how radically his situation has changed. Their purpose is to stun him, to terrorize him into quick submission, and to extract those magic words "Yes, I'm guilty, I confess," around which they will build their case.

But the effect of Galkin's tirade was the opposite of what he intended. Now that my moment of weakness had passed, I saw him for what he was: my enemy. His aim was to separate me from everything and everybody I cared about, to deprive my life of its meaning, and to leave me without dignity or hope.

And now he made his final mistake: he mentioned Avital.

"Your wife is waiting for you," he said. "You want to join her? That depends only on you."

Galkin had just given me a gift—a window to the world, and a graphic reminder that I wasn't alone after all. For I immediately pictured how Avital and her brother Misha would hear the report of my arrest. Four days ago, surrounded by tails, I had managed to receive a call from Israel. Avital's roommate answered, and told me that Avital and her friends had taken the *Izvestia* article very seriously, that they had organized a support committee on our behalf, and she had just left for Geneva and America to publicize my situation. One after another, her friends took the receiver and offered words of support. But I was bitterly disappointed that I wasn't able to speak to my wife, as I felt that this might be my last opportunity to hear her voice before I was arrested.

Now, as I imagined her in Switzerland, I smiled. I was grateful that I had managed to get off a letter only yesterday, and was hopeful that she might actually receive it.

I looked at Galkin: "I demand that you write down my statement in the protocol." I had learned years ago that when you were dealing with the KGB, nothing counted unless it was entered into the official transcript.

"What statement?"

"The one I made when we began."

"That wasn't a statement," said Galkin. "That was slander. We won't write that kind of thing."

"Then there is nothing more to discuss," I replied.

This unleashed another long speech, which boiled down to the fact that Galkin felt very sorry for me. But I was no longer listening. By now I was exhausted, and all I wanted to do was sleep. Finally Galkin phoned for a guard to bring me to my cell.

Once more I was led down a series of long, narrow corridors and steep staircases. As a newcomer to prison, I was first taken to the showers. Although I was freezing, there was no faucet to regulate the water temperature. I knocked for the guard and asked him to turn up the hot water. "More." He complied. The water began to scald me, but the chills didn't go away.

Maybe I'm feverish, I thought, as I became tempted by a truly dangerous notion—that it wouldn't be so terrible if I was sick for a week or two. This thought was harmful because it betrayed my fear, my wish to escape my situation. I could no longer hide the fact that I was afraid. And if fear was my primary emotion, it could lead me to do whatever they wished.

I wanted to get to a bed as quickly as possible to confront my fear and grapple with it during the night. Tomorrow would probably bring a new interrogation, and until then I had to work on myself until I was ready.

The guard gave me a mattress, a blanket, a pillow, a mug, a spoon, and a bowl, and led me, with all my earthly possessions, to a cell. The cell was bare as iron—narrow and cold—but I didn't even want to look it over. I dragged the mattress over to the cot and pulled the blanket up over my head.

Only a few hours ago I had been sitting among friends, drinking a toast, speaking with foreign correspondents, and feeling connected to the entire world. And now I was enclosed in a small iron box inside a larger box, with long rows of one-eyed cells like so many Cyclopses—a box with no escape, where I might have to spend the rest of my life.

The guard, who was observing me through the peephole, immediately opened the food trap and informed me that I was forbidden to cover my head, even though a bright light was burning above me and remained on all night. I would have to lie with my eyes closed and get used to the light and the cold. At the time, it didn't occur to me that I could cover my eyes with a handkerchief or close the window. To my surprise, I immediately fell into a sound, dreamless sleep, and didn't wake up until I heard shouting the next morning.

Later, toward the end of my sixteen-month stay at Lefortovo, when I was familiar with the entire structure of the prison, I often wondered in disbelief when I recalled my first groggy hours in my new home. That first interrogation with Galkin, where did it take place? And although I remembered climbing several steep and narrow staircases to the sixth or seventh floor, in reality the investigative wing at Lefortovo was only three stories high, and the staircases were quite ordinary.

And what about Galkin's office, which had seemed so enormous that night? During the months that followed I was in every conceivable office in the investigative division of Lefortovo, but I never again saw anything like that room. Nor did I ever see Galkin again.

If not for the protocol of the interrogation on March 15, 1977, signed by Galkin and stating that I refused to reply to the essence of the charge, I could have sworn I had dreamed all of this.

Lefortovo

2

WAKING up the first morning after my arrest was genuine psychological torment—no less real than the physical suffering I experienced later on. The moment of awakening is always the most difficult part of the prison routine, especially during the first few days. Completely immersed in your former life, you still maintain the unconscious and irrational hope that this nightmare is about to end, that some official is even now on his way to your cell to announce that a terrible mistake has been made.

After my sleep was interrupted by a loud banging in the corridor and the shouting of a guard, I lay still, hoping to fall back asleep or, better yet, to wake up all over again—this time in Slepak's apartment. But the clanging grew louder and louder until finally the food trap opened and the guard ordered, "Get up!"

I sat up. My head felt heavy and there was an ache in my heart. In my mouth was a bitter taste I didn't recognize. My body felt sickly and weak, and I was still shivering. My eyes focused on the toilet. Good, I thought, at least I won't have far to go.

Lined up against the wall were three iron cots. In the middle of the cell was a small wooden table with a stool. High above me was a window, with bars behind the glass, and then a steel shutter, which almost totally blocked out the sunlight. A bulb on the ceiling burned twenty-four hours a day—proof that light is not always friendly.

There was also a sink. They had already given me a small towel, too short to serve as a noose in case I became suicidal. Suicide was a major concern at Lefortovo, which was why you had to leave your metal cup and spoon on the table at night so that the guard could see it; otherwise, you might sharpen the spoon and use it to cut your veins. I had already discovered that you weren't allowed to cover your head at night, as your face had to be visible at all times. And soon I would see that the stairwells in Lefortovo were covered with steel netting, in case a prisoner decided to hurl himself down.

As I sat on my cot in the cold cell, I noticed that the top window-pane was open. I wanted to close it, but it was too high up. Although I was freezing, it didn't occur to me that day, or the next, that I could pick up the stool, put it on my cot, and climb up to close the window myself. Nor did I realize that I could push the table aside and take four or five steps around the cell. Instead, I walked by squeezing my way between the cot and the table.

Even a laboratory monkey could have solved such primitive prob-lems, but I felt powerless in this hostile environment. During the first forty-eight hours I tried not to touch anything in the cell, as if minimizing all contact with my surroundings somehow proved I didn't really belong here. With all I had to think about, it was easier not to tamper with anything in this bleak new world or to leave any trace of my presence.

The guard brought me breakfast, my first prison meal, which consisted of black bread, hot porridge, and weak tea. But I didn't feel like eating, and didn't touch the food. The next morning, when the guard opened the door, he handed me a pail and asked, "Any bread?"

I silently gave over the first day's entire ration of 450 grams. "Never mind," he said cheerfully. "Soon you won't be leaving any."

Instead of eating, I waited—for new developments, new threats, further interrogations. Although my body was slack, my mind was burning. Concentrate on future interrogations, I told myself. Pre-pare for the unexpected. Be sure to . . .

But it was no use, as my thoughts carried me far outside the prison walls. Instead of soberly analyzing my situation, I quickly tumbled into a fantasy world where I imagined how individuals in Israel and elsewhere were reacting to news of my arrest. Many people knew the truth, I reminded myself, including the foreign correspondents, Jewish tourists from the West, my friends and fellow activists in both the Jewish and dissident movements, a handful of diplomats, and a number of American politicians who had been to Moscow.

They all knew who I was and what I had done. They all understood that my only crime was that I wanted to leave the Soviet
Union and join my wife in Israel. Nobody will be fooled by these
trumped-up charges of espionage. The wave of protest and indignation will be overwhelming. The Kremlin will have no choice but
to . . .

I caught myself and tried to laugh at these wildly optimistic
speculations. This was no time for wishful thinking! I was facing
a long and difficult struggle, and I had to prepare. There would soon
be a second interrogation, and a third, and many more after that,
where the KGB would try to pressure and intimidate me so that I
would plead guilty, repent, and give false testimony against my
friends.

But even as I tried to focus my mind, my thoughts wandered off
anew. Solzhenitsyn's case popped into my head. Three years ago he,
too, was brought to Lefortovo and accused of treason, and on the
very next day they expelled him to the West. And only last month
they had arrested my friends Yuri Orlov and Alexander Ginzburg
from the Helsinki Watch Group. This had been greeted by outrage
throughout the free world, and even the White House had protested.

And now my own arrest on a charge of treason was a direct
challenge to the Americans, so the public outcry would be even
greater. With the Helsinki Review Conference coming up in Belgrade, the issue of Soviet compliance with the Helsinki Accords was
sure to be in the news. The Soviets were stuck. Maybe they'd put
all three of us on a plane and ship us out of the country.

Lord, what nonsense was creeping into my head! Tolya, grab
hold of yourself! This is no time for foolishness; you've got to
concentrate.

Suddenly the door clanked. It took at least half a minute before
the bolts were removed and the locks turned, which gave me plenty
of time to imagine the possibilities: interrogation? expulsion? release?

My caller introduced himself as Major Stepanov, deputy head of
the political section of the prison. He looked like a simple country
fellow with a plain face and a turned-up nose, and he spoke with a

comical Volga accent. But his homespun speech was littered with official bureaucratic phrases, quotes from Lenin, and even references to Plekhanov, an early Marxist theoretician. Under normal circumstances I would have been fascinated to encounter an official with such contradictory qualities, but this wasn't the time to engage him in conversation.

"Have you any requests?" he asked.

"Yes, give me back the picture of my wife."

"That will be decided during the investigation."

"But the investigative section told me it was your decision."

"I don't know about that. You can submit a request in writing. Anything else?"

"I'd like books from the library and a chess set."

"Books are no problem, but you're alone in here. What do you want with a chess set?"

"The rules stipulate that the prison must provide a chess set for every cell, without specifying how many people there must be." The prison rules were posted on a cardboard sheet on the wall of my cell. I had read them several times, and although I absorbed very little, the word "chess" jumped out at me.

Stepanov tried to object, and we argued for a long time. In the end, however, he agreed with me; incredibly, rules were rules. Soon after he left, a guard brought me a chess set and I arranged the pieces on the board. I immediately began to feel better, for I have always used chess to escape from pressure and anxiety.

I was a chess prodigy as a child, and I loved the way the game gave me power over grown-ups. My mother taught me the moves when I was five, and soon chess became my greatest passion. Before long I was beating my older brother, Leonid, as well as my parents, and I started seeking partners outside the family.

I quickly reached the rank of candidate-master, and for years my dream was to become a great chess player. But I was always ambivalent about this goal, because the more time I spent on chess, the more I suffered from doubts: Did it really make sense to spend so much time playing games? And yet whenever I neglected chess, I missed those moments of free play and fantasy, those challenging opportunities to test my intellectual powers, and the special delight I took in defeating my opponents.

Now, at the table in my cell, I began to analyze a variation of the French Defense, my favorite chess opening. Its distinctive feature is that black opens with his king's pawn, but advances only one square instead of the customary two, thereby yielding the center and inviting his opponent to mount an early attack. But while black is exposed to strong pressure during the opening moves, he eventually has the resources to mount a successful counterattack. If he can withstand white's initial assault, black's prospects are excellent.

Unable to rein in my thoughts, which threatened to gallop off again in various wayward directions, I started whipping the pieces around as if I were playing both sides in a blitz match. When I reached the endgame I caught myself and returned to the opening position that had intrigued me in the first place. But then it happened all over again: unable to restrain myself, I raced ahead.

Ten minutes passed, then twenty, then thirty. Finally, I began to calm down. I moved the pieces much more deliberately and took time to consider each move. I formed some ideas and reached some conclusions and counterconclusions. Gradually, my feverish state of mind gave way to a sustained analysis.

Once again the door clanked and for a moment I lost control of my thoughts. Interrogation? Liberation? No, merely an officer who brought in a paper stating that my case had been transferred from the Moscow KGB to the national office. The document was signed personally by Yuri Andropov, head of the KGB. When I asked what this meant, I was informed that, among other things, Galkin would no longer be my investigator.

I was delighted to hear this, although in retrospect I don't understand why. It must have been because Galkin lost his temper last night. If so, how naive I was then! At least with a screamer you knew where you stood. I soon learned that the KGB has far more subtle and effective ways to manipulate a prisoner.

The chess, together with the document signed by Andropov, had a sobering effect, and now that I was less agitated it was time to sit down and think things over. Whether or not they actually believed it, the KGB had already made a public claim that I was a spy. But what evidence could they possibly have against me?

My motto had been "No secrets." Before meeting a correspondent from the Western press, I would call him at his office, where the line was certainly bugged, to tell him, for example, that sixty refuseniks from half a dozen cities had signed a petition to the U.S. Congress in support of the Jackson Amendment, which linked Soviet-American trade to human rights.

That way, if my tails detained me on the way to deliver the statement, the correspondent would file a report on my detention, which would attract more attention to the document itself. If nobody stopped me, I always made sure to give over the documents right under the noses of the KGB. No secrets.

Each time I handed another document to a correspondent under the sullen gaze of my tails, I again rejoiced in the feeling of freedom that we, a small group of Jewish activists, had won for ourselves in the land of slavery. Every few weeks the KGB would bring me in for a little chat, where they warned me about my activities and tried to intimidate me. But I knew all their arguments in advance, and I tried to apply an Indian proverb I had found years ago in a chess book: "When you're riding on a tiger, the most dangerous thing is to stop."

In September 1976 I was picked up at the Moscow train station just before leaving for Kiev to attend the annual memorial service commemorating the mass murder of Soviet Jews by the Nazis at Babi Yar in 1941.

"There's a great deal I could tell you, Anatoly Borisovich," said the officer in charge. "I would be happy to explain why your application for a visa was denied, and what your prospects are. Unfortunately, you have many English-speaking friends," he continued, referring to the foreign correspondents, "and you tell them everything. But what I want to say concerns only you, and you must not repeat it to anybody else. If you promise to keep it to yourself, I'll tell you what I know."

"I'm sorry," I replied. "But I'm much too afraid of your organization to have any secrets with you. Tell me whatever you wish, as long as you understand that as soon as this meeting is over I'll report every word of it."

"*Please,*" he said, "I really *do* want to tell you. But you must promise."

"Please, I'd *love* to know, believe me. But it will remain a secret only until I reach the first public telephone."

We went back and forth like a pair of characters in a comic

operetta. Finally he said with a sigh, "I can see you're not a serious person, even though it's in your own interest to have this information."

So I never did learn what the great secret was. But I had no intention of violating my most basic principle, as I knew that complete openness was essential if I was to continue riding the tiger.

Still, I was well aware of the dangers I faced. Every interview I gave to a foreign correspondent or any one of the hundreds of documents I signed was enough to get me arrested on a charge of anti-Soviet activity. But how could my activities result in a charge of *treason*, with its implication that I had some secret contact with Western intelligence services? As recently as two weeks ago this was unthinkable.

And now, mulling it over in my cell, I reached a similar conclusion—that my activities were simply too public to support a charge of treason. (In retrospect, as I look back on my first few days in Lefortovo I am shocked at my own naiveté about Soviet justice. On the other hand, perhaps naiveté is an essential component for the person who rejects the spiritual slavery of his society and struggles against a powerful regime. Perhaps it guarantees that you won't be frightened to death or paralyzed by fear. Naiveté helps draw you into the struggle, where you're able to meet the growing danger head-on, with a firmer resolve.)

Presumably, my interrogators would be looking for some hidden element in my contacts with foreigners. But were there any secrets?

To some extent, yes. When I gave a statement to a correspondent, his news agency would use, at best, only two or three lines from it and would mention only two or three of the signatories. If we wanted to transmit the entire text to Soviet Jewry or human rights support groups in the West—say, for example, a twenty-page review of Soviet emigration policy, or tapes and photographs of a refusenik family—we had to find safe and effective ways to send it. So the one thing we never revealed was exactly how, when, and with whose help this material found its way out of the country.

While these items were leaving the Soviet Union, other publications came in from abroad, including Jewish novels, histories, prayer books, Bibles, Hebrew textbooks, Israeli newspapers, and Russian-language newspapers and journals published in Israel. These were often confiscated, but the activists who distributed unofficial or samizdat literature generally stayed a step ahead of the authorities. By the time a history book or a Jewish magazine was discovered and seized, a dozen people had already read it. Some books had been read by so many people that the pages were falling out.

But that was the whole point. We had an expression: The books must *work*. It was unthinkable that they should simply lie on a shelf and collect dust.

In many cases, the confiscated books or articles had not only been read but photocopied as well. I am not referring here to the copying machines that have become so common in the West. In the Soviet Union, such equipment is carefully guarded, and it's considered a crime to use such a machine for private purposes. (Years later, when I finally arrived in Israel, one thing that amazed me was that you could bring any document to the local photocopy center and purchase as many copies as you pleased.)

Our only choice, then, was to *literally* photocopy books and journals by taking a picture of each page and then developing the film ourselves. This was an awkward and time-consuming procedure, but my first Hebrew textbook, *Elef Milim* (A Thousand Words), was published just this way.

Of course I had no intention of discussing these details with the KGB. In my previous encounters with them, my attitude had been simple and defiant: "You persecute people because of their convictions. You operate outside the law and outside morality, and we have nothing to talk about." This posture had become an ingrained part of my character, so I knew how to conduct myself after my arrest.

Or so I thought. But five days before they took me away I had received a visit from Valentin Turchin, a leading Soviet cybernetician and a founder of the Moscow chapter of Amnesty International.

When I told Turchin that I was planning not to talk to the KGB after my arrest, he was incredulous. "This isn't just a charge of anti-Soviet activity," he replied. "We're talking about espionage! There will be all kinds of distortions and falsifications, and these must be exposed and refuted."

He was right, of course: it was unthinkable not to respond to a charge of espionage. And now, in my cell, I had to solve a difficult problem: How could I refute this charge without also revealing information that the KGB could use against me or my friends? In theory, there had been plenty of time to formulate an answer before my arrest. In reality, however, I hadn't been able to think about it.

"Exposed and refuted," Turchin had said. But to whom? To the KGB? To the court? No, they knew the answers even before they asked the questions. And the more I told the KGB, the easier it would be for them to take a compromising phrase from my testimony and turn it against me.

So then, exposed to whom? To history? I was trying to mock my own self-importance, but in fact I felt a genuine historical responsibility. As soon as the *Izvestia* article appeared, I and my fellow "traitors"—Slepak, Dina Beilin, Alexander Lerner, and Ida Nudel—concluded that we now faced the threat of new anti-Semitic show trials along the lines of the notorious Doctors' Plot. Shortly before Stalin's death, the regime had accused a group of Jewish physicians of plotting to poison the Soviet leadership with the help of the CIA. Stalin had planned to deport millions of Jews to Siberia, but he died before the program could be put into effect.

To us the espionage charges in *Izvestia* seemed to be cut from the same cloth. And now, as I looked down at Andropov's signature, I understood that the KGB had promoted me to a new position. Instead of being the spokesman for a small group of aliyah activists, I was now accused of disloyalty in a charge that extended to all the Jews of the Soviet Union.

Very well, I thought, but what about the question Turchin had raised? I resolved to limit my testimony to general points, such as the meaning, the tasks, the goals, and the nature of our activities. But I wouldn't give any concrete information, such as who wrote what statement and under what circumstances, or who collected signatures for a petition or letter, or who gave what material to whom.

Say, for example, that they got hold of one of the packets of information I sent to Michael Sherbourne, a London schoolteacher, who was enormously helpful to our struggle.

"Is this your packet?" they might ask.

I would refuse to answer.

But wait—wouldn't that imply that our activity really *was* secret?

Then what if I answered, "Yes, I sent it." In that case, wouldn't I be helping them compromise the foreigners who helped us deliver these packets?

Well, I decided, I'll give a general answer about the meaning and nature of my activity, but I'll refuse to discuss concrete facts. But then how should I respond if they then reach into the packet and take out some obviously forged document, such as a report about a Soviet military target? If I protest that this couldn't possibly be part of the packet, I would then be admitting that the material came from me.

As I sat there, weighing these various possibilities and fearing that at any moment they would summon me to an interrogation for which I wasn't prepared, I looked at the chess set on the table. Five years ago, as a student at the Moscow Institute of Physics and Technology, I had written a thesis entitled "Simulating the Decision-Making Process in Conflict Situations Based on the Chess Endgame." The examination commission had paid me a flattering but definitely exaggerated compliment, concluding that I had designed, in their words, "the first chess program in the world capable of playing the endgame." An important element in my program was a hierarchical list, a "tree" of goals and conditions for attaining them. And now, as I stared at the chessboard in my cell, it occurred to me that I could take a similar approach in the game I was about to play against the KGB.

What are the goals of *this* game? I asked myself. Clearly it was impossible to establish a goal of "minimizing the possible punishment," for that would mean submitting to the will of the KGB. After some thought, I decided upon three goals, and I sketched them out on a scrap of toilet paper, part of the daily ration of rough tissue paper the guard had given me at breakfast:

Obstruct _____ Study _____ Expose

My first goal was to obstruct their investigation. Second, I wanted to study their approach. Finally, I hoped to expose them—either through some contact with the outside world, or through an open trial.

Looking at my three objectives, I realized that I had attempted too much. Unfortunately, it wasn't in my power to obstruct, so I neatly crossed out that word and replaced it with a more modest goal: Not to cooperate.

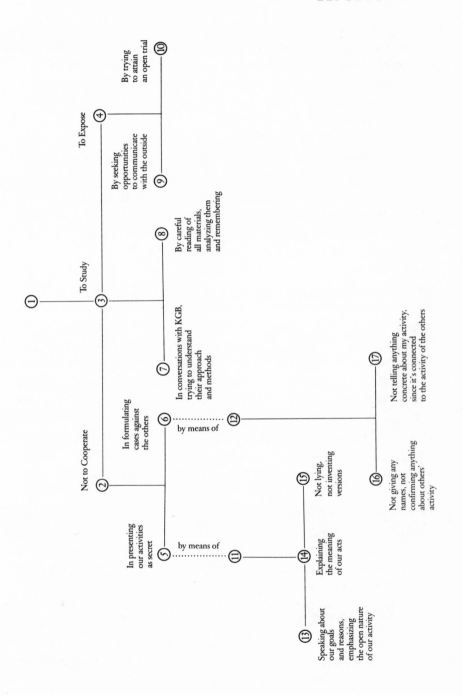

① ③ To Study

② Not to Cooperate

④ To Expose

⑩ By trying to attain an open trial

⑨

By seeking opportunities to communicate with the outside

⑧ By careful reading of all materials, analyzing them and remembering

⑦ In conversations with KGB, trying to understand their approach and methods

⑥ In formulating cases against the others

⑤ In presenting our activities as secret

⑫ by means of

⑪ by means of

⑰ Not telling anything concrete about my activity, since it's connected to the activity of the others

⑯ Not giving any names, not confirming anything about others' activity

⑮ Not lying, not inventing versions

⑭ Explaining the meaning of our acts

⑬ Speaking about our goals and reasons, emphasizing the open nature of our activity

But not to cooperate with *what?* With portraying our activity as secret, and gathering testimony from me on other refuseniks. After dividing the first goal into more elementary ones, I sat there for a long time and drew up an entire diagram of ends and means, with each goal divided into more elementary parts until my "tree" took the form of the above sketch.

As I look back on it now, my tree seems like pseudoscience, a pathetic attempt to impose order on my racing and chaotic mind. But at the time it was tremendously important, as the familiar terminology from my scientific training helped me adjust to my new reality. After hours of scattered thoughts, I was finally able to organize my impulses under the rubric of a logical plan. This alone was comforting, and gave me a sense of control.

My plan was far from perfect, however, as I immediately noticed a serious contradiction between point 14 (to explain the meaning of my actions) and point 17 (not to reveal concrete facts and circumstances). But then, as I reminded myself, it was the job of theory to point out contradictions, while the function of practice was to resolve them.

The food trap clanked for lunch—or perhaps it was supper—and I quickly flushed the paper down the toilet. I spent the rest of the day and all of the next one sketching my tree and using it to respond to a variety of questions I expected to be asked. I kept drawing the tree and destroying it until it became imprinted on my brain, ready to act as a censor for any answers I might be asked to give.

Prisoners in Lefortovo are allowed one hour a day for exercise, and on my second morning the guard took me out to a special area that consisted of a series of adjoining rectangular stone courtyards, each one measuring five meters by three meters with a bench in the middle. The walls were three meters high, and were covered with a rough cement so that you couldn't write on them. Overhead was an iron grating, which was covered by a wire net. Above the courtyard, on a raised catwalk, a guard paced back and forth to make sure there were no conversations between prisoners, and that nothing was tossed from one yard to the next.

During the exercise period I kept busy by jogging, bending, stretching, and doing push-ups. Before my arrest I had never bothered much with fitness, but in Lefortovo I became more systematic about taking care of my body. I even brushed my teeth carefully—something I had always been too rushed for in the past. But here such tasks were essential, a way to maintain control over my situation. Prison life encourages laziness, and I had to fight against it.

On one side of the exercise area was the prison; on the other was the investigative division. The prison building was in the shape of an enormous letter K, as Lefortovo was one of the so-called Katherine prisons, among the first in Russia, which were built during the reign of Katherine the Great in the late-eighteenth century. In Russian, she was known as both Katerina and Ekaterina, and in her honor these buildings were constructed in the shape of an E or a K.

I could hear the click of typewriters from almost every room of the investigative department. Looking up, I could sometimes make out faces perched above neckties with cigarettes dangling from their lips. They're sewing up cases, I thought. Despite my impatience, I hoped the interrogations would be delayed as long as possible. Was I afraid, or merely tired? It was hard to say.

On the evening of my third day in Lefortovo I was still waiting to be interrogated when the guard brought me a surprise: my first monthly food package from home, which contained five kilos of vegetables, fruits, sausage, and cheese. The most gratifying part of the package was the mandatory itemized list that Raya, my sister-in-law, had prepared. I stared at it for a long time, for although it was only a list, it was still a note from home. Reluctantly, I signed it and gave it over to the guard.

For the first time since I arrived I had an appetite, but before I could finish my first tomato the door opened again.

"With your things," said the guard. He explained that I was to collect all my belongings, as they were moving me to another cell.

My new cell contained one enormous difference: it was occupied. Another prisoner's possessions were hung up and strewn about, there was food in plastic containers, and he even had rags for cleaning the floor and the sink.

Tearing himself away from some kind of calculation, a man of about forty, with large bags under his eyes, stood up to introduce himself: "Shneivas, Efim Abram-Abelevich." He was of average height, plump, with a blotched and sagging face. Heart problems?

I wondered. High blood pressure? He turned out to have both.

Shneivas, a Jew, greeted me in a mixture of Yiddish and Russian: "A *Yid?* Wonderful. I'm tired of being with *goyim.*" He immediately combined our food supplies, which was generous of him because as a veteran *zek* (an acronym, designating a prisoner, that was left over from Stalin's time), he had far more food than I did. Then he proceeded to give me all kinds of practical advice: which of the two empty cots would be more comfortable in the warm weather, how to keep butter cold, what was worth buying in the prison store, and what time of day was best for washing the floor. (The stone floor retained moisture, so this was not a trivial matter.)

Shneivas was serving his second term in prison, so he knew how everything worked. The next morning, as I watched him gobble up his porridge, I wondered: Will the day ever come when I, too, will look forward to these meals?

Within hours we were addressing each other in the *ty* form and using our nicknames, Fima and Tolya. When I told him who I was and what I was being charged with, Fima looked shocked: "This is the first time I've seen a Jew fight against the Soviet regime," he said, giving me a string of compliments.

"But do you realize what's in store for you?" he asked. "Your forehead will be smeared with iodine."

"What do you mean?"

"They'll shoot you."

"What's the iodine for?"

"So your blood won't get infected!" Shneivas laughed long and hard to see a novice caught in what must have been an old prison joke.

Over the next few evenings, Fima told me the story of his life. He spent his early childhood in Leningrad during the siege. First he survived the hunger of the war years, which was followed by the hunger of the postwar years. Somehow he got hold of a used car, which was a great rarity during the 1950s. He teamed up with a prostitute: she would pick up a traveler at the port or the railway station and take him "home," with Fima playing the role of taxi driver. The man's luggage would remain in the car and Fima would disappear with the goods. The victim was helpless, as he couldn't very well tell the police he was robbed while visiting a prostitute.

Later, Fima switched to more solid work, selling scarce and fashionable foreign goods, such as shoelaces, ladies' shoes with stiletto heels, and plastic raincoats, on the black market. By the early 1960s, he was involved in more serious crimes. With the help of a well-placed police officer in one of the Central Asian republics, he began to buy up *mumie,* an organic substance found in mountain caves that was thought to strengthen the body. He sold the stuff in Leningrad, but was eventually caught and sent to prison camp for three years.

Then he moved to Moscow, where he found a legitimate job as an inspector of stores and warehouses at a salary of 150 rubles a month. But his real income was much higher, as Fima was also a black-market currency dealer. He carried out his operations only two or three times a year, with an American friend who was the Moscow representative of a commercial firm. This went on for ten years, and Fima acquired vast sums of money. He lived well, but not so lavishly as to attract unwanted attention. But one of the dealers with whom he did business was arrested, and they came for Fima as well.

Thus far, Fima's stories, which he spun out at great length, were so full of realistic detail that I believed most of what he told me. But I noticed that from the moment of his arrest his anecdotes became simplistic and predictable.

In one such episode he told of the KGB's showing him a photograph of himself picking up a cigarette butt at a deserted spot at the side of a road. Supposedly, Fima's American friend flew into Sheremetevo Airport and immediately drove to Moscow. Fima, who was waiting in the crowd, followed in his own car. At a deserted stretch of the road the American signaled with his horn and tossed a cigarette butt out the window, whereupon Fima pulled over, made sure he was alone, and picked up the butt, which contained a note outlining the details of their next deal.

In another of these stories, the KGB played Shneivas a tape of a conversation between himself and the American—a conversation, Fima claimed, that was held in the bathroom with the water running. The point of these tales, of course, was that the KGB knew everything, so it was pointless to resist their pressures.

Whenever he told me stories about the KGB, I felt he had an interest in my giving up as soon as possible. But it was difficult to know whether this was the result of a special assignment on his part or simply the normal response of a man who had surrendered and needed to believe he was no worse than anyone else.

I was well aware, of course, that the KGB used stool pigeons in the cells. And earlier this month, I myself had been betrayed by an informer: the author of the *Izvestia* article was Sanya Lipavsky, a physician who had helped many refuseniks with medical care, access to telephones, and numerous other favors.

But I always found it difficult to transfer my general hatred of informers to specific human beings. Besides, the premonition that your fellow citizen is working for the KGB operates like a cancer in Soviet society. While many people do work as informers for the regime, the mere fact that this is always a possibility does not, in my view, constitute adequate grounds for suspicion.

In captivity, I made up my mind to follow the same rules as in freedom: while I was careful not to help potential informers in their work, I would try not to assume the worst about my neighbors. Inside the prisons and camps, as well as in the "large zone," as the zeks cynically refer to the rest of the country, informing was so common that the intrigue alone could drive you crazy. Besides, no matter what kind of person Fima was, his pain over being separated from his wife and children was genuine, and I tried my best to console him. Equally sincere, in my view, was his involuntary feeling of solidarity with the refuseniks as I described our long struggle against the KGB.

Fima's favorite topic was his numerous romantic and sexual adventures, which he loved to recount in salacious detail. I tried to cut him off on several occasions, but my reaction produced only amazement: "You have to know how to talk about such things in the camps," he said. "If you don't join in, nobody will respect you." Before long, Fima's stories lost the psychological nuances that had made them interesting, and began to resemble the plots of bad movies—especially when popular actresses from both cinema and theater started appearing as his partners.

"Don't you believe me?" he would ask.

"Of course," I would reply, so as not to offend him. And indeed, when he returned from an interrogation, claiming that he just had a face-to-face confrontation with some famous singer who said that

Fima had given her a diamond ring, it was hard for a new zek like myself to understand why anyone would make up something like this. In time, however, I learned that such fantasies were common among nonpolitical prisoners. To hear them talk, you would have thought that every one had had affairs with the most popular actresses in the Soviet Union.

It was also possible that Shneivas had another purpose in mind: at one point, having apparently grown tired of talking, he suggested that I tell a few stories of my own. I declined, explaining that I didn't like to speak about such things and that I didn't have much to say in any event.

But Fima was strangely persistent, and when I continued to resist, he resorted to demands and finally to threats: "You better watch out, you'll have a hard time in the camps if you don't tell stories." At that point I had to answer him more firmly.

Later, I became familiar with the KGB's interest in the private lives of its wards. In prison, of course, the walls have ears, and the authorities can learn a great deal from a prisoner's private conversation even if he reveals nothing significant about his case. In the struggle for your soul, the KGB tries to provoke tension and suspicion between husbands and wives, and among prisoners and their friends and relatives. Eventually, I came to see that Fima's attempts to have me talk about my personal life may have gone well beyond his own prurient curiosity.

Interrogation

3

O N my third morning in Lefortovo the food trap opened with a clang and a guard pointed at me with the cell key—a key as thick as the barrel of a gun.

"Name!" he demanded. He checked my name on his form. Then, "To a summons!"

This, I learned, was the procedure for taking a prisoner to an interrogation, and during the hundred and ten times I was questioned, it never varied.

In the center of the prison, where the four corridors of the letter K converged, stood a signalman with a red flag. His job was to ensure that no two cells were ever opened simultaneously. When he waved the flag once, my cell door could be opened. A second wave meant I could proceed.

After being searched, I walked slowly down the long corridor with my hands behind my back. The guard followed, snapping his fingers as loudly as possible or banging two keys together. This was a warning: I am with a prisoner.

Then it was up a winding staircase, where I crossed over to the investigative department and into an entirely different world. Whereas the prison was dark and all the guards wore uniforms, here there were windows and telephones and men in business suits.

From time to time, when a similar finger-snapping was heard from the other end of the corridor, they locked me in a special closet that resembled a telephone booth. If there was no closet nearby, I might be taken up or down to another floor, or even back to my cell. But this was rarely necessary.

The signalman and the other precautions were there to enforce a basic rule of prison life—that no prisoner awaiting trial could know who else was being held. (This was why the guard always asked your name and never said it himself, for if he happened to make a mistake, you might inadvertently learn the identity of a fellow prisoner.) If you passed another zek in the corridor, there was always the possibility that some quick message or gesture might be exchanged. Or you might see a witness from your own case who would somehow let you know that he wasn't cooperating with the authorities, even if your interrogators insisted that he was.

At some level, every Soviet citizen lives in fear of the consequences of his actions, for he knows there is no presumption of innocence on the part of the KGB. That is what makes interrogations so sinister.

At the same time the nature of these sessions has changed enormously since the Stalin era. From my older friends, and from samizdat memoirs, I knew about endless nocturnal interrogations in Lefortovo, as well as crude beatings and more refined tortures to pressure the accused into signing a confession and giving "testimony," which was then used against his companions. In some cases, prisoners were brought to Lefortovo and summarily shot. Now, however, both quick executions and torture are officially forbidden, and the KGB is a paragon of Soviet legality.

Lefortovo is no police station: officially, fists aren't permitted here, and they don't yell at you. True, they can torture you with the cold and hunger of the punishment cell, but even there they address you formally. The prison guards called me Citizen Sharansky, and the KGB officers, including my interrogators, always addressed me as Anatoly Borisovich, which was more polite and less ceremonial. Never in my life was I addressed so often by that honorific, which normally wasn't used for people my age.

Years later, in a prison camp, I learned that I had been one of the lucky ones. As they led me down the deathly silent corridors of Lefortovo, I had no idea that next to the freight elevator was a room lined with rubber. If "state interests" demanded it, and if the KGB was certain that Western public opinion had no interest in their victim, they would bring him here, where the beatings were carried out by the very same officers who addressed me so politely. And while my interrogators tried to assure me that our Helsinki Group reports on Soviet psychiatric abuses were false and slanderous, in the very next office other interrogators were showing my fellow prisoners terrifying pictures of people whose faces were distorted by pain, and telling them, "If you don't want to spend the rest of your life on a cot in a lunatic asylum, you'd better testify."

Where they had once used force, the KGB now preferred to engage you in long conversations, which often lasted the whole day. They kept you here for weeks, months, even years, trying to manipulate you with explanations, threats, promises, hints, and more threats. The point of these incessant interrogations was twofold: first, to create an aura of legitimacy to mask what was still a legal farce, and, second, to induce you to reveal as much information as possible, even if it was already known to the investigators. Everything you told them was written down in the protocol, which you would then be asked to sign. Later, carefully selected and twisted excerpts could be used to pressure the next person: "You see? Sharansky has already told us all about this."

My first interrogator, Major Anatoly Vasilievich Chernysh, seemed to be in his early forties. He was only slightly taller than I, and almost as bald. Chernysh was clearly concerned about losing his hair, and one day he asked whether I had ever tried to restore mine. For me, however, this topic had been moot since the age of twenty-two.

Chernysh had a small head and tiny eyes, but they were observant and, I must admit, intelligent. At first he reminded me of a hamster—later, a rat. His office was long and narrow, and he sat behind a large desk, beneath the hammer-and-sickle insignia. I sat near the door, behind a small table. Between us, along the drab wall, was a bookshelf filled with the standard works of Marx and Lenin, assorted legal volumes, and professional and party journals. There were portraits of Lenin and Brezhnev, and of Felix Dzerzhinsky, the first head of the Soviet Secret Police.

Chernysh began by informing me that a team of eleven investigators had been set up to handle my case. (Later, the number grew to seventeen.) Hearing this news, I felt overwhelmed and depressed. Why so many? Instead of closing my case, they were apparently gearing up for something enormous. "If this is how the KGB uses its personnel," I replied sarcastically, "then there's obviously no danger of unemployment."

"What can we do?" replied Chernysh. "You and your accomplices were engaged in criminal activity over many years, and now we have to investigate it all." He said this calmly and politely, but every word heightened the tension. I realized I had better get used to the idea that from now on my friends were "accomplices," and that our struggle to emigrate to Israel constituted "criminal activity."

Then Chernysh repeated the question that Galkin had asked me when I first arrived: "What can you tell us about the essence of the charge?" I gave my same reply, but in contrast to Galkin, Chernysh calmly recorded my answer and read it back to make sure he had it correctly.

Only then did he try to pick apart my response: "You say you 'informed international public opinion,' and that you 'drew attention to . . .' By what means?"

I hesitated briefly to make sure my reply conformed to the principles of my tree. "I organized press conferences and met with Western correspondents and politicians. I also sent letters to the appropriate Soviet organizations. This was all done openly, and the material I transmitted was designated exclusively for public use."

"Who else participated in this activity?"

"I refuse to answer because I don't want to help the KGB prepare a criminal case against any other Jewish activists or dissidents who, like me, have committed no crimes."

"If you really committed no crimes," said Chernysh, "then what are you afraid of? If your activity was open, speak openly. You're forcing me to think there was something secret in all this."

"Our activity *was* open and public," I replied. "You have copies of letters with our signatures that we wrote for publication. If you want to know who was involved, you can read the names yourself. But for some reason you need *me* to testify about the participation of others. Why?"

Chernysh politely reminded me that he was the one who was asking the questions. He continued: "Exactly what kind of letters and appeals were sent? When and to whom did you send them?"

Again I had to pause: What kind of answer did my tree indicate? While I didn't plan to deny any of my activity, I also had no intention of helping the KGB prepare a dossier on us.

"I refuse to answer," I told Chernysh, "because I don't want to help the KGB draw up criminal cases against Jewish activists for their legal and open activity."

He duly recorded my reply, read it aloud, and then launched into a little speech. He didn't want to frighten me, he said, but it was his unpleasant duty to explain my situation. He had handled several previous cases that resulted in *rasstrel*—execution—although he always hoped to avoid such an outcome.

And now, as he looked at me and thought about my various talents, about my young wife who was waiting for me in Israel, and my elderly parents who had pinned so many hopes on me—at this moment, despite our ideological differences—he found it difficult as a fellow human being to think that I might be executed. He didn't want to encroach on my views or change them, but I had to understand that my fate now depended on only one thing—the nature of my testimony.

Chernysh had been pacing around the room, but suddenly he grabbed a chair, sat down at my little table, and looked me right in the eye. I was leaning back with my arms folded over my chest, trying to appear calm and indifferent. Inside, however, I was trembling with anxiety. It was that word *ras-s-strel*—especially the way Chernysh pronounced it, with a hissing sound—that grated on my ears and made my knees shake. Each time he said it the muscles tensed up in my chest and shoulders and I had to clench my teeth to hide my tension.

Some people associate *rasstrel* with a firing squad, but for me the word has always conjured up a different image: a prison official leads you down to the basement, and when you get to the bottom of the stairs he shoots you in the back of the head. That's how things were done in Stalin's time, and that's what I thought of every time Chernysh uttered that terrible word.

Over the next few weeks Chernysh diligently sought out ways to insert *ras-s-strel* into the conversation. When I asked for my Hebrew-Russian dictionary, which had been seized during the search of my apartment, he expressed surprise: "What do you need that

for? Given your conduct, they're going to shoot you anyway."
When Brezhnev delivered another speech denouncing the Ameri-
cans after Cyrus Vance's unsuccessful visit to Moscow at the end of
March, Chernysh said, "See for yourself. It's right here in black and
white that we won't permit any interference in our internal affairs.
The Americans won't save you from *ras-s-strel.*"

Back in the cell, Fima would tell me about his case and ask about
my own. The conclusion of his stories was always the same: Don't
let them smear your forehead with iodine. There it was *ras-s-strel,*
here it was iodine. I just wanted to be left alone.

I lay down, covered myself with my overcoat, turned toward the
wall and fell asleep. On days when there were no interrogations, I
slept right through except for meals and exercise. When interrogations were scheduled, I fell asleep as soon as they were done. By law
there were no sessions past ten at night—this was one of the post-
Stalin reforms, along with the official ban on beatings and torture—
but when the interrogation dragged on past noon and they brought
me back to the cell for lunch, I used the time to doze for another
forty or fifty minutes. When I returned to Chernysh's office I was
barely able to suppress a yawn.

Chernysh was convinced I was faking and trying to appear indifferent, but my fatigue was real. Never in my life did I sleep as much
as during those first three weeks in Lefortovo. I had never needed
much sleep, but ever since the *Izvestia* article appeared I was exhausted, and now I was sleeping as much as fifteen or sixteen hours
a day. I would doze off immediately, but it was a fitful sleep, as my
mind was filled with interrogations, both past and future, and with
anxiety over friends and loved ones. Mostly I thought about Avital.
Where was she now? What was she thinking about at this very
moment? What was she doing? What was the weather today in
Israel? And Mama—how was *she* coping with all of this? And what
about Papa, whose health wasn't all that strong to begin with?

One morning, about twenty days after my arrest, I woke up and
suddenly realized that I no longer wanted to sleep. Instead of feeling
crushed or tired, I was full of strength. I even did exercises and
doused myself with cold water from the sink, although our cell was
so chilly that Fima and I slept in warm underwear and covered
ourselves with a blanket and an overcoat.

It wasn't that my problems had disappeared. I still felt weighed down by a sense of responsibility and by the uncertainty of my situation. But now, for the first time since my arrest, I felt determined and ready to struggle.

Invigorated by this new energy, I decided that my first priority was to sort out my feelings. Why was I so anxious before each interrogation? I invariably expected some terrible surprise—a mysterious document, perhaps, or the unexpected testimony of a close friend that would finally make clear why they had accused me of treason. But nothing of the sort ever happened. Instead, Chernysh would ask a few questions and then launch into a long discourse about the hopelessness of my situation.

Before my arrest I had trained myself not to pay attention to the threats of the KGB interrogators I occasionally met with. Instead of answering their questions, I told them only what I wanted them to hear. In their presence I felt like a chess player facing a much weaker opponent. They did exactly what they were supposed to, and I knew all their moves in advance: their threats and warnings, their attempts at blackmail, their flattery and their promises.

But now my former confidence had disappeared. So far, at least, I hadn't said anything I regretted. But who knew what would happen later, when they switched from the opening artillery barrage of all these general questions to a more detailed, frontal attack?

Analyzing my first few sessions with Chernysh, I came to the obvious conclusion that I hadn't been psychologically prepared for a charge of treason—and especially for the horrifying possibility of *rasstrel*. My only hope was to quickly become accustomed to that idea, to steel myself against it. Just as the skin on my feet used to toughen up every summer during my childhood, when I walked around barefoot, I now had to toughen up my ears and my heart until the sound and the prospect of *rasstrel* meant nothing to me.

As a dissident, I had gradually grown accustomed to words like "arrest" and "exile," which no longer had the same dramatic power over me as they once did. Now I had to get accustomed to the word *rasstrel*, but I had to do so on my own—and fast. Any word loses its mystique when you use it often enough, so I started talking about *rasstrel* with Fima at every opportunity. As for Chernysh, I still remember how amazed he was the first time I turned the tables on him and blurted out, "What's the use of all these conversations when you're just going to shoot me anyway—*rasstrel?*"

He was shocked. Until now this word had been his exclusive weapon, while I had avoided any mention of it. Chernysh seemed to think I was testing him, and he began to ramble on about how these were not empty threats, and how his duty was not to coerce me but simply to explain the situation. But the atmosphere had changed. At first it was awkward, but as we went along I was able to insert *rasstrel* into almost every conversation, whether it was appropriate or not. Before long my plan began to pay off, and neither the word itself nor our conversations about it caught me off-balance. Within weeks, *rasstrel* had become a word like any other.

While the interrogations had their own routine, there were occasional surprises. One morning Chernysh brought in excerpts from the treason laws of Western countries. "You see?" he said. "Acts that go against the interests of the state are prosecuted everywhere. And there's no point in alluding to the West because their guidelines are even stricter."

I glanced at the pages he showed me, but I couldn't see much difference in the formulations. "I don't understand all the legal terms," I said, "but I know this—if the Western nations had an equivalent to our laws on 'anti-Soviet activity,' then the Communist Party would be outlawed in these countries, and all their members would be arrested."

Chernysh took a moment to think this one over. "Of course it *ought* to be that way," he conceded, "but the capitalists tolerate the Communists because they're afraid of the people's anger." This idiotic answer—the same moronic drivel I used to hear back in kindergarten—reminded me of how primitive my adversaries could be.

Chernysh's next tactic was to tell me about two other prisoners he had recently dealt with who had decided to cooperate with their investigators. They were both foreigners, a Dutchman and a Frenchman, and were arrested for passing out dissident literature. As I could see from the protocols of their interrogations, each had loudly insisted on his rights, but soon recanted. Then, after returning home, both men had repudiated their confessions, and the

Dutchman had even written a book about his imprisonment. Chernysh's message was obvious: Recant, and you, too, will be released. Then you can say whatever you like. "Goddamn foreigners," I muttered. "How glibly they recant and write books."

Chernysh didn't mention Yakir and Krasin, but they were on my mind a great deal. In 1973, when I first became an aliyah activist, dissident circles in Moscow were in shock from the confessions of Pyotr Yakir and Viktor Krasin, two leaders of the democratic movement who had survived Stalin's labor camps. At a major press conference that was broadcast on radio and television, Yakir and Krasin condemned their own dissident activities, including *Chronicle of Current Events,* the journal of the human rights movement. Both received conspicuously light sentences, while their friends and colleagues who did not recant were punished more harshly. Although I later witnessed many cases of prisoners cooperating with the KGB, the case of Yakir and Krasin was the first time I had seen this process in sharp relief, and it remained with me.

Sitting in my cell, I asked myself the obvious question: Why *not* recant and then repudiate it after I was released? But I already knew the answer. First, any confession I made would mean betraying my friends. When Yakir and Krasin decided to cooperate with the authorities, it was enormously demoralizing for the dissident community. I had no desire to undermine the movements I believed in, or to do anything that would leave my fellow refuseniks and dissidents with an even greater feeling of hopelessness, or of the KGB's omnipotence.

Second, I knew that the only reason the world paid any attention to a small group of Soviet dissidents and Jewish activists was our strong moral position. While collaborating with the KGB might be understandable, it would severely compromise that stance. The moral righteousness of our struggle was our greatest asset, perhaps our *only* asset. To cooperate with the KGB would mean letting down our growing number of supporters in the free world and undermining their continued determination to help us.

Finally, on a more practical level, I knew that each time the KGB made a political arrest, it required permission from the political leadership. If I recanted, it would only make it easier for the KGB to receive permission to initiate new repressions and another round of arrests.

Recalling these arguments in my cell, I found them as compelling as ever. But even if none of them was true, and I could somehow surrender to the KGB without any damage to my friends and our supporters, I still couldn't confess to crimes I hadn't committed. For behind all these valid and rational arguments was a barrier of the spirit that blocked all roads to surrender.

To put it simply, there was no way on earth I could ever return to my former life as an assimilated Soviet Jew, a loyal citizen who said one thing but thought another as he tried to act just like everyone else. That was all behind me now. For the past four years I had been a free man, and it was unthinkable that I would ever give up the marvelous sensation of freedom that came over me after I returned to my roots. For now I had purpose, I had perspective, I had peace of mind.

And although we were separated by time and space, I had Avital.

4

Breaking Through
to Other Worlds

FEAR and isolation are the KGB's two main weapons against prisoners in Lefortovo. I had already begun dealing with my fear—especially of *rasstrel*. Now I had to come to terms with my feelings of isolation, which were growing more intense by the day.

No mail was allowed in or out of Lefortovo. No visitors were permitted. Communicating with other prisoners was strictly forbidden, except for your cell mate, who could always turn out to be an informer. Aside from your interrogators, your only contact with the outside world was through reading *Pravda*, which the guard handed you through the food trap. Twenty minutes later he took it back and delivered it to the next cell, checking first to make sure you hadn't written any messages inside.

The isolation of Lefortovo was so severe that I actually looked forward to reading *Pravda*, which would have been unthinkable in my former life. My friends among the foreign press gave me copies of *Time, Newsweek,* and the *International Herald Tribune,* and there was no point in looking at *Pravda* if you had access to real news. But here at Lefortovo I read it straight through—even the boring articles on Soviet agriculture and economy. It was all propaganda, of course, but through the art of reading between the lines, which is known to every Soviet citizen, you could still learn a great deal.

What worried me most about my isolation was that if it continued, I would inevitably, perhaps even unconsciously, start adapting myself to the world of my interrogators. And once that process began, helped along by my fear of being killed and by Fima's constant chatter about the possibility of reaching an agreement with the KGB, I would gradually abandon my own world and my own values. The next step was all too clear: I would begin to "understand" my captors, and would try to reach an accord with them. Unless I stopped this process, it was only a matter of time before I succumbed.

After all, there was so much they already controlled: when I slept, what I ate, when I was interrogated, when I exercised—not to mention the larger question of whether I would live or die. When they brought me here a few weeks ago I had firm and clear views, and a perspective on the world that protected me. Now, however, I was cut off completely (and possibly *forever*) from the world that nurtured those views and the people who shared and supported them.

Ironically, it was Chernysh who made me aware of how important it was to maintain a link to my own world. He interrupted one of my interrogations to call his son, who seemed to be around fourteen, and who evidently wanted his father's permission to go to the movies.

"Did you finish your homework?" asked Chernysh, who at that moment sounded exactly like my own schoolteacher fifteen years earlier. "Did you merely go over your lessons, or did you really learn them?"

Another time, I overheard Chernysh making arrangements with his wife for an evening at the Bolshoi Theater. And later on, in my presence, two investigators from my case discussed plans for a summer house.

Even today I can't say whether my exposure to these conversations was accidental or part of the KGB's plan. In any case, my initial reaction was sharply negative. How could it be, I wondered, that the same people who were threatening me with execution and plotting against me every day could also be responsible fathers and family men? But then I remembered that beyond these prison walls life went on. Although my entire physical world now consisted of a small cell, the exercise yard, the corridors of Lefortovo, and Chernysh's office, *these* people, the masters of my new world, were full participants in that other life. They probably loved their children just as my parents loved me, and adored their wives just as I adored

Avital. They read books and attended the theater and the cinema—which meant, I concluded, that they were capable of empathizing with other human beings.

If this was true, I told myself, maybe they didn't really want me to die. After all, Chernysh and his colleagues had shown an interest in me that went well beyond my dissident and Jewish activities. They had examined my personal photographs that had been confiscated in the search, including one that showed me giving an exhibition of simultaneous chess, and when Chernysh told me of his great respect for chess players, he was probably telling the truth.

On another occasion, Chernysh confided that he knew how hard it was for me to be apart from my wife, because he was once separated from his wife for several months and found it very painful. Although I wasn't so naive as to take such remarks seriously, they added to my feeling that perhaps Chernysh and his colleagues really did prefer to avoid a tragic outcome and reach some suitable compromise.

When I finally realized that I was actually thinking along these lines, I became disgusted with myself. Suddenly it was clear that I was becoming aware of all the human areas that the KGB men and I had in common. While this was natural enough, it was also dangerous, for the growing sense of our common humanity could easily become the first step in my surrender. If my interrogators were my only link to the outside world, I would come to depend on them and to look for areas of agreement.

I had heard such arguments before—that we had to find a common language with the KGB because in the final analysis, despite everything, they were human beings, too. Yakir and Krasin had probably come to a similar conclusion. But however tempting it was to think otherwise, there was no way to cooperate with the KGB without taking that first step on the road to betrayal. It wasn't that they were less than human. Nor was it simply a matter of our respective attachments—that they worshiped the Soviet Union while we dreamed of Israel. No, the real differences between us were far more profound.

For the KGB a person was a means of attaining a specific goal—a goal so important that any number of bodies (not to mention souls) could be sacrificed to achieve it. For us, however, the person *was* the goal. What we hoped to achieve was nothing less than man's rebirth. By reclaiming our national and historical roots we hoped to advance from spiritual slavery to genuine freedom.

As long as I kept these differences in mind, I felt secure in the knowledge that the KGB could never reach my soul. But now, in my cell, I was painfully aware that my defensive wall was beginning to show cracks—cracks that let in such dangerous leaks as "They, too, are human beings." I could patch up these cracks, but that was not sufficient; I had to find out what was causing them.

The only way out was to hold on fiercely to my own world. No matter how difficult it was, I had to preserve the link with my former environment and my values. Since I obviously couldn't accomplish this in the physical world, I had to find another way. Yes, I decided, instead of feeling guilty about my various mental escapes, I ought to be using them to my own advantage.

When I was first brought to Lefortovo, I immediately began to focus on the people who were dear to me: Where were they now, and what were they doing at this very moment? But each time I mentally returned to the cell I became angry at myself, as I was convinced that these flights from reality were a sign of weakness. Concentrate on the present, I told myself. Prepare for the next investigation. But it was no use, for an hour later I'd be drifting off again.

But now I realized that instead of driving away all thoughts of my past life and my loved ones, I should be doing just the opposite. I ought to be surrounding myself with my memories of these people in an effort to return to *my* life, rather than the one the KGB wanted to impose on me.

Before my arrest, Slepak had been teaching me how to calm down and take a quick nap in the middle of the day. (He had read somewhere that President Kennedy used to do this in the White House.) You lay on your back and slowly relaxed your body, muscle by muscle, while saying to yourself, "I am calm, I am completely calm, my left hand is getting warm," and so on. The first time Slepak demonstrated this technique, he practically fell asleep on the spot.

My own initial attempts had backfired, for as soon as I began, the muscles I was trying to relax would tense up. I also found it difficult to focus attention on one spot without moving on. I never did complete the course, which was interrupted by my arrest. Several years later, in Chistopol Prison, I finally mastered the process.

Now, however, I began using Slepak's technique for a very different purpose. Instead of talking with Fima, I lay on the cot and pretended to sleep. Then, slowly, very slowly, I began reviewing my life. Along the way I stopped at every episode I could remember, as if it were just another muscle in my body, and I didn't leave it until I had recalled all the significant details. When I concentrated, I found that I could "brake" my thoughts and dwell on the important moments, adding more details each time. Soon I was back among my friends and loved ones, pining for Israel and working with my fellow activists in our movement.

Of course my most precious memories were of Avital, and I lovingly recalled the first time I met her. It was a Saturday in the fall of 1973, and I was standing outside the Moscow synagogue when a tall and lovely young woman came up who introduced herself as Natalia Stieglitz. Her brother, Misha, had recently been arrested during a demonstration and sentenced to fifteen days, and a mutual friend had told her that as one of the regular demonstrators I might be able to explain the usual procedure in these cases.

Natasha, as she was known, made an immediate and powerful impression on me. She seemed uncomfortable in this crowd—and in this country. As she huddled against the snow in her thin jacket she reminded me of a flower that wants to open but is afraid of being destroyed by the cold. But although she seemed painfully shy, Natasha exuded a tremendous feeling of warmth. And something in her eyes told me that despite her demure and even timid manner, she was already a free person. I felt a deep affinity for her, and I knew at once that I had to see Natasha again.

I told her all I knew about what usually happened when demonstrators were jailed, and tried to reassure her that Misha would be fine. These detentions were routine in our lives, and when I explained the process she seemed relieved. I also pointed out that some refuseniks were given exit visas following their fifteen-day sentences; this turned out to be true for Misha, who left the country at the end of November.

Then I asked if she was studying Hebrew.

"I've been trying to learn it on my own," she replied, "but I'm not getting anywhere. What do you suggest?"

"Maybe you could join our class," I said. "What level are you on?"

"And you?" she asked, avoiding my question.

"I know about a thousand words."

"That's exactly my level," she immediately replied.

It didn't take me long to discover that she was stretching the truth by around nine hundred and ninety words. But I was thrilled when I realized that she wanted to join the class so we could be together.

Our Hebrew class met weekly, and I still remember the very first sentence we learned from our teacher, Micka Chlenov: *Anachnu yehudim, aval anachnu lo m'dabrim ivrit* (We are Jews, but we do not speak Hebrew).

Micka was an ethnographer who knew six or seven languages and had taught himself Hebrew. When the KGB learned that Micka was teaching Hebrew, they approached the director of the institute where Micka worked and told him to advise Micka to stop meeting with us.

"Let's approach this as scientists," the director had said to Micka. "We both know that all languages and civilizations have life cycles. Take the Etruscans, who once had a great civilization. But is there any sense in reviving their language today?"

"I'll tell you the truth," said Micka. "If I were an Etruscan, I'd probably be teaching their language, too."

Professionally, Micka had to pay a high price for his involvement with our movement. Although he himself never applied for a visa and therefore didn't lose his job, this outstanding scholar of ethnography was never permitted to receive his doctorate.

Micka was such a dynamic, entertaining teacher that when you sat in his class you felt you were already in Israel. He used to bring in Hebrew tapes he had recorded from Kol Yisrael, the Israeli radio service. (So few people in the Soviet Union knew Hebrew that the authorities didn't bother to jam these broadcasts.) He would also bring in articles from Israeli newspapers and Hebrew record albums brought in by tourists.

Our class was a marvelous combination of fun and serious learning. There was homework, of course, as we had to study a list of

new words and prepare stories in Hebrew. If you failed to prepare
your assignment, you had to bring along a bottle of wine. Once a
week, several classes joined together for *dibburim* (conversations)
where the rule was *Rak ivrit* (Only Hebrew).

Micka also taught us some basic information about Judaism and
especially Jewish holidays. At that point I had little interest in
religion, and Micka himself was not a believer, but as we learned
about the historical events behind Hanukkah, Purim, and Passover,
I was fascinated and inspired to discover that all we were going
through—and much worse—had already happened to previous generations of Jews. In those days Jewish history was meaningful to me
mostly because of the many striking precedents and parallels it
offered for our own lives.

At first Natasha and I saw each other only at the synagogue and
in class. I could have tried to rush her, but I was reluctant to tempt
fate. From the day we met I felt we were kindred spirits, destined
to be together, and I was transformed. I saw her as a sign from
God—although back then I wouldn't have phrased it in those
terms—that I was on the right path and that this new life I had
recently entered into was my true destiny. I could never have met
her in my previous life, where someone like Natasha simply could
not exist.

On November 13, 1973, exactly a month after we met, she moved
her belongings into my small rented room.

"Are you sure this is love?" she asked me that day.

"I know this," I replied. "We need each other and we can't go
on living apart."

Those were the best days of my life. I had so much—love, a cause,
and a community. All I lacked was an exit visa.

In the spring, Micka Chlenov and two other Hebrew teachers
organized a Passover Seder, which Natasha and I attended. This was
the first Seder I had ever been to. Our teachers explained the various
symbols, such as the matzoh and the bitter herbs, and I as the
youngest participant was given the honor of asking the Four Questions. I was twenty-six years old, but in terms of my Jewish life I
was a mere child.

The special relevance of the Passover story to a group of refuseniks in Moscow was so obvious that nobody had to point it out. We

sat there enthralled as we discussed the story of our ancestors, enslaved and oppressed in Egypt, a powerful land where they were unable to practice their religion or learn about their heritage. Then, through a series of miracles, they succeeded in leaving this place of bondage, eventually reaching their homeland, the land of Israel. That night I came across a moving line in the Passover liturgy that would stay with me forever: "In every generation, a person should feel as though he, personally, went out of Egypt."

(It would be twelve long years before I could spend another Passover with Avital. Finally, in the spring of 1986, the two of us held our own Seder in Jerusalem. For the first time ever, I conducted the ceremony. Avital asked the Four Questions.)

During the course of these heartfelt recollections, I slipped imperceptibly across the border between real life and fantasy, between past and present. There's Avital with her brother, Misha, leaving Switzerland for America. Now they're in New York, where they meet Jerry Stern, an American Jew whom I met just after Avital left, the first in a long list of American and European Jews who helped maintain the link between us. Jerry takes them down to Washington for meetings with Javits, Humphrey, Drinan, and other members of the House and Senate who know me from their visits to Moscow. Diplomats and foreign correspondents come into view and talk about my activities. I try to linger with these people, and together we recall every such meeting, every declaration. But these images soon lead me back to Moscow, back to the past, back to my final interviews and my arrest.

When the dream was over and I was back on my cot, the cell no longer seemed so depressing or so frightening, and I no longer felt alone. My friends were with me, and our life went on. I could return to my world whenever I wished, and I often did so during the months and years that followed.

It was around this time that I composed a short prayer in my primitive Hebrew: "*Baruch atah Adonai, eloheinu melech ha'olam, ten li mazal lagur im ishti, ahuvati, Avital Sharon, b'Eretz Yisrael. Ten l'horim sheli, ten l'ishti, ten l'kol mishpachti, ko'ach lisbol kol k'shaiim ad p'gishteinu. Ten li ko'ach, g'vurah, sechel, mazal v'savlanut latzeit mikeleh hazeh, l'hagiah l'Eretz Yisrael b'derech yashar v'ra'ui*" (Blessed are You, Adonai, King of the Universe. Grant me the good fortune to live with my wife, my beloved Avital Sharon, in the Land of Israel. Grant my parents, my wife, and my whole family the strength to endure all hardships until we meet. Grant me the strength, the power, the intelligence, the good fortune, and the patience to leave this jail and to reach the land of Israel in an honest and worthy way).

From that day on, every time I was led to an interrogation I said the prayer twice. When I exercised, and later in the punishment cells, I chanted it like a psalm. Soon I started reciting it every night before I went to sleep. I did this for almost nine years—until the day I walked over the bridge to West Berlin and rejoined Avital.

The prayer was the only part of the daily routine that was mine; everything else in Lefortovo was determined by the prison authorities. They woke you at six, when the guard opened the food trap. Then you washed up, cleaned the cell, and made your bed. You weren't supposed to lie down between wake-up and breakfast, which was at seven, but this rule was not enforced. During the day, if you weren't called to an interrogation, you could read, write, or think about your case. There was an hour for exercise, usually in the morning. Lunch was at twelve, supper at five. In the evening you could play chess or dominoes with your cell mate. Lights out— although the lights were never actually turned off—was at ten.

Twice a week they brought you hot water, a mirror, soap, and a razor to shave, and of course they watched you the whole time. (Shaving was compulsory, although any prisoner who came to Lefortovo with a beard or a mustache had to keep it until the trial in order that witnesses could identify him more easily.) Once a week, on Saturday, they took you for a shower and changed your sheets and pillowcases.

As Soviet prisons go, Lefortovo was efficient and relatively humane. It was strictly an investigative prison, where those arrested by the KGB were held before their trials. Only a few weeks before I was arrested, Yuri Orlov was brought here, although, of course, I never saw him or any other political prisoner. Few of my fellow inmates were dissidents; most had been convicted of currency violations, smuggling, or other illegal contacts with foreigners.

Early in April, Fima initiated a new approach in his attempt to have me reach an understanding with my interrogators. "It's certainly a despicable thing to turn in your friends," he said. "But you should also consider yourself. If you don't give the KGB anything, they'll smear your forehead with iodine. Think about it: they need something to show their superiors. Decide exactly what you can tell them and what you can't, but don't discuss this during interrogations, for who knows what they'll squeeze out of you? Write a statement to the procurator general. Say as much as you can, and then stop. You'll be safe, for how can they kill you after you've helped with the investigation?"

When Fima had first started in on this topic, I ignored him by drifting off to sleep. And now I left him behind in other ways, too, as I rejoined Avital and my friends at every opportunity. But Fima wouldn't let up, and before long I found myself listening to him. Indeed, why *not* write a statement as he suggested? Although it wouldn't be exactly what he had in mind, wasn't this an ideal way to formulate my position exactly as I wished? Then, in future interrogations, I could simply refer back to this statement, which was far easier than coming up with new answers each time, and far safer than allowing the particular circumstances of each session to influence what I said.

When I told Fima I had decided to take his advice, he was beside himself with pleasure. Although it was my turn to clean up, he immediately started bustling around, dusting and sweeping the cell. When the guard arrived with our meals, Fima approached the food trap for both of us so that I wouldn't be interrupted. "Don't stop writing," he said repeatedly. "Stick with it. You're saving your own life, and that's no joke."

In my statement, which went on for ten or fifteen pages, I explained such points as the reason why we maintained detailed lists of personal information about refuseniks, which was to let the world know who these people were and about their plight, and why we were in touch with the foreign press. I stressed that all our activities were both legal and open, that the goal of all aliyah activists was to live in Israel, and that everything we did was aimed at that target. I wrote that my involvement in the Helsinki Watch Group was a natural outgrowth of my other activities, and that, just like my efforts on behalf of refuseniks, this work, too, was necessary because the Soviet Union was violating international agreements it had signed. I stressed that I had no intention of discussing any concrete details, as I didn't want to help the KGB prepare cases against other Jews as they were now doing against me.

I added that I was aware that my fate had already been determined, and that if *Izvestia* said we were criminals, the authorities would somehow find a way to "prove" that charge. Because the case had already been decided, I refused to cooperate with the investigation. (This was not mere rhetoric. It was well known that never in Soviet history had a court acquitted a defendant who was brought to trial on political charges.)

While my statement ultimately had nothing to do with saving my life, it certainly simplified the interrogations. From then on, whenever I confirmed my participation in either the aliyah movement or the Helsinki Watch Group, I usually concluded by saying, "I refuse to testify in detail for reasons that are given in my statement of April 19, 1977."

Chernysh reacted laconically: "What are you trying to prove by such statements? You're putting on a good performance, but you should be thinking about saving your life."

As for Fima, as soon as I completed my statement the topic disappeared from his conversation. The next day, however, he introduced a far more interesting idea. "Today I started talking with the guard," he whispered. "I want him to take a note to my wife. She'll pay him a hundred rubles and he'll bring back an answer. There's something I have to warn her about."

I was astonished. "You can really bribe a KGB man with a hundred rubles?"

"You know so little about life," he replied smugly. "Believe me, everyone loves money and everyone takes it. This guard delivered a letter for my previous cell mate. He trusts me. He's afraid of you, of course, so he'll approach me only when you're not around."

Fima's guard, a withered and bony man of around sixty, was the oldest of the lot. Like his colleagues, he worked on a fixed schedule: two days on the first shift (seven in the morning until three in the afternoon), then two on the second (three until eleven), followed by two more on the third (eleven to seven), and then two days off. It was impossible to make an arrangement during the night shift because I was there, and in general it was difficult for the guard to open the food trap without arousing the suspicion of the shift supervisor. Fima and the guard could talk only if I was summoned to an interrogation during his shift, no officials were in the corridor, and the supervisor was busy. In short, it wasn't going to be easy.

Surprisingly, we were wrong about that. I was summoned to three interrogations that week, each time during this guard's shift. While I was gone, Fima was able to come to terms with him on everything. He would pass on the note on an upcoming morning when the old man handed us our daily allotment of toilet paper.

At the last moment Fima came to me with an offer. "You probably need a contact even more than I do," he whispered. "If you like, I can hand over your note first. This will give me a chance to make sure our channel works."

Although I was expecting it, Fima's offer upset me, for now there could be little doubt that he was working for the KGB. I realize that many former zeks will be angry at this observation, for how could I still have had *any* doubts? Wasn't Fima's very first remark, where he warned me about the iodine, more than enough to make it clear where he stood? Of course he was working for them! But I didn't want to rush to conclusions, and as long as there was any other possibility I tried to give him the benefit of the doubt.

I thought long and hard about Fima's offer, and in the end I decided to send a message to Slepak, who lived in the center of town, where the guard should have no trouble finding him. I concluded that no matter how unlikely it was that Slepak would ever receive my note, I had to take advantage of this potential opportunity. If the world knew about the nature of the charges against me, this would completely neutralize the threat of execution. Or so it seemed to me then.

And what if the note ended up in the hands of the KGB, which I had to admit was the most likely outcome? Well, whether or not they found anything useful in it was obviously up to me. Besides, what was there to be afraid of when I already faced a possible death sentence?

Fima's only request was that he wanted to add a few lines at the end to his wife. Before his arrest, he explained, they had agreed upon a code for transmitting messages through the monthly food packages, where certain quantities and kinds of food would signify specific information about the outside world. Five packages of cheese, for example, might mean that nobody else had been arrested in his case. "You had plenty of time to prepare for your arrest, but you probably didn't think of that, did you?" he said in a condescending tone. At the same time, he carefully monitored my reaction—or did it only seem that way?

"You're right," I assured him. "I really missed a good opportunity. Now I'll have to be more explicit." I don't know whether Fima believed me, but unfortunately it was the truth. Before my arrest I had plenty of time for final interviews and farewells, and for hypothesizing with friends about the possible course of events. And yet I hadn't done the most natural and simple thing of all, which was to establish a prearranged code with my family or friends.

My letter to Slepak was in English, as Fima didn't want the guard to know it came from me. I wrote:

> Shalom, it is I, Natan Sharon. Don't ask any questions and don't say a word to this man. Just read the letter, write out your answer, and give it to him with a hundred rubles. I'm being charged under Article 64-A, and they're threatening to kill me. A team of investigators is interrogating me about our documents on the Jackson Amendment, our meetings with senators and congressmen, the lists of refuseniks, and so on. I'm discussing the purposes and aims of our movement, but nothing concrete. The more the public knows about all this, the better. Let everyone know that none of our activity was secret. From here, at least, the situation appears dangerous, although my health is fine and my mood is good. Please give my love to my wife and my mother, and all my friends.

During the next few days there was no opportunity to hand over the note. Either our guard was stationed in some other part of the corridor or one of his colleagues was close by and the guard signaled to Fima to be careful. Because we could be searched at any moment, I wrote out a new version of the note every night. In the morning, after another unsuccessful attempt to pass it on, I destroyed it. (At this point I hadn't yet developed the art of writing microscopic texts, which could be swallowed or disposed of at a moment's notice.)

The first time I wrote to Slepak, I had almost no doubt that the note would go straight to the KGB. But each time I rewrote it I was increasingly optimistic and excited by the prospect that it might actually reach its destination.

On April 29 we were finally successful. The guard opened the door in the morning and shoved in a bucket for trash. Although cells were supposed to be opened only in the presence of at least two guards, our man's partner was nowhere in sight. I had already arranged with Fima that I would be lying down on my cot, facing the wall and reading a book. Fima emptied the trash into the bucket, held out his hand for the toilet paper, and handed over my note. At last!

When the door closed and I turned around, I noticed that Fima's hands were trembling with excitement. He tried to tear the toilet paper in half, as usual, but this time he couldn't do it and the pieces fell to the floor. Fima cursed fiercely, but with obvious relief. His agitation and his joy were contagious. Perhaps this wasn't a provocation, after all?

In any case, it would take time to receive an answer. The guard had two days off, and with the May Day holidays approaching, there could be a change in the schedule. I had no interrogation on the twenty-ninth, and the next three days were off-days. Meanwhile, I pictured Slepak receiving the message, contacting my family, calling together my friends, and sending the note through foreigners to Natasha in Israel. I visualized press conferences, declarations, protests.

The day after he handed over the note Fima's mood underwent an abrupt change. After anxiously pacing back and forth in the cell, he told me he had decided to reveal to his interrogators another hiding place, where he had stashed away some gold coins between the bricks of his balcony, as there was still a discrepancy between what the KGB knew about his income and the amount he had actually given them. Fima hoped to be allowed to go home to reveal his secret, which would give him an opportunity to see his wife and family. He wrote out a statement to his investigator, but the shift supervisor refused to accept it. Today was Saturday, and all statements had to be submitted on weekday mornings. "Submit it after the holiday," Fima was told.

But Fima refused to wait. He became so determined to submit his statement immediately that his face turned red, he clutched his chest, and a nurse had to come to administer medication. Finally his statement was accepted, and a few hours later Fima was taken to an interrogation. He returned tired but satisfied. Immediately after the holidays they were going to take him home so that he could lead them to the gold.

During the next three days Fima had no contact with the guard who had helped us. We passed him in the corridor on the way to the exercise yard, but he was stuck at the other end. "They must have made a switch because of the holidays," said Fima. "Don't worry, he'll be back."

On May 3, right after breakfast, the guard on duty looked into our cell and pointed his key at Shneivas: "To a summons." This was strange, as they didn't usually start so early in the morning.

"I'm going home," said Fima as he quickly put on his suit, his white shirt, and his shoes. (In an investigative prison you're allowed to wear your regular clothing—except for your belt, tie, and shoe-laces—until the sentence.) Then Fima left with the guard and I never saw or heard from him again.

Two hours later, the shift supervisor came to the cell to ask for Fima's things. As I handed them over I was left with so many questions. What was Fima so frightened about on April 30, and why did he suddenly want to see the investigator? And why did they move him away from me so quickly, without even letting him collect his own belongings?

Questions, questions, and more questions. So many mysteries piled up over the years about my fellow prisoners. How complicated and confusing some of these people were! And how few about whom I could unequivocally state that he's a friend or he's an enemy. I soon learned that it was best not to seek answers to such questions. You had to remain true to yourself, to be guided by your own conscience and reason, and to let life and the passing of time sort everything out.

But back then I still found these questions intriguing. Pacing back and forth in the cell, I considered various possibilities and selected the conclusions that suited me. Why had they pulled us apart so suddenly and so quickly? Perhaps it was in response to some exter-nal event that the KGB had not expected. If so, wasn't it only natural to assume that this might have been some statement that my friends had made about my case as a result of my message to Slepak? Perhaps the authorities were trying to determine the source of the leak, and now that they were interrogating Shneivas, they could no longer return him to the cell with me.

But how could I know for sure that my note had reached its destination? The guard dealt only with Shneivas, and had never come near me. Never mind, I thought. In a few days I'll send out a feeler, and if he really did pass on my note, perhaps he'll nibble at the bait. I had no special plan in mind, but I would find some way to let him know it was I who had sent the note.

In the midst of these speculations I noticed that Shneivas's box of sugar was still in the cell. I called for the guard, who informed the shift supervisor. The latter shifted the matter to the duty officer, who acted with the wisdom of Solomon: if Shneivas asked for the sugar, they would give it to him.

I took this as another good omen: obviously they suspected the sugar was some kind of prearranged signal between Shneivas and me. If they were afraid we had conspired together, that meant they didn't trust Shneivas. In that case, Shneivas wasn't working for them—unless, of course, he was working for them but had tried to help me anyway, and was then burned by the guard and lost their trust. If so, then my note was now in their hands. Well, I thought, that isn't so terrible, as I wrote it with the knowledge that they'd probably read it. But despite these rationalizations, I quickly tried to think of some evidence to indicate that they didn't have the note.

As I mulled over these various possibilities, I was startled to hear the food trap open: "To a summons!" A summons? Now, when it was already past four in the afternoon? Soon it would be suppertime and the end of the working day in the investigative division. I had never been summoned this late before. What kind of interrogation lasted only thirty or forty minutes?

On my way to meet Chernysh I slowly recited my prayer. Normally it helped me concentrate, but this time I could barely control my anxiety. Bristling with impatience, I entered the office and took my usual seat at the small table in the corner of the room. Now, I thought, I'll finally learn what happened to my note.

5

"We Don't Let Heroes Out of Lefortovo Alive"

C HERNYSH began by removing a sheet of paper from an envelope on his desk. Then he stood up and walked over to me. What was this? I wondered anxiously. My note to Slepak? Slepak's response?

"What do you have to say about this document?" Chernysh asked as he placed it in front of me and sat down at my table to monitor my reaction. I glanced down and quickly saw that it wasn't written by me—or by Slepak.

The session that followed was the shortest one I underwent in Lefortovo, and I remember it especially vividly. It was the day I thought I caught the outlines of the case the KGB was trying to make. It was the day I was confronted by the highest-ranking KGB official I met in Lefortovo, who harangued me, warned me it was hopeless to resist, and offered me the opportunity to save my own life. And it was the day I tested all the skills of resistance I had developed up to that point.

Chernysh's paper turned out to be a fundamental part of the KGB's supposed evidence in my case. I immediately recognized the handwriting of Ina Rubin, Vitaly's wife. The document, which began, "Dear Tolya," was evidently a letter to me from Israel, where Vitaly and Ina had been living for the past year or so. There were a few lines about Natasha, with the hope that I would soon be joining her. There was also a reference to a clipping about me from one of the Israeli papers—I think it was *Ma'ariv*—that Ina had enclosed. At the end of the letter, which I had never seen before, she added that it would be a good idea to distribute the questionnaire on the back of the page to refusenik scientists, as this could help them in advance to find work in their specific fields when they arrived in Israel.

Turning the letter over, I found a list of routine questions: What was your education and when was it completed? What courses have you taken for retraining or improving your professional skills? When and where did you work, and what, exactly, did you do? What articles or books have you published? What languages do you know? In what areas would you like to work?

Aha, I thought, at last they're getting to the point. Until now I hadn't seen any link between the questions my investigators had asked me and the charge of treason. But the questions on the back of Ina's letter—especially those asking the scientists about their professional experience—could easily be connected to the wild charges in *Izvestia*. There, Lipavsky had claimed that Alexander Lerner had been assigned by the CIA, through Vitaly Rubin, to collect information about secret enterprises in the Soviet Union, and that Lerner had entrusted me to carry out the mission.

When the article appeared, we all wondered how the KGB would ever try to prove such a ridiculous charge, and I had been asking myself the same question in Lefortovo. But now I felt that this seemingly innocent letter from Ina Rubin might actually be the tip of a monstrous iceberg being fabricated somewhere in the depths of the KGB. Knowing how they worked, I realized that they might try to link the question asking refuseniks where they had worked to some alleged attempt by the Americans, or perhaps the Israelis, to uncover state secrets.

Secrets, after all, were the KGB's favorite excuse for denying exit visas, even though most refuseniks had little or no exposure to classified information. In a story I once heard from Slepak, which later became a legend (in 1984, I even heard it from a fellow zek in camp who had picked it up in America and had never heard of Slepak), Volodia had been told by a KGB officer, "We can't allow you to leave because you know state secrets."

"What secrets?" Slepak had asked. "Where I worked, we were ten years behind the West."

"Aha," said the officer. "That's the secret."

"But that secret is known by every schoolboy," Slepak had protested.

"But you know it better," he was told.

Slepak, at least, had been involved in electronics. But what about Rubin, who was denied a visa for years on the same grounds, and whose "secrets" were limited to the works of Confucius!

I had no doubt that the questions on the back of Ina's letter were completely innocuous. Years later, when I arrived in Israel, I checked, and just as I expected, they were part of a standard questionnaire filled out by Soviet scientists who emigrated to Israel and were looking for work. It was clear that Ina had simply copied them down.

But why had I never seen this letter before? Could it be that I had received it and somehow forgotten to read it? This was possible, but unlikely. Could it be a forgery? So far, every document they had shown me was authentic. But if they relied only on the truth, they'd never be able to prove the charges.

I wasn't sure how to respond. If I told Chernysh the letter was forged and it turned out to be genuine, I would be helping them prove we had something to hide. But if I acknowledged receiving the letter—well, who knew how they intended to use it in building their case against me?

"Where was it found?" I asked Chernysh.

"You'll find out in due time," he replied.

"You still haven't presented me with a list of items and documents that were confiscated from my apartment." I was playing for time, hoping to gather from his reaction whether the letter had been found among my possessions. But Chernysh was too smart for that.

"Don't be upset, Anatoly Borisovich," he said with a condescending and slightly ironic smile. "A list is being drawn up of the items confiscated at your apartment in Moscow and at your parents' residence in Istra, and you'll have a chance to examine it. Still, one would think that you knew what documents you wrote and what letters you received."

He was still awaiting my answer. "Well?"

Slowly and deliberately, I took a clean sheet of paper and began to write—and immediately edit—my reply, keeping in mind the tree, and especially the points "Don't lie" and "Don't help them represent our activities as secret."

I wrote as follows:

I am seeing the letter that was presented to me for the first time. If it was really written by Ina Rubin, her desire to help refusenik scientists find work in Israel seems perfectly natural to me. Indeed, Vitaly Rubin himself, who for many years was groundlessly refused permission to emigrate, was able, while still in the Soviet Union, to maintain professional contacts and to continue research in his area of expertise in preparation for working at the Hebrew University in Jerusalem. Moreover, it was the solidarity and struggle of his fellow scholars that helped him finally get out of the Soviet Union and arrive in Israel, where he was able to continue his work at the university in Jerusalem.

After I dictated the statement to Chernysh, he framed my response in his own words and read me the result: "This letter was written by Ina Rubin. Her desire to help—"

"Wait," I said, "that's not what I said."

"What's wrong, you don't recognize Ina Rubin's handwriting?" he asked in annoyance. Instead of arguing, I simply dictated my statement again, refusing, as usual, to answer other questions.

After several unsuccessful attempts to edit my answer, Chernysh said, "Wait here while I take the protocol to the typist." He summoned another investigator to sit with me until he returned.

This was unusual, for normally Chernysh sent me back to my cell while the protocol was being typed. If the working day was already over, he had me sign the sheets the next morning. That was fine with me, for during the night I could reflect on my answers and, if necessary, clarify them at our next session.

Chernysh had been gone for no more than five minutes when an official came in whom I had seen before but never met, and who pretended to be looking for Chernysh. Colonel Viktor Ivanovich Volodin was the coordinator of all KGB cases against political dissidents, and Chernysh reported to him regularly, sometimes even interrupting an interrogation to run to Volodin with a report. Volodin was elegant and sporty-looking, and although his hair was gray and thinning, he looked much younger than his fifty-odd years.

When Volodin saw that Chernysh had left, he "accidentally" noticed me and approached my little table with a friendly smile. "Well, Anatoly Borisovich. How are you feeling? What were you discussing today with Anatoly Vasilievich?"

In the wake of Chernysh's attack, I resumed my defensive posture: "If you have the right to interrogate me, then do it according to the rules. Without a protocol I have nothing to say."

"I certainly have the right to interrogate you," Volodin replied. "But now I simply want to talk with you. You're wrong to start up like this because a lot depends on me."

"I don't want to get into an argument," I replied. "I don't want anything to do with you." My answer came out automatically, but even before I finished the sentence I was already regretting my tough stance. Why not talk with Volodin? Perhaps I could learn what happened to my note to Slepak. Besides, for the first time since my arrest I was feeling that same confidence I had in the old days when I knew how to handle myself with the KGB. But having given Volodin my answer, I didn't want to back down. Fortunately, he was persistent. He sat across from me, his chin cupped in his hands, and gave me a pensive, inquiring look.

Just then Chernysh returned with the protocol, and Volodin grabbed the text and read it. Then, in a fit of anger, he cried out, "Is this the honest answer of a fighter for Jewish rights? In your place, I would have said, 'Yes, I engaged in such activity. I conducted—or did not conduct—these surveys with those people—'"

"Go right ahead," I interrupted. "Please, record *your* answer in the protocol."

"No, I'm only telling you what yours should be if you want anyone to believe you."

"My response is in the protocol. You don't have to feed me answers."

"You see?" said Volodin. "It's always the same with these dissidents. They scream about freedom of speech and openness, but as soon as they end up with us, they clam up. Where has all your oratorical ardor disappeared?"

"Oh, yes," I replied. "This is really freedom of speech, Soviet style. You grab a man, cut him off from the rest of the world, stick a pistol in his ribs and say, 'Now, let's discuss things openly.'"

Instead of acting insulted, Volodin seemed pleased to have gotten a rise out of me.

"Do you understand what lies in store for you?" he asked.

"Yes," I replied with a broad smile. "They've already explained that I'm definitely going to be shot. *Rasstrel.*"

Good, I thought, my training is working. I can speak about *rasstrel* as if it had nothing to do with me, and without losing control of myself or the conversation.

Volodin, of course, had a different reaction. "You talk about *rasstrel* with a smile? Then you still don't appreciate the seriousness of your situation." Whereupon he launched into an extended monologue about how the KGB had long tolerated the hostile activity of a handful of Zionists who were struggling against the Soviet Union.

"Lerner, Beilin, Slepak, Lunts, Rubin, Brailovsky—I can name them all," he assured me. "There aren't as many of you as people think, but you cause enormous harm and you blacken our motherland by the day and by the hour. You entered into a real conspiracy with the American Zionists and with Israel. Together with the American Zionists, you forced the Congress to pass the Jackson Amendment, which caused enormous damage to the Soviet Union. Did you really think nobody would answer for this? You also gathered subversive and secret information and transmitted it to the West—"

Here I was forced to interrupt: "Of all people, you in the KGB surely know that I never gathered any secret information. All my activity was open."

Volodin paused, thought for a moment, and said, "Is that so? Even when you sat in a car with an American correspondent with the windows shut tight?"

It sounded familiar, but there was no time to think about that now, while Volodin was still talking. But this reference must have been important, because he turned to Chernysh and said, "Anatoly Vasilievich, when you get to that point in the interrogations, be sure to remind Sharansky of his words."

Volodin turned back to me. "We tolerated you for a long time. We warned you and your friends. But even our patience has its limits. You ought to know our Soviet history. *In every case where somebody was charged with crimes such as yours and did not confess and repent, he was executed.* Well, not *every* case. There were times when there was no death penalty, and the accused received twenty-five years. We're not threatening you. I'm merely explaining your situation, which is my duty as an investigator."

It felt good to stay calm while a high-ranking KGB officer was trying to intimidate me. I studied Volodin, watching him from the sidelines as if I were a film director on a movie set. Now there could be no doubt that all my mental conditioning had paid off. As Volodin's speech began to die down I decided to throw another log on the fire. "What's left for me to think about when everything has already been decided? I was declared a spy in the Soviet press even before my arrest."

Volodin seemed to interpret this remark as a cry of despair, and his response was cynical and frank: "All the more reason, then, for you to understand the gravity of your situation. Yes, we announced to the entire world that you're a state criminal, and we shall never take it back. Your situation is hopeless. Besides, you're not such a hero as to sacrifice your own life. Look at Krasin. He strutted like a rooster, and he wasn't even threatened with *rasstrel*. He lasted three months, but you won't survive that long. How can you be compared with Krasin?" he said with a scornful wave of the hand.

This, too, was part of their game, but they couldn't reach me with such primitive tactics. In fact, Volodin's mention of Krasin came as a pleasant surprise, for every time I thought of Yakir and Krasin it strengthened my resolve not to listen to the KGB.

And now, having finished with the stick, Volodin introduced the carrot. "We are not bloodthirsty," he said. My interrogators were especially fond of that phrase, and repeated it often. "Our only goal is to defend state interests. You're young, and your wife is waiting for you in Israel. If you help us suppress the antigovernment activity of the Zionists and the so-called dissidents, you'll receive a very short sentence—maybe two or three years. Perhaps you can even be freed right after the trial. We can make a deal about everything. We are not judges, of course, but we do have some influence in the courtroom."

I felt like a chess player who has lured his opponent into a trap. For Volodin had just made explicit what his subordinates had only hinted at: the conditions and the reward for my surrender. They were much as I had expected, and it felt good to hear them spoken aloud. Now I could no longer restrain myself. "Why wait for the trial?" I asked. "Why not release me even sooner, as you did with Irina Belogorodsky?" I was referring to a colleague of Yakir and Krasin who confessed her guilt after being arrested, and was of considerable help to her captors. By a special order, she was actually pardoned before the sentencing. In other words, they absolved her of the crime even before the court "decided" that she had committed one! But the irony floated right past Volodin.

"Of course it can be done before the trial," he replied. "It all depends on you. So you remember her case, and the case of Yakir and Krasin? Then you know we played straight with them, and did exactly as we had promised. I directed that case."

This I hadn't known. But it was obvious that Volodin had a similar scenario in mind for me.

He continued: "I showed Krasin more than seventy examples of slander in his documents, and he finally recanted. He and Yakir appeared at a press conference, admitted their crimes, and were released. Krasin wanted to leave the country, and he did."

"Yes," I said, knowing exactly where I wanted to take this conversation. "But is it true that you had promised not to use their testimony against other dissidents?"

"Slander and lies!" Volodin shouted, fearing that I now doubted his word. "With the evidence I had we could have jailed many people. But we are not bloodthirsty. We arrested only those who absolutely refused to stop their hostile activity. But I made no promises."

"Just as I thought," I said in a conciliatory tone. "Then Krasin lied both times. He lied when he spoke against the dissidents at the Moscow press conference, and he lied again at a press conference in New York when he spoke against the KGB. So why should I lie twice? It's better if I don't lie at all!"

By now I was smiling, for it seemed that I had successfully steered the conversation to a close. "My supper turned cold long ago," I said. "It's time for me to leave."

Only now did Volodin realize that he hadn't succeeded in controlling our conversation. "So you want to play the hero?" he said spitefully. "Go ahead, be a hero. Only remember—*we don't let heroes out of Lefortovo alive!*" He shouted these words, so they would echo in my head for a long time.

I returned to my cell in a state of agitation. Over the next two weeks I continually replayed my conversation with Volodin, recalling everything he said and every response I made. I was pleased with myself; I had listened calmly to all the KGB's threats and promises, and they hadn't reached me at all. I had regained my old form—or so it seemed. Therefore, I told myself, the most difficult part was now behind me.

Of course I was wrong about this.

That night I was so wrapped up in thinking about the conversation with Volodin that I almost forgot about my note to Slepak. Falling asleep, I caught myself thinking that perhaps he had received it after all.

Over the next few days, as I looked back on my dialogue with Volodin, what pleased me most was how I had handled our conversation. Humor and irony had always helped me to maintain distance between myself and the KGB.

The KGB can actually be a rich source of amusement because it pretends to be far less powerful than it really is, while those Soviet institutions that *seem* powerful—the courts, the legal profession, the parliament (known as the Supreme Soviet)—are actually elaborate frauds whose power is mostly theoretical. When you meet the KGB directly and it tries to mask its real power, the absurdity of the situation becomes apparent.

The first time I had laughed at the KGB's expense was in the fall of 1973, when I found myself stuck in a broken elevator with two KGB tails, a man and a woman. It was a Sunday, so it took hours for someone to respond to the emergency buzzer.

I immediately started teasing my companions. "I feel bad for you," I said. "Here it is Sunday, a fine time to have a drink with your friends, and you're stuck in this dirty elevator."

The man tried to smile, and soon started in on a familiar theme. "There are plenty of good Jews in the Soviet Union," he said.

"How about you?" I asked. "Are you Jewish?"

"Can't you see what I am?" he said.

"Of course I can. And I see that you're a Jew."

"Me? Don't be ridiculous."

"You may fool some people," I said, "but you can't fool me. I can see from your face that you have Jewish blood. Don't be upset; after all, there are plenty of good Jews in the Soviet Union."

He grew agitated, and began staring at his reflection in the elevator wall and checking the size of his nose. I noticed that his partner was beginning to enjoy his discomfort. Later, when the elevator was repaired, he ran to the car and immediately began studying his face in the rearview mirror.

The first time I saw a refusenik being followed by tails, I thought it must be terrible to have these people after you. But as with anything else, you get used to it. Later, when the tails were with me most of the time, I actually felt safer in their presence, especially at night. Officially, of course, these people did not exist, and whenever I mentioned tails to KGB officials, their position was, "Nobody is following you. You must be paranoid."

Actually, the tails were so real they were virtually part of the family. Once, on a bus, I got into a conversation with my tail. "Whatever became of Valera?" he asked, referring to a former refusenik whom he used to follow.

"He lives in Israel," I replied. "And he's very happy there." When my companion started asking about Valera's new life, with particular attention to his job and salary, a woman standing near us on the bus started shouting, "Shame on you! Why must we listen to this Zionist propaganda?" But her outburst was directed not at me but at my tail—which embarrassed him greatly and gave me enormous pleasure.

The most fun I ever had at the KGB's expense came on November 7, 1974. November 7 is a major Soviet holiday celebrating the anniversary of the Revolution. Many Muscovites go to Red Square for the traditional military parade, which is followed by a mass patriotic demonstration by hundreds of thousands of Muscovites from every organization and institute in the area who are required to attend.

I had been planning to leave town that day for Riga and Minsk, to prepare a report on refuseniks in those cities. But a week before the trip I was summoned by my boss at the Institute for Oil and Gas. "As you know," he said, "during every holiday a senior person has to remain here and be responsible for the institute." Normally this assignment was given to a party leader or some equally loyal citizen, so why were they asking me, the only dissident in the entire place? Obviously the KGB wanted to keep an eye on people like me, as the regime didn't want any unauthorized demonstrations to spoil the unity of this great holiday.

"I'm sorry," I said, "but I have other plans. I won't even be in Moscow on November seventh."

An hour later my boss called again. "If you really plan to leave," he said, "you'll have to show me your plane ticket." I could see that he was embarrassed at having to do the KGB's dirty work.

"Fine," I replied. "I'll stay here on November seventh, and I'll take the next two days off."

"Good," he said, with obvious relief.

On November 7, from eight in the morning until four in the afternoon, I was to sit in the director's office and take care of any emergencies that might arise. Three tails followed me to work, as the KGB knew I was planning to leave Moscow that evening. But because no outsiders were allowed in our building, my tails had to remain in the car.

The director had a large and luxurious office on the third floor, and I took great pleasure in the fact that I, an outcast in Soviet society, was now acting director of the Institute for Oil and Gas— even if only for one day. Before he left, the director handed me a sheet of instructions that listed names and phone numbers of various organizations, including the local KGB, in case there were any problems.

A few minutes later the phone rang, and an official from the regional committee of the Communist Party was on the line. "What's going on?" he demanded. "Your banners aren't here yet."

"I'm sorry," I replied, "but that's not my responsibility."

A moment later, obviously assuming he had dialed a wrong number, he called back and repeated his question, adding, "Do you understand what I'm talking about?"

"Yes."

"And you're in charge at the Institute for Oil and Gas?"

"Yes."

"Then let me explain the situation again." He went on to describe some administrative problem at the demonstration, but I wasn't paying attention. It was bitterly cold outside, and I was feeling sorry for anyone who had to be there.

"Let *me* explain something," I said. "This isn't my problem. I have other things to do, so leave me alone."

After a brief pause he called again. "What's going on over there?

Are you already drunk?" It was a reasonable question, as there's always a lot of drinking on this holiday.

"No," I replied, "I'm perfectly sober."

"Are you a party member?"

"No, I'm not."

"A Komsomol member?"

"No, thank God."

"Then what the hell *are* you?"

"A Zionist."

He hung up.

A little later, the security guard called from downstairs to report that a group of men who had been sitting in a parked car had come into the lobby to warm up. Although she had asked them to leave, they insisted on coming inside. She had no idea, of course, that their real purpose was to keep an eye on me.

"Let me check on it," I said.

I called the regional office of the KGB, whose number the director had so thoughtfully provided. "This is Sharansky, Anatoly Borisovich," I said. "I am responsible today at the Institute for Oil and Gas. Downstairs in the lobby are three KGB men who are following citizen Sharansky, Anatoly Borisovich. They say they have the right to be in our building, but this goes against our rules. Did you give them permission to enter?"

There was a long pause. "Wait a minute, what's your name again?"

"Sharansky, Anatoly Borisovich."

"And who are they following?" I'll never forget that question, because this was the only time I ever heard the KGB admit that their tails existed.

"They're following Sharansky, Anatoly Borisovich," I said.

"What?" he shouted. "You're making fun of us! It's only noon and you're already drunk! Do you think that by calling from a public telephone you can get away with this? We'll track you down—just wait!" He hung up, but I had my answer.

I called the guard: "Tell those men that I spoke to their boss, and he didn't approve of their being in the building. If they don't leave at once I'll notify the police and have them evicted. Call me back in five minutes and let me know what happens."

She called back to report that they had left. I walked over to the window and looked out: yes, there they were, back in the car. I always treasured that moment, that wonderful feeling of giving orders and having the KGB obey me.

Eventually I came to feel a comic sense of responsibility for the behavior of my tails. One afternoon, on a bus, my tail was drunk and abusive, and started saying nasty things about Jews and dissidents. I felt angry and insulted that he was failing to treat this important state mission with the proper seriousness. It would have been easy to sneak away, but instead I went to the nearest public phone and called the KGB office.

"The man following me is drunk," I said.

"Nobody is following you," I was told.

"Look," I said, "I'm standing near the Kirovskaya subway station, and he's down the street. I'll wait here for ten minutes so your people can come and check."

The KGB car was nearby, and a few minutes later one of the other tails came out and replaced the one who was drunk. It was months before I saw that fellow again.

Of course, making fun of my KGB tails was far easier than laughing at those who now had the power of life and death over me. But having adopted the appropriate tone with Volodin, I vowed to continue not taking my captors too seriously.

Three days after my sudden divorce from Fima, the guard opened the door of my cell and gave the familiar order: "With your things." My new cell mate, a melancholy man, was sitting at the table and setting up dominoes, and I later learned that he was trying to divine the answer to his marital problems.

He stood and introduced himself: "Timofeev, Mikhail Alexandrovich." He was about fifty, tall and thin, with large bags under his eyes and a tired, sad face. His movements and his conduct reflected the caution and solidity of a veteran zek and a crushed man who had landed in the midst of new misfortunes. Timofeev had already spent over two years in Lefortovo during his investigation and trial on a bribery charge and a year in prison camp. Now they had brought him back for an investigation in another case.

When I explained that I had been arrested under Article 64-A, he asked, "What kind of article is that?" But before I could answer, he shrieked in amazement: "Treason? What did you do, try to cross the border?"

"No, I'm a Zionist."

"A Zionist? Yes, that's a . . ." He was perplexed. "I've had many Jewish friends," he said, "but this is the first time I ever met a Zionist." He put away the dominoes, stretched out on the cot, and told me which of the two unoccupied cots would be more comfortable in the warm weather. "I don't feel so well now," he explained, closing his eyes, "but there will be plenty of time to talk." He was certainly right about that, as Timofeev and I spent almost ten months together.

In addition to being a loyal Soviet citizen—perhaps the most loyal of all those I met in the Gulag—Timofeev was a Stalinist, for whom ideology had long since turned into dogma. I found it amazing to meet and to actually live with someone who believed that Stalin was a great man who had been slandered by envious rivals, that the Soviet regime was the most just and democratic in the world, and that all those Sakharovs and Solzhenitsyns were just so many Judases who had sold out to the capitalists for a few silver coins. No wonder he regarded me with astonishment and distrust.

Soviet dogma was so sacred to Timofeev that he would easily rearrange new information to conform with his vision of the world. I once mentioned that Fanny Kaplan, who was accused of trying to kill Lenin, had been shot without a trial.

"What are you talking about?" he said. "Don't you know that Lenin personally pardoned her? As soon as he regained consciousness he gave the order to spare her life."

I burst out laughing. This was the version they had told us back in kindergarten, a fairy tale about kind old Grandfather Lenin. The truth, which was published only after Stalin's death, was that, a few hours after the assassination attempt in 1918, Fanny Kaplan was quickly executed in the Kremlin courtyard by the commandant of the Kremlin without so much as an interrogation.

I expressed genuine surprise that Timofeev, whose work required him to keep up with political literature, was not aware of this, and I mentioned several books as well as a play, which had been running in Moscow for years, that included this fact. But Timofeev refused to believe it. This story was something he had known since childhood, and had even taught as a Komsomol leader as an example of Lenin's extraordinary humanity. Moreover, he assured me, one of his acquaintances had actually met Fanny Kaplan in a sanatorium. Fortunately, the prison library contained the memoirs of the Kremlin commandant, and I showed Timofeev the page where he described how he personally shot Fanny Kaplan. Only then did he believe me.

At first Timofeev was disheartened by this new information, but a few days later he announced that Fanny Kaplan *had* to be executed, that the Revolution required it, and so on, as though he had completely forgotten what he had said earlier. His reversal on Fanny Kaplan was typical of dozens of other topics that came up during our time together. Timofeev exemplified the predicament of a man who was forced to live in the cramped and constricted quarters of a loyal Soviet consciousness.

But despite his fierce fundamentalism, Timofeev had never been able to take full advantage of his connections or his convictions. For as much as he loved Stalin and the Soviet regime, he also loved women, friends, soccer, and singing. He even wrote poetry—an interest he cultivated in prison.

He suffered deeply from his political and social fall. "What a biography I wasted," he would say with real bitterness. "My life could have been written up in *An Activist's Notebook.*" I found it difficult to suppress my laughter. How could I possibly sympathize with a man whose greatest ambition in life was to see himself written up in a miserable little magazine for low-level party workers, which featured tedious biographical sketches of loyal Communists?

The farce turned into real drama, however, when Timofeev told me about his family life. A few years after his arrest his third wife, a young woman, left him. Until then *he* had been the one to leave—not only his two previous wives but innumerable other women. His wife had returned, but their relationship was still tense. Timofeev expressed his turmoil in dozens of poems, some of which, to my surprise, were quite good and very moving. He suffered from a heart problem, diabetes, and an ulcer, but sometimes in the evening, when his health permitted and he felt inspired, he would perform for an audience of one, reciting his poems or singing lyrical songs he had once sung while accompanying himself on the guitar, surrounded by many friends.

But most evenings he preferred to forget his troubles by playing dominoes. Because cards were forbidden in prison (they were considered a form of gambling), the zeks had invented "prison points," a card game played with dominoes, which Timofeev taught me. He was a compulsive player who didn't lose interest in the game even when I began beating him.

After serving half his sentence in a prison camp, Timofeev had suddenly been transferred back to Lefortovo. Around the time I met him, he was presented with a new charge—divulging some kind of official information. He took this very hard, and I turned away so as not to witness the tears in the eyes of this seemingly strong man.

"Do they really want to make a traitor out of me?" he said bitterly. "I was a genuine Communist. Our entire state rests on people like me."

It became clear, however, that the state simply wanted to give him yet another opportunity to serve its interests. Timofeev was an expert on copyrights, and when several officials were arrested for foreign currency violations in connection with authors' royalties from abroad, Timofeev was rearrested on some ludicrous charge. He was terrified, and didn't need to be asked twice when, after the first threatening interrogations, he was led to understand that his help on the second case could lead to a pardon on the first one. After debating for a few evenings in the cell as to whether it was moral to turn in his friends, he soon convinced himself that it was actually his duty to do so. And so Timofeev became the right-hand man of his investigator, Major Baklanov, who consulted with him on everything. Baklanov was the party organizer of the investigative division of the KGB, while Timofeev was also a former party worker. Both were lawyers, and both were big fans of sports and primitive humor. In short, they had much to talk about, and during interrogations Timofeev could drink a little coffee, listen to music on the radio, and check out the latest issue of *Soviet Sport*. Baklanov even gave Timofeev the opportunity to meet his wife. It was not surprising that he soon began to live from one interrogation to the next, like a young lover who can barely wait for the next tryst.

Timofeev also maintained good relations with Petrenko, the head of the prison. Back in 1973, immediately after his arrest, my cell mate had faced the problem of officially registering his marriage. He and his wife had lived together for several years, but had somehow neglected to take care of this detail. Now, however, it was urgent that the marriage be made official, because in the camps only a "legitimate" wife was permitted a private meeting with a prisoner.

Naturally, the investigators used the opportunity to engage in a little blackmail, demanding that Timofeev give them the necessary testimony before he could register. He quickly agreed, thus earning the remarkable privilege of marrying his own wife. Moreover, instead of riding to the registration office in the prison's Black Maria, Timofeev was driven in Petrenko's personal Volga sedan. After a few minutes of freedom the new bridegroom was taken back to prison, where Petrenko sent his congratulations via the duty officer.

Although it had been three years since all this happened, my cell mate still took pride in recalling Petrenko's generosity. In the years ahead I saw many other examples of this same phenomenon: the more a prisoner was broken, the more important it was for him to have some kind of evidence that the authorities respected him.

Despite the many differences in our beliefs and attitudes, and despite our completely different postures while under investigation, Timofeev and I got along reasonably well. We shared food and other items, and did our best to distract each other from sad and unpleasant thoughts. In the evening, over dominoes, we told each other about recent interrogations. We both spoke cautiously, not only because Big Brother was listening but because neither of us could ignore the striking contrasts in how we viewed the world.

Was Timofeev an informer? I listened carefully to everything he said, but despite his obvious loyalties, he never tried to get information out of me or to persuade me to change my position. I was therefore in no great rush to decide.

Escape

6

THERE was no escape from Lefortovo, but one way or another, the subject was constantly on my mind. In addition to vivid fantasies of a physical flight, I escaped from prison in other ways as well—through books, thanks to a remarkable prison library, and through my continuing mental forays into the past.

My most compelling visions of a genuine escape occurred after the appearance of a new interrogator, Senior Lieutenant Alexander Samoilovich Solonchenko, who took over from Chernysh at the end of June. Of the seventeen investigators involved in my case Solonchenko was both the most junior in rank and the youngest. He was also the most knowledgeable. Chernysh, meanwhile, moved on to coordinate the work of the investigating team and to question some of the key witnesses.

Solonchenko was a broad-cheeked man with small eyes and a round face who favored austere suits with fashionable shirts and ties. His office, room 58, was a large square room with a large window overlooking the exercise yards. It was a well-appointed space with a crystal chandelier and a plush sofa near the defendant's table. There were family photographs on the desk and a standard portrait of Lenin on the wall.

From the start, Solonchenko tried to establish an atmosphere that was correct but informal. He liked to demonstrate that he and I had much in common and could understand each other; when I asked his age, for example, he replied, "A little older than you." He enjoyed talking about his student years, which were almost the same as mine. "I remember how difficult it was to sit the whole day with books and notebooks preparing for exams," he once told me. "So if you ever feel tired, don't be embarrassed to stand up and do some exercises."

I didn't need to be asked twice. From then on I regularly engaged in gymnastics at interrogations, choosing the most tense moments as opportunities for limbering up. When Solonchenko posed an unexpected question, I would write it down, begin to ponder my answer, and then say, "Excuse me, I think my leg is cramped." While he sat and waited, I would stand and massage my leg muscles. Then, as Solonchenko tapped his fingers on the table, I would begin to do knee bends. For my finale, I occasionally performed head-stands against the wall.

"Really, Anatoly Borosovich, this is too much!"

"Nothing is too much," I would reply, standing on my head. "Actually, it's quite beneficial. You want me to give you a helpful answer, don't you?"

I would sit down, give my regular "helpful" refusal to testify, and feel terrific. Before long, Solonchenko withdrew his offer, claiming that gymnastics were forbidden by the boss.

Still, he tried to maintain a casual ambience. Sometimes he'd tell a joke, and often I'd reciprocate. While Solonchenko's jokes were generally about sex, I was more interested in teasing him about politics. I once told him a well-known story about how the Polit-buro members were so unhappy when the American astronauts landed on the moon that they called together the heads of the Soviet space program: "The Americans have reached the moon, so you must arrange a flight to the sun."

"What?" the scientists protested. "Our astronauts will burn to death."

"Do you take us for fools? Everything has been taken into ac-count," replied the chairman. "We've decided to send them at night!"

Another popular joke I told Solonchenko described a news bulle-tin from the year 2000: "Here are the headlines," says the an-nouncer. "Riots continue in Northern Ireland. There has been an exchange of gunfire on the Golan Heights. But all was calm last night on the Sino-Finnish border."

He usually laughed at my jokes, but when I told a mildly anti-

Brezhnev story in the presence of one of his colleagues, Solonchenko didn't respond, and for the rest of the day he was cool to me.

As spring turned into summer, I continued to work at maintaining all possible connections to my former life. It was easy to joke with Solonchenko, which was helpful in maintaining my distance from the KGB. But the isolation in Lefortovo was terrible, and I tried to concentrate on everything that connected me to my former life. If only they'd allow me a Hebrew textbook, I thought, although I knew it was out of the question. One evening, however, I realized that if I could retain a connection with my friends without actually seeing them, then I could certainly study Hebrew without a textbook. I immediately resolved to draw up a list of every Hebrew word I could remember. This task occupied me for two or three weeks, as my vocabulary turned out to be larger than I realized— approximately fifteen hundred words.

The next step was to find a way to actually use these words, which was admittedly difficult in a world where my social contacts were limited to Solonchenko and Timofeev. So I began to translate silently everything I heard and read. Naturally, this dragged out my interrogations with Solonchenko, as I would write down his question and take a long time to respond. "Wait," I'd tell him, "I have to translate your question into Hebrew."

"Maybe you'll do that later?" he'd reply. "We don't have unlimited time." But I refused to be rushed.

Long after I gave up on my note to Slepak (years later, he told me he had never received it), I still couldn't shake the irrational and totally groundless hope of contacting my friends. One morning, as I was strolling in the exercise yard, I glanced up at the large window of Solonchenko's office. This time my eyes seized upon a detail I hadn't noticed before: an old rusty drainpipe, which came down from the roof and broke off about half a meter from the window.

Staring at that pipe, I recalled the time in 1974 when I had left my key in the third-floor room that Natasha and I were renting, and I had to break in through the window. I had clambered along just such a pipe, ignoring Natasha's shrieks and warnings. Now, looking up at Solonchenko's office, my imagination quickly took over. I pictured myself leaning out the window—but, no, I couldn't reach the drainpipe with my hands. I'd have to jump from the window, grab on to it, pull myself up and climb up the wall.

The first time the idea entered my mind, I was able to drive it away. But then some kind of autonomous process took over, independent of my will. In the exercise yard, I began studying every dent in the wall of the building along the pipe from the window all the way to the roof. And as I walked along the corridors of the prison, to and from my interrogations, I tried to imagine where and how I could possibly climb down along the drainpipe on the other side of the building.

During interrogations I began to imagine that Solonchenko would leave the room for a moment and the door would slam shut, or that he'd suddenly collapse in a faint. (His face would often flush; perhaps he had high blood pressure?) Or—and this was the most improbable scenario, but as time went on it entered my mind with increasing frequency—he'd turn his back to me and I'd bang him on the head with . . . perhaps a water pitcher!

I knew, of course, that all of this was nonsense, an idle fantasy, and I quickly fled from it. And yet I kept returning to it and taking it further—especially at night, as I was falling asleep, or early in the morning. I pictured myself alone in Solonchenko's office. How much time would I need? One second to kick off my shoes; three more to open or break the window; about a minute to jump to the pipe, shinny up, and crawl to the roof. To run silently along to the other side of the building (which is why I had to kick off my shoes)—about half a minute. To climb down the drainpipe on the other side, then to run to the nearest side street and grab a taxi . . .

But how would I explain to the taxi driver why I was without shoes and had no money? Yes, I'd tell him that the door to my apartment had accidentally slammed shut and that I had to go to my relatives for the keys and would pay him when we arrived. Perhaps I'd carry my shoes with me, and put them on after I landed on the ground.

But where could I go? As soon as my escape was discovered, the apartments of all my friends would be closely watched. After a long process of selection, I settled on the apartment of a distant relative who was above suspicion. I worked out the safest route for the taxi to reach her, which would circumvent the center of town and the main roads. My friend Felix Kandel lived nearby; I'd send him a message and he'd invite a few correspondents to his apartment. Perhaps my parents, too? No, better not to involve them, as they'd probably be under tight surveillance.

Yes, I'd go over to tell Felix and the correspondents about my case. Then we'd *all* go to the KGB, because my purpose was to expose my captors, not to hide from them. Back in March, when everyone knew that my arrest was only a matter of time, Slepak had proposed that I go underground. But I rejected it then and I rejected it now. My goal was to continue my open struggle to emigrate to Israel.

Each morning I would resolutely toss off all these fantasies of escape. But on my way to the interrogation I'd suddenly notice that my shoes were untied—in order to kick them off more quickly. Fine, I told myself, I'll tie them when I get to Solonchenko's office. But somehow I always left this task until the end of the session, when it was time to return to the cell. I would be angry at myself for this childish behavior, but the next time I'd "forget" to tie my laces all over again. This pattern continued until the rusty drainpipe outside Solonchenko's office finally broke off.

Strange as it may seem, Lefortovo had a magnificent library with excellent service. Every ten days the librarian came to your cell with a catalog; you filled out a form, and he brought any three books you requested. Each volume was marked with a rubber-stamped message: INTERNAL PRISON OF THE NKVD. ANY DAMAGE DONE TO BOOKS OR MARKINGS OF THE TEXT BY PENCIL, MATCHES, FINGERNAILS, ETC., WILL RESULT IN THE WITHDRAWAL OF LIBRARY PRIVILEGES. This was to prevent any possible contact between cells.

In the late 1930s, during the height of Stalin's purges, members of the Moscow intelligentsia had started to disappear—including devoted and loyal citizens who had created the "new man," and couldn't understand why this new man was now trying to kill them. All their property was confiscated, including, of course, their libraries. As a result, many valuable books wound up in the hands of the KGB, and were kept at such unlikely institutions as Lefortovo

Prison. The best books made their way to the shelves of the administration, and over the years more and more of them were simply stolen by prison officials. During the sixteen months I was at Lefortovo the old leather-bound classics were gradually crossed out in the catalog and replaced by modern accounts of factory workers, military heroes, and cosmonauts, and biographies of Soviet leaders.

Ironically, the books from czarist times were in much better condition than those published in the 1930s. In the newer books, introductions or commentaries had been torn out if they had been prepared by anyone who was later judged to be an "enemy of the people." But those writers who were fortunate enough to have died before the Revolution were left alone, so their books remained untouched.

Mostly I read the classics. I have always been a bookworm, and as a child I read voraciously. Guided by my father, I had dutifully passed through the writings of Homer, Virgil, and many of the ancients, and had retained enough to understand some of the classical metaphors. As far as I knew, however, "real" literature did not begin until the eighteenth century. Before then there were only Shakespeare, Dante, and two or three others.

But now time had changed its pace, and as a prisoner I had an opportunity and even an obligation to think things over and weigh them carefully. My new inactive life and the silence of the prison provided an ideal environment for my encounters with such familiar strangers as Homer, Sophocles, Aristophanes, Virgil, Cervantes, Rabelais, and many more authors from long ago. When I found that the prison library included nothing by Chekhov or Dostoevsky, or any of my favorite Western writers, I resolved to fill the gaps in my education and to make my way through the classics of the ages.

It took me several weeks before I was actually able to escape through my reading. At first I progressed with difficulty, as if I were studying early literature from a distance. I enjoyed the books, but I remained where I was.

The breakthrough happened accidentally. I was reading a comedy by Aristophanes in which one of the characters turns to another and says something like "Aha, you have a Corinthian vase. That makes you a traitor." (Corinth was then at war with Athens, where Aristophanes lived.) I laughed aloud as I became aware of my connection with people who were separated from me by twenty-five centuries.

As I continued reading I found that the feelings and thoughts of many classical authors and their heroes seemed remarkably appropriate to my own predicament. I was inspired by Ulysses, with his wit, his stubbornness and his enormous curiosity—even on the edge of the abyss. (During the interrogations there were times when my curiosity was so powerful that there was simply no room left for fear.) There was Gargantua, whose physical strength and laughter broke through all the borders of this world. And Antigone—pressed by fate, she refused to violate the basic, eternal values, and saw her mission as bringing love, not hate. And Don Quixote—a dreamer who enjoyed life to the fullest, in contrast to the dull players around him. Even his own author portrayed him as a madman among rational people, but where was real life—with him or with them?

All of these characters, it seemed to me, hurried toward me from various countries and across the centuries. "You see," they told me, "there is nothing new in this world of ours. But how much there is that is worth living for—and, if necessary, worth dying for as well."

At the time, my interrogators were advising me to read through the Criminal Code. But I was in no hurry to do so. Later, when I became my own attorney, I felt the insufficiency of my knowledge of the law. But there was no doubt that reading Xenophon's book about Socrates and his speech to the court in Athens taught me far more than I learned from studying the Soviet legal codes.

Books were important, but the best weapon against the isolation was always my own memory, which I continued to activate through Slepak's system. Many of my thoughts were of Avital, and as July 4, the date of our wedding anniversary, approached, I often thought of that amazing and unreal day. In the spring of 1974, when Avital and I appeared at the registry office to apply for a marriage license, we were told we could be married in a month. But the following day an official from the same office contacted us and said, "We're sorry, a mistake has been made. Because of the differences in your ages, you must wait in another line, which will take four months."

I was furious. At the time, when we were all intoxicated with the optimism of the Jackson Amendment, four months seemed like an eternity. And there could be no doubt that this "delay" was political. The difference in our ages was only three years, and even the Soviet Union doesn't ask people to delay their weddings for such reasons. Somebody must have informed the registry office that I was a troublemaker, and the KGB had decided to play on our impatience.

Then another idea came to mind. Instead of a Soviet marriage, which was no more meaningful than any other bureaucratic formality, we would try to arrange a Jewish wedding. Yes, this would be a perfect symbol of the new life we had already begun and planned to continue in Israel. Soon our struggle to get married began to take on an almost mystical meaning: if we succeeded, then we'd always be together.

But when I approached the head of the Jewish community, he informed me that the authorities had instructed the synagogue officials not to help "anti-Soviet" elements. "You're seen as a Zionist and a troublemaker," he said. "And you aren't even going through official channels. I'm sorry, but we can't help."

On the morning of June 19, Avital and I planned to go to the synagogue to investigate one other possibility. First, I went to the Institute for Oil and Gas to explain that I had to be absent for two hours. When I arrived, there was a message from the personnel department asking me to come up to the second floor to check on some documents. Climbing the stairs, I was stopped by two men who showed me their papers from the Moscow Investigative Department.

"Please come with us for a brief discussion," one of them said.

"Another time," I replied. "Right now I'm busy."

"Please come now," he said firmly, grabbing my arm. I understood that resistance was pointless. They took me to a black Volga and drove for two hours to a jail in the town of Volokolamsk. There was no mention of a charge, but I knew that President Nixon was about to come to Moscow for a visit, and I assumed the authorities had probably arrested a number of aliyah activists for fifteen-day terms to avoid any embarrassing protests.

I demanded to see the head of the prison. "Now you'll have the opportunity to rest a little," he said.

"Why was I taken here?" I asked.

"You must ask the people who brought you," he replied. "We have no idea."

"But I didn't even bring books!"

"Don't worry, we'll give you books," he said. And they did—everything in their library that was worth reading. But there was no charge, no explanation, nothing. And as far as Avital knew, I had simply disappeared.

(When I failed to return, she contacted the institute and was told only that I had left the building. Later that day, she called around and learned that many of our friends had also vanished. It soon became clear that these were preventive arrests, although such arrangements are against the law in the Soviet Union and are never admitted to.)

There was a radio in the jail, and it was reported that Brezhnev and Nixon were holding talks. On July 3, when the newscaster said that Nixon was leaving Moscow, I expected to be released. They let me go later that day. I had just started reading a novel by John O'Hara, and while I was obviously eager to return home, I didn't want my captors to be setting the rules of the game.

"Let's go," they said. "The car is waiting."

"I've been waiting for days," I replied. "Don't rush me." I continued reading for another half hour.

Meanwhile, on the seventh day of my imprisonment, Avital was suddenly given an exit visa to join her brother in Israel. But the visa was valid only until July 5, and at first Avital refused to accept it. But every refusenik knew the rule that if they gave you an exit visa, you had to use it, as you might never be allowed another one. In a desperate last attempt to find somebody who could perform our wedding after my return, Avital ran to the synagogue. She found Girsh Manevich, an elderly scholar who was active in synagogue affairs. He explained that there was nothing he could do, as the leaders of the synagogue didn't want to antagonize the KGB.

But when she showed him my picture, he broke into a smile. "Tolya is your fiancé?" he said. "I know him well. For him I'll do it."

I had helped Manevich send his articles to Israel. He also used to enjoy chatting with me, as I was one of the few young people who paid attention to the older men. And now our conversations were yielding wonderful results. He found a rabbi for the wedding, and started teaching Avital about the rituals. Although our entire lives revolved around Israel and Judaism, neither of us had ever been to a Jewish wedding.

During my incarceration, of course, I knew nothing of these developments. On July 3, I was driven to a police station in Moscow where a KGB man lectured me on my behavior.

"But what should I tell them at my job?" I asked.

"You *were* at your job," he said with a smile. I was too eager to get home to enjoy this splendid example of Soviet logic. When I finally arrived home Mama was there, and she told me through her tears that Avital had to leave in just thirty-six hours! Then Avital returned and informed me that she had just arranged our wedding.

I spent the next day in a fog. But we were determined to get married, for if not now, when? Avital and I rushed around town buying wedding rings, inviting guests—some of whom were only now starting to return from *their* jails—and making the necessary arrangements. The frantic last-minute preparations kept our minds occupied, but the tension was growing.

The wedding took place in our apartment, late in the day. The rabbi warned us that the ceremony had to begin before sundown, as we were entering the three-week mourning period in the Jewish calendar when weddings and other celebrations were forbidden. But he wouldn't start the service until there was a *minyan*, a quorum of ten men. (Years later, I learned that a *minyan* isn't really essential for a wedding.) As the sun was setting I frantically went out on the street in an attempt to round up a tenth Jew. Just then my brother arrived and we were able to begin.

Most of the evening was a blur, but I remember standing under the *chuppah*, the wedding canopy, repeating the nine Hebrew words of the marriage ceremony, and then breaking the glass—the symbol that even in times of joy we remember our moments of sorrow. And so it was for us: the happiness of our marriage and the sadness of Avital's departure.

Early the next morning we took a taxi to the airport. I felt over-whelmed by powerful, complex, and contradictory feelings that were impossible to sort out. We were approaching the end of our feverish race with time, with the KGB, and with our own fate. Last night the *chuppah* had crowned our victory, and now we were together forever. We were taking a step toward freedom, standing with one foot in Israel.

Until this moment my immersion in the struggle had left no time for doubts. But now, in the taxi, I was feverish: Were we making a terrible mistake? What if this step, which we believed was moving us toward freedom, was actually drawing us closer to the abyss?

Squeezing Natasha's hand, I said, "I'll be there within six months at the latest." I spoke loudly, trying to jam my nervousness, and then repeated the familiar arguments: the promises from OVIR (the visa office), the international situation, and the coming ratification of the Jackson Amendment. Natasha nodded silently, but I could see my words weren't reaching her. In her other hand was the *ketubah,* our marriage certificate, and for her it was this, rather than my arguments, that guaranteed our future together.

We discussed what Natasha would do when she arrived in Israel. First to a kibbutz to rest, then to our friends Elana and Benjamin in Tiberias, then to an intensive Hebrew course, and then—

"There'll be no 'then,' " I interrupted. "Before you finish learning Hebrew I'll be there. We'll find an apartment and begin our life."

"Where?"

"In Jerusalem, of course."

By the time we reached the airport our anxiety had almost disappeared. The customs officials were surprised that Natasha was carrying only one small bag, but neither of us had many possessions. We had been concerned about the *ketubah,* for according to Soviet law no documents can be taken out of the country. But the customs man looked at it, asked what it was, and said, "Fine." The entire procedure, which often takes hours, was completed in fifteen minutes, which seemed to confirm the *ketubah*'s special power.

Natasha's flight was called, but for a long time we couldn't separate. Finally I said, "See you soon in Jerusalem," and we parted. The tears we held back were tears of joy and hope. As she started to move down the long corridor, for a moment—but only for a moment—I was overtaken by a horrible feeling of weakness, as in a dream, when you want to run up to something and touch it, but you can't.

I took a taxi home from the airport. It was two in the afternoon, but I collapsed on the sofa and slept like a dead man.

Exactly two years later, on July 4, 1976, our wedding anniversary coincided with a great event in modern Jewish history. A few days earlier, an Air France plane had been hijacked by a group of Arab and German terrorists. The plane landed in Uganda, where the Jewish passengers were removed and held under guard. All of us were greatly disturbed as we listened to news reports on the BBC and Voice of America. It was terribly frustrating, but there was nothing we could do.

On July 3 I read an article in the newspaper about riots in the Sudan. That night I dreamed that Israel used the Sudan riots to establish a beachhead, and that a column of Israeli tanks was on its way to the Entebbe airport in Uganda. In the middle of the battle I woke up.

I turned on an English-language broadcast on Voice of America. I remember thinking that my English must be worse than I realized because they were talking about an "unprecedented rescue operation, a spectacular raid at Entebbe." What was going on here? Were they reporting my dream? No, it was too good to be true. Was I missing something?

That evening Avital called my parents' home in Istra to mark our anniversary. "Did you hear what happened?" she exclaimed. By then we all knew. Avital held out the phone so that I could hear Israelis celebrating in the streets. We both felt as if this event were a personal present in honor of our anniversary. "If the hostages can come here," she said, "I'm sure you will, too. If such miracles are possible, what's there to be afraid of?"

The next day I called several of the foreign correspondents. "Aren't you going to congratulate me?" I asked.

"Oh, yes, yes, it's wonderful," one of them said. "And now Rabin will be reelected."

It was sobering to realize that to the correspondents Entebbe was just another news story. Moreover, my friend was wrong, for a year later Rabin's party lost the election.

For the Jews of the Soviet Union the Entebbe hijacking was enormously significant. Earlier in the week we had felt so much fear, frustration, and humiliation, and the added outrage that the Soviet Union was in fact supporting the hijackers. The press had been full of hatred toward Israel, and the rescue itself was described as a "military operation by Israeli pirates against peaceful Uganda." The newspapers maintained that innocent people were killed and the passengers were seized *against their will* and taken to Israel.

I was so eager to learn what had really happened that I asked several foreign correspondents to save the articles from the Western press. When Robert Toth brought me the account in the *Herald Tribune*, with a photograph of Yonatan Netanyahu, the young Israeli officer who had led the mission and was killed by gunfire during the rescue, I felt an immediate connection with him. His kind and modest smile looked out from the photograph, and I cut out the picture and put it on my wall. I was determined to learn everything I could about Entebbe and this young hero. Somebody brought me an instant book from America called *Ninety Minutes in Entebbe*, and with the help of this book and all the clippings, I volunteered to give a lecture about the Entebbe rescue to one of our refusenik seminars.

Several weeks later, more than fifty people, ranging from senior professors to teenagers, crowded into Felix Kandel's apartment. With the help of maps and photographs, I spoke for three and a half hours about almost every aspect of the operation. I had never considered myself a great public speaker, but my audience was spellbound, as if they themselves had been rescued.

I still remember two or three small details that I found intriguing and included in my lecture. Because there were so many contradictory "facts," I used a principle I had learned from friends who worked for the Associated Press—that every detail had to be corroborated by at least two sources. And when I described how Shimon Peres, the minister of defense, finally gave the signal for the planes to take off, even though the cabinet was still discussing the matter, the entire room sighed in relief.

The Israeli commandos had no idea what would happen at the Entebbe airport. They had expected a blackout and had trained in the dark, but the airport was fully lit. When the plane landed and the steps came down like a crack of thunder, there was a moment of enormous tension. Would they be met by a shower of bullets? The room was hushed as I described how the plane landed and a black Mercedes drove out with black-faced soldiers. Apparently there had been no black Mercedes in all of Israel, so the Israelis had to use a white car and paint it black. Nobody in the Soviet Union knew these details, and people were enthralled. When I finally finished, Mark Novikov, a former colonel in the Soviet army, jumped up and embraced me as if I myself had been the pilot of the Israeli rescue plane.

I had read that Yonatan Netanyahu was twenty-nine when he was killed, which had a special meaning for me in Lefortovo because I was twenty-nine at the time of my arrest. The worst that can happen is that they'll kill me, I thought, and that had already happened to him at my age. If Yonatan could face death, so could I.

Enemies and Friends

7

WHO was Sanya Lipavsky? I knew this much: he was the informer who had betrayed us, and given his outrageous allegations in *Izvestia* it was clear that he would be a main witness against me. But who was he really? Was he a Jewish activist who was broken by the KGB shortly before my arrest, or had he been deceiving us for a much longer period? Early in May, Chernysh inadvertently presented me with the answer.

During an interrogation about statements we had made in support of the Jackson Amendment, Chernysh showed me the typed text of one such document from February 1976, which many of us had signed. I confirmed that I was one of its authors, but as usual I refused to answer specific questions. Chernysh then handed me a rough draft of the same statement—a crumpled sheet with a typed text and handwritten signatures. Looking at it, I was shocked: How had *this* ended up with the KGB?

I remembered taking a rough draft of this particular statement over to Vitaly Rubin's apartment, as he was my nearest refusenik friend with a typewriter. As I dictated Rubin typed up several copies with a complete list of the signatories. I tore up the draft, crumpled it, and tossed it in his wastebasket.

Fifteen months later, this same rough draft lay on the table in Chernysh's office—only, now it was carefully smoothed out and pasted together.

Suddenly I recalled that just as I was leaving Rubin's apartment Sanya Lipavsky was coming in. Of course! Lipavsky must have fished the rough draft out of the wastebasket and given it to his masters. In that case, he had been betraying us for at least a year.

At the time, Lipavsky's presence at Vitaly Rubin's had seemed perfectly normal. I don't know how they first met, but Lipavsky was their family doctor, and over time he had become almost like a son to Vitaly. Lipavsky told us he had applied for a visa and had been refused because he lived near a space research center, and although that seemed preposterous, it was no more absurd than many other refusals.

Sanya Lipavsky was a sweet and slightly unctuous man with a trim mustache who had worked his way into our group by being helpful. In addition to the Rubins, he had attended to many other refuseniks who required medical attention and had lost their jobs. He had even made several trips to Minsk to treat Yefim Davidovich, the former Red Army colonel who was stripped of his rank after applying to go to Israel. When my friend Lida Voronin was in the hospital with a concussion, Lipavsky came to see her and insisted she be given a different medication; she soon recovered. If you had any kind of medical problem, Sanya would arrange to have one of his colleagues treat you either for free or for a modest sum.

Lipavsky offered us other important help, too, especially with telephones. We were constantly seeking additional phone lines for our overseas calls, because if you called more than a few times from any one apartment, the phone would be disconnected. Sanya offered us another route. One of his colleagues, who performed abortions, would occasionally ask his patients to let us use their telephones, and these women were usually happy to do their doctor a favor.

And when we needed nourishing food to send to our friends in Siberian exile, it was Lipavsky who found top-quality sausages, which were scarce even in Moscow. Now, with the wisdom of hindsight, I realized that those sausages had probably been supplied by the KGB.

Lipavsky and I were never close, perhaps because I was deeply involved in the political side of the struggle, while he showed little interest in these matters. I was also uncomfortable with his obsequious manner. Still, who could not appreciate all the ways he helped us?

But now, as I thought about Lipavsky in my cell, I recalled two or three warning signals we probably shouldn't have overlooked. In

1976, when Vitaly and Ina Rubin finally received permission to emigrate, Vitaly told me that Lipavsky was eager to replace him as a member of the Helsinki Watch Group. Even then I found this puzzling, as Lipavsky had always stayed in the background. It was odd that he suddenly wanted to step into the lion's mouth.

At the time, I was annoyed—not so much at Lipavsky as at Vitaly, for trying to promote Lipavsky to a position for which he was obviously unsuited. But nobody took the proposal seriously, and I simply assumed that Lipavsky believed that his membership in the Helsinki Group would somehow make it easier to receive an exit visa.

Another warning came early in 1977, when Dina Beilin asked Lipavsky to fly to Uzbekistan in central Soviet Asia to attend the trial of refusenik Amner Zavurov—one of the few times he was asked to perform a political act. (Lipavsky was chosen because he had lived in Tashkent and spoke Uzbek.) After agreeing to go, Sanya immediately disappeared for several days. Later, he told us a long story about being detained at the airport by the KGB, and how he had then gone home to rest, where his telephone wasn't working.

Nobody believed him. I assumed he had simply lost his nerve, but Dina thought it was far more serious. She was always the first to spot suspicious characters. And Raya, my sister-in-law, who was far removed from our movement, once said to me, "Tolya, I can't understand what this man is doing with you. He's a shady character, and very different from the rest of your group."

"Maybe you're right," I replied. "No doubt there are informers among us. But if we start worrying about who they are, there's no end to it."

Certainly Lipavsky was different. For one thing, he dressed more formally, like a bureaucrat, always wearing a suit. For another, he was one of the very few refuseniks who owned a car. He explained that he had bought it with money coming in from relatives who lived abroad, and we believed him.

My final contact with Lipavsky came early in 1977. I was looking for a place to live, and when Sanya invited me to share a room he had just rented in central Moscow, I quickly agreed. How fortunate, I thought, that he's always available when we need him. I moved in mid-February, and my new roommate disappeared a few days later, allegedly on urgent family business. His next appearance was in *Izvestia*.

But why did Lipavsky betray us? What is it that makes a man do such a thing? Loyalty to the Soviet system? Hatred toward us? The answer is almost certainly no. The only explanation I have is that he made a deal with the KGB. We knew that his father had been sentenced to fifteen years in prison for economic crimes, and I had heard that he had originally been sentenced to death. But the connection between his father and his betrayal of our movement didn't become clear until 1979, when David Shipler, head of the *New York Times* Moscow Bureau during the last two years before my arrest, filed a story from Jerusalem. In Israel, Shipler had learned from a former Soviet official that Lipavsky's father had been sentenced to death for stealing fabric from a textile factory, and that Sanya had volunteered his services to the KGB in order to save his father's life. This incident had occurred back in 1962—fifteen years before the *Izvestia* article!

While I was in Lefortovo the CIA confirmed that Lipavsky had worked for them during 1975, reporting on the Soviet scientific community. Lipavsky had mentioned his CIA connection in the *Izvestia* article, and it was obviously arranged with the full knowledge of the KGB. Apparently the aliyah activists weren't the only victims of his deceit.

Lipavsky was the most damaging of the informers in our midst, but he wasn't the only one. I met Leonid Tsypin in 1973, when I first joined the aliyah movement. I was immediately impressed by those refuseniks who held public demonstrations, although I soon came to understand that not everyone in our community shared my view. There was, in fact, a rift between the demonstrators and the "chiefs," as the demonstrators referred to the older and more cautious leaders. This split was intensified after a group of demonstrators were beaten by the KGB; when the chiefs failed to rally to their support, the demonstrators were furious.

Two of the younger demonstrators, Leonid Tsypin and Arkady Lurie, were considerably more militant and antiestablishment than the others. They resisted every opportunity to build bridges between the two camps, or even to meet with their counterparts on the other side. "We'll never sit down with those people," they said contemptuously. Later, we discovered that Tsypin and Lurie were informers and provocateurs, employed by the KGB to monitor our activities and undermine our movement.

Lurie was unmasked quite early, but Tsypin was involved with us until 1976. He was only twenty when I met him, but this young man with the red beard and the black-framed glasses claimed to have been a refusenik for two years. Although Tsypin betrayed us over a period of three years, he was an important model for me as I first entered the movement. He was hardly an admirable person, but the fact that he was younger than I, and displayed what seemed to be genuine courage, had a positive influence on me. To a novice like myself, even the staged performance of an informer could be inspiring.

After Tsypin was unmasked, one of the more "respectable" activists told me he had suspected Tsypin for years.

"Why didn't you warn us?" I asked.

"Would you have listened?" he replied. Unfortunately, he was right. The rift between the two sides was so great—thanks in large measure to Tsypin himself—that we would never have believed these charges against him. And the fact that Tsypin had dealings with the foreign correspondents made him appear even more important and above reproach.

But we did know that Tsypin was a difficult character. He was often drunk, and he appeared to be deeply involved in shady financial transactions. He wasn't reliable, either, and even I, who was tolerant on principle, preferred not to depend on Tsypin. Sometimes he would promise to deliver documents or letters to foreign correspondents, and we would later learn that they were never received, although he swore he had handed them over. In 1974, when a group of us traveled to prepare reports on refuseniks in other cities, he refused to go with a companion. Not wanting him to end up drunk, we teamed him up with a partner. But Tsypin made a terrible fuss and insisted on going alone.

Although the evidence seemed to point to Tsypin as an informer, there was always a counterargument to be made: Would the KGB conceivably enlist somebody who was careless, unkempt, and frequently drunk? Although Tsypin was suspicious, he just didn't seem to have the personality of a provocateur. Our mistake was to assume that the KGB was trying to improve the morality of its informers. And even if he was an informer, how could we keep him away? He claimed to be a refusenik, and anybody could be part of our group.

Eventually, when I was absolutely convinced that Tsypin was an informer, I said to Lev Gendin, a veteran refusenik who knew him longer than anyone else and who shared my doubts, "There are too many suspicious things about Tsypin. Let's collect all the facts and get rid of him."

A few days later Gendin told me he had spoken to a girl who had lived with Tsypin years earlier. "Yes," she told Lev, "I knew he was working for the KGB." According to her story, their telephone would ring and a voice would ask, "Is this the Cinema Baikal?" To which Tsypin would answer, "You must have the wrong number," and would then leave to meet his contact. When she realized what was going on and asked him about it, he replied that he was on an assignment from the Israelis to penetrate the KGB. She was only eighteen at the time, and she believed him. To make his story more convincing, Tsypin would listen to shortwave broadcasts on Kol Yisrael, the Voice of Israel, and pretend to write down secret messages. Even now, as she told all this to Lev, she asked him hopefully, "But maybe he was telling the truth?"

Eventually we learned the whole story. At the age of seventeen, Tsypin had been found with Jewish or dissident literature, and the KGB had threatened him and turned him into an informer. We started boycotting him until he eventually disappeared. Months later, at a party, a girl asked me if I knew Leonid Tsypin.

"Yes," I replied.

"And did you know he was working for the KGB?" she asked.

"Yes," I said. "And how did *you* know?"

Apparently Tsypin had turned up at a teachers college outside of Moscow. The heads of this college were sympathetic to dissidents, and a number of people who had lost their jobs were employed there. Tsypin had enrolled as a new student, but people in the dean's office quietly passed the word that the KGB had engineered his admission and that he was dangerous.

The next time I saw Tsypin was at my trial. But one morning, during the eleventh month of my investigation in Lefortovo, I stepped into my interrogator's office and saw a haggard-looking but familiar face across the room.

Lipavsky! He had changed so dramatically that it was hard to believe that less than a year had passed since we had last seen each other. He had grown noticeably grayer, his cheeks sagged, and there were bags under his eyes. As always, his appearance was neat and his trousers were carefully pressed. But there was no trace left of his unfailingly ingratiating smile.

Lipavsky sat through the entire session, which lasted until late in the evening, without once looking at me. Even when he spoke to me, he awkwardly looked only to the right, toward my interrogator. When another official entered the office and we exchanged nods and a dry "hello," Lipavsky fussily jumped up and greeted him in a servile manner. Judging from his frightened and tense expression, you might have thought he was there not as a witness but as a defendant.

I was astonished by his appearance. After all, Lipavsky wasn't exactly a newly repentant "Zionist accomplice," crushed by fear and self-loathing. I expected that after showing his true colors, he would have sighed with relief, looking younger and more relaxed because he no longer needed to play a role. I'll never know what he really felt, and whether he actually suffered for what he had done to our community.

Although Lipavsky gave a great deal of testimony to my investigators, in our face-to-face meeting they wanted him to repeat only those episodes that related directly to the gathering of espionage information at the behest of American intelligence services. In order for the KGB to prove its case against me, it had to be demonstrated, first, that my friends and I had carried out orders from abroad; second, that our lists of refuseniks were truly secret; and third, that I had been directly involved in the transmission of secret data.

Even before my arrest the *Izvestia* article had shown me how they would prove the first point—by contending that I was receiving instructions from the CIA through Vitaly Rubin and Peter Osnos, the Moscow correspondent of the *Washington Post*. The "proof" for the second point had come just five days ago, from experts who determined that "in their aggregate" and "as a whole" our lists of refuseniks contained state secrets. I wondered how they would handle the third item, when it was Dina and not I who retained the lists.

My question was answered when Lipavsky testified that Lida Voronin had typed the lists of refuseniks at my request. Lida was a close family friend who participated actively in dissident life. After moving in with friends in the suburbs, she offered me her small room in the center of Moscow and returned only for flying visits. (Most of her possessions, including her typewriter, were in the suburbs.) It was here, at her apartment, that the KGB confiscated my most valuable property—several hundred letters and postcards that I had received from Avital during our two-and-a-half-year separation. But that was not enough for them, as they also decided to "find" lists of refuseniks in order to link them to me.

When Lipavsky was finally finished—and his testimony was much longer and more complicated than I have indicated here—I thought of how upset and indignant I would have been had I heard such nonsense during my first few weeks at Lefortovo. By this time, however, I was a seasoned veteran, and was able to listen carefully and to analyze this so-called evidence in preparation for my trial. As I watched this wretch Lipavsky I wondered whether I would assault him if I had the chance, and concluded that I would not. All I felt was contempt.

Although Lipavsky was certainly a principal accuser in my case, the KGB wanted me to believe that my real problem was Robert Toth, the Moscow correspondent for the *Los Angeles Times.* In fact Toth was my close friend, and our relationship left a profound mark on both of our lives.

Chernysh first mentioned Toth in the middle of June, and his questions and allegations about him continued for weeks. Unlike most of the other sessions, however, this particular interrogation involved no specific documents and no small talk. Chernysh needed some answers, and was evidently in a hurry to get them.

Soon after Robert Toth first arrived in the Soviet Union in the summer of 1974, we met at the home of Sasha Lunts and hit it off immediately. Two and a half years later, after Ginzburg and Orlov were arrested shortly before the *Izvestia* article appeared, Bob was so concerned about my safety that he had me call him twice a day as a way of letting the KGB know that the foreign press was keeping an eye on me.

I eventually came to know dozens of foreign reporters, but I was especially friendly with Toth, in part because he cared so deeply about the problems of Soviet Jews. Although he couldn't always show the depth of his concern in his articles, there was no more reliable individual when it came to keeping our friends in the West informed about our activities and our problems. Although Bob wasn't Jewish, his wife, Paula, was, and Bob jokingly referred to himself as an associate member of the tribe.

Bob was a few years older than most of the other correspondents and was more family-oriented. He and Paula had three young children, the three J's—Jessica, Jane, and John—and I was impressed that Bob was able to turn down an invitation to play a Sunday game of tennis with the American ambassador because he and Paula always spent Sundays with the children. I loved to visit their family, and I especially enjoyed playing with the kids.

I once turned to Bob in an effort to assist Elena Sirotenko, a fellow refusenik and a close friend. Elena loved a young Armenian nationalist named Paruyr Ayrikian, who was in prison. The authorities wanted her to leave the country, but she refused to go while her lover and future husband was still in jail. Soon she began receiving threats of rape and murder on the telephone and in the mail, saying she had better get out.

When I asked Bob if he would write an article about Elena's predicament, he replied that although the Armenian connection was important to readers in Los Angeles, with its large Armenian population, he had recently written a story on this subject and didn't think he could do another. So, instead, I arranged to call him on a well-bugged telephone and tell him about Elena's predicament. He agreed, and we discussed it in detail for half an hour; he asked me to keep him informed about the case, and stressed that it would be of great interest to his readers. Not long after that conversation, Elena Sirotenko stopped receiving threats.

As I helped Bob gather material for his articles I learned a great deal from him, especially when it came to understanding the Western mass media. Our conversations were especially useful in helping me act as a bridge between the aliyah activists and the dissidents, on one side, and the foreign press, on the other. It was tempting to think of the reporters as our allies, but as Bob patiently explained to me, the real relationship between them and us was considerably more complicated. He helped me understand that although most of the foreign correspondents were genuinely sympathetic toward refuseniks and dissidents, the issue of human rights was only one of many topics they were expected to report on, and not necessarily the most important, either.

Even when the foreign press did cover human rights, they couldn't act as a mere amplifier for our voices in the same way that the Soviet press did for the regime. Many dissidents and refuseniks, who had no experience with a free press, expected the foreign correspondents to publish whatever they said or did, and couldn't understand, for example, that reporters were under pressure to file stories that were new and interesting, and that the mere fact that a refusenik or a dissident was arrested or imprisoned was not enough to guarantee coverage in the West. Sakharov, in particular, was continually frustrated that the foreign press seemed interested in only a few well-known cases, and virtually ignored lesser-known dissidents who were in even greater danger.

But the foreign correspondents were expected to present a variety of perspectives and viewpoints, and to report on conflicting approaches, even when the results were not as flattering to our image as we might have wished. I came to understand this point in June 1975, at the end of an official visit to the Soviet Union by a group of fourteen United States senators. I was informed in advance that before they saw Brezhnev and other top leaders, the senators wanted to meet with a group of refuseniks. This was wonderful news, because, in addition to describing our problems to a group of very influential American politicians, we now had the opportunity, through the Americans, to communicate our concerns to the highest levels of Soviet leadership.

Shortly before the meeting, however, we encountered a serious problem. For several months our movement had been seething with a heated conflict between the *politiki,* who favored emigration as the top priority, and the *kulturniki,* who wanted to strengthen Jewish culture in the Soviet Union. My own sympathies, and those of most of my friends, were with the *politiki.* For one thing, I have never believed in the possibility of a real Jewish life in the Soviet Union. For another, we considered it dangerous to shift the focus of our struggle from aliyah to culture, because the authorities would find it easy to deceive the West with a sham liberalization, just as they had deceived the Christian world with the help of the official Russian Orthodox Church.

But I also had many friends among the *kulturniki,* and because of my special relationship with the press I made sure to keep the lines of communication open to all factions. Moreover, the split was more theoretical than practical, as both sides appreciated, and to some extent even supported, the other side's position. But as often happens in these situations, the division between the two groups was heated up by personal ambition and pride.

A few days before the senators arrived I learned that the *kulturniki* planned to request their own meeting. I spent the next few days in a desperate attempt to persuade them to abandon the idea, but with no success. Their request reached Senator Jacob Javits, who resolved the problem with one wise remark: "My hotel suite has two rooms," he said. "Whoever wants to can sit in the other one." In the end there was only one meeting, but the tension surrounding it unexpectedly revealed both the depth and the seriousness of our internal conflict to the correspondents, who hadn't realized the full extent of the discord.

Bob Toth was the first to react. "I'm going to write an article about the split in the Jewish movement," he told me.

I reacted with horror, viewing his plan as a form of treachery. "Don't do it," I pleaded.

"If I don't," he replied, "somebody else will. I'm not the only correspondent who knows about it."

Toth quickly interviewed two of the principal opponents—Mark Azbel and Sasha Lunts—and wrote an article that appeared under the headline SPLIT AMONG ACTIVIST SOVIET JEWS BREAKS INTO OPEN OVER TALKS WITH U.S. SENATORS.

When the story appeared, many refuseniks were alarmed and some were enraged. Some of our supporters in the West reacted with trepidation, but soon passions cooled and the discussion of "emigration or culture," both in the West and among ourselves, continued on a higher level—calmly, and without personal attacks. Bob had been right to insist that in the final analysis his article would not aggravate the split but would actually help repair it. We were unfamiliar with the healing mechanism of a free press, so we feared it.

In the article, Bob reminded us it was the split itself, and not the publicity about it, that was dangerous to our cause. "Whatever the merits of the arguments," he wrote, "the split is bad enough, on its face, that Soviet interests are served by keeping the principal figures of both groups here, indefinitely perpetuating the division, rather than letting them emigrate." This was a valuable warning, and Bob's article was a vivid reminder that both groups were working for the same goals.

At my interrogation on the morning of June 13, however, it was a different article by Bob Toth that Chernysh wanted to show me. The previous November, Bob had told me that he wanted to research an article about refuseniks who worked in enterprises that cooperated with Western firms. For us this was a highly sensitive subject, as many Jews were denied exit visas on the basis of security considerations, or on the frequently absurd claim that they had access to state secrets. And yet whenever official Soviet bodies concluded treaties, trade agreements, or scientific exchanges with Western countries, they would declare that these same research facilities where refuseniks had worked were "open" and had no connections with the military.

Bob decided to write about the issue, and Dina Beilin, who maintained our lists of refuseniks, helped him select the most suitable cases for the article. But when it was published, I was shocked by the headline RUSSIA INDIRECTLY REVEALS ITS CENTERS OF SECRET RESEARCH, which made it sound as though we were actually giving away secrets. After seeing such a headline, I couldn't read the article objectively. I met with Bob and really carried on.

"That headline!" I shouted. "It literally urges the KGB to sever our ties with the West."

"I don't write the headlines," he replied. While Bob was sympathetic to our concerns, he clearly thought I was overreacting.

In the summer of 1978, a full year after Chernysh showed me this article, I was sitting in my cell on the eve of the trial. I read the text of my indictment to my cell mate, a professional swindler. When I reached the part about Toth's article, he interrupted: "Just a minute, didn't you say this Toth was your friend? How could he write such an article?" I explained that the editor, and not the correspondent, wrote the headlines.

"Correspondent, editor, what does it matter? I'd never have anything to do with people who don't understand the Soviets. Do you think anyone in the Politburo actually reads these articles? Andropov showed it to them and said, 'It's time to arrest them for treason. They're betraying us. We knew it long ago, but now they admit it themselves. Here's the article.' The leadership read the headline, shrugged their shoulders, and consented to the arrest." My cell mate had never engaged in politics or met with foreigners, but he understood exactly how the system worked—far better than the American Sovietologists and other so-called experts.

Although I wasn't arrested because of Toth's article, it did provide the KGB with another pretext for charging me under Article 64-A. So I wasn't surprised when Chernysh showed it to me on June 13. He had only one question: Who gave Toth the information for his article? Pausing for a moment, he suddenly blurted out, "Beilin?"

As Chernysh stared at me, searching for a reaction, I wondered if he actually knew something or was merely bluffing. After all, it was no secret that Dina handled lists of refuseniks. I started to speculate on various possibilities, and then abruptly cut myself off. What did it matter if Chernysh knew or not? Our actions were not criminal, so there was nothing to discuss.

But Chernysh had clearly decided to impress me with his knowledge. He pulled a piece of paper out of an envelope—from a distance it looked like a tournament chart—and said, "Well, perhaps you will nevertheless tell us about your secret meetings with Toth?" He paused, and then slowly, smiling and shifting his gaze back and forth between the chart and me, he started reading: " 'With Naumov—at the apartment on M. Poryvaeva Street, from September; with Zinovev—at his apartment from ——; with Akselrod—at the apartment of L. Ulanovsky, from ——; with Petukhov—at the apartment . . .' " Here he stopped as if taking a breath, and waited. "As you see, we know everything," he said. "What can you tell us about these meetings?"

There were, of course, no secrets at these meetings. Toth had interviewed all these people over the past six months, and their names were well known to the KGB as refuseniks or dissidents. The only exception was Petukhov. He was a loyal and well-placed scientist with an interest in parapsychology who was afraid that somebody would learn about his meetings with Toth, which were arranged at his own initiative. The common element was that in all of these meetings I had been present as a translator.

To Chernysh I merely said, "I sometimes helped Toth as a translator when he conducted interviews. But I refuse to speak about these meetings, since they concern other people and not me. I only want to emphasize that there was no discussion in my presence about any issues connected with state secrets."

I was sent to my cell, but half an hour later, just before lunch, I was summoned again. Chernysh began by saying that now, finally, the director of the prison had agreed to give me back the photograph of my wife, which I had been doggedly trying to recover since I first arrived at Lefortovo. He added that he had talked with my mother over the phone, and that everyone at home was well. At the same time, he handed me the typed pages of that morning's interrogation and said, "Sign quickly, then off to lunch," before continuing on about my wife's photograph.

It didn't take long to see why Chernysh was trying to distract me, for in the protocol it appeared as if I, rather than Chernysh, was naming the people Toth had met with. And my remarks about refusing to give specific testimony had been dropped altogether. When I protested, Chernysh became infuriated. "Look what I did for you," he said. "I ran around like a little boy trying to get back your photograph, and you make a fuss about these details? You have already spoken of your position many times, so why repeat it? What does it matter which one of us named the people Toth met? If there was nothing secret about these meetings, what are you afraid of?"

Let him talk, I thought. Meanwhile, I was trying to understand what Chernysh had to gain by this kind of deception. I was led away and then summoned a third time, right after lunch, to sign the protocol. This time the whole section about Toth's meetings had simply disappeared. I shrugged my shoulders and signed.

Back in the cell, I continued to ponder these unusual events. What was going on with the protocol? Suddenly I understood: *they intended to show the protocol to somebody else, to convince him that I was testifying.* That's why they wanted me, rather than Chernysh, to list Toth's meetings, and it also explained why they omitted my customary refusal to testify. But who was the intended reader of this distorted protocol? Dina Beilin? Petukhov? Toth himself? Here I had to laugh, for the idea that the KGB could interrogate a foreign correspondent was patently absurd.

In my heart, I actually hoped it was Dina or one of my other friends. For one of my greatest fears was that my case would be conducted in total secrecy, and that the authorities would try to create the impression that Sharansky was being tried for such terrible crimes that nothing could be reported about them. But if my friends were summoned and were asked the same questions as I was, they would be able to deduce what I was being charged with, and could then inform the world. But not even in my wildest fantasy could I imagine that an American correspondent would be interrogated about my activity.

Punishment Cell

A T the end of June, during an unscheduled search of our cell, the guards confiscated my toothbrush for being slightly sharpened at one end. The previous evening, Timofeev had rubbed it against the metal cot so I could cut the sausages and cheese from my monthly food package. Zeks weren't allowed to keep knives, of course, and Timofeev, who had false teeth, had no toothbrush of his own.

On July 4, my third wedding anniversary, Major Stepanov came to the cell. "You violated the rules of conduct," he snapped. "Prepare yourself for punishment." I was being sentenced to ten days in the punishment cell for making a sharp weapon.

The guards ordered me to remove my clothing. After examining it, they permitted me to put on underpants, a T-shirt, and thin socks. They handed me a torn, thin jacket and a pair of pants, and offered me a choice between slippers or huge boots without laces. I chose the boots.

The punishment cell was in the basement, where the darkness was broken only by a dull lamp over the door so the guard could see me through the peephole. The cement floor of my cell measured about two meters by one and a half. In the middle was a little cement stump that was almost too small to sit on. The walls were moist with large wet spots, and the damp plaster was peeling off. The moisture quickly penetrated through my clothing. At first I didn't feel the cold, but I could see that the night would be difficult.

There was no cot. Before bedtime the guard came in and removed the lock from a heavy, rough-hewn wooden plank that sprang from the wall like a berth in a railroad car. I lay down, but I already knew that between the dampness and the cold I wouldn't be able to sleep. In the corridor two guards sat throughout the night. They were supposed to guard several punishment cells, but only mine was occupied, so they sat in their sheepskin coats, drank tea, talked, and tried to keep warm. I had no coat, of course, and no hot tea, so I kept moving with vigorous exercises. Whenever I managed to warm myself up, I lay down again, hoping to fall asleep before I started freezing.

It was no use. Without getting up, I stretched my feet and massaged my muscles. This helped, but only as long as I kept it up. Finally, having decided to pay no attention to the cold, I stretched out on the "cot" and began to review the day's interrogation. But soon my muscles began to twitch convulsively, and my feet started rising up and falling back on their own as my heavy boots banged against the wood.

In the years that followed I learned dozens of little tricks: how to bring a pencil into the punishment cell, how to divide my food between a "hungry" day and a "full" one, and how to breathe by pulling my shirt over my head in order to warm myself with my own breath. I also learned how to demand my rights—a procurator's visit to the cell, a thermometer, and warm underwear.

From my work on the Helsinki Watch Group, I knew that, according to prison regulations, when the temperature in the punishment cell falls below 18 degrees centigrade (65 degrees Fahrenheit), the prison is required to supply warm underwear and a padded jacket. These instructions, however, were almost never adhered to. Of the 403 days I eventually spent in punishment cells, I had a padded jacket for no more than fifteen or twenty, although the temperature at night was almost always below 18 degrees. Anyone who tries to survive for a few days in a cold basement in thin clothing and with hot food on alternate days—not more than 1,500 calories—will know that even 18 degrees is no blessing.

For some prisoners the worst part of the punishment cell is the hunger. For others it's the boredom. For me it was the cold. Finally the night passed and the guards came to lock up the wooden plank. They led me into the corridor, where they had been sitting in their padded jackets. How warm it was here! I washed my hands and face in the cool water—slowly, in order to delay my return to the cold punishment cell.

Back in the cell, I did my exercises and waited for breakfast. A guard explained, as I already knew, that in the punishment cell I would receive a diminished ration of hot food every other day, alternating with bread and water. Today was a bread-and-water day, but I wasn't hungry. The important thing was the mug of hot water, which I could use to warm up.

I sat on the stump, swallowed some water, and then began pressing the warm mug against various parts of my body—my chest, my feet, and even, with some difficulty, my back. I had a strong desire to sleep, but I was too tired to sit on the stump, as there was nothing to lean on. And the cement floor was simply too cold.

I knew all along that I hadn't been sent to the punishment cell because of a sharpened toothbrush. When it was confiscated, and I asked Timofeev what to expect, he had replied from the elevated perspective of three years in Lefortovo: "We always did it and nothing happened. If it was sharpened like a real knife, they might take it away."

"And if they took it away, what happened then?"

"Nothing. We'd make a new one a few days later."

No, the toothbrush was only a pretext. The real reason I was being sent to the punishment cell was connected to this morning's interrogation, when Solonchenko had returned to the topic of Robert Toth. When I look back on my first stay in the punishment cell, it's the interrogations that I remember most vividly, for never was I questioned so vigorously as during these ten days. As bad as it was, the punishment cell was merely a tool to increase the pressure of those interrogations.

A few hours before my punishment was announced, Solonchenko had dropped two bombshells. He had led up to the first one by maintaining that it was an established fact that Western intelligence services used correspondents, dissidents, and Zionists for their own purposes; the only question was who had helped them naively, and who had done so knowingly. "Now that I'm familiar with all the evidence," Solonchenko had said, "I find it difficult to believe that an intelligent man like yourself didn't know or suspect anything about Toth's espionage activity."

Toth's espionage activity? The phrase shocked me. Relax, I told myself, it's just propaganda. But Solonchenko had a second surprise for me. Settling himself in an armchair about two meters to my right, he said, "Your friend Toth, that so-called correspondent, is now with us. He's under arrest, and he's testifying."

What? Bob under arrest? They had to be bluffing! But for the first time in two months I no longer felt in control.

"What case is he testifying about?" I asked.

"Both his own and yours," said Solonchenko. "He was caught red-handed, and he wants to live. When a man works for money rather than ideology, he cracks quickly."

"Well, it will be interesting to hear his testimony," I replied as coolly as I could.

"Why should I read it to you if you still refuse to cooperate?" Solonchenko asked. He then launched into a short digression on how an intelligent man shouldn't be too dogmatic. "You took a certain position, but the situation changed. Think it over. Is it really in your interest to remain silent when the foreigners who took advantage of you are testifying and rushing to save their own lives?" Solonchenko spoke vehemently, but I just wanted to be alone so that I could concentrate on the significance of these new "facts." Fortunately it was time for lunch, and Solonchenko summoned the guard to take me back to my cell.

So they claimed that Toth was arrested and that he was testifying. Could this be true? And even if it was, what kind of evidence could he give against me?

But why was I allowing them to distract me with these questions? Was I responsible for the activities of a foreign correspondent, even if he was my friend? The only thing that mattered was that I knew for certain that I had done nothing illegal with Toth and had never engaged in espionage.

Did I give interviews? Yes. Did I help him write articles? Certainly. About what? About Jewish emigration. About why refuseniks were denied exit visas. About Jewish culture in the Soviet Union. About Ilyinka, a forlorn Jewish village whose inhabitants were refused permission to emigrate to Israel. About the lives of refuseniks in exile. About a new book by Yuri Trifonov, a novelist. About purges in the Institute for Sociology. About Soviet censorship. For some of these articles Bob had interviewed loyal Soviet citizens who provided information on condition that their names were not used. But even if the authorities knew about these meetings, what could be secret or criminal in a conversation about literature or sociology?

True, there was that stupid article about "secret centers of research." What had we given Bob for that? The same old list of refuseniks we had been distributing for years to various organizations both in the Soviet Union and abroad—a list that was available in almost every American synagogue. In 1975 we had given that same list to Congressman Sidney Yates of Illinois, who, at our request, had personally handed it to Brezhnev. So what was there to be afraid of?

In June, Chernysh had mentioned several people whom Toth had interviewed, but I concentrated on Petukhov, the only one of the group who wasn't a dissident, and who wanted to avoid publicity. Knowing of Toth's interest in parapsychology, Petukhov had contacted me to request a meeting with Bob. I called Toth, who was eager to interview him. Bob had already interviewed Eduard Naumov, a popularizer of parapsychology, and he hoped that Petukhov would describe the attitude of Soviet scientists toward parapsychologists.

Petukhov told Bob he was conducting certain experiments, and that he hoped to publish his results in the West because his Soviet colleagues didn't take his work seriously. He handed Bob a scientific paper he had written and asked him to send it to an appropriate American journal. In return, he promised that when the experiments were completed, Toth would be the first journalist to write about them.

Perhaps, if there had been more time, I would have asked myself some difficult questions about Petukhov, such as why he had insisted that his meetings with Toth take place in my presence, and why he needed me at all, given that he spoke excellent English. Perhaps I would have asked myself how a Soviet scientist could send an article to a foreign journal without receiving permission from a whole range of official bodies, or why he had tried to tell Bob about a secret institute in a closed city until I intervened. But all this occurred during a tumultuous period in my life, and Petukhov was merely one of hundreds of individuals who flitted past me in the months before my arrest. I knew the KGB was capable of provocations, but I also knew that if they wanted to arrest me, they could always find a pretext.

Lying on my cot during the lunch break, I wondered, Was Petukhov simply an ambitious parapsychologist, or was he a provocateur? And what about Bob? If he *had* been arrested, it was either a serious provocation or else— No, the thought that Bob might be a spy was so distressing I didn't want to think about it. Perhaps it was all a bluff, and there wasn't any testimony from Toth. After all, Solonchenko had refused to read it to me.

When I returned to Solonchenko's office for the afternoon session, I was so eager to learn whether Toth's testimony really existed that I violated one of my principles and took a small step toward cooperating with the KGB. "All right," I said, "as an exception, after hearing the testimony of Toth and those who met with him, I'm prepared to confirm or refute facts that concern me personally."

Now that it seemed I might be giving in to the pressure, Solonchenko immediately tried to apply more. "If you want your testimony to be taken seriously," he said indignantly, "then give it. We'll be the ones to compare it with the testimony of others. If there are discrepancies, we'll inform you and you can refute them. But this is no time to be fussy like an English queen." Solonchenko loved to compare me to an English queen, or to the princess and the pea, asserting that I demanded too much of the KGB and too little of myself. But I wasn't going to compromise any further, and I returned to the cell, having left the game in the same position. An hour later Stepanov came in to announce my punishment.

After my first sleepless night in the punishment cell, a guard came to announce, "To a summons!" For the first time since my arrest I was overjoyed to hear these words. I didn't care what awaited me at the interrogation as long as I could warm up. Each day except Sunday I was taken from the punishment cell to an intense session with Solonchenko.

On that first morning, when I entered Solonchenko's luxurious office in my punishment-cell rags and sat down on the chair, my body continued to twitch involuntarily for a long time. Solonchenko solicitously asked how I felt and complained about Petrenko's arbitrary nature. "It's too bad Volodin is sick," he said. "He's the only one who can restrain Petrenko."

"Now let's drink some tea," he added, pouring two glasses of aromatic—and more important—*hot* tea, which had been brewed right there on the table in a small electric kettle. Solonchenko gave me a cup, sugar, and some cookies. "But don't tell Petrenko I fed you in violation of regulations," he said softly. "They won't praise me for that." As soon as I had finished the feast, he removed the empty cup and all traces of his hospitality.

When this hypocrisy was repeated for the second or third day, I couldn't resist a comment. "You know," I said, "as a kid I saw many war movies, and the SS officers usually interrogated our man in the following way: one would beat him savagely, and then the other, invariably in white gloves, would bend over the battered victim and say, 'Ay-ay-ay, what swine.' He would summon a doctor, give the prisoner something to drink, and would begin interrogating him politely. But these were primitive films from the Stalinist era. Can't you find a more original script?"

At first Solonchenko seemed offended, but thinking it over, he said with uncharacteristic humility, "Yes, I understand, it's hard for you, and you need to take your anger out on someone. I'm not insulted, as I'm not responsible for putting you in the punishment cell. It would be more pleasant for me to interrogate you in a normal state, not when you're so sleepy and cold."

When the next interrogation also began with tea and cookies, I decided to challenge Solonchenko from another direction: "Why cookies and tea all the time? Aren't there any sausages or cheese in the KGB cafeteria?"

He burst out laughing. "Well, Anatoly Borisovich, you certainly won't die from shyness," he said, and proceeded to the questions.

At one point Solonchenko suggested that I might want to move over from my chair to the sofa, where it was softer and warmer. But when I did, the soft springs drew me down, my head began to spin, and I started losing control. I stood, limbered up, and never sat on the sofa again.

Back in the punishment cell, where no books were permitted, I had a great deal to think about. I reviewed my daily interrogations, and continued reliving scenes from my past and repeating my prayer about the future. And I soon found another way to keep busy: I sang.

Ever since childhood I've been completely tone-deaf. In kindergarten, during the music period, when the other children were learning some simple song, the teacher would say, "Wait a little, Tolya dear, you'll sing later on." Petulantly I awaited my turn. After kindergarten came school, and summer camp, and the institute, but my turn never came. Whenever I joined a group of singers, it was clear to everyone that Tolya should sing later on.

In recent years, however, I could no longer restrain myself from singing, as Jewish and Israeli songs were an inseparable part of my new life. When we sang "Heveinu Shalom Aleichem" (We Bring You Peaceful Greetings) or "Hinei mah tov u'mah na'im shevet achim gam yachad" (How good and pleasant it is for brothers to be together), I knew that my friends were always ready to forgive me for spoiling the tune.

In the punishment cell, having tried yet again to escape in my imagination to happier days, and to find refuge there from the cold and anxiety, I began singing a haunting song that a visiting American Jew had taught us a few months earlier. The words had been composed by Rabbi Nachman of Bratslav, the eighteenth-century Hasidic master:

Kol ha-olam kulo gesher tzar m'od,
V'ha-ikar lo l'fached klal.
(The entire world is a narrow bridge, and the important thing is not to be afraid at all.)

I felt that my turn had finally come, that the "later on" my kindergarten teacher had promised me had finally arrived. For now I could sing at the top of my voice without hurting anyone's ears or ruining an ensemble. As for the guards, let them suffer. These songs were the easiest and quickest way of feeling that I was back with my friends.

Petrenko came down to the punishment cell every day. "How's he behaving?" he would ask the guard on duty.

"All right."

"What does he do?"

"He sings."

"What does he sing?"

"Some garbage. It's not our language."

The door opened. "Well, Sharansky, you're singing?" said Petrenko.

I continued to sing.

"Are we going to violate the rules again?"

I continued to sing.

"You don't want to return to your cell?"

I continued to sing.

"Well," he said to the guards, "if he's singing, he must like it here. Let him stay a little longer."

Then Stepanov came to see me. "Sharansky, if you sign up for a meeting with the director and tell him you're sorry and you won't do it again, he'll probably let you go back to your cell."

I was willing to speak to Stepanov, who was more like a guard than an official. "Won't do *what* again?"

"Make a knife. It's bad for you in here." Then, looking around, he turned to the guard and pointed to the floor of my cell, which was strewn with plaster. "Why is it so dirty? Give him a broom and let him sweep it up."

"A broom?" I replied. "And what if I make a gun out of it?"

Stepanov smiled tensely. "Yes, humor is good, we understand that." But all the same, he told the guard, "Forget the broom."

Several other officials and guards tried to persuade me to apologize, but I had no intention of doing so. Obviously the plan was to keep me in the punishment cell during the investigation about Toth. If I apologized, would Petrenko really let me out? If so, this would have been a victory for them—a small one, but a first step. Once I started apologizing or asking for favors, I would become dependent, and my elaborate system of defenses would begin to crumble.

Meanwhile, Solonchenko continued pressuring me to testify. When he finally accepted that I wouldn't budge from my position of July 4, he began to read me a part of Toth's testimony. I stopped him and asked, "From what date?"

"You were interrogated about him on June thirteenth, and he was interrogated on the fourteenth," he replied, apparently guessing the reason for my question. Indeed, this explained why Chernysh had been in such a hurry to hear my testimony that day. The doctored text, which I had refused to sign, was intended for Toth.

Toth's testimony contained nothing damaging to me or to anyone else. I had no doubt that his words were genuine, but it was a mistake for him to give any answers to the KGB because of the perverse ways they could be used. I returned to the punishment cell and paced for hours in the darkness, trying, despite the cold, to concentrate on the interrogations—and on Bob. He had once published an article about the SALT II talks that included data nobody else had. When I asked how he had learned this information, he answered with professional aplomb, "I never reveal my sources of information." He had a highly developed sense of professional ethics, so why was he talking to the KGB about innocent conversations with Soviet citizens? He had every moral right to tell the KGB exactly what he had told me: "I never reveal my sources."

Could it be that Solonchenko was right, and that something really *had* changed out there in the world I had left behind? I searched for an explanation for Bob's behavior. He had probably been told that I had already testified. Lacking any experience in dealing with the KGB, Bob believed them and wanted to show there was nothing criminal in our meetings.

I had no intention of repeating Bob's mistake, and the next time Solonchenko read me an excerpt from Toth's testimony, I asked to see it. When I pointed out that Bob's signature was missing, I was shown the English version, which he had signed. I found it encouraging that they wouldn't show me the entire text, and I took this to mean that even at Toth's interrogations not everything had gone according to their plan.

Solonchenko continued to lecture me about the links of foreign journalists to the CIA, and how they gathered intelligence under the pretext of researching and writing articles. "You never noticed that?" he said. "As much as I want to believe you, I find that difficult to accept."

Back in the punishment cell, I kept wondering why they had interrogated Bob, and why he had agreed to testify. And if Toth was talking to them, what about his colleagues? I remembered how David Shipler of the *New York Times*, with whom I was also very close, had once hesitated when I asked him for a favor. Both he and

Toth had been tremendously helpful, but now, deprived of sleep and anxious about Toth's testimony, I saw only the dark side.

And what about Peter Osnos of the *Washington Post*, who knew me so well, and who knew Lipavsky better than any of the other correspondents did? And yet during our last telephone conversation, only days before my arrest, he had said, "Those charges in *Izvestia* are ridiculous, right?" As if he didn't know!

And what about the German correspondent who was afraid to interview three Soviet Germans who, like us, were fighting for their right to emigrate? Anxious to be repatriated, they had come to Moscow secretly, in the hope of giving Western journalists lists of those seeking to leave. I had set up an interview with a German correspondent, but as we drove to the apartment where these people were staying he noticed my tails in the rearview mirror and said, "We're being followed, I'll go another time."

I pointed out that the tails were following me, not him, and that the people he was scheduled to see were Germans, like himself. But apparently the sight of the tails was more powerful than my arguments, and he refused to come. I got out of his car and made my own way to the Germans. I felt terribly awkward when I explained why I had come alone, and I hoped they believed me.

When I recalled this episode in the punishment cell, my anger swelled up again. Although I was on excellent terms with most of the foreign newsmen in Moscow, during these dark and cold nights I regarded them with suspicion and distrust.

Not until the eighth night in the punishment cell did I manage to sleep, and then for only a few minutes at a time and no more than an hour in all. Sitting in Solonchenko's office after another cold and sleepless night, I put my head down and dozed.

"I hope I'm not disturbing you, Anatoly Borisovich," he said.

"No, not at all," I replied, without lifting my head. "Go on, pay no attention to me." But not even the fatigue could remove my anxiety about what had gone on outside the walls of Lefortovo during the past three months. Had the KGB really managed to implicate us in some kind of espionage plot? I worried about this constantly, both in Solonchenko's office and in the punishment cell.

On the previous day Solonchenko had shown me a list of refuseniks in Dina's handwriting. As usual, I made some general comment on our need for such lists, but refused to give any details. But the next morning, when Solonchenko gave me the protocol to sign, I found a reference to the handwritten list, which I had allegedly described as "a rough draft of a list of refuseniks that was shown to me earlier." I knew for certain I had said nothing of the kind.

"Excuse me," I said, "but where did you get these words? I simply refused to testify."

Solonchenko, however, insisted that he remembered the interrogation better than I did, and that I must have been tired. "O.K.," he said, "if you want, write a note at the end saying, 'It should be read in the following way.' "

Inadvertently Solonchenko had given me a good idea: "Yes, I really am tired," I said as I took the protocol. In front of the space for my signature at the end of the page was the usual phrase "The protocol is recorded correctly from my words. There are no comments."

This time, however, I wrote, "The interrogation took place on my seventh day in a punishment cell, where I could not sleep because of the cold and was given hot food every other day. I am reading this on the eighth day in the punishment cell. My physical state is such that I cannot certify the accuracy of a single word that is written here."

"In the future," I told Solonchenko, "give me the protocols to sign on the same day, so there won't be different readings."

On the following day Solonchenko again tried to force me to sign the "corrected" text of an interrogation. This time he implied that Dina Beilin had been arrested, and that somebody in our movement had allegedly reevaluated his position. "There's no sense in lying to you," he said. "We don't arrest people like you or Toth for no reason. We hold the aces and now we can play with an open hand."

The time had passed when I would feverishly begin to analyze such remarks on the spot. Now I simply tried to remember everything Solonchenko said so that I could analyze it back in the punishment cell.

Just then Volodin came into the office. "Oh, my," he said, noticing my punishment-cell outfit. "I was sick, and I just returned to work today. They told me you were in the punishment cell. Had I been here, of course, I would have intervened. Perhaps I could have managed to avert it. But Petrenko is an arbitrary fellow who doesn't listen to us at all. The punishment cell, yes, that's bad. You know, even if everything works out and you wind up in prison camp, arriving with a bad personal record is no good at all."

I burst out laughing. "What's this? First I'm going to be shot, and now I should worry about a bad personal record? Why don't you choose one or the other to threaten me?"

"No one is threatening you," Volodin said. "We are simply explaining your situation. If everything works out and they don't shoot you—well, everything depends on *you*. When are you going to give proper testimony?"

"I *am* giving proper testimony," I replied.

"Sometimes your memory is so good that you can play chess blindfolded or rattle off numbers at a press conference. Then you land here and suddenly your memory fails. You don't remember anything, you don't know anything."

I was insulted. "Excuse me, Viktor Ivanovich, but you must be confusing me with someone else. If I forgot anything, I would say so. In the majority of cases, I remember everything very well and have said honestly that I refuse to answer. You can find whatever you want in my testimony, but you won't find any lies."

Volodin laughed, as if appreciating my joke. "So you honestly refuse," he said. "But something also happened to Beilin's memory. As soon as these fighters for human rights wind up with us, they start forgetting things. Beilin, Nudel—they act like wound-up toy soldiers and hysterically say the same thing over and over. You, however, are an intellectual, a thoughtful man. But you're acting like a cowardly and stupid ostrich, hiding your head in the sand and telling us you don't see anything or know anything."

I remained silent, trying to retain everything he said and to understand where he was leading. Apparently inspired by my attention, Volodin continued, becoming increasingly assertive and energetic. "You think you're a hero, a fighter for Jewish interests. Yet you yourself will betray these interests, because you lack the courage to face the truth squarely. During the time you've been in Lefortovo, a great deal has changed. We can't tell you everything, but there's no point in lying to you."

He continued: "Pressel, Toth, Osnos, Krimsky, Friendly, and

your other friends have all been exposed as CIA agents." Joseph
Pressel was an officer at the American embassy, and the others were
all American journalists—Osnos for the *Washington Post*, Krimsky
for the Associated Press, and Friendly for *Newsweek*. Although I
was fairly sure Volodin was lying, I listened carefully.

"We have been following these people for a long time," he added,
"but the interests of state security forced us to wait. At last they've
shown their true colors. And how do all those fighters for human
rights who helped them—even if out of naiveté—look now? And
how naive could *you* be, after all the warnings we gave you?

"You want to go to Israel? That's your business. But renounce all
these Pressels, Toths, and Shiplers who used you for their own
purposes. You'll not only alleviate your own situation, but you'll
also help those Jews who listened to you, believed you, trusted you,
and have now wound up in similar situations. *This* is genuine courage.

"Take Lerner. He's a respectable man. He realized that you
dragged the Jews into a swamp, and he's already thinking about how
to get them out before it's too late. As you know, his desire to spite
the Soviet regime was stronger than anyone else's. He admits he
made a mistake, and that he allowed Western secret service agencies
to use him for criminal purposes."

"Well, then," I interrupted, "if that's the case, why not arrange
a face-to-face confrontation between Lerner and me? Perhaps he'll
explain to me what I myself don't yet understand." I was being
provocative, of course, because I was saying, in effect, You're lying
to me about everything. If Alexander Lerner had recanted, you
would let me meet with him.

After a brief pause Volodin said, "If you like, this can be arranged.
Alexander Samoilovich," he said to Solonchenko, "coordinate it
with those who are working with Lerner and arrange a personal
confrontation."

Did this mean they weren't bluffing about Lerner? I tried not to
show my feelings, but Volodin seemed inspired by my reaction.
Whether I liked it or not, he said, I too would have to recant, and
the earlier I did, the better it would be for me and the others.

"In May," I reminded him, "you predicted that I would last no
longer than Krasin. But three months have now passed, and I hope

you'll be wrong this time too." I spoke sharply, letting him know it was senseless to continue. In fact, I was eager to leave as soon as possible so that I could weigh and consider all of this new "information."

Volodin was silent for a long time. "You continue playing the hero," he said slowly. I immediately remembered these words from our previous conversation when he had added, "But we don't let heroes out of Lefortovo alive." This time, however, he spoke roughly and derisively: "Never mind, as soon as you see the pistol you'll start crapping all over yourself."

This childish phrase seemed ludicrously inappropriate. I harrumphed, and confidently turned to Solonchenko. "Citizen Senior Lieutenant, in my opinion the Citizen Colonel has fizzled out. He has used up all his arguments and I won't detain him any longer."

Volodin burst out laughing, while Solonchenko didn't know how to react. Then Volodin leaped up lightly from the sofa and said, "Oh, that Anatoly Borisovich, what a humorist," and walked spryly toward the door. Before he left, he stopped and turned to me. "Perhaps I should speak with Petrenko about letting you out of the punishment cell," he said in an unusually friendly tone.

I tried to answer him in an equally congenial way: "Is it really worth it to you, Viktor Ivanovich, to give Petrenko so much satisfaction for only two nights? We'll manage to survive it somehow."

Again he smiled politely. "If you reconsider, tell Alexander Samoilovich. I'll come to you immediately." Then Volodin disappeared behind the door.

Of my last two days in the punishment cell I remember very little, except that I spent hours pacing almost in place—three small steps in each direction. Otherwise, trying to ignore the cold, I sat still until my feet became numb. At night I lay on the cold plank, escaping in sleep for no more than an hour before I awoke to find myself still in the punishment cell.

I spent most of my time thinking. Securely shut off from the external world, and with no hope of either receiving or sending any kind of message to my friends, I had been trying to retain my values and the feeling of closeness to those who were dear to me. But if Volodin was telling the truth, there was a danger that this world existed only in my imagination.

Did his arguments have any basis in reality? And how could I find out? Volodin confidently promised a face-to-face confrontation with Lerner. If it took place, it would, of course, clarify a great deal. But what the hell did I need to clarify? I shook my head, stood up, did some warming-up movements with my hands, and again resumed my "psychotherapy" of reviewing the past.

Let's start with absolute values, I told myself. My mainstay, of course, was Avital, and I again thought back to our nine wonderful months together.

"Are you sure this is love?"

"I know that we need each other and can't go on living apart."

I recalled one of the first postcards Avital had sent me from Israel: "Here the sun is so bright that you immediately realize what a gloomy, terrible place we are leaving." That line stayed with me throughout my imprisonment.

More recently, Avital had written me, "We have to bear it just a little more, Tolenka. It's very hard for us now, but it could be a lot worse. My being here is a sign that nothing bad will happen to us."

Yes, I thought, it's good that I urged her to leave.

In the world of mathematics, in game theory, there is a theorum about an optimal strategy that guarantees minimal losses. This strategy is possible because of a fact proved in another mathematical field, topology, that however you replace one system of coordinates with another on a globe, at least one fixed point will always remain.

During my years of imprisonment I searched for my own optimal strategy. It, too, depended on the existence of one fixed point. The coordinates in my life changed many times, and there were moments when I doubted almost everybody. Archimedes called for one fixed point to move the world. For twelve years I continually relied on my own fixed point—Avital—even as our globe was spinning, throwing us madly from one situation to another.

9

The Game

THE KGB made a big mistake when they put me in the punishment cell. Their objective, of course, was to intensify the psychological pressure, and at first their plan succeeded. But gradually, in this harsh setting, with no distractions and no human companionship, I was able to focus all my energies into new strategies of resistance.

As I paced around the tiny punishment cell during the final forty-eight hours of my confinement, my thoughts were of how to recover some self-control, which I felt I had lost in recent sessions. I saw two possible responses. The first was to barricade myself in my own world and to terminate all communication with the KGB. I admired the simplicity of this approach, but how long could I maintain such a position? Moreover, I was reluctant to follow an inflexible strategy that left no room to improvise.

The second alternative was more elegant, but also more perilous: I would seek some kind of proof that they were lying to me. If I was successful, I could throw away my doubts and regain control of the interrogations. At the same time, I couldn't allow myself to start bargaining with them—as in Give me a face-to-face confrontation with X and I'll tell you something—for such arrangements were invariably a prelude to concessions. Could I possibly discover whether they were lying to me without making any deals?

Again and again I brought to mind fragments of conversation from my interrogators, who had made it abundantly clear that they wanted me to believe them: that I might be sentenced to death, that Lerner had recanted, that Toth was a spy, that Dina Beilin had been arrested, and that our movement was in disarray. In the final analysis, it was fear that was supposed to convince me. That phrase, *They want me to believe them*, kept whirling around in my head.

I don't know exactly when and how these thoughts grew into a logical argument, but the process began in the punishment cell and continued after I returned to my regular cell. I developed a simple plan: because they were so eager for me to believe them, if I appeared to let slip some information as if I knew it for a fact—for example, that Dina Beilin hadn't been arrested—then, assuming I was correct, they couldn't deny that fact without risking their credibility. (Unless, of course, they thought I was guessing.)

I arrived at the following scheme: I would blurt out fact X. They wouldn't deny it if, and only if, two conditions were met. First, it had to be true. Second, they had to suspect I had some opportunity to discover it, which meant that I had to make them believe I had some contact with the outside world. How would I do that? By telling them something that from their point of view I had no other way of knowing.

Before leaving the punishment cell, I had decided to blurt out a series of such "facts," spacing them over several interrogations so that the KGB would be forced to believe I had an outside source of information. I would reveal these items in order of decreasing probability, starting with one that was virtually certain to be true.

But once the punishment period was over, my perspective changed dramatically. Timofeev had saved some food for me, and as soon as I was coddled in my warm cell with someone to talk to, books to read, food to eat, and all the other comforts of Lefortovo (which really did seem like comforts after the punishment cell), my recent plans to outwit the KGB seemed childish and irrelevant, a product of those ten miserable days.

At this point fortune smiled on me. By chance, my July food package from home included a collection of mathematical and logical puzzles by Martin Gardner, the well-known American scientific writer. (It was the only time I was ever permitted to receive a book from home.) I eagerly leafed through it, joyfully anticipating an opportunity to escape even further from the world of the KGB.

Timofeev looked through it too. "How can you solve these?" he asked in astonishment. "They talk about one thing and ask about something entirely different!" In fact these simple puzzles could be solved by a bright teenager.

Timofeev began reading me problems from Gardner's book and watching me solve them in my head. I don't know what he enjoyed more—the apparent absurdity of the puzzles or the fact that they nonetheless had a solution. With each new puzzle I would think, Here's a man who graduated from a Soviet law school—the same one, incidentally, as my investigators'—and spent his life in the Soviet system, and yet he can barely understand logic. My interrogators are just like him.

Unlike them, I had enjoyed solving such puzzles ever since childhood. But what good were all my logical skills unless I could put them to use now, when it really mattered?

The editor's notes to the book gave an example that generalized logical problems of a certain type. In the town of X there are N families. All the husbands are wise, and they spend their mornings thinking. Every afternoon they implement their decisions. All of the wives in this town are unfaithful. There is a rule in this town that if a husband should learn that his wife is unfaithful, he kills her that day. But while each husband knows about the unfaithfulness of all the other wives, he believes his own wife is an exception.

One day a traveler arrives, looks around, and announces, "There is an unfaithful wife in this town." Although the traveler imparts no new information, in exactly n days all n wives are killed by their husbands. Explain why.

(The solution isn't important to our story, but for those who are interested, it goes as follows: Let $n = 2$, which means there are only two wise men. On the morning of the second day, each one reasons as follows: If my neighbor knows there is one unfaithful wife, and he didn't kill his own wife, then he assumes that my wife, not his, is unfaithful. He and I are the only ones in this town, so my wife obviously betrayed me with him. This proof works for any n with the help of mathematical induction.)

I had first heard this problem from Sasha Lunts, who had cited it to illustrate the fact that the disclosure even of information known to everybody can have serious consequences. For the solution to this problem takes into account not only the information itself but also the probable response of other people to it. That's what must happen here, too, I decided. The key is that I give my interrogators no new information but get some from seeing their reaction.

For a long time I mulled over various developments that had probably taken place in the outside world: that my fate had been discussed at the Helsinki Review Conference in Belgrade in October; that Avital had been to Washington, where she had met, among others, with Congressman Robert Drinan, with whom we had become friendly, and who had probably become active in my behalf; that the KGB was telling witnesses in my case that my involvement as a Jewish activist was merely a cover for my espionage activities. None of these "facts" was ideal, however; the first two weren't all that difficult to deduce, and I wasn't entirely sure that the third one was true. In the end, I decided to blurt out all three during a single week, and perhaps even during a single interrogation. But when I tried to think of a natural way to slip them into the conversation, I felt like a budding actor facing a possible flop.

I don't know how I would have resolved the problem had fortune not come to my rescue a second time. On July 20, as I was being brought to Solonchenko's office, I heard a door slam behind me. I turned around and saw a guard, two KGB officers, and—or so it seemed—the thin face and bald head of Veniamin Grigor'evich Levich, the renowned physicist and the highest-ranking refusenik scientist in the Soviet Union. But I didn't get a good look at him, as my guard pushed me lightly from behind and the apparition vanished.

At the interrogation that followed, Solonchenko read to me once more from the testimony of Tsypin and Lipavsky. "It's always the same duo," I said, "Tsypin and Lipavsky." This wasn't the first time I had teased the KGB that they had no other witnesses.

"Don't worry," Solonchenko replied. "Soon you'll hear from somebody else."

At the end of the session, Solonchenko said, "Next time let's talk about the Rossiya Hotel. You can tell us about your meeting with the American senators."

"Well," I replied, "as always, I prefer to listen. I'll be interested to hear what your duo will say about a meeting they didn't attend."

As I left his office I was struck by the fact that Solonchenko had warned me in advance about the topic of our next meeting. He had never done this before, preferring to begin each interrogation by saying, "The investigation possesses data about——" This was always followed by a long pause, during which he'd look at me enigmatically. I don't know why he deviated from the pattern on this occasion, but the results were most significant.

Back in the cell, I began to think: If that really was Levich in the corridor, why were they interrogating him? He rarely signed collective letters of protest or participated in our demonstrations, and our paths seldom crossed. The only exception that came to mind was that he had attended the meeting with the American senators at the Rossiya Hotel—yes, of course it was Levich!

At my next interrogation, as always, I confirmed my participation in the meeting with the senators, but refused to say anything else.

"With which one of the duo shall we begin?" asked Solonchenko, who was making every effort to adapt himself to my terminology and style.

"With the first one, of course."

"Fine, let it be the first. I'm always willing to be amenable to you."

In his testimony, Lipavsky made some wild claims about a meeting I allegedly had with Senator Javits's aide at a time when the aide wasn't even in Moscow. As usual, I refused to comment on the testimony "no matter how far from reality it is." (I generally used this phrase to describe outright lies, which I preferred not to designate as such lest I inadvertently imply that the rest of the testimony was accurate.) After recording my answer, Solonchenko rose, paced around the room and said, "You always complain you're bored with the testimony of the duo. Well, let's hear the testimony of another participant in the meeting with the senators."

Smiling with self-satisfaction, he reached for some papers on his desk. Here was my chance. Looking at my notes, I said, in the most ordinary tone I could manage, "Levich, Veniamin Grigor'evich. When was that interrogation, did you say?"

As soon as the words came out I was frightened. Did they sound natural? Did Solonchenko realize I was playing a game? Raising my eyes, however, I saw that I had struck my target. Although Solonchenko was still looking at me, his smile had vanished and his gaze had turned wary and malicious, like that of a man who had suddenly been deprived of his just reward. Placing the papers back on his desk, he said, "Wait a minute, you seem to have let the cat out of the bag, Anatoly Borisovich. How do you know we were talking about Levich?"

These were probably the most pleasant words I had heard since my arrest. Although my heart was rejoicing, I was afraid to believe the apparent ease of my victory. But in a considerably bolder and more insolent tone I said, "You just told me you were going to read Levich's testimony, and I asked you the date. Do I have the right to this information or not?"

Solonchenko sat down. "Well, well," he said pensively. "You can be sure I'll find out how you learned about this."

Levich's testimony contained no revelations, and Solonchenko's only purpose in reading it had been to convince me that Tsypin and Lipavsky weren't the only witnesses he could produce. But the dramatic effect had been spoiled. He read perfunctorily, recorded my refusal to comment, and sent me back for lunch.

I knew I had to follow up on my success as soon as possible, before Solonchenko discovered I had seen Levich in the corridor—assuming the guard would admit his mistake. According to my plan, after I had managed to implant suspicion about my links with the outside, I had to blurt out another fact. But what? That Bob Toth wasn't actually sitting in a cell in Lefortovo? No, that would be too difficult for them to admit now, as Toth was central to my case. That no other refuseniks had been arrested? No, I wasn't sure about that. I finally settled on Lerner. They asserted that he had been broken and had begun to cooperate, but I had my doubts.

In the afternoon session Solonchenko's opening remark hit me like a cold shower. Consulting a note on his desk, he said with a smile, "On July twentieth you were interrogated from two o'clock and Levich was interrogated from two-twenty, so you could have seen him in the corridor. That's the whole puzzle, right?"

"Yes? Can one really see other people in the corridor?" I answered quickly, with a simulated carelessness. In reality I felt like a chess player who has planned a beautiful combination and suddenly gets hit with an infantile checkmate. But while Solonchenko had called check, it wasn't yet mate. His voice lacked confidence; he was merely stating a hypothesis.

"Of course you can't see other defendants in the prison, but sometimes there can be a slipup with the witnesses," he said, continuing to monitor my reaction.

"Aha," I replied. "That means that everyone I've seen in the corridor is a witness and not a defendant. Thank you for this important information."

"Are you telling me you've seen *many* people in the corridor?"

"I don't know, probably around twenty."

We both laughed and got down to business, but I was interested in only one question: Had I succeeded in sowing doubt in Solonchenko's mind, or was he convinced I had seen Levich in the corridor?

"By the way," he said, "when Levich was shown the list of refuseniks, he was unhappy to find his own name there. He condemned that kind of activity."

"Really?" I replied. "But in the corridor Levich told me just the opposite." I said this as boldly as possible, trying to stretch the idea of my having seen Levich to the point of absurdity.

Solonchenko reacted immediately: "So you *did* see Levich in the corridor." I was thrilled, for this meant he still wasn't sure!

"Certainly," I replied with a laugh. "Where do I get all my information? From you, Alexander Samoilovich, from the people I meet in the corridor, and from Naumov. Now, there's a man you can rely on. He contacts me every morning at the same time."

I uttered this nonsense casually, almost without thinking. The absurd notion that Naumov, that unrecognized popularizer of parapsychology, was sending me mental messages through the thick walls of Lefortovo seemed to bridge the gap between Solonchenko and me. We laughed together, each one rocking in his chair.

As the session began to wind down I knew I had to release my first trial balloon now, before Solonchenko knew for certain I had seen Levich. I wasn't sure what to say, but when Solonchenko called the guard to take me back to my cell, I knew that if I was going to play the Lerner card it was now or never. With a voice slightly hoarse from excitement, I said, "All the same, it's good to see that you in the KGB aren't as all-powerful as you'd like. You can't break everyone."

"Who do you have in mind, yourself?"

"Not only me. I can imagine—well, take Lerner, for example.

You really wanted him to cooperate with you, and you'd love to arrange the face-to-face meeting you promised me. But it won't happen. So far you're no match for this man." I stressed the phrase "so far," which I had prepared in advance to leave Solonchenko a way out. After all, he couldn't directly admit he was lying.

Solonchenko stopped rocking in his chair and tapping his fingers. He looked at me intently and began to blush. Chuckling with satisfaction, I didn't take my eyes off him. My heart was bursting from excitement, for I knew that the train of thought I had imagined in my cell was now racing through his head: *If he really knows something and I lie to him now, then my words will lose all their power.* . . .

After a pause that seemed like an eternity, Solonchenko swallowed the bait: "That's just it—*so far.* Right now we don't need him, but when he has to answer for his sins, we're convinced he'll do it more cleverly than you. As for a face-to-face confrontation, we simply don't need it now. Why should we help you save yourself? You're an intelligent man who's responsible for his own actions. You should be able to evaluate your situation and that of other refuseniks and decide what's best for you and for them. . . ."

Solonchenko didn't stop talking until the guard arrived, as if he was afraid I'd break in with some new and disturbing comment. But I had no intention of interrupting. His words were like music to me, and I was euphoric. So they had been lying about Lerner all along, which meant they had probably lied about the others as well.

I was terribly pleased with myself. Suddenly, all my abstract, logical analysis, which I had viewed mostly as a means of distracting myself from this gloomy reality, had yielded a concrete result. Now that they suspected I had a link with the outside world, they would be forced to confirm my next guess—assuming it was correct— which would make them even more convinced I had such a link.

So I was finally able to make good use of the interest in games, puzzles, and logic that began when I was a child, reading the stories of Sherlock Holmes. What delighted me no less than the ice cream I forced Papa to buy me on the way home from kindergarten was Holmes's solving of puzzles and his ability to defeat evil without leaving the table. I was both amazed and inspired by the mind of the great detective as I began to appreciate the immense power of the human intellect.

I remembered posing two difficult questions to Papa: First, which animal was stronger, the elephant or the whale? And second, was there anyone in the world as clever as Sherlock Holmes? When my father explained with a smile that Sherlock Holmes was merely a literary hero, I concluded that the smartest man in the world was Arthur Conan Doyle. After all, I reasoned, Doyle had to solve these mysteries before he could write about them. My father was too kind to point out that Doyle had to first create the problems he then "solved."

I was jubilant as I fell asleep to the sweet memories of Papa and Sherlock Holmes, but my ordeal at Lefortovo was far from over. Most of my struggle still lay ahead of me, including many difficult days and some moments of real fear. But never again did I experience the terror of those first few months, when it seemed that nothing depended on me, and I wasn't sure I had the strength to resist.

From here on, the atmosphere of the interrogations changed completely and forever. I heard their promises and their threats, but they no longer reached me. I switched roles from being an actor—no, not even that, but one of a crowd of extras—to being the producer who watches comfortably from the sidelines. The goals I had formulated earlier had now turned into axioms that could not be violated. And when the KGB repeatedly tried to undermine these axioms, I was so involved with my "game" that I didn't even notice.

"Think it over, Anatoly Borisovich" was how Solonchenko ended every interrogation as he delivered yet another lecture about the might of the KGB and the hopelessness of my position. And thinking is exactly what I did. I thought constantly about how to reinforce their suspicions about my contact with the outside world, and wondered what other information I could learn from them. Already, in the week after the game began, by using the same technique I had made Solonchenko admit that no other refuseniks had been arrested after me. Over time, I learned a great deal. But would anything have changed had I not known these things? I hope not, and I believe that the record of my interrogations would have remained the same. Officially, my game left no tracks.

But it's difficult to imagine how much more effort I would have had to expend without it, and how much more arduous the interrogations would have been. The game may not have altered my case, but it performed wonders for my morale. I started going to interrogations as if I were off to the theater.

I must stress again, however, that this game took place in my own mind, and that only one side was playing it. During my long years in other prisons, where I came to know many other zeks, I saw that everyone who ventured to play games with the KGB invariably lost, whether these games involved seeking a common language, trying to strike bargains, or looking for an honorable compromise. My game succeeded precisely because it fenced me off from the KGB and helped me hide in my own world. The other games I witnessed and heard about put the defendant on the same level as his captors and eventually delivered him into their hands.

In August I received confirmation that the first moves in my game had struck home. This time, when the guard brought my regular monthly food package, I was presented with a blank sheet of paper and told to draw up my own list. I protested, because seeing the handwriting of one of my relatives was the only way of making sure that he or she was still alive; it was almost like receiving a letter. But the guard insisted that there was now a new procedure.

But I soon saw that this new procedure did not extend to my cell mate or, as I later learned, to the other residents of Lefortovo. And when I noticed that the labels on every container had been torn off, I had to laugh. Not so long ago, through Shneivas, the KGB itself had informed me that information could be conveyed from the outside by changing the type of provisions in the package or varying their amounts. At the time, I admitted in all sincerity that I hadn't dreamed of making an arrangement. But now it was clear that they suspected I had a link with the outside, which made me even more certain that Lerner had not been broken and that no other refuseniks had been arrested. Had my guesses been wrong, I told myself, the KGB would not have hastened to confirm my hypotheses, even at the risk of undermining their own efforts.

As if to corroborate my optimistic conclusion, during the second half of August the KGB conducted three searches of our cell that were unprecedented in their thoroughness. They removed all the library books and checked them. They tore off every label, probed every fold of clothing, and tapped the walls and the furniture. They even brought in a special instrument to test for metal, and another to check for hidden cavities in objects. I remained calm, trying to hide my pleasure behind a mask of indifference. Occasionally I egged them on with remarks like "Do you think we don't know how to hide things?"

Timofeev, who had no idea what was going on, grew irritable. "This is my fourth year in Lefortovo," he complained, "and I've never seen anything like this. What are you looking for, a receiver?"

Suddenly the leader of the search grabbed him by the arm. "Why did you mention a receiver?"

Poor Timofeev became frightened, and after the search he was summoned for an interrogation. When he returned, he looked at me warily for a long time. That evening, during our game of dominoes, he suddenly whispered, "Either I don't understand people at all and you're not who you seem to be, or our KGB has gone completely crazy with spy stories. A receiver, no less!"

He chuckled maliciously, but did not elaborate, and I asked no questions. "Don't take any of this to heart," I said. "By the way, it's your move."

Several days later he suddenly blurted out, "They say you'd sell your own father to get your name in the Western press. Is that true?"

"Judge for yourself" was all I found to answer. Our relationship remained stable, cautious, and semifriendly.

The only prize the KGB men seized during these searches was a twisted paper clip that had slipped behind the hem of my jacket. Because a paper clip is a sharp metallic object, it was forbidden in the cell. Petrenko came by and questioned me in a menacing voice: "Where did this come from?"

I told him I wasn't responsible for the quality of work of his employees who searched me when I first came to Lefortovo. "You were there," I reminded him. "You should have supervised them."

Petrenko was curt: "If you don't want to live in peace with us, you have only yourself to blame, and you'll be strictly punished."

I knew the paper clip wasn't the real issue, but I didn't know then that two weeks earlier Petrenko had received an official letter from the investigative department of the KGB, demanding that he terminate my link with the outside world. I had no desire to return to the punishment cell, so at my next meeting with Solonchenko I announced that I was tired of this nonsense of a good investigator and a bad Petrenko. "Last time it was a toothbrush," I said. "Now it's a paper clip. Petrenko may be a blatant anti-Semite, but he can't act independently of you. If I'm taken to the punishment cell again, I'll consider it one more attempt to pressure me, and I'll refuse to attend further interrogations."

Solonchenko listened silently and wrote something down. Several days later Petrenko flew into our cell during the lunch hour. "Sharansky," he said, huffing and puffing, "have you any complaints against the prison administration?"

"Of course I do."

"What are they?"

"Well, for example, despite the rules, I still haven't been given the photograph of my wife."

"That's disgraceful. I'll look into it. They'll give it to you," he blurted out, as if he had forgotten all his former refusals. "If there are any complaints or questions, sign up for a meeting and we'll resolve them. I came to inform you that the prison administration has no claims against you. If there were misunderstandings in the past, I regret it. Continue eating, and hearty appetite!" After barking these unusually kind words in his normal commanding tone, he turned and shot out of the cell.

Timofeev collapsed in laughter on the bed. "An apologetic Petrenko? That's unprecedented!" Before I could comprehend what all this meant, a guard opened the food trap and pushed through the picture of Natasha that Papa had taken just before our wedding. As I held it my hands were shaking from excitement and joy.

In the words of the Russian proverb, the appetite returns with eating. Now that I had the photograph, why not demand that they bring me Shapiro's Hebrew-Russian dictionary, which Mama had tried to deliver via the prison administration? Supported by Timofeev, who urged me to strike while the iron was hot, I sent a request to Petrenko for a meeting. To my surprise there was no answer. The next day there was also no reply. On the third day I was informed that Petrenko had resigned as head of the prison, a post he had held for more than fifteen years, which was now taken over by his deputy.

I never saw Petrenko again. Although it was tempting to think I had a hand in ruining his career, officials at the highest levels of the Soviet system lose their jobs not because they have committed mistakes, but because they are victims of internal intrigues or power struggles. Only after it has already been decided that an official will be relieved of his position is he presented with a list of his transgressions, even if they were committed at the behest of his superiors.

Apparently, something of the sort happened this time, too. Presumably, when they decided to get rid of Petrenko, they accused him of doing a poor job of isolating me from the outside world and of giving me a pretext for accusing the KGB of anti-Semitism. Perhaps they also criticized him for infuriating me by his stupid behavior and thus complicating the work of the investigation. In any case, during the months ahead my investigators and even the procurator let me know on several occasions that they condemned Petrenko's working methods and that his departure was no accident.

August and September were the easiest and most interesting months I spent in Lefortovo. I would enter Solonchenko's office with a smile, inspired by my prayer, which I had managed to recite twice on the way from the cell. In September I was also carrying the photograph of Avital in the side pocket of my jacket.

"Well, Anatoly Borisovich, again in a good mood?"

"Of course, Alexander Samoilovich. With such good news arriving from the outside, how could I not be happy?"

"Yes? Where is it coming from now?"

"Naumov still contacts me every morning. He's a very punctual fellow."

We both laughed, each of us rocking in his chair without taking his eyes off the other.

"So what are you going to tell me today, Anatoly Borisovich?"

"For heaven's sake, how could this happen, Alexander Samoilovich? Why should I suddenly tell you things? I thought we had an understanding—you talk and I listen."

"But perhaps for the sake of variety you'll tell me something. Please let me listen today."

"Oh, no, please allow *me*. . . ."

I thought of this introductory part of the interrogation as the Manilov-Chichikov routine, after the characters in Gogol's *Dead Souls* who dawdled at great length at the door, each trying to let the other enter first. But whereas in Gogol's novel the two men eventually went through the door together, I never permitted myself to violate the etiquette of the investigation. Solonchenko was always the first to talk: "The investigation possesses data about——" and here he'd mention some document, demonstration, or press conference. I would confirm my participation or authorship, and would limit my remarks to the general meaning of the document or event without revealing any specific facts or names. The testimony of the duo would be read, and I would either refuse to comment on it or would repeat what I had said earlier.

This was followed by the free-form part of the conversation, where each of us would parade his homework. While Solonchenko discussed the moral qualities of my "accomplices," I waited for a suitable moment to remind him that I knew more than he thought about developments in the outside world. At one point, Solonchenko asked about Father Robert Drinan, the Massachusetts congressman whom I had brought to the homes of Andrei Sakharov and Sasha Lunts.

"Here's something interesting," I said. "At the same time you're saying he's one of my accomplices, in *Pravda* they're praising him and some of the other Americans I met as fighters for peace. If Father Drinan and his friends knew you were labeling them as participants in a Zionist conspiracy, they'd probably work even more actively for my release. As it is, he's my wife's prime supporter in Washington."

Here I was extremely lucky. While I had no doubt that Drinan was helping Natasha, as he had been doing even before my arrest, I couldn't imagine how accurately I had hit the bull's-eye. I eventually learned that shortly after my arrest Father Drinan had agreed to serve as chairman of an International Committee for the Release of Anatoly Sharansky.

Solonchenko merely replied, "Don't hope too much. No matter what your wife does, she won't manage to deceive anyone even if your friends do help her. By the way, their numbers are continually decreasing." Even this thin comment was enough to show me that Avital wasn't idle, and that she wasn't alone in her struggle.

In mid-September, Solonchenko told me that the refusenik community was intimidated and demoralized by my arrest, and that tongues were beginning to wag.

"That's interesting," I replied, and then played another card, "because you're telling my friends the same thing about me. Presumably, you're equally far from the truth in both cases."

After a long pause, Solonchenko replied in a cold and haughty tone, "Anatoly Borisovich, if I were in your place I wouldn't rely on dubious sources of information. You should know how dangerous that is. Here you are in jail, and yet how many times did your friends assure you we wouldn't dare to arrest you?"

I was thrilled that Solonchenko now seemed to accept that I had a contact with the outside, and that he didn't even consider it necessary to hide this assumption from me. His only goal was to sow doubt about the quality of my information.

Once, after our usual opening routine, when Solonchenko suggested that I talk and he would listen, I said, "Well, O.K., if you want to switch roles just once, I'm willing. In that case, however, let's also change places, even for only ten minutes. I'll sit in your seat and you can sit in mine."

"Why would you want to do that?" he asked.

"I'd like to use your telephone. I'll call, say, the office of the *New York Times*. They probably miss my voice over there."

I had prepared this comment in advance, expecting Solonchenko to say, "There's no use hoping. They're all afraid of your name, and your friends haven't been there for a long time," or something along those lines. Then I'd try to demonstrate my "knowledge" that this wasn't true. Perhaps I'd even drop the name of Robert Toth in order to learn what was happening to him. But suddenly I ran up against Solonchenko's own homework.

"I've been meaning to ask you for a long time, Anatoly Borisovich. You enjoy the theater, don't you?"

"Yes," I replied, "very much."

"You probably like the Taganka Theater?" he asked, referring to the favorite theater of the Moscow intelligentsia that was as daring as a troupe could be while staying within the official limits.

"You guessed it again," I said, trying to catch his direction.

"And what genre do you enjoy the most?" he asked with an ironic and good-natured smile, gesturing vaguely in the air as if to say, Look, here we are in the theater.

"You're right, Alexander Samoilovich," I replied, for now it was clear what he was getting at. "Farce is my favorite genre, and I especially enjoyed the Taganka production of *Tartuffe*. But since you won't take me to the theater, I'll have to make do with these performances."

But I wasn't going to have the last word this time. "Let me remind you, Anatoly Borisovich, that you're forgetting the first rule of the theater. Remember what Chekhov said, that if we are shown a gun in the first act, then in the final act it must go off. Well, you were shown a gun in the first act, but now you're behaving as if the final act will never arrive. I assure you, however, that every play comes to an end, and this one will, too."

That exchange, however, was an exception. If some passerby had glanced in on office 58 during those days, he would have seen what seemed like two old friends, rocking in their chairs as they recalled happy days from the past and exchanged private jokes. Solonchenko would rock on the back legs of his chair, sometimes leaning against the wall with his shoulders and usually tapping on the desk with his fingers. I tried to imitate him, but my awkward tapping sounded like a poor parody. To compensate, I would rock on one leg, pushing off from the wall on my left and then from the wall behind me. Eventually the leg of my chair broke and, in mock horror, I begged Solonchenko not to betray me to the director of the prison.

Magnanimously, he promised to take the blame on himself. "If the director finds out about this," he said with a laugh, "you won't get out of the punishment cell until the trial, and perhaps not even until the iodine marks the spot on your forehead." The farce continued, and so did my game.

But it was still months before I was able to get them to reveal the truth about Toth. I would often write down a draft of my answer before dictating it, and in November, when the questions became increasingly sinister, I was especially careful with each word.

"Why are you so cautious, Anatoly Borisovich? Are you afraid?" Solonchenko asked me.

This was my cue. "Why should I be afraid? I see which direction you're going in, for it's easy to *deduce* from your conversations. Even *Pravda* hints the KGB is patching together a case about an international Zionist conspiracy. Naturally, I'm trying not to assist you in this dirty work."

As I had hoped, Solonchenko pounced on the word "deduce."

"Why do you have to deduce?" he asked. "Why do you need to live with guesses and hypotheses? We're not hiding anything, and in time you'll learn it all. But you're wrong to think these deductions can help you."

He said more, but now that he had accepted my gambit, I moved on: "So you think it's pointless to make deductions? I can see that you've never dealt with logic. You can't even imagine how much I can learn from a careful analysis of conversations. I can give you an example."

I pretended to hesitate and to ponder whether or not to reveal my secret. Then, as if the desire to boast had triumphed over my doubts, I continued with a self-satisfied expression: "I couldn't say this earlier, but now that it's no longer current I can tell you about it. Do you remember that back in July we discussed Robert Toth and you read me his testimony?"

Solonchenko nodded. He was clearly intrigued.

"You told me then that Bob was arrested. Of course I didn't know whether it was true. I listened to you carefully, however, and after two or three weeks, I knew for sure that it wasn't."

When Solonchenko tensed up and froze in his seat, I quickly added a line I had prepared in advance to make his admission easier. "Of course I don't know whether Toth was ever seized, but at some point in August I knew he was free."

Solonchenko took the bait. Lifting his head, and slowly choosing his words, he said, "I can assure you that everything we needed from Toth we got. He sat in jail as long as was necessary and confessed everything. Why should we detain him any longer? The Americans have their spies here, and we have our people over there. You, however, are not simply a spy. You're a Soviet citizen—and a traitor. An entirely different fate awaits you."

Here I tried to make a wry face, although I'm not sure I succeeded. I had started this game back in July, in the hope of finding out whether they were lying to me about Bob's arrest. And while I had forced them to take back several of their lies, only now had I finally achieved my original goal.

Solonchenko had partially recovered his composure and started rocking in his chair. "It can't be that you learned about Toth from me," he said. "We'll find out, and very quickly, how and from where you learned this."

I laughed, for now, at long last, I was free to tell him. "From you, only from you, Alexander Samoilovich!" The fact that to this extent, at least, I was telling him the truth only increased my pleasure. "After all, except for you and Naumov, I had no one to talk with. You can't imagine how much I can learn by analyzing your words. A whole science exists for this purpose, called mathematical logic. I can even explain how I deduced from your comments that Toth was free. Are you interested?"

"Go ahead," he replied, with an expression that indicated that he didn't believe a word I was saying, but why not listen? I told him the problem about the wise men who killed their faithless wives. "If you solve it," I said, "you'll understand the logic I used."

But now my thoughts were far away, and from an especially dangerous state criminal I changed back into a seven-year-old boy who used to sit near the grown-ups playing chess in the park until somebody left and I'd have a partner, whom I would quickly and proudly defeat.

Solonchenko meticulously recorded the text of the problem of the wise men. "Fine," he said, "we'll solve it at our leisure," and quickly sent me back to the cell. But he never mentioned the subject again.

Timofeev did not approve of my casual attitude toward the KGB. "They know their stuff," he said, "and you can be sure they're working nonstop, riveting together one volume of evidence after another."

Sunday interrogations were rare in Lefortovo, but Timofeev was delighted when, on the very next Sunday, he was summoned to meet with Baklanov, his interrogator. He went off as happily as always, but returned as gloomy as a cloud. This time he didn't wait for our game of dominoes to begin talking.

"Well, I got fucked because of you," he whispered as soon as the guard closed the door. "You show them how smart you are, and I'm the one who suffers. When did I ever tell you anything about your friend Toth?"

Timofeev explained that this time he had also talked with Baklanov's boss, who told him, "We are accommodating to you, Mikhail Alexandrovich, and helping you maintain a link with your family, but this can end at any moment. We're not providing such amenities in order to help Sharansky."

After Timofeev assured them of his loyalty and noncomplicity, the KGB men changed their tone and tried to ascertain how I could have learned about Toth. Perhaps Timofeev had mentioned something he had read in the newspaper?

"But I read only *Soviet Sport,*" he told them. The session ended amicably, but Timofeev was distressed that he might have lost their trust. I felt sorry for him, although I was delighted to hear that I was evidently correct about Toth.

I consoled Timofeev and expressed my indignation at those idiotic investigators who talked too much and then looked for a scapegoat. While I had no specific plans to continue the game, I was so worked up by the incident with Timofeev that I decided to amuse myself a little longer. "I'm sorry you became the innocent victim of my relations with the KGB," I whispered to him. "If you like, I can protest that they're turning you against me. I'll tell them you're upset with me and that you suspect I slandered you. That will be yet another proof of your noncomplicity."

After thinking it over, Timofeev said, "Well, I suppose it can't hurt."

I arrived at the next interrogation in a deliberately sullen mood, and didn't respond to Solonchenko's inquiries about my bad temper. Soon after the start of the interrogation, Solonchenko was joined by Mikhail Ivanovich Iliukhin, the assistant procurator general who supervised the KGB investigative department. Iliukhin, whose official role was to demonstrate that everything was going "according to law," became a regular participant during the final months of the interrogations. He, too, noticed my dark mood, but Solonchenko spoke first: "Yes, somehow Anatoly Borisovich is down in the dumps today."

This was my cue. "You want to know why? You turned my cell mate against me, and now he's after me with his fists because he thinks I slandered him. I already explained that *you*, and nobody else, had informed me that Toth was free. What does Timofeev have to do with it? I demand that the procurator halt the KGB's attempts to poison the atmosphere in our cell."

Iliukhin was dumbfounded, while Solonchenko blanched and seemed genuinely frightened. Iliukhin spoke first: "Alexander Samoilovich, do you know what he's talking about?"

"Yes, you see—" Solonchenko began timidly, but quickly switched to a more aggressive tone. "Anatoly Borisovich had the gall"—this was the first time Solonchenko had ever used such an indelicate word when conducting official business—"to claim that I informed him that Robert Toth was free. That's a lie; I don't know where he learned it. As for your cell mate," he added, turning toward me, "I don't even know who he is."

As the interrogators liked to remind me, they were prohibited from knowing who was in the cell with the prisoner they were interrogating.

"I don't care whether you know or not," I replied. "I demand that you stop turning him against me in search of a scapegoat who will take the blame for your blunders."

Iliukhin spoke up in a strict, procuratorial voice: "The prison administration and not the investigative department is in charge of the isolation of prisoners. If the investigative team has any suspicions, they can turn to the prison administration."

"But that's exactly what we did when Volodin sent a letter to the head of the prison on this matter," Solonchenko replied defensively. Then he retreated again: "And I know nothing more about it."

That was how I learned about the letter in which Volodin demanded that Petrenko terminate my contact with the outside world—a letter I read for myself half a year later as I was studying the documents of the case. What further proof did I need that my game had yielded the desired results?

I returned to my cell with a slight feeling of sadness. My game was almost certainly over, and a boring period would probably follow. It turned out, however, that even the gloomy confines of Lefortovo could be full of fascination and intrigue.

10

Tactics of Intimidation

WHILE I was playing out my game the KGB pressed on with its own tactics, trying new moves to manipulate me into worrying about the evidence they were gathering against my friends and me.

In the beginning of August Solonchenko took out a document and said, "You keep insisting that Tsypin and Lipavsky speak for us. Tell me, for whom does this man speak?" Then he read the following sentence: "Previously we tried to provoke Marchais against Brezhnev, but now let's try to reach Mitterrand, which could be even more sensitive for Marchais."

Solonchenko watched intently as he tried to determine whether I recognized these words. I did indeed; I had spoken them in Alexander Lerner's apartment, when Vitaly Rubin and I came by to collect Lerner's signature for an appeal to François Mitterrand, the French Socialist leader. (We had previously written to Georges Marchais, head of the French Communist Party, suggesting that he meet with a group of refuseniks during his forthcoming visit to Moscow, but he had not responded.)

Nobody doubted that Lerner's apartment was bugged, and nothing indiscreet had been said that night. But when my remark, read from a transcript, was taken out of context and repeated here, in the office of a KGB investigator, it sounded damaging and conspiratorial.

This time it was I who paused. In a dry and precise tone, and without revealing that I recognized the sentence in question, I replied, "Please include your question in the protocol and indicate exactly what document was read to me, when it was composed, and so on." (In other words, if you intend to use tapes of bugged conversations, then say so openly). I knew that KGB operatives liked to cover their tracks, and that officially it wasn't so easy to get authorization for bugging.

Solonchenko quickly retreated. When the session ended, he said, "I hope you understand that there are cases when the procurator gives permission to record conversations. It's one thing to participate in a little slander, but quite another to engage in treason. But we'll get to that. In the meantime," he concluded as always, "think it over, Anatoly Borisovich, think it over."

Over the next few days I was obsessed with how the KGB might use tapes of my conversations against me. Again and again I tried to imagine how some sentence or phrase taken out of context might sound. What if I had given material about refuseniks to a visiting member of Congress and had said to a colleague, "I passed some information to Congressman X," or "I sent a package of information abroad"? Even the most innocuous remark could sound suspicious if the KGB chose to link it with a specifically tailored fabrication by Lipavsky.

But each time I began speculating along these lines I stopped and asked myself: Why am I bothering with such nonsense? Instead of the KGB scaring me, I'm doing it for them! If they really wanted to, they could fashion a criminal case out of anything, including the Communist Party program.

Still, it was difficult to stop thinking about these taped conversations, especially when I remembered Mark Morozov. A few weeks before my arrest, Morozov, a Moscow dissident, had shared with some of us a sensational secret—that a KGB agent had offered to pass on information about the KGB's intentions. At first nobody believed Mark, and the hotter heads drove him away altogether, saying they didn't want to become entangled in KGB provocations. But specific information began to arrive from Morozov's source about impending searches and arrests, and some of it turned out to be true. I was among the few who continued to have contact with Morozov. Even if he was being used, as I assumed he was, I believed it was important to determine exactly what information the KGB was hoping to give us.

Two days before the publication of the *Izvestia* article, Morozov asked me to come to his apartment, and wrote two messages on the slate: first, that a member of our group—he didn't know who—was a major squealer for the KGB, and, second, that the KGB had recorded my recent conversation with Robert Toth, which took place in his car, and which they believed could be used to compromise both of us.

I viewed these warnings as merely another attempt to intimidate and demoralize me, but when Lipavsky's article appeared just two days later in *Izvestia,* I recalled Morozov's comment about Toth. Although Bob and I had held several conversations in his car, neither of us could recall discussing anything secret or suspicious. "It's probably just a provocation," I said. "They want us to be afraid of them."

But now that Solonchenko had informed me that the taping of conversations was officially permitted, I recalled Volodin's words back in May: "No secrets?" he had said. "Even when you sat in a car with an American correspondent with the windows shut tight?" I couldn't help wondering, What would they fashion out of my conversation with Toth?

I worried about this for some time, which was exactly what the KGB wanted. But no such tape ever appeared during the investigation or at the trial. The KGB probably calculated that among my many conversations with Toth there were surely some I might prefer to conceal, and that my fear might lead me to start talking. In an attempt to explain what I really meant, I might easily incriminate myself. Later, I heard of cases where people were caught in just this kind of trap.

Their next tactic also concerned Toth. During a rare Sunday interrogation, Solonchenko gave me two sheets of paper whose text began approximately as follows:

On March 14, 1977, the custodian Citizen Zakharov, while cleaning the courtyard of the building at 12/24 Sadovo-Samotechnaya Street, where the office of the newspaper the *Los Angeles Times* is located, found typed material with handwritten corrections, which he brought to the reception room of the KGB on March 15, 1977. Having looked over this material, KGB investigator Sharudilo sent forty pages for expert evaluation to ascertain whether the handwriting was that of correspondent Robert Toth.

This was followed by the standard description of such documents, which consisted of the first and last words on each page. Although the contents were not revealed, it was possible to conclude from the few words that were quoted that this material dealt with the KGB, refuseniks, dissidents, and my arrest. Solonchenko looked at me, smiled from behind his desk, leaned back in his chair and said, "Well, Anatoly Borisovich, that's how it is."

Having recently felt myself to be in control of our conversations, I didn't want to lose the initiative. Stifling my anxiety, I said with an ironic smile, "So you probably have very good janitors working for you who can find anything you want. All you have to do is dictate the text." And then, in my eagerness to repulse Solonchenko's attack and to take the wind out of his sails, I moved too fast.

As I looked through the pages "found" by Citizen Zakharov on March 14 a thought had occurred to me that I couldn't restrain myself from expressing. "What a remarkable broom your janitor has," I said. "It was twenty-four hours before my arrest, and he had already found Toth's report about it. It's really true," I continued with a laugh that sounded more nervous than I had intended, "there are no accidents in your work."

As Solonchenko approached my table and bent over the papers, I saw by his distraught face what a stupid gaffe I had just committed. The KGB had made an error that nobody had caught, and I, like a fool, had brought it to their attention. Now they'd find a way to fix it. At the trial—assuming my trial was open—I could have used this crude blunder to expose their methods.

While I was cursing myself Solonchenko was struggling to come up with a suitable response. Finally he said, "Don't quibble over technical details. You don't even know what arrest the text refers to. Perhaps it was an impending arrest. You yourself said you were expecting to be arrested. But that's not the issue. The important thing is, this is no joke. It's a matter of national security. The American espionage network in Moscow has suffered a defeat. We have serious evidence confirming that you and other Zionists had a link to this network. So think it over before it's too late."

But it was clear that Solonchenko had lost his initial enthusiasm. He was obviously upset about something, and quickly sent me to my cell.

This time, however, I took little pleasure in his discomfort. Ever since my childhood I've been a terrible chatterbox. I remembered how Papa used to pick up my brother and me from kindergarten—he was six, I was four—to take us to the movies. Afterward, Papa and I would discuss the film, and it was such a pleasure to show off to Papa that I understood it. Papa supported me, as he also liked to talk, but Lenya, who was embarrassed by our public garrulity, would whisper to me, "Shut up, you damn chatterbox."

As I returned to the cell I repeated to myself with a bitter smile, "Shut up, you damn chatterbox!" and resolved to keep stricter watch over my tongue in the days ahead.

Later, at the end of November, Solonchenko showed me a section of the papers that were "found" by Zakharov. "Look it over," he said. "You'll see that even Toth realized your activities were illegal."

This time I was presented with a rather long telex, which included a rough draft and then a final copy of Toth's article about my arrest, both in English and in a Russian translation. Reading it with great excitement, I learned for the first time what had happened back at Slepak's apartment as I was driven to Lefortovo, searched, and interrogated. Dina Beilin had phoned the KGB to determine where I was. Masha Slepak was upset because I had forgotten my satchel. Lerner said he would wait until the following day before making a statement to the press. Although over half a year had passed since that evening, I felt as if I were once again among my friends. Don't worry, I wanted to call to them, I'm holding up!

Of course I wasn't being shown Zakharov's "discoveries" in order to inform me about events in Moscow on the evening of my arrest. What they wanted to show me was a brief postscript to the article, a note from Toth to his editor that read approximately as follows:

Nick, we may have a problem. *Izvestia* accused a group of Jewish activists of collecting secret information about the jobs of refuseniks. This was the topic of my article in November, and Sharansky helped me openly then. One correspondent told me I was a dupe to write such an article, although he agreed there was nothing criminal in it. Sharansky told me a few days before his arrest that somebody mentioned a tape that the KGB allegedly has of my conversation with him, although he thought this was a provocation.

Regards—15-03-77-22-00

After reading Toth's addendum several times, I thought, Well, Bob, if you were a dupe, it wasn't when you wrote that article but when you added this note. Why didn't you include this information in the actual article? I helped you openly, so you should have written about it openly and not given the KGB a pretext to assert we had any secrets!

I wasn't surprised to see that the Russian translation of Toth's words contained several inaccuracies and errors. The most significant one occurred at the end of the postscript, where the word "Regards" before the string of numbers was translated as "All this concerns case number . . ."

It didn't take Sherlock Holmes to conclude that these numbers represented the date and time of dispatch of the article. The investigative team, however, came up with a different meaning. "You see," said Iliukhin, "the CIA even opened a whole file on you with a ten-digit number."

I smirked, but I had no interest in arguing with him. By this time my game was over and I was merely an observer. Nor did I say anything more about the timing of Zakharov's discovery, although each sheet carried the stamp of the reception desk of the KGB and the clearly impossible date of March 15, 1977.

In September Solonchenko initiated a new approach to impress upon me that the KGB knew a great deal about the personal lives of my fellow Jewish activists. His intention was obvious—to show that A was a coward, B a philanderer, C was greedy for money, and D was pursuing his own glory. These descriptions didn't come out of thin air, but were carefully thought out and derived from both informers and bugged conversations.

For it was true that among ourselves we occasionally discussed the fact that A wasn't always a model of bravery, that B didn't necessarily display the habits of a monk, or that C may have received more money from abroad than he and his family actually needed. As for D, who really did seem to be pursuing glory, Solonchenko would say, "You may be surprised that this document still exists, but your friend D was so narcissistic that he saved everything, which helped us considerably."

I, meanwhile, was portrayed in a very different light. Never in my life did I receive as many compliments as I was given by the KGB during those weeks: not only did I decline to take part in various squabbles, but I had evidently treated my comrades with far more respect than they deserved. I was so intelligent and good-natured, in fact, that were it not for some of my views and judgments, I would have been an excellent fellow. The conclusion of these conversations was always the same: Look, nobody is pure, but some, who sinned more than others, are currently enjoying life in Moscow or in Israel, whereas you must answer for all of them. What injustice!

Although this onslaught seemed much weaker than the previous, more aggressive swoops, it was both longer and more methodical. It was designed not only to force me to doubt my friends and to weaken my ties with them, but also to set the stage for a time when my feelings of hopelessness and isolation would be so powerful that I might be receptive to a compromise.

A few weeks later Solonchenko and Iliukhin finally got around to Avital. We were discussing documents from the OVIR which showed that refuseniks were denied permission to emigrate either "because this went against state interests," or "because this was not a case of reunification of families."

"What about my wife?" I asked. "The investigative team showed such touching concern about our speedy reunification during the early months of my interrogations."

"What wife?" said Iliukhin. "You don't have any wife!"

"We'll get to your so-called wife," said Solonchenko. "No matter what she calls herself, she didn't even want to send you an invitation."

I was actually pleased at their sharp reaction; it meant that Avital was probably giving them something to get angry about. Two weeks later they read me a certificate from the Moscow synagogue claiming our marriage was invalid. They also showed me an interview with Avital in a Canadian women's magazine. The photocopy was made in such a way that it was possible to read only a few words from the interview, where Avital had said, "We weren't able to arrange a *chuppah* in the Moscow synagogue."

"You see," said Solonchenko, "even your so-called wife confirms to the Western press that you didn't have a *chuppah*. You had neither a civil nor a religious wedding, so all this is a lie and a provocation."

I carefully examined the fuzzy reprint of the interview. The text was framed by tiny alternating photographs of Avital and me, which formed a border around the article. I was dying to see through the paper to her real face, and to hear the words as she had spoken them. Instinctively, my hand slipped into my pocket for the photograph.

Avital had anticipated this problem about the marriage. A few weeks before she left, she and I, together with other Jewish activists, had demonstrated in front of the Lebanese embassy to protest the terrorist murder of twenty Israeli schoolchildren in the town of Ma'alot, near the Lebanese border. The police put all of us on a bus and drove us to a "sobering station," which was standard procedure following a demonstration. Avital was the last to leave because she told them nothing, not even her name. I was waiting for her, and on the way home I told her we must do everything possible to get her visa as soon as possible.

"But what about registering?" she had said. "If I leave before we register, they'll claim we were never married."

"What's important?" I had replied. "That they know we're married, or that we know?"

The KGB's next tactic was surprising in its sophistication. At the beginning of October the interrogations came to an abrupt halt. A week passed, then another, and soon four weeks went by and it seemed as if the investigators had forgotten me. But one evening, during our game of dominoes, Timofeev whispered, "Today, it seems, Baklanov told me a joke for you." Then, in a normal voice, he said, "Baklanov told me a joke today. 'Do you remember the one from the peak of the Zhids' flight?' he asked me. 'Two Jews are standing together and a third one comes up to them and says, 'I don't know what you two are talking about, but I know for sure— we must emigrate.'

" 'Yesterday,' continued Baklanov, 'I heard an updated variation of that joke. Two Jews are standing together, and a third one comes up to them and says, "I don't know what you two are talking about, but I know for sure—we must confess. I've already signed a statement." Yes, difficult times have arrived for the Jews.' "

Whereas Timofeev merely suspected that this joke was meant for my ears, I had no doubts at all. I remembered the first one clearly, which had made the rounds in Moscow in late 1971. It was amusing and had some spice to it, but only because it circulated shortly after the trial in Leningrad of a number of Jews who tried to hijack a plane to Israel, which was followed by a vigorous anti-Zionist campaign that ignited talk about emigration in virtually every Jewish household. This new variation of the joke, assuming it really existed, could make sense only in an atmosphere dominated by public recantations of Jews for their "Zionist delusions."

I expected a sequel to this joke, and I wasn't disappointed. A few days later Timofeev told me about a conversation of Baklanov's that he had "inadvertently" overheard. "No," Baklanov had said, referring to one of my investigators, "Sharudilo can't go with us on Sunday. They've decided to finish with this Zhids' bazaar once and for all. He's been sitting for a month without a break, but he'll get a long vacation later to make up for it." Timofeev didn't think this remark was intended for me, but I disagreed. It was no accident that Baklanov used the vulgar term "Zhids" instead of "Jews," as required by the KGB's hypocritical but official code of ethics. By his choice of language he was indicating his trust in Timofeev.

In retrospect, I believe that Timofeev's role in the KGB's game was unusual. I have no guarantee, of course, that he wasn't an ordinary informer, but he seemed unlikely to have agreed to such a role. Although he was a loyal Soviet citizen and a confirmed Communist, he maintained his own principles of honesty, decency, and zeks' solidarity. I could imagine Timofeev as a prosecutor at my trial, but not as an informer. And while he never volunteered to use his meetings with his wife to help me send a message to the outside world (and I never asked him to), he did consider it his duty to transmit any information he received from the KGB that might help me make the "correct decision."

The KGB, of course, was more than willing to take advantage of this channel. At the end of October they allowed him to meet with several highly placed officials, including his old friends and colleagues from the Central Committee and the Interior Ministry. Timofeev had been hoping they would help arrange a pardon, and Baklanov was kind enough to leave them alone in his office. Timofeev returned late, excited and encouraged. As he went on at great length with boring gossip from the lives of his colleagues, I listened partly out of politeness and partly out of a belief that this time, too, the KGB would send me a greeting.

I was right. When we sat down to our nightly game of dominoes, he whispered, "There was also something said about you. When they asked who my cell mate was, I didn't gave your name, but simply said, 'One of the so-called dissidents.' "

"Many of them are in prison now," one of Timofeev's friends had said. "They've finally stopped treating them with kid gloves and started going after them seriously. They've been grabbing these people all over the country."

"And what will happen to them?" Timofeev had asked.

"Well, these aren't Stalinist times, so there won't be any mass executions. But apparently those who went too far in their games with foreigners will be shot."

"Not that!" Timofeev had cried out. Whereupon his friend from the Central Committee, whom Timofeev described as very well informed, explained, "What can we do? The longer they sit in the jail, the more capital they earn in the West and the more dangerous they become when they leave the country. This way we'll get rid of our enemies and intimidate the others. They're now more arrogant than ever; they openly mock our system and make alliances with our enemies."

I had no doubt that Timofeev's friends were part of the KGB's plan, and that a new attack against me was in the works. These days, however, there were no interrogations, which meant no opportunities to expose their lies and build up my morale. I stopped thinking about the investigation and returned to my books and the marvelous world of literary heroes.

In November my interrogations resumed in an expanded format. Iliukhin, the assistant procurator general, was often present at the sessions, and starting in January he was always with us. In his early fifties, Iliukhin was a short, plump man with a gray and sleepy demeanor. It soon became clear that he had joined us for cosmetic purposes—to enable the KGB to maintain that everything was being done by the book and that they were working under the direct supervision of the procurator's office.

Iliukhin made a pretense of showing concern, and as soon as we met he asked if I had any complaints about the investigative team.

In my presence, he reminded Solonchenko that the protocol had to be signed on the same day it was written. Iliukhin's conduct at the interrogations, however, was something else. For example, when I was asked about my relationship with Andrei Sakharov, I replied, "I am well acquainted with the Nobel Peace Prize winner Academician Andrei Dmitrievich Sakharov. I consider his activity in defense of human rights in the USSR to be correct, and I refuse to provide any testimony about him."

At this point, Iliukhin suddenly burst out: "We shall not write in the protocol that the anti-Soviet Sakharov is a winner of the Nobel Peace Prize! That award was an anti-Soviet provocation. He has Soviet prizes, too. Why don't you enumerate *them?*"

I was astonished by Iliukhin's reaction. "The *anti-Soviet* Andrei Sakharov," I replied, "father of the *Soviet* hydrogen bomb, is the recipient of the highest *Soviet* titles and awards, and I have no objections whatsoever if the investigator wishes to enumerate them in his question. But I will formulate my own answer, without any prompting."

But Iliukhin didn't permit the investigator to record my answer. I refused to sign the protocol, and only at the following interrogation, when Iliukhin was absent, did Solonchenko give it to me to sign in my own version.

Normally, however, Iliukhin was sluggish, and had difficulty following the line of the interrogation. Sometimes he brought in papers—apparently material from another case—and like a schoolboy stealing time during one class to prepare for the next one, he would furtively read these sheets during my interrogation. Occasionally he even dozed off, waking up whenever his head jerked down. Each time this happened I would give Solonchenko a conspiratorial wink and lower my voice so as not to awaken our visitor. Solonchenko responded with an understanding smile.

The first time Iliukhin fell asleep Solonchenko and I burst out laughing the moment he left the room. Then, fearing he might be undermining the authority of the regime, Solonchenko hastily added, "You are mistaken to take this man so lightly. It's entirely possible that he'll be the prosecutor at your trial, which means your fate will depend on him."

"So what?" I replied sarcastically. "The prosecutor can sleep. The

KGB decides." Solonchenko merely shrugged his shoulders, but in the future he was more cautious and respectful toward Iliukhin.

December and January were devoted primarily to "exposing the slanderous nature" of documents I had signed, including reports on Jewish issues and documents from the Helsinki Watch Group on Soviet violations of human rights. Solonchenko spent countless hours solemnly reading me all this material, and each time he would conclude, "As you see, here, too, you slandered us."

In one of these reports we had described the miserable conditions of political prisoners in Soviet prisons and labor camps, with the names of approximately a hundred zeks who were prepared to confirm our information.

To refute the "slander" in our report, the KGB worked long and hard to prepare their own documents. They produced statements from the heads of prisons and camps, and from doctors, who testified about the excellent medical services and healthful food. They even collected testimony from the prisoners themselves, all of whom attested to how well they were treated, how tasty the food was, and how only a small number of "Zionists" and "anti-Soviets" provoked conflicts in order to depict themselves as victims and thus attract attention in the West.

"You prepared your reports from hearsay," said Solonchenko, "and you've never been to a prison or a camp. This is the testimony of people who are really there. What further proof do you need?"

In time I came to understand that the KGB was correct on one point—that our Helsinki reports on political prisoners didn't always correspond to reality. As I would discover, reality was much worse, much harsher than we had described it. We wrote about how inhumane it was to keep a prisoner in a punishment cell for thirty days, when even the law decreed that this torture should not last for more than fifteen. But I had yet to learn for myself what it meant to lose consciousness in a punishment cell after a hundred days of such abuse. Or to go for years without visits or letters. Or how cruelly and mercilessly the camp machine tries to grind down anyone who seeks to retain his own system of values or convictions.

All of this still lay in the future. Now I simply informed Solonchenko that I had personally talked with many prisoners who had returned from camps, and with their families, and that I trusted their testimony more than the statements produced by the KGB. More-over, I added, even my brief experience in the punishment cell of Lefortovo was enough to refute the KGB's testimony. One of their "witnesses" had stated that during the 150 days he had spent in punishment cells he hadn't once suffered from cold or hunger. But having spent only ten days there, I was prepared to confirm that this was genuine torture by cold. Moreover, the prison officials had often told me that Lefortovo was a resort when compared with the rest of the Gulag system, and for once I knew they were telling the truth.

"Yes, of course it's a resort," said Solonchenko, eager to confirm this idea for his own purposes. "You simply can't imagine what awaits you after the trial, even if you're lucky and they don't shoot you. You can't imagine it, so you pretend you're not afraid."

He wasn't bothered by the glaring contradiction between these words and the testimony he had just read me. But Iliukhin noticed, and made sure to add, "There, too, however, everything is done in accordance with the law."

Solonchenko and Iliukhin also tried to show me that our Helsinki Group reports on psychiatric repressions were false, and they read me extracts from the medical records of several individuals whose cases we described, as if the very fact that they were holding in their hands an official document was sufficient proof of its legality.

I wasn't an expert in the Soviet use of psychiatry as an instrument of repression, and always relied on the experience and research of my fellow Helsinki Group members, just as they relied on me when they signed documents about Jewish emigration. But I remembered my meeting with the poet Natalia Gorbanevsky, one of the seven brave people who demonstrated in Red Square to protest the 1968 invasion of Czechoslovakia, and the founder of the samizdat journal *Chronicle of Human Events.* She had been confined to a psychiatric hospital as punishment for her dissident activities, and shortly before she emigrated to France, she told me, "The worst part is that they keep you for an unlimited period, and you understand that this can last forever. They give you pills, and if you don't swallow them, they give you an injection. After that, you can't concentrate on anything. You tell yourself, 'I must write a letter today,' and you tell yourself this for a day, a week, and a month, but you can't force yourself to sit down and write it."

Among others, our group had reported on a little-known and truly absurd case concerning a Ukrainian named Sedykh. His family had moved to Canada, but after World War II they decided to return to the Soviet Union. Sedykh, who was fifteen at the time, wanted to go back to Canada. When he refused to serve in the Soviet army, he was sentenced to several years in a camp. Later, he settled in the Ukraine and raised a family, but he never abandoned his efforts to return to Canada. In the early 1970s, when the gates of the USSR opened slightly, Sedykh began to push harder.

The authorities, however, told him that in order to emigrate he needed an invitation from relatives in Israel. Why? he asked. He hadn't needed one when he came over from Canada. And why Israel? He wasn't a Jew; he was a Canadian of Ukrainian ancestry. These questions were completely natural for a healthy peasant mind, but Sedykh ended up in a mental hospital. According to the specialists in punitive medicine, he suffered from an "idée fixe of emigration from the USSR to Canada, despite the lack of invitation from relatives." I don't recall exactly what cure was prescribed.

On another occasion, Solonchenko tried to refute our document on criminal persecutions of Baptist peasants. A woman named Tatiana Barin had been convicted of teaching religion to children, which is punishable by a prison term of up to five years. Naturally, we had spoken out in her defense.

Solonchenko read me excerpts from her criminal file, including the testimony of a nine-year-old schoolgirl: "After school Papa and Mama brought me to Auntie Tania. She told us that Jesus Christ taught that we should love all people—both bad and good. She gave us little booklets and pictures. I liked it better at Auntie Tania's than at school. There no one yells or fights. Everybody loves each other."

Poor girl, she told the "uncle" investigators about Auntie Tania in the presence of the schoolteacher, so that everything was according to law. She didn't realize that she was giving evidence against Auntie Tania, and was helping these "uncles" put Auntie Tania in prison. What do the investigators feel when they take such testimony? I wondered.

"What are you turning these children into?" I said. "New Pavlik Morozovs?" Pavlik Morozov was a boy who, during the time of collectivization in the early thirties, informed the secret police that his father was hoarding grain. The father was exiled, and the boy was killed in revenge by his father's relatives and subsequently glorified as a Soviet hero.

Solonchenko simply didn't understand what I meant. For him, Pavlik Morozov was a hero, the model of the new Soviet man. Iliukhin replied for him: "According to Marx, religion is the opiate of the masses. We won't permit anyone to poison our children."

They also read me the criminal case of a seventy-five-year-old Baptist who had been preaching for approximately thirty years. This was his fourth or fifth arrest, and each time he would declare in court, "I did God's will and I shall continue to bring the divine word to the people." After several years in prison, he would go back to doing what he felt he must.

"Fine," I interrupted. "You and I have different attitudes toward religion. But in strictly human terms, don't you feel any respect for this old man who stands up for his convictions?"

Solonchenko looked at me in astonishment. Then he smirked and said, "Anatoly Borisovich, what do you need this pathos for? Isn't it obvious that this guy is nuts?"

I was genuinely surprised. "Why, because he's a believer?"

"Listen, we're not kids, you and I," snickered Solonchenko. "These days everybody knows that religion is a mental deviation from the norm. As long as he leaves others alone, we tolerate him. But if he bothers people, we have to isolate him in a prison or hospital."

No matter how hard the KGB tried to isolate me from my world and draw me into theirs, their very existence was enough to remind me that we were separated by an enormous wall. And although Solonchenko was undoubtedly sincere in his vision of Soviet religious freedom, and although he smiled at me as we both rocked in our chairs, it was clear that we lived on different planets.

The Evidence

11

FINALLY the investigation was over, and I was presented with a document called "Charges in the Final Form." It consisted of three elements: Article 64-A—high treason in the form of rendering aid to a foreign state in carrying on hostile activity against the USSR (this covered all statements that I and others had signed in support of the Jackson Amendment, statements on behalf of refuseniks, and meetings with American senators and congressmen); Article 64-A—high treason in the form of espionage (this consisted of maintaining lists of refuseniks "under the orders of the CIA," and passing those lists to foreigners); and Article 70—anti-Soviet activity (this new charge covered my work as a member of the Helsinki Watch Group).

Which of the allegations was the most serious? The espionage charge, with its sensational reference to the CIA, showed that the Soviets, no less than in Stalin's time, were capable of complete fabrication. The charge of high treason in the form of assistance to refuseniks had a basis in real meetings and activities, even though there was nothing criminal in our work. But the use of this charge showed me that the KGB was prepared to bring similar cases against anyone in our movement. Now, *that* was serious.

The accusations were supported by evidence collected by the seventeen investigators in my case. Volodin informed me that there were fifty-one volumes of my file, and showed me one, which consisted of more than three hundred pages of typed text in a cardboard binding. "Case no. 182," it read. On the upper right-hand corner it was stamped "Secret."

"Why secret?" I asked. "There were no secret interrogations. Does this mean the trial will be closed?"

"No, it's a routine stamp. Everything in the KGB is secret." Later the evidence was marked "Top Secret"—presumably to give the impression that there were real secrets in my file.

"We're giving you two weeks to examine it," said Volodin. "That's more than enough time, as you're familiar with the case."

"I'll take as much time as I need," I replied. When my interrogators tried to hurry me along, I replied calmly, "I didn't interfere with your work, so don't prevent me from trying to understand whatever it was you concocted here."

After eleven months of deprivation, it was thrilling to have so much information. I spent the next three and a half months studying the case. For more than a hundred days, from morning until evening, with breaks for lunch and supper, I sat in office 58 and pored over the testimony of some three hundred witnesses from almost forty cities and towns who had been questioned by the KGB.

What, then, did I learn from studying these fifty-one volumes?

The question I had most wanted to answer was What was really going on in the outside world? Had the KGB succeeded in crushing our movement or in convincing my fellow activists that I was a spy? My game had shown that they hadn't, but what if I had played the game only with myself? Perhaps the KGB had been laughing to themselves all along, while breaking one Jewish activist after another?

The first fifteen volumes contained the testimony of the witnesses. Half of them were refuseniks, and I leafed through their interrogations first because only from them would I learn the truth. The refuseniks conducted themselves in a variety of ways, but after I read a few volumes the picture was clear: to my enormous relief, the KGB had not succeeded in crushing our movement or in obtaining mass recantations.

On the contrary, all of my friends had held out, and several, including Beilin, Slepak, Nudel, and Leva Ulanovsky, had clearly tried to make accusatory speeches against their interrogators. I knew this because their testimony was quickly cut off with the sentence "The witness refused to answer the essence of the question."

Some refuseniks, of course, preferred not to remember anything, as in "I don't remember whether I signed that letter." Some even added, "But if my name was used for purposes hostile to the Soviet Union, then I condemn this." For the most part, however, these were people from distant provinces who were not connected to me in any way and did not play a significant role in the aliyah movement.

My closest friends were interrogated last. The KGB officials had started with those who, in their opinion, could be counted among my "opponents." But they must have been disenchanted quickly, as the aliyah movement was united in opposing them. From reading the protocols of the interrogations of more than a hundred refuseniks from thirty cities, towns, and villages, it wasn't even possible to say who was a *politik* and who was a *kulturnik*, who was a demonstrator and who was active in scientific seminars. No, I thought, the KGB wasn't able to finish off the "Zhids' bazaar" after all.

While I was reading through the evidence my interrogators sat with me and studied Brezhnev's memoirs. The second book of the three-volume set had just appeared—it dealt with Brezhnev's experiences as a political commissar during the war—and reading it became a national obligation. *Pravda* wrote about it constantly, and later, when the final volume appeared, Brezhnev was awarded the prestigious Lenin Prize for Literature, which was normally reserved for great writers. My investigators had to attend discussion groups about the book in the evening, and I took great pleasure in watching these otherwise powerful people acting like schoolchildren who were afraid of failing their exams.

Meanwhile, I ordered one folder after another from the prison store and quickly filled them up with notes, copying out everything that seemed worthy of future study. I was told that I wouldn't be allowed to take any notes with me from Lefortovo, but even so I filled both sides of some fifteen hundred sheets of paper. I studied the case while I copied the material, and continued to study it in my cell.

The investigators had gathered a great deal of confiscated material from refuseniks—especially documents connected with foreigners—and had drawn up a long list of more than three hundred tourists who had "criminal" contacts with me: Soviet Jewry activists like Irene Manekovsky from Washington, Glenn Richter from New York, Connie Smukler and Enid Wurtman from Philadelphia, June Daniels from Des Moines and many others.

Some American tourists had apparently been detained by the authorities, and, when pressed, had signed incriminating documents and apologies. All had repudiated these documents upon returning home, but in my file this material was presented as "proof" of their CIA connections.

There were also numerous "character references"—KGB profiles of tourists, correspondents, diplomats, and members of Congress, designed to show they were Jewish and part of the international Zionist anti-Soviet conspiracy. Some of the material was more revealing than the KGB intended. There was, for example, a document in which the KGB asked the telephone company to list the international calls of Sharansky and his friends over a three-year period—who called whom, who spoke to whom, and what was discussed. This showed just how pervasive the surveillance had been.

I was especially moved as I read the interrogations of Mama and my brother. (I felt terrible for Papa, who answered the summons by writing that he could not appear at the interrogation because of poor health, but I was proud that he nevertheless condemned my arrest and demanded my release.) My family were loyal Soviet citizens, and my arrest had drawn them unexpectedly into a confrontation for which they were not prepared. Not even knowing what a KGB interrogation was, how would they conduct themselves when they turned out to be relatives of a "traitor"? Would they repudiate me? Would they deny that they knew anything about me?

On the contrary: instead of defending themselves, they attacked, demanding justice for their son and brother. But, Mama, why did you explain to these predators what kind of chess player I was, and how I learned Lermontov's epic poem "Borodino" by heart at the age of four? Were you trying to evoke their sympathy? But I was proud of my family, for they challenged the KGB and insisted on my innocence.

When I came to Lipavsky's testimony, I studied it as carefully as historians pore over ancient texts, trying to understand what was invented and what was genuine, and what the intentions were of those who guided the author's hand along the way. In his initial interrogations, Lipavsky had pointed to Lerner as the ideological leader of our "conspiracy," with Dina Beilin as the chief executor and my own role limited to that of disseminating information that other people had generated. Later, in the fall, when it was apparently decided to limit the trial to me, Lipavsky was called back to change his testimony and redistribute the roles. Now Beilin's central role was shifted over to me, which made it necessary to transfer the handling of the lists of refuseniks from Beilin to Lida Voronin.

And I finally learned how Robert Toth had ended up in the hands of the KGB. On June 11, 1977, four days before Bob was scheduled to leave Moscow at the end of his three-year term, Petukhov had called him at home to say he had finally received the long-awaited results of his experiments. They arranged a meeting, and according to a "casual passerby," whose testimony was also in my file, Petukhov had taken some papers out of his briefcase to give to Toth. The witness, who found this incident suspicious, asked two other bystanders to direct him to the nearest police station. In a striking coincidence, these two men turned out to be police investigators, who, with the help of the police, detained both Toth and Petukhov.

An expert was brought in who testified that Petukhov's material, which Toth hadn't even looked at yet, was secret. Toth said he was unaware of this, and actually asked whether he could remain longer in the USSR to testify in behalf of Petukhov if Petukhov was taken to trial! This naive but noble gesture immediately restored all my former sympathy for Bob. He wasn't prepared for an encounter with the KGB—and who in the foreign press corps was?—but he was still a man of integrity. Poor Bob, I wondered, how was it that you still didn't understand that you, rather than Petukhov, were the victim of a provocation?

Petukhov testified that all his meetings with Toth took place at Toth's initiative, and that I had played a fundamental role in organizing them and keeping them secret. Toth was interrogated for two days, and now that I knew what had preceded these sessions, I was better able to understand the atmosphere that led Bob to testify. But to my astonishment, the protocol of Bob's first interrogation hadn't even been translated into English. Under the Russian text was a note by Toth saying, "It has been explained to me that in accordance with the Criminal Procedural Code of the USSR I am obliged to sign, although I do not read Russian and cannot understand what is written here."

Justice was restored in Toth's second protocol, as he was permitted to sign an English translation. But it didn't take me long to find a key difference between the English version that Toth had signed and the Russian version signed by Volodin and Chernysh. While Toth had testified that part of the information used in his article "Russia Indirectly Reveals Its Centers of Secret Research" had come from me, the Russian translation said that part of the information received from me was used in Toth's article. Although it appeared to be a subtle difference, the translation supported the KGB's contention that the information published in Toth's article was only a cover, and that I had given Bob other, genuinely secret information as well.

I also discovered that Zakharov, the janitor, had "found" even more than the KGB had originally let on. His discoveries also included a list of the workplaces of refuseniks and a multitude of other material connected with refuseniks, including several pages neatly torn from Robert Toth's notebook. Apparently Zakharov had checked Toth's entire office, including his notebooks, before making his "find." Every page that he handed to the KGB carried the stamp of the KGB reception desk and the same date, March 15, 1977.

As to the problem I had stupidly pointed out—that Zakharov had "found" Toth's article a day before it was written—there had been plenty of time to prepare an explanation. My file contained a letter from the investigative division asking how this could be, as well as a letter back from the reception office explaining that the secretary had made a mistake and that the actual date was not March 15, but April 15.

As I read and analyzed all these materials I wondered again, Why were there so many blunders? Why were so many stitches still visible after the operation? Were these people incompetent, or were they simply in too much of a hurry? The possibility that the KGB had been in a rush to arrest me had occurred to me before. After all, they had finally been able to place Lipavsky and me in the same rented apartment, which could have provided a marvelous opportunity to slip some genuinely secret information into a package that I was planning to hand to a foreigner. They would have caught the foreigner and me red-handed, and Lipavsky would not even have had to reveal himself.

Instead, just as the KGB's many years of trying to infiltrate Lipavsky into the aliyah movement were about to bear fruit, he promptly disappeared, whereupon *Izvestia* printed his letter without any opportunity to set up the case. This preparatory work had to be done *after* my arrest, which explains why they threw both Petukhov and Zakharov into battle, why they had to transfer the preparation of lists from Beilin to Voronin, and why they had to fuss with Lipavsky's testimony and alter some of Toth's.

But why the rush? After the Helsinki conference the Soviet Union found that the issue of human rights had suddenly become an international concern. The Helsinki Watch Group was established, and the protests of Soviet Jews became more energetic and visible than ever, now that leading American political figures were openly supporting the aliyah movement. Moreover, one of President Carter's first acts was to exchange letters with Andrei Sakharov. Things had changed so dramatically that I no longer had to think up ways to interest the press in the statements and letters of refuseniks or dissidents; the correspondents literally tore them out of my hands.

Apparently a decision was made in the Politburo to launch a counterattack. Because the Jewish movement represented a much greater danger than the other dissident movements, it had to be crushed more forcibly. The Jewish activists would be charged not as "anti-Soviets," like Orlov, Ginzburg, and other Helsinki Group activists, but as traitors—which would be easy enough in an anti-Semitic society. Because I had so many links with foreigners, they decided to start with me. When the command to strike came from on high, the operative wing of the KGB had to move so quickly that most of the preparations were completed only after my arrest.

Early in February the investigative team had presented the last and, in their view, most serious proofs of my "traitorous activities." After being shown documents revealing the alleged complicity of certain American diplomats at the Moscow embassy, I was given a KGB report on thirty-seven Moscow-based foreign correspondents with whom "Sharansky maintained a criminal link." There were also individual descriptions of Alfred Friendly *(Newsweek)*, George Krimsky (Associated Press), Christopher Wren and David Shipler *(New York Times)*, Peter Osnos *(Washington Post)*, Philip Short (BBC), and Philip Caputo *(Chicago Tribune)*, all of whom were said to be working for American intelligence.

These reports were prepared in the fall of 1977, but the one on Robert Toth was dated March 11—four days before my arrest and the official start of my case. I read with great interest that Toth was a Jew of Hungarian origin, although he wasn't the only non-Jew who was converted to Judaism by the KGB; Shipler, Friendly, Krimsky, and Caputo were all depicted as Jews so that they could be part of the "Zionist conspiracy." (Osnos was Jewish by birth and did not require a KGB conversion.)

According to the report,

> [Toth] constantly shows an interest in places that are off limits to foreigners. Appears knowledgeable in matters related to defense and economics. Conducts polls of Soviet citizens on secret topics. Citizen of the USSR Sharansky, A. B., is particularly helpful to Toth in his criminal contacts with Soviet citizens. Competent organs possess an instructional letter to Toth from the head of the American D.I.A. [an acronym I had never seen before, which stood for Defense Intelligence Agency]. It states in particular that at operational sessions, the head of the D.I.A., General Wilson, recommended that his agents pay special attention to Toth's materials. It also follows from the letter that Toth held meetings with General Haig, the head of NATO, and that more such meetings are scheduled to take place in the future.

"As you see," I was told, "there is a direct thread linking you to the head of NATO. In legal language this is called espionage."

This was certainly curious. I recalled that Bob had known Haig back when Bob was a White House correspondent and Haig was Nixon's chief of staff. But what was the D.I.A.? If Toth reported to the Defense Intelligence Agency, then perhaps he really was a spy. Or was this merely a reference to Bob's newspaper articles, which were surely of interest to intelligence experts? If the allegation involved more than Toth's articles, I thought, they would have been more specific. But what guilt could the KGB ascribe to me? And what materials did they think I passed on to Haig?

I didn't have to wait long for an answer, as they soon presented me with another document "found by the janitor Zakharov"—a short list of refuseniks that included their places of work. Not knowing whether this list was genuine, I had given my standard answer explaining why in *our* lists of refuseniks there couldn't be any secrets. Then came the decisive blow: they read me the conclusion of a commission of experts that our lists contained "information about the location and departmental affiliation of a series of enterprises of the defense branches of industry, about their secrecy and about other enterprises linked with defense sites which in their aggregate comprises state secrets and as a whole constitutes a state secret of the Soviet Union."

"In their aggregate," "as a whole"—it was clear that these formulations lacked conviction. If my trial is open, I thought, I must find a way to refute all this. Meanwhile I maintained a depressed silence. I didn't understand why this document had such a dispiriting effect on me, as it contained nothing more than the same old empty charges dressed up in legal language. Still, I found it frightening to read through these official papers about "information comprising state secrets," "espionage," and the transmission of "secret information" to the Defense Intelligence Agency and to NATO.

Perhaps the most frightening thing was the simplicity of these charges. During these past eleven months I had expected that at any moment some mysterious iceberg would float to the surface, some kind of carefully worked out KGB scheme that would implicate me in espionage activity, complete with incriminating photographs in the spirit of Soviet detective novels.

But their main "evidence" kept coming down to the same old lists of refuseniks, which Lipavsky maintained in his testimony were compiled on orders from abroad and were strictly secret. But what about the lists I had personally delivered to the Central Committee of the Communist Party and to the minister of the interior, which, at our request, the senators had delivered to Brezhnev? Would they claim that these, too, were strictly secret?

"Nothing like that ever happened," replied Solonchenko when I raised the question. "You fabricated all this during the investigation."

His remark was oddly soothing, as it provided one more reminder that the investigative team created its own facts, and that the people I was dealing with were impervious to logic and common sense.

Later in February Solonchenko declared, "The investigation has established unambiguously that you are a traitor. You are again reminded of the content of the Criminal Procedural Code of the USSR. In pronouncing its sentence, the court will consider heartfelt repentance as a circumstance mitigating guilt. What do you have to say about the charges brought against you concerning the conspiracy to commit especially dangerous state crimes?"

So the circle was finally closed, as we had now returned to the same question that was raised at my very first interrogation. Eleven months had passed since the night of March 15, and over a hundred interrogations had taken place, but although the formulation had become more refined and more aggressive, my answer was approximately the same: "I committed no crimes. My activity in drawing public attention to the violation of human rights in the USSR does not violate Soviet laws, since it did not pursue the goal of violating the sovereign independence or military might of the USSR. The false charges brought against me by the KGB are based on false testimony, juggling with facts, and an intentional distortion of the meaning and nature of our Jewish emigration activity."

Solonchenko was taking down my answer, but Iliukhin motioned for him to stop. "Think it over again," he told me. "This is a very important interrogation for you!"

I harrumphed, shrugged my shoulders, and gave a scornful smile. Although I was exhausted, I was also calm, detached, and satisfied that the case was finally coming to an end.

"Why are you smiling?" said Iliukhin. "Is it nerves? What's the matter, don't you realize you're a spy? What are you counting on?"

I ignored him, as I was no longer interested in talking. My only concern was that my reply be recorded correctly in the protocol. As the guard led me away I heard the tired and irritated voice of Iliukhin from behind the door of office no. 58 just before it closed: "He's impossible!"

That's a real compliment, I thought, returning to the cell, where I fell asleep almost immediately.

Included in my file were hundreds of pages of the *Congressional Record*, with speeches by both senators and congressmen in defense of Soviet Jewry. Wasn't this the best proof of a conspiracy? My American friends used to joke that nobody actually read the *Congressional Record* because it was so boring, but in Lefortovo I devoured it greedily and gratefully. As I read the speeches of Father Robert Drinan and Joshua Eilberg, Henry Jackson and Jacob Javits, Abraham Ribicoff and Elizabeth Holtzman, Christopher Dodd and Frank Church, I recalled Avital's and my own meetings with these people and I knew they were continuing the struggle.

Presumably to stimulate my memory, the KGB had obligingly included among the evidence some of Avital's letters and postcards to me in which she mentioned her talks with some of the American politicians, wrote that she had heard my voice over the radio, or read one of my interviews in the press. There were about twenty pieces of mail from Avital out of more than four hundred that the KGB had confiscated during a search, and I was only sorry that she hadn't made such "incautious" remarks in every one of them, for then I would be reading them all. The remaining postcards and letters, which were of no interest to the investigative team because they didn't mention "criminal activity," were, in the official jargon, "destroyed by burning."

One entire volume of my file consisted of articles and reports from the Western press, and excerpts from foreign radio broadcasts that mentioned our activity and either quoted me or alluded to me as the source of information. The transcripts of the radio broadcasts were sometimes interrupted by the phrase "could not be heard further on account of heavy jamming."

"What can I say?" I told the investigator. "You people have a tough job. One section of the KGB jams the broadcasts and another suffers from it."

Yet another volume included photographs taken by an American citizen named Gold that were confiscated upon his departure from Moscow. The film, which was developed by the KGB, included reports in Dina's handwriting based on interrogations of refuseniks in my case. Dina had summarized dozens of these sessions, noting what questions were asked, what documents the KGB was interested in, and how they formulated the charge. Wonderful Dina! In effect, she had reconstructed the charge against me so that the whole world could know what was going on.

I spent a long time studying and rereading the volume with Dina's material. I was reluctant to part with it, but only because I couldn't imagine what a stupendous surprise awaited me next. Among other things, I was being charged because of my role in the television film *A Calculated Risk,* produced by Granada in London in 1976, which featured lengthy interviews with Slepak and myself, and which was widely shown in Western Europe and on public television in the United States.

A film crew from London had come to Moscow as tourists, and I had accompanied them around the city in their rented car. Along the way I pointed out where various demonstrations had occurred in support of Jewish and German emigration. I showed them the lamppost in front of KGB headquarters where a German woman had chained herself and her five children. I arranged an interview with a refusenik who was underground to avoid a draft call. I took them to a Passover Seder in Lerner's apartment, and much more.

I could see that the KGB took this film very seriously, for as soon as I was arrested they got in touch with the Foreign Ministry. Three days later the Foreign Ministry passed on a videotape of the film that was received from the Soviet consulate in New York. An accompanying document from one of the consular officers attested to the great harm the film had caused to the prestige of the USSR, and similar documents had arrived from Soviet embassies in England, France, and Denmark.

The film was included as evidence because "Sharansky took part in the illegal filming of a foreign movie containing the slanderous fabrications of the defendant about the situation of national minorities in the USSR." Naturally I was eager to see the film and to recall just what "fabrications" I had uttered. Because the investigative team was obliged to familiarize me with all the documents used in the charge, I demanded that they show me *A Calculated Risk.*

They had no objections, and told me I could see it as soon as the videocassette operator returned from vacation. Meanwhile, I stumbled onto something even more interesting. Apparently there was also a Granada film about *me,* made after my arrest, entitled *The Man Who Went Too Far.* My file mentioned an interview filmed in London with my friend Michael Sherbourne, a prominent Soviet Jewry activist, in which Michael said, "Sharansky was a dedicated Zionist. Over the course of three years I spoke to him about a hundred times, and he sent me many letters and documents about the situation of Jews in the USSR."

Fine, I thought, if you really want to quote Michael Sherbourne, go right ahead! But if the film has the "validity of evidence," as the file also indicated, then I had the right to see this one, too. At first they resisted, and I had to pressure them by refusing to sign documents concerning my reviewing of the evidence. Finally the memorable day arrived. I was taken to Captain Gubinsky's office, where Solonchenko, Volodin, and Iliukhin had already gathered. The operator brought in a Japanese video machine and inserted the cassette of *A Calculated Risk.*

On the screen I saw myself, Slepak, and Alexander Lerner. Who could have imagined, I thought, when I gave that interview in 1976, that I would be seeing it for the first time two years later in Lefortovo? The film was like a tiny window into the recent past, which now seemed so distant.

Then they ran the second cassette and I went into a fog. For there, on the screen, was a demonstration in my behalf in London, near the Soviet embassy. And leading the demonstration was Avital! Her Hebrew was fluent.

"Already nothing remains from the Russian," commented Gubinsky in surprise.

Then Michael Sherbourne appeared, and Ludmilla Alexeyeva, and various English Jews, some of whom were familiar. I barely took in what they said. And then again—Avital. The film ended.

"Show it again," I said, almost pleading.

"What, you liked it?" said Iliukhin spitefully. "Once is enough. A prisoner under investigation may not watch television."

He quickly brought me back to reality, and I immediately changed my tone. "I have the right to familiarize myself with the evidence of the case," I said curtly. "I must understand every sentence, every word of the documents you are using against me. I have no legal experience, so I can only guess how you are going to build your charge. My command of English and Hebrew wasn't good enough for me to grasp everything the first time. Let me see it again."

After some hesitation they repeated the videotape. Again Avital was coming toward me. I didn't want her to disappear.

"Play it back, I missed a few words."

The operator put the machine into reverse.

An hour passed, then a second, then a third. My companions were growing increasingly angry, but I was unyielding. Again and again I forced them to repeat the videotape. Again and again Avital led the people to the Soviet embassy in London . . . no—to Lefortovo prison to demand my release!

Finally, Colonel Volodin's patience ran out and he began to yell at me: "That's enough! What do you think, that your fate is in the hands of those people and not ours? They're nothing more than students and housewives!"

Students and housewives. Thank you, Citizen Colonel, for providing me with such an excellent formulation. Today, whenever I appear before audiences in Jerusalem and in New York, in Paris and London and many other cities where people demonstrated in my behalf, I thank them for their efforts and I remind them of their strength and their power. And I always remember to tell them what Volodin said, for in the end the army of students and housewives turned out to be mightier than the army of the KGB.

The Lawyer

12

As soon as the investigation was completed I would have the right to a lawyer. In early January, when my case was nearing an end, I wrote a statement: "Since I am in isolation and cannot choose a defense counsel for myself, I entrust my proxies to do it for me—my mother, Ida Petrovna Milgrom, and my wife, Avital Sharansky."

When the investigation was over, Volodin informed me that my family had refused to choose a lawyer, and that I had to accept one who would be chosen for me from the Collegium of Advocates. Because the statute under which I was accused called for capital punishment, a lawyer could be appointed even against my will. I reminded Volodin that the same law gave me the right, in the event that difficulties arose in selecting a lawyer, to meet with my family and to explain my requirements to them.

"We won't give you a meeting, you can be sure of that," he replied curtly.

"Then let me explain to them in a letter just what kind of lawyer I need."

"No, you already wrote your statement. That's enough."

"Well . . . I'll have nothing to do with any lawyer chosen by you."

Here Volodin made some gesture to Solonchenko, who suddenly excused himself to use the bathroom.

"If I were in your place, Anatoly Borisovich," said Volodin, moving closer to me, "I would think it over very carefully. You may think the appointed lawyer is one of ours, but by law he is *required* to defend you, *required* to analyze the case and find arguments in your defense. Under these conditions it would be difficult to apply the maximum punishment. Although the KGB doesn't participate in the trial, the court certainly takes us into consideration. I'm telling you clearly: if you agree to accept the lawyer we give you, you won't be given the death sentence."

So here was yet another generous offer from the KGB! For some reason they were far from indifferent as to whether I would cooperate with their lawyer. I could imagine only one explanation—that the case had attracted enormous attention, and that my friends abroad were demanding that I be given a real defense counsel.

I had no hope that they would permit a foreign lawyer to defend me. I also knew very well that the KGB firmly controlled the choice of lawyers admitted to "their" cases. Only a lawyer with KGB clearance was permitted to participate in political trials, although the need for such clearance wasn't mentioned in any law. Moreover, lawyers who went too far in the defense of their clients had been known to lose their clearance.

Obviously, no serious lawyer would dare to defend my position, as this would mean exposing the fabrications of the KGB. Instead, he would try to "reestablish the truth" by trying to show that the actions attributed to me were committed by other members of our group, and that I was the unwitting victim of more experienced Zionist provocateurs. I certainly didn't want that kind of "defense," and I fervently hoped that my family would refuse to submit to the KGB's blackmail. Only much later did I discover how strongly my mother had been pressured, not only by the KGB but also by many well-meaning friends who believed that a KGB-appointed lawyer would make things easier for me.

On March 16, a year and a day after I arrived in Lefortovo, I was sitting in Solonchenko's office, buried in the volumes of my file, when Volodin and Iliukhin came in. With a hesitant cough, Volodin said, "Anatoly Borisovich, we have decided to give you another opportunity to write to your family to specify which person you entrust with selecting a lawyer."

I paused, wondering what such generosity really meant.

"Fine," I replied, "but I must also explain what my requirements are."

"No, that's impossible. You may write only that you entrust the selection of a lawyer to so-and-so."

"But I wrote such a statement several months ago."

"Write another one," he said. "Your mother is here now and we'll give her the note. You can add a few words that you are well."

I was so shocked and excited that I could hardly catch my breath. With trembling hands I wrote:

Mama dearest!

At the beginning of January I told the investigative group that I entrusted the selection of my defense to you and Natasha. I rejected the lawyer they offered me. If you don't succeed in finding a lawyer, I shall conduct my own defense. Don't fear for me. I lovingly kiss all of you and Natasha.

Tolya
March 16, 1977

Volodin read the note and frowned. "We are not discussing your lawyer," he said. "Rewrite it. The first sentence is entirely sufficient. You may also add that you are healthy."

He tried to hand me the note, but I kept my hands behind my back and defiantly shook my head. "You're making it very difficult for me and my family to find a lawyer," I said. "I won't shorten the note."

Volodin handed the note to Iliukhin. He read it, looked at Volodin, and they both left the room without indicating whether they would give it to Mama. Meanwhile my heart was almost bursting from the excitement. Would the wall of silence finally be broken? Would my family see my handwriting? Would they understand from my note that I wasn't making any compromises with the KGB?

About an hour passed before Captain Gubinsky reappeared with my note.

"Rewrite it with the correct date. This is 1978, not 1977."

I was delighted that the problem was so trivial, and I offered to correct my original version.

"No, rewrite it!"

I rewrote the note word for word with the correct date. An hour later Gubinsky returned with a paper in his hand.

"What's your nephew's name?" he asked.

The question caught me by surprise. "Sasha," I replied.

"Read this and sign that you have seen it."
Mama's handwriting!

My darling son!
    I read your note and everything is clear. We are doing everything possible to find a lawyer for you. Don't worry about us, we are all alive and well. We are with you constantly. Sashenka loves you and is waiting for you.

Your mama

I held the note in my hands for a long time, reading it several times and then simply looking at the left-slanted letters of this handwriting that I knew so well. Sitting there in front of my captors, I tried not to cry. Somebody spoke to me but I remained silent, fearing my voice would betray me. Finally I asked hoarsely, "Why can't I take it with me?"

"It will go into the file. Sign that you read it, then give it back."

Gubinsky left with the note and I continued studying the file. But I absorbed nothing. Only now did I realize how deeply I had been oppressed all these months by a thought I had succeeded in driving away: How are my aging parents? Are they still alive? Now I knew that they were alive and probably well. (Mama had withheld the fact that soon after my arrest Papa had suffered a serious heart attack.)

What was this sudden generosity on the part of the KGB? Only a year had passed since my arrest and already they were permitting us to exchange notes! I hoped it was because of the international commotion over my case, and that the demand to permit a lawyer of my choice to defend me was so strong that the KGB was forced to show some signs of legality.

But I was upset that Mama hadn't mentioned Avital in the note, although I assumed the censor had taken out the name. I had no way of knowing that Iliukhin had warned her, "If you want your son to see this note, don't mention his wife." At the last moment, she had substituted the name of my six-year-old nephew instead of Avital. Even so, I had finally broken through that wall and communicated with Mama!

Around nine o'clock in the evening the investigator summoned the guard to take me back to the cell. It was Anatoly—a young, slender, towheaded fellow with a smiling face. In the presence of his superiors he followed the rules strictly, but when we were alone he was good-natured and friendly. He seemed bored by the prison routine and welcomed any opportunity to amuse himself. I was happy to reciprocate, and because we shared the same name, we called each other "Namesake."

We walked into the dark and empty corridor. All the offices had been closed long ago, and the lights turned off. Although we couldn't meet anyone on the way, my namesake was nevertheless required to snap his fingers to signify that he was leading a zek. Tonight, however, his snap was weak and could barely be heard.

"What's the matter, Namesake," I said, "did you forget how to snap? It's time to fire you! Look!"

I snapped with my right hand and then with my left. Then, to my surprise, I switched to a dancing step, swaying to the left and to the right and clicking my fingers like castanets.

My namesake was clearly enjoying this. He burst out laughing, removed two large metal cell keys from his belt and struck them together as we skipped along. We sped through the hall like a pair of Spanish dancers and continued down the stairs and up to the iron door that separated the investigative wing from the prison corridor.

Laughing and panting, my partner reached for the bell which informed the traffic manager that a zek was at the entrance to the prison.

"Why are you so happy, Namesake?" he asked. "Did they promise to release you soon?"

"Well, a year has already passed, so if they don't smear my forehead with iodine, I have only fourteen years left," I answered cheerfully, gasping for breath.

"You're putting me on," he said, but just then they gave us the "clear" signal and my namesake instantly turned back into a guard, crying "Hands behind your back!" as we entered the prison corridor. I led the way solemnly and decorously, like a commander inspecting his troops—only, in our case the troops consisted of one-eyed cells that stretched along the corridor. The way had been cleared for us as if we were honored guests, and the iron netting in the stairwells protected us from harm. Kind old prison from Katherine's time! Where had all your gloominess gone?

A few weeks later Volodin and Iliukhin entered Solonchenko's office, smiling festively and accompanied by a large middle-aged, gaudily made-up woman.

"Here's a lawyer to help you, Anatoly Borisovich," said Volodin. "Now it will be easier for you to make your way through all those volumes."

"Dubrovsky, Silva Abramovna," said my defense counsel as she introduced herself to me.

A Jew to defend me? Well, they really did a good job of planning, I thought. Much later my family learned that the KGB had used four criteria to select a defense lawyer from the Moscow Collegium of Advocates: in addition to having clearance from the KGB, my lawyer had to be a party member, a woman, and a Jew. The KGB evidently believed that I was more likely to establish a relationship of trust with a Jewish woman, and I remember thinking that here was a rare case in Soviet life when the fifth line on the passport, the one that specified nationality, was not an obstacle but a plus.

Silva Abramovna, alternating between acting like a mother and an older sister, began to shower me with compliments about how clever I was.

"Excuse me," I asked. "Did you meet with my family?"

"N-no."

"But I entrusted *them* with the selection of my defense counsel. It's difficult for me here in complete isolation to know anything about one lawyer or another. Why didn't you meet with them? If they choose you, then I will too."

"Yes, but . . ." She paused and looked at Volodin, who said, "Your family doesn't want to meet with anyone."

"That's not true," I replied, "but there's no point in arguing. I will agree only to a defense counsel who is approved by my mother or my wife."

"Anatoly Borisovich, you are the first man to refuse me," said Silva Abramovna in a playful tone that didn't suit her age.

"Yes, this is very unpleasant for me," I agreed amiably, "as I am apparently increasing the number of Jewish refuseniks by one more."

Everyone burst out laughing except for Dubrovsky, who didn't appreciate my reference to her nationality. Adopting a more businesslike posture, she looked at Volodin as if to say, What next?

They suggested that I sign a prepared paper to the effect that I had refused a lawyer. I added a correction: "I reject the lawyer selected for me by the KGB." This concluded my first and last meeting with Silva Dubrovsky.

Several days later, however, they brought me a document saying that she had been appointed to defend me. Volodin explained: "Your case carries a maximum sentence of capital punishment, so we can't leave you without a defense counsel."

On several subsequent occasions I was informed that my lawyer was looking over the file and wanted to meet with me to discuss my defense at the trial. I invariably replied, "She's not my lawyer, she's yours. *You* talk to her."

In February Timofeev suffered a minor heart attack and was taken to the hospital. I never saw him again, and never learned if he received his pardon. My new cell mate was the former assistant to the minister of the Soviet automobile industry. He was a large, athletically built, brown-haired man of around forty or forty-five. He was disheartened but, unlike Timofeev, not yet broken.

"Kolosar, Leonid Yosifovich," he introduced himself and immediately added, "A victim of slander and conspiracy in the highest department of the ministry and in the procurator's office of the USSR."

I gave my standard reply: "Article 64, Zionist."

"Well," he said, "it's clear that you're a Jew, but nobody could guess you're a Zionist. Did you really fight against the Soviet regime?"

Before I could answer, Kolosar added that he was a Ukrainian, but had many Jewish friends.

"If you like," I said, "you may speak to me in Ukrainian." I grew up in the Ukraine and studied Ukrainian in school, which turned out to be an important factor in our relationship. As Leonid Yosifovich later admitted, during his years in Moscow what he missed most was his native language.

Night after night I listened with fascination as Kolosar described the rigid hierarchy of life at the highest levels of Soviet society. His boss, for example, an intimidating man who was accustomed to dressing down the factory managers, turned into a little boy whenever he had to report to Prime Minister Kosygin, even on routine matters. In preparation for the call, Leonid Yosifovich would bring in all the necessities—documents, medicines, and drinks. Then, at the appointed time, he would dial the number.

"Comrade Kosygin is on the line."

Kolosar's boss would pick up the receiver, stand at attention, and begin to speak. If all went well, when the call was over he would make do with some relatively light medication and would lie down on the sofa for ten or fifteen minutes. But if Comrade Kosygin was dissatisfied with anything, then the minister would have to be taken home immediately on account of his heart. Sometimes an ambulance had to be called, and in the end he really did suffer a heart attack.

Kolosar recalled his boss with humor, but also with warmth. The minister had accepted him as a member of the family, and Kolosar looked after his personal affairs, such as renting a restaurant for his daughter's wedding or buying scarce goods for him in the special stores.

Of course I had heard about these stores, which are restricted to high officials, but until I met Kolosar I had no idea how complex and carefully structured the system actually is. Even among ministers there are three separate categories, depending on how important they are, and each one has access to a different type of special store. As Soviet officials climb the career ladder and, in theory, come closer to the Communist ideal, they are entitled to a growing number of luxury goods at lower and lower prices.

I learned that other privileges, too, are assigned strictly in accordance with rank. A minister, if I remember correctly, may receive two tickets to any theatrical production, whereas a deputy minister can do so no more than once a week. The head of a central board can receive tickets every two weeks, and so on, and although these people rarely attend the theater, they value their privileges highly. If you are demoted but retain the same privileges, it's considered only half a demotion. The real tragedy is to be demoted to a position with a lower-level special store, for it can be very difficult to work your way back.

Kolosar told me that he had once asked his boss, who, as mentioned before, had terrible heart problems, "At your age, why don't you retire?"

"If I die at my post," his boss had replied, "the funeral meal will be held in the Central Building of the Soviet army, the obituary will appear in *Izvestia* with the signatures of the entire Politburo, and they'll bury me in the Novodevichy Cemetery. But if I die in retirement, then the funeral meal will be in an ordinary restaurant, the obituary in a trade paper with the signature of the new minister, and I will be buried at Vagankov."

Another fascinating topic of Kolosar's was how zeks were used to supplement the labor force. Apparently, every ministry submitted an annual request for forced labor. Even the automobile industry, which was not especially "zek-consuming"—this was the first time I had heard that cynical phrase—employed 120,000 zeks, which was only half as many men as Kolosar's boss had requested. There were also 180,000 "chemists." Whereas a zek is a slave, a chemist is only half a slave. In effect, he's a serf who must live wherever he is sent and work wherever he is told—generally in places that are harmful to his health, such as chemical enterprises, which is why these people are commonly known as chemists. Unlike other zeks, however, the chemist is paid for his work. He lives in a special hostel and must be there in the evening, but he is allowed to receive visits from his family.

"Was there any discrimination against Jews in your ministry?" I once asked Kolosar.

"In such cases we would say, 'He didn't pass the vision test— minus seven or minus five,'" he explained. "The seventh line on the application lists your party affiliation, and 'minus seven' means you're not a member. The fifth line lists your nationality, and 'minus five' means you're a Jew. But many of the ministers and other higher-ups are married to Jewish women. Even Brezhnev." (This was true.) Kolosar and his colleagues even had a theory to explain this phenomenon: Jewish women didn't permit their husbands to drink, and skillfully guided their men through the intrigues of officialdom. Several years later, in the labor camp, I heard a different explanation from a former intelligence agent, who told me of a secret Zionist women's organization that was working to infiltrate the highest echelons of the Soviet regime through mixed marriages. The name of this organization—and here he leaned toward me and whispered—was Hadassah.

Kolosar was an avid chess fan, and I joyfully exchanged dominoes for chess pieces. He played with passion and abandon, and after a few test games, we came to the following agreement: I would cede him a rook, and we would play three games. If I won the match, he would do the next cleanup. If he won or if our game ended in a draw, I would clean up. As a result of this arrangement our cell was always in model shape, for Leonid Yosifovich washed the floors with great diligence.

My fourth and final cell mate in Lefortovo was a professional swindler named Leonid. He was a short man of about thirty-five with a sporty build and intelligent, mocking eyes. Having served several years in prison as a young thief, he returned to Moscow with the intention of finding a job that was more challenging and more secure. His sharp, lively mind, his understanding of people, and his facile ability to fit into a variety of molds could have steered him toward a career in the theater or in sociology. Instead, he became a swindler, and had been arrested twice. A swindler, however, is not a thief or a bandit, and his prison terms were relatively short. Leonid was serving his term elsewhere, and had been brought to Lefortovo to testify in the case of an associate who was a currency dealer.

He was unfamiliar with the KGB, and viewed them with respect and fear. But he also had a highly developed curiosity, and listened eagerly as I told him about my own experiences with the KGB, both before and after my arrest. I was equally curious about his world, and he was delighted to tell me about it. "I'm only revealing what the authorities already know," he said, "but we swindlers are constantly at work and are continually inventing new techniques." He was clearly proud of his profession, and if you could set aside the moral element—which I could not, and which frequently led me to be horrified at Leonid's heartlessness—it was a fascinating occupation.

In one of Leonid's more complex scams, his victims were Jews who had succeeded in leaving the Soviet Union. Several years ago his team of "specialists" had approached Jews from the provinces who planned to emigrate to the United States and Canada, and who wanted to ship their valuables, which they weren't allowed to take with them. So Leonid and his friends represented themselves as corrupt employees of the Moscow customs office. They rented an apartment in the heart of the city where they received clients.

Leonid told me he bargained harshly and at length with these people. They wanted to pay him 10 percent of the value of the goods, while he insisted on 20 percent.

"But why argue if you're getting one hundred percent in any case?" I asked.

"So they'll know they're dealing with a serious person!"

The clients left Moscow and returned to negotiate further. In the end they accepted the conditions of the "customs official" and sent a small part of their valuables abroad, which arrived safely.

"How was that?" I asked.

"We also know real customs officials," he replied.

Believing in the reliability of the channel, the clients then left for North America, having entrusted all of their remaining valuables to Leonid and his team. I wasn't surprised to hear that this operation had been crowned with success. In addition to growing rich on Jewish emigrants, Leonid himself hoped to utilize the "Jewish channel" to leave the Soviet Union.

"Why?" I asked.

"After all my arrests, my opportunities here are very limited," he said. "My friends who left write that it's easy to find work in Europe, and even easier in America. Although the Americans are business-minded, they're as naive as children. That's why I'm learning English."

"But how will they let you go? You're a Russian, and you don't have any relatives abroad."

"That's no problem. They're happy to send criminals abroad." Leonid planned to arrange an invitation from Israel, and assumed the authorities would let him out with a wink.

He saw life as a vast theatrical stage, and he not only played his own role with zeal, but viewed everybody else in terms of their roles in the drama. "You'll serve your time," he once told me, "and then you'll get out and join your wife. You'll probably write your memoirs in Israel. And when you do, I have one request—please don't reveal my family name. My daughters think that their father works at the space center and that he had to leave on business for a few years."

I don't know what astonished me more—that such a cynical man was concerned about his daughters' opinion of him, or that at this particular moment, on the eve of my trial, when I still didn't know if I would live or die, Leonid was thinking about some illusory future for me and a book of memoirs.

July 4, 1978. I woke up, mentally sent congratulations to my Avital, and settled back to wait for something to happen. After all, on July 4 something *always* happened. Four years ago was our *chuppah*. Three years ago I met Professor Richard Pipes of Harvard University, an encounter that would be discussed at my trial. Two years ago, Entebbe. Last year, the punishment cell. This year, however, the whole day passed in tense expectation. Was my premonition deceiving me?

Sure enough, about twenty minutes before bedtime, the door clanged and the duty officer brought in the final summary of charges and evidence, a document of forty pages. The trial was imminent, and I had to prepare.

From morning to night I sat with my notes, picking out all the material mentioned in the text of the charge. But I was unable to concentrate. Unexpectedly, the same feelings I had experienced during my first few weeks in Lefortovo—a burden of responsibility and a lack of self-confidence—had returned to engulf me. That was my reaction to the merciless formulations of the indictment, such as "The main goal of Sharansky and his accomplices was a struggle against the existing system in the USSR, a struggle financed and inspired by capitalist circles of the West and Zionist organizations who cooperated with them."

For sixteen months I had been dreaming of an open trial, but now I was suddenly frightened: even if the trial was open and my mother and brother were allowed to attend—I didn't count on more than that—would I be able to mount a convincing refutation of these monstrous accusations that had been made against our entire movement? The harsh language of the charge made an impression even on me, although I knew perfectly well that it was constructed of paper and lies. Would I succeed? Would I be given the opportunity to present the truth to my family, and through them, to the world?

Before I spoke, there would probably be interrogations of witnesses and the reading of documents. Then I realized that I didn't even know how a trial proceeds. I had never attended one, not even as a spectator. I had stood many times near the closed doors of "open" trials of dissidents, but these doors were firmly guarded by the KGB. I had read the materials of trials, but had never witnessed one with my own eyes. I didn't have the vaguest notion about what to expect.

I tried to recall books I had read and movies I had seen about trials. There was Tolstoy's *Resurrection,* about a jury trial in Russia at the beginning of the twentieth century, and I recalled that the jury deliberated at great length before announcing its verdict. Then there was *Judgment at Nuremberg,* the Stanley Kramer film—a trial of Nazis, this one, too, with a jury. Each defendant had a defense counsel, and the room was full of reporters and movie cameras.

No, it seemed that books and movies would not be helpful. My cell mate hadn't attended any political trials either, but he had been tried three times and knew the general procedure: first they read the indictment and then they ask you what you think about it; they would probably discuss each document and episode separately.

That calmed me somewhat. If that's the case, I thought, it means there should be sufficient opportunities to expose their methods— assuming, of course, that the trial was open. I wrote down brief points of my reply to the charge, but I wasn't able to turn this into a speech. During the five days that remained before the trial, I rushed from one document to another, from witness to witness, from conclusion to conclusion.

When I first arrived in Lefortovo, I had learned to cope with my fear by constructing my own world—a world where I was the master and there were no surprises. But now, on the eve of my trial, I could no longer remain in my shell. I was going out into *their* world, and the forthcoming battle would be fought on enemy terri- tory.

My head was filled with questions. What was Avital doing now? My parents? My brother? Did they know about the impending trial? Would I ever see them again? Would the trial be open? It was as if the dam had burst, that dam I had constructed in the first weeks of the investigation to restrain the chaotic stream of thoughts and analyze everything that was happening to me. Then I had to fight against fear. Now I was fighting against an acute nervousness over the approaching exam. This was the big one, I told myself—the most important test of my life.

13

The Trial

THE next morning, as soon as I awoke they brought me break-fast.

"They're taking you to the trial," Leonid explained.

I hadn't finished eating when they brought me a razor and hot water. I shaved.

"You're going to the trial," said a prisoner official. "Does your shirt need to be ironed? Your jacket?"

They took my shirt and brought it back ironed. Following Leonid's advice, I decided to go without a jacket. My cell mate deftly rolled up my sleeves.

"It's hot and stuffy in the courtroom," he said. "This way you'll be more comfortable." He even made me some sandwiches to take along.

I grabbed a folder, which I had filled with excerpts from my file, and followed the guard to a transit cell where zeks are held as they come in or out of the prison.

Captain Minaev came in. On his belt was a holster, and the handsome white handle of a pistol was clearly visible. It was the first weapon I had seen since my arrest.

"I'll be accompanying you," he said. "If you have any papers, give them to me."

"But I'll need them in the courtroom."

"You'll receive them there."

In the small prison van they locked me in a "pencil box," a dark metal closet with a bench where it was impossible to turn around or stand up. Traveling with me were Captain Minaev, two master sergeants, and the head of the medical section. The head of the prison would also be at the trial, but he rode in his own car.

I recited my prayer as I rode in the pencil box. I recited it again when I entered the court building, having managed only a momentary glance at the bright sun and vivid greenery. I recited it once more as I waited in a holding cell before going up to the second floor of the courtroom.

The whole scene appeared staged and unreal—the rows of plain-clothes KGB men, the visitors with special passes who rushed ahead of me, and especially the buffet with black caviar and other scarce products that had been quickly set up for the guests. To assure myself this wasn't a dream, I touched the handle of Minaev's pistol. "This must be fake, right?"

He twitched abruptly and grabbed my hand. "Stop your jokes!" he ordered.

Yes, it was real, although I couldn't take it all in. What next? Whom would I see? What would I say? My thoughts jumped around, unable to focus. The closer we came to the courtroom, the greater was my anxiety. In the end, everything disappeared from my mind except for one phrase, half question and half assertion, which I began to repeat like an incantation: Now I'll see Mama.

Near the entrance of the courtroom was the defendant's bench, where I was seated between two master sergeants. The room was full and all eyes were on me. It had been well over a year since I had seen so many people. Although I could barely distinguish individual faces, I felt the hostility of the crowd. There were no familiar faces here—no Mama, no brother, no friends. I was bitterly disappointed and felt very alone.

I turned to the left, but the judge's dais was not yet occupied. To the left of the dais was the prosecution. Near me, I saw Silva Dubrovsky, the lawyer. So the KGB had decided to "defend" me with their own forces? I wasn't happy to see her, although she gave me a warm smile and tried to say something encouraging. I turned away.

Who are my prosecutors? I wondered. Was that really Iliukhin, sitting decorously at the table opposite me? Yes, but today he was merely helping Solonin, the senior assistant of the procurator general of the USSR. I had seen Solonin several times before in the corridors of Lefortovo, and I knew him as a sickly-looking man who was haughty and probably nasty. They were clever in thinking this one up. Solonin, who officially supervised the KGB, would now support all their falsifications.

Despite my disappointment at the absence of familiar faces—or perhaps because of it—I quickly snapped out of my fog. With hateful eyes to my right, the prosecutors opposite me, and the "defender" selected by them on my left, the KGB pressed in on me from all directions. But this only brought the picture into sharper focus as the crowd began to break down into a collection of individuals. Searching their faces, I saw not only hostility but genuine curiosity as well.

The first two rows were filled with spectators in hard-to-find foreign clothing. Most likely they were KGB officials and particularly trusted correspondents of APN (Novosty Press Agency), *Pravda*, and *Izvestia*. Behind them sat the common people. From following other political trials, I knew that at nearby factories the authorities had distributed special passes to trusted comrades among the Komsomol and party activists. These people were delighted to attend, not only because they were excused from work but also because this gave them the opportunity to enjoy the special and rare treats at the buffet.

"Rise! The court is in session!"

Three men—the judge and the two people's assessors—took their places. (The assessors are representatives of the people whose role, at least in theory, is to keep the judge honest.) But all three faces were mostly hidden behind the fifty-one volumes of testimony, which had been placed on the table.

After some formalities that I didn't understand, the judge turned to me and demanded, "Last name, first name, patronymic!"

I rose. "As I declared earlier, I will not participate in a closed trial."

Before I could continue, the judge interrupted: "But the trial is open, don't you see?" He waved his hand toward the spectators.

"For whom is it open? For the APN correspondents and the KGB? Where are my relatives? Where are my friends? Perhaps you'd like to tell me they didn't want to attend?"

But the judge was clearly prepared for this question: "As you can see, there are no empty seats, although for your family, of course, we would find room. But your mother and brother cannot be present in the courtroom because they will be called in later as witnesses. As for your father—where is the defendant's father?"

An usher standing at the door replied, "The defendant's father could not travel from Istra to Moscow because of his health."

"Well, you see, what do you want from us? We did everything in our power."

What's wrong with Papa? I wondered, but my anxiety about him was quickly driven out by another feeling. Even more convincingly than Minaev's pistol, the insolent cynicism and hypocrisy of the producers of this show reminded me of the kind of people I was dealing with. I felt a surge of anger, which calmed me down and restored my ability to think logically.

"I read the list of witnesses, and neither my mother nor my brother was mentioned. And there has been no petition to summon them from either the prosecution or the defense."

"I petition!" shrieked Solonin.

Raising my voice, I drowned him out easily: "Aha, the procurator petitions! But I don't intend to enter into discussions about the legal details of this farce. I declare once again that I shall not participate in this trial until the following conditions are met. First, a member of my family must be present in the courtroom. Second, the lawyer selected for me must not participate in the trial. If I cannot select a lawyer, I prefer to conduct my own defense rather than relying on a procurator in the guise of an attorney."

I sat down and ignored the judge's remark that nobody had imposed a lawyer on me, and that neither my family nor I wanted one. Finally the judge inclined his head toward the assessor on his right, who nodded, and then toward the assessor on his left, who also nodded. I now understood why, in the zeks' slang, the assessors were known as "nodders." But only toward the end of the trial would I come to appreciate how accurate that epithet really was. For during the entire proceeding the assessors never asked a single question and didn't even open their mouths. All they did was nod to the judge each time he looked their way.

"Ten-minute recess," the judge announced. "The court is retiring to confer."

They took me to a special holding cell. I knew that nothing was actually being decided now, and that all the important decisions had already been made. To distract myself, I read the various inscriptions and curses scratched and written across the walls of the cell.

Suddenly my eyes lit upon a *magen David,* the star of David, with an inscription beneath it in Hebrew: *Asir Tziyon Yosef Begun. Chazak ve'ematz!* (Prisoner of Zion Yosef Begun. Be strong and courageous!)

Begun, a Hebrew teacher and a veteran of our movement, had been arrested not long before me on a charge of parasitism, a common charge against refuseniks dismissed from their jobs. Begun must have been tried in this building and waited in this very cell, where he had left a greeting to support whoever would be here. Thank you, Yosef.

I returned to my seat in the courtroom, and when I looked up, suddenly—Lenya! My brother was sitting two meters away in the front row! He gave me a broad grin and showed me a fist with his thumb turned up to indicate that everything was fine.

Without tearing my gaze from his face, I said, with a stupid smile, "You've put on weight!"

"Stop your talking!" the master sergeant warned me.

I wanted to ask Lenya about Mama and Avital, but just then I realized that if they had permitted him to come in, *they definitely wouldn't shoot me.* No *rasstrel.* I had long ago convinced myself that they could execute me only if nobody knew exactly what the charge was. I felt utterly relieved, and only now did I understand that my fear of *rasstrel* had never fully disappeared.

Now the judge was asking the procurator's opinion about my dismissal of the lawyer.

"The case carries a possible sentence of death," he replied. "Therefore the accused is supposed to have a lawyer. But insofar as Sharansky insists, the procurator's office does not object to his defending himself."

Two turns of the judge's head toward the assessors; two nods.

"The lawyer may leave the courtroom."

Silva Dubrovsky left with a friendly smile, wishing me all the best. Now I, too, was ready to smile and to thank her for her good wishes. It wasn't her fault; they ordered her to participate and she had no alternative.

Finally the trial began.

The judge read the indictment, which dragged on for approximately forty minutes. While listening to the familiar text I kept looking at my brother. He divided his attention between me and the judge, gave me encouraging smiles, made some soothing gestures, and tried to concentrate on the judge's words. Listen, Lenya, I begged him mentally. Listen carefully and remember as much as you can!

But just as I had feared, the menacing tone of the text affected him. He became increasingly gloomy, and began to shake his head. Don't plead guilty, he seemed to be saying. Of course, I realized, here in the outside world nobody knew whether or not I had been broken. When the text of the indictment mentioned "subversive Western radio stations that used the slanderous information of Sharansky and his accomplices," Lenya brought one hand to his ear and pulled it, while pointing to me with his other hand, as if to indicate that these stations were now making a big fuss about me.

The man next to him, who was specifically assigned to Lenya, grabbed him by the arm and rebuked him.

Finally the judge finished reading the indictment. He turned to me and asked, "Do you plead guilty?"

I rose, saw my brother's tense expression, and almost joyfully proclaimed, "I do not plead guilty. I consider all the charges brought against me to be absurd."

The judge immediately declared a recess. Before leaving, however, I exchanged smiles with my brother and held up Avital's picture, which I had taken from my pocket. Lenya was surprised and delighted, and tried to show me something before they stopped him. But the tension seemed to have abated.

Lunchtime. They brought my guards food from the special buffet, including ham, cheese, black caviar, and fruit. I'd been wondering whether they would offer me any of these items and had decided against accepting it if they did, but they brought me the usual prison slop. They had specifically delivered one portion of soup so as not to violate the rules by allowing a prisoner to enjoy real food.

Still, my mood was excellent, for what enormous changes had occurred in just half a day! I had seen my brother, and everything appeared to be in order at home. He heard the text of the charge and saw that I didn't yield. Even if they removed him from the courtroom, which wouldn't surprise me, they could no longer fool anyone.

The session resumed after lunch, but Lenya was no longer in the front row. Had they removed him? No, there he was at the very back, near the wall. He barely managed to catch my eye through the rows of people in front of him. His guardian was still with him, and was looking not at the proceedings but at Lenya.

The judge suggested that I respond to the essence of the charge, so I took out of the folder the sheet with my basic arguments. I spoke briefly, leaving the details for later, so that my brother could catch the essence of the charge and my defense without having to remember too many details at once. I made several points with regard to the first part of the charge—treason in the form of aid to capitalist states.

First, that our documents about Soviet Jews were true and not slanderous. Soviet Jews really *are* subject to forced assimilation and cut off from their own language, culture, and religion. Can you name a single school where it's possible to study Hebrew or even Yiddish? I asked. Can you name a single Hebrew book published in the Soviet Union? A book on Jewish history? A Hebrew Bible?

Second, Jews who apply to emigrate become victims of arbitrary repression, a situation that led to the rise of activists who work to draw the world's attention to their predicament.

Third, the question of emigration from the Soviet Union is an international matter, as confirmed by the Declaration of Human Rights, the Helsinki Accords, and other agreements that the Soviet Union has signed. But our open struggle to have these accords taken seriously was regarded as treason.

Fourth, I pointed out that the Jackson Amendment was a humane act of the American Congress, the first real link between human rights and Soviet-American relations. Attempts to accuse Jewish activists of treason for supporting the Jackson Amendment were just as misguided as repressions against the members of the Helsinki Group, who demanded that the USSR meet its obligations under the Helsinki Accords.

Fifth, there was nothing treasonous about contacts between Soviet Jews and Jewish organizations abroad.

Sixth, the word "Zionist" was being used as a legal term that was equivalent to "anti-Soviet" or "treasonous." But Zionism is simply the national liberation movement of the Jews for creating their own state. If Zionism was illegal, what about the state of Israel, which the Soviet Union recognized as soon as it was founded?

Seventh, American diplomats and correspondents were said to be my accomplices in treasonous activity even though there was absolutely no proof that they were spies. The KGB stated that the Soviet press cited examples of their espionage activity, but these articles merely asserted that the "competent organs" were familiar with this activity. But even if one of them *was* a spy—and there was absolutely no evidence of this—how did this implicate me?

I started to say that the KGB committed even cruder distortions and falsifications in the second part of the charge—treason in the form of espionage—but I was interrupted by the judge: "We shall deal with espionage at the closed session, about state secrets."

"But there are no secrets in the file!" I protested. "The only documents that were declared secret are the lists of refuseniks. I don't intend to read these lists in the courtroom, but only to speak about the methods of the investigation. I insist that you let me address this matter in the open session."

But the judge was adamant, and after two quick nods from the assessors he declared a recess. As I left, Lenya had his thumb up again. He was smiling joyfully and was apparently relieved. His guardian angrily pushed down my brother's hand.

After the recess the judge asked me if I was prepared to give concrete and true testimony for each episode of the charge.

"Yes, of course. For every episode I can say something about the methods of the investigation. For example, let's look at the first so-called treasonous document—our letter to the U.S. Congress from July 1974, which speaks about preventive arrests of Jewish activists during President Nixon's visit to Moscow in June 1974. I was one of those arrested—or, rather, abducted, as they held me and several other refuseniks in prison for fifteen days with no trial and no explanation. Yet in the indictment it asserts that this statement is slanderous and incorrect. And indeed, they didn't give us any papers indicating we were arrested. So were there preventive arrests or not?"

I began to explain that upon my return from prison I successfully demanded that I be paid for my forced absence from work during my incarceration.

"I'm not asking about that now!" said the judge. "Explain precisely who prepared this document and all the following ones, and under what circumstances."

I refused to answer this question, and in order that Lenya could take it all in, I explained my position thoroughly.

Solonin, the procurator, began to ask questions:

"You say that emigration is forbidden, so how is it that approximately one hundred fifty thousand Jews have emigrated?"

"Emigration *is* forbidden. Only family reunification is permitted, so you need an invitation from a relative. Second, the process of applying for an exit visa is extremely difficult. Third, refusals are arbitrary. Fourth, refuseniks are harassed. But even under these conditions, one hundred fifty thousand people have left, which shows how badly people want to emigrate."

"Why do many of those who have left now appeal to Soviet institutions abroad, begging to go back?"

"Only a handful want to return, and in these cases the Universal Declaration of Human Rights is violated a second time, as it gives each citizen the right to leave his country of residence *and to return to it.*"

Solonin was not prepared for this answer, and when he heard it he looked lost. I recalled my meeting in the fall of 1976 with the minister of internal affairs. "If it were up to me," he said, "I'd let them all go. But of course I wouldn't let any of them come back."

"Why do you criticize the state of affairs in the USSR but not in the West?" asked Solonin.

"It's clear," I replied, "even from the Soviet press, that every citizen in the West can freely criticize the society in which he lives. There's no need to worry that the world won't learn about human rights violations there. In the USSR, however, such criticisms are punished. If people aren't willing to risk their freedom and perhaps their lives to give out this information, the world will never know the truth."

"In the telegram you sent to President Ford on the occasion of the American Bicentennial, you praised America, the main capitalist power of the West, while saying nothing about unemployment, poverty, and prostitution, those festering sores of the Western world. Isn't that hypocrisy?"

"Yes, I really did express my gratitude to the American people for their devotion to the principles of liberty, and especially to the principles of free emigration. As for criticizing faults, the congratulatory telegram of the Soviet government on the occasion of the Bicentennial also said nothing about prostitution or unemployment."

"Why did you invite to your press conferences only representatives of the mass media organs that are hostile to the Soviet Union?"

"I don't know what you mean by hostile organs of the mass media, but we sometimes invited correspondents of Soviet papers and of Communist papers in the West. Why not ask those representatives of the Soviet press who are sitting in this room why they never once wanted to come?"

"You say that in the Soviet Union Jews are not given the opportunity to enjoy the benefits of Jewish culture. Then for whom is the journal *Sovietische Heimland* published?"

"I ask the same thing: For whom? After all, although Yiddish is considered the official Jewish language, it isn't taught in a single Soviet school, not even in the so-called Jewish Autonomous Region. So it's not surprising that the average age of the readers of this journal is well over sixty."

My responses seemed to surprise Solonin, who kept on changing the subject without going into further discussion. But he asked his final question with great enthusiasm: Was our marriage ceremony performed according to all the requirements of Judaism? He read a document from the Moscow synagogue saying that "the *ketubah*, or marriage certificate, which was allegedly given to Natalia Stieglitz and is being shown around in the West, is a fake."

I considered arguing the point, but quickly stopped myself. That was all I needed—to discuss my marital status with them!

The first day of the court session was over, and the judge announced that tomorrow's session would be closed. I left without tearing my eyes away from my brother, and on my way out I heard him shout, "Shalom! Avital!"

They quickly led me past the ranks of KGB into the van, which was parked right up against the back door of the court. As before,

I was locked in the pencil box. It was pitch-black, but as the car picked up speed and made a turn, a sliver of daylight suddenly appeared in the narrow crack between the wall of the pencil box and the door. A narrow shaft of light hit my eyes, and numbers and letters started flashing like an electronic coded message. These were license plates, I realized, black letters on a white background, starting with K04. A white background indicates a foreigner's car, K means a correspondent, and 04 means an American. Terrific! This means my "accomplices" must be waiting for news by the doors of the courtroom! Now Lenya would go out and tell them everything. I felt a wave of fatigue, and deep relief. Even the fact that tomorrow's session would be closed didn't cloud my joy. Yes, I thought with satisfaction, Avital must really be giving them a hard time if they brought up our *chuppah* at the trial.

Back in the cell, I immediately asked for *Pravda*, but the guard replied that it hadn't come today.

"He's lying," said Leonid. "I heard them giving it out to the other cells."

The next day I demanded that the judge explain why they had stopped giving me *Pravda*. Several hours later, during the recess, Povarenkov, the new head of the prison, personally brought me yesterday's issue. There were two articles of note, and they appeared together—one about the start of hearings in the Supreme Military Tribunal against somebody named Filatov on a charge of espionage and one about the start of hearings in the Supreme Court on a charge of espionage against Sharansky. I didn't know who Filatov was, but I assumed he was a real spy, and that they were deliberately linking the two cases in the public consciousness. To some degree they succeeded, as years later, in the labor camp, I was asked about my "co-defendant" Filatov.

On the second day of the trial the hall was empty except for two men with recording equipment. When Solonin asked about the lists of refuseniks, I replied that I was prepared to answer all his questions at an open session.

"It will be worse for you," he said dryly. "I won't be asking these questions there."

They began the interrogation of witnesses. Officially this day had been set aside to consider the charge of espionage, but it soon became clear that this was merely a cover for the interrogation of witnesses whose conduct or preparedness the authorities were not completely confident about.

Lipavsky was the first witness, and again he didn't look at me. When the judge inquired as to his address and his place of work, he answered evasively, "I live in Moscow and I work in my specialty."

After a short pause the judge decided not to insist on further clarification. What is Lipavsky afraid of, I wondered, an assassination attempt? I learned later, from an acquaintance who ran into him not long before the trial, that Lipavsky went around with a guard. Apparently the KGB had started to believe their own stories about a Zionist conspiracy.

Lipavsky took out some paper and said, "Here, I wrote this down to remember it." He spoke like a first-grader reciting poetry, hastily but diligently, and "with feeling." He rarely looked at the paper, but nearly devoured the judge with his eyes. His testimony differed little from what he had said five months ago at our face-to-face confrontation, except that this time it was considerably briefer.

The judge asked, "You were recruited by the CIA and worked for them. Is that correct?"

"Yes." Lipavsky spoke slowly, evidently trying to make some decision. "Should I describe how they recruited me?"

"No, that's not necessary. Tell us, when you shared a room with Sharansky, were you already working for the CIA?"

"Yes, of course," Lipavsky exclaimed with relief. "I have been working for them for a long time." I could see that he was terribly fearful of making a mistake, of misjudging exactly what it was that they wanted from him.

"I see," said the judge with satisfaction. He looked at me ominously, and then turned back to the witness. "Tell me, Comrade Lipavsky, who was Sharansky's closest friend among the diplomats?"

"Pressel."

"And was Pressel linked to the CIA?"

"Absolutely. I said to him several times, 'Why don't you take the information I prepared from the hiding places?' He avoided answering, but it was clear that he knew where the hiding places were."

"Well," said the judge with obvious satisfaction, "the picture is clear."

He offered the floor to the procurator for questions.

"Was the assignment to prepare a list of refuseniks received from abroad?"

"Yes, of course. I myself attended the meetings with the two congressional aides when they suggested to Lerner and Sharansky that they find some new way to stop trade between America and the USSR, as the Jackson Amendment wasn't sufficient. Then, in my presence, when we were in the Lenin Hills, Lerner presented the idea of total pressure on the USSR to Rubin, before Rubin left for Israel."

"So this was Lerner's idea?"

"No, no! It was Sharansky's idea!" explained Lipavsky, barely hesitating as he discarded the remains of his initial testimony about our collective crime. He continued: "Then we received three letters from Rubin with the assignment to prepare lists of refuseniks."

"How did Sharansky transmit the lists to the West?"

"Through Pressel and Toth. I know this from his own words."

But this was clearly insufficient for the procurator, who needed direct evidence and tried to get it through a leading question: "In your presence did Sharansky transmit lists of refuseniks over the telephone?"

Lipavsky was confused, but after some tense reflection he answered decisively, "No! What are you talking about? This was really secret work!"

It was clear that they hadn't worked it all out in advance. In the charge they said that I *had* transmitted lists of refuseniks over the telephone and the owners of the telephones had "confirmed" this. I petitioned that Lipavsky be summoned to the open court session.

"We shall consider this petition," replied the judge. "But keep in mind that there we shall not ask you questions concerning the charge of espionage."

Realizing that I might never see Lipavsky again, I couldn't miss this opportunity to expose the clumsy work of the KGB. "When were the American congressional aides in Moscow?" I asked him.

"I don't remember the exact date."

"And when did Rubin leave?"

"In 1976."

"No, in what month?"

"I don't remember exactly."

"Which came first, the visit of the congressional aides or Rubin's departure?"

Lipavsky shrugged his shoulders and the judge intervened: "The witness told you he doesn't remember exactly. Why is he required to recall dates? Next question!"

"Of course he isn't required to recall dates," I replied. "But Rubin left in June of 1976, whereas Dodd and Popovich arrived in the fall. In other words, the effect preceded the cause by four months! Here I have the right to doubt not only Lipavsky's memory for dates . . ."

Lipavsky blushed and his hands began to shake. He looked at the paper and turned it over several times. The judge was also embarrassed, and quickly asked, "Any more questions?"

Of course I had questions that undermined Lipavsky's testimony, but they all touched on the same subject—proof that I personally did not engage in the preparation of lists of refuseniks. But my questions would only bring up the matter of who did prepare them, and I didn't want to move the conversation in that direction. I therefore responded, "I shall ask Lipavsky the remaining questions at the open session."

At the judge's orders, Lipavsky remained in the courtroom, taking a place in the second row. The next two witnesses were supposed to confirm that I used their telephones to transmit anti-Soviet and espionage information to the West. Both women testified that Lipavsky, both personally and through mutual friends, requested that every two or three months they allow their telephones to be used for a conversation with Israel. Both confirmed that I was among those who came to their apartments for this purpose. From here on, however, their testimony differed sharply from the protocols of the investigation. The witnesses now asserted that they didn't know what was discussed in these conversations because they weren't in the room and heard only fragments. As for transmitting lists of refuseniks over the telephone, they knew nothing about it.

The judge decided that the time had come to show his authority. "Come here," he said to each of the women, "and read what you testified at the investigation! Here is your signature under the testimony. You were warned about criminal responsibility for giving false testimony. If you now say that your previous testimony does not correspond to reality, then we must charge you for giving false evidence."

The two women showed identical reactions: fear, embarrassment, and then timid responses, such as "Well, a year has passed since that testimony" and "I really don't remember clearly."

"But you probably remembered better then?"

"Probably."

"That means we shall consider as valid the testimony you gave then."

The witnesses meekly sat down, choosing seats that were far from their "friend" Lipavsky, from whom they overtly turned away.

The judge's actions in pressuring the witnesses were completely illegal. Moreover, by law, it is precisely the testimony in court and not at the preliminary investigation that is accepted as valid. The KGB had scheduled a closed session precisely for this kind of trick. I protested and demanded that the two women be summoned to the open session of court.

Following a recess, Tsypin entered the empty courtroom. He had changed little in the year and a half since I last saw him. Like Lipavsky, he avoided my gaze. He was very tense, and I noticed that he clenched his hands, which had begun to shake.

Once, back in 1974, Tsypin and I were interrogated together after a demonstration. I noticed then that as he reached for an ashtray his hands trembled so much that the ashes of his cigarette scattered over the table. I was surprised, for Tsypin was a veteran demonstrator. What was he afraid of? Perhaps he feared being exposed? But if that was true then, why was he afraid now? Perhaps it's the fate of the Tsypins and the Lipavskys of this world to spend their whole lives in fear.

Tsypin's testimony wasn't interesting, and I limited myself to the standard petition to summon the witness to the open court session. To my surprise, I felt neither hatred nor malice toward him—only scorn.

The witness Adamsky, a refusenik from Vilna. This should be interesting, I thought. Of the one hundred or so refuseniks interro-

Avital. The picture was taken by my father at the end of June 1974, a few days before our wedding and her departure for Israel. After my arrest I finally retrieved the picture from prison authorities and kept it with me throughout my captivity.

Avital, shortly after her arrival in Israel. This is another photo I obtained with great difficulty from my captors and kept with me until my release.

My father. I kept this photograph in front of me during
my prolonged hunger strikes.

Photo by Alexander Lunts

My Psalm book, a present from
Avital that became a talisman
during all the years in custody.
It is the only piece of property
I managed to take with me from
the Soviet Union.

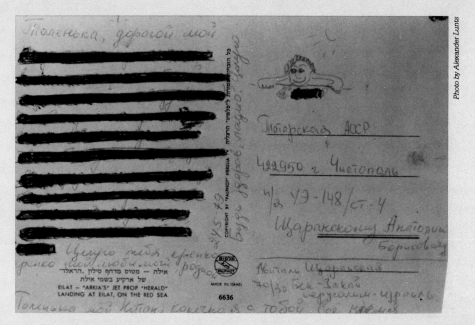

A postcard I received from Avital in 1979. Everything but the greeting and the signature has been censored.

The front of Chistopol Prison, where I was transferred after my conviction. The picture was secretly made by my brother, Leonid.

Avital shows me Israel shortly after my release in 1986.

My brother, Leonid.

Rachel, my daughter, and my mother in Jerusalem.

gated during my investigation, only Adamsky had said anything really damaging. (His testimony was similar to Lipavsky's, except that, implausibly, he had placed these alleged events two years earlier.) After reading his testimony, I had tried to summon Adamsky for a face-to-face confrontation in order to determine whether he was a squealer whom we had missed or a well-meaning man who had yielded to KGB pressure as the result of an uninterrupted thirteen-hour interrogation.

Adamsky glanced around at everyone and settled on me. I could see that he was afraid of the proceedings and sympathetic toward the defendant.

"You planned to emigrate to Israel?" asked the judge.

"I planned to, and I still plan to."

"What do you know about the activity of Sharansky and other refuseniks?"

Adamsky replied that he had signed letters and petitions that I had also signed. It seemed that both the judge and the procurator were afraid to ask him questions, so I rose and read from the copy I had made of his testimony.

"Do you stick to this testimony?" I asked him.

A glance at the witness showed that my question was rhetorical. His face was now even more frightened, and his half-opened mouth and widened eyes expressed not even surprise but genuine shock. After a pause he whispered, and then repeated more loudly, "I don't know anything of the sort."

The judge intervened quickly and decisively.

"Approach the table."

Adamsky came forward.

"Is this your signature?"

"It's mine."

"This was almost a year ago, so you probably remembered better then. If you repudiate it, then we must bring you to trial for giving false testimony at an investigation."

Adamsky returned to the witness stand. "No," he said, "I don't repudiate it. I'm only saying that now I don't remember anything of the sort and cannot confirm that testimony."

"But you agree that you should have remembered better then?"

"Probably . . ."

"We shall go according to that. Is it clear?" Then, turning to me, he asked, "Are there any questions?"

"Yes," I replied, turning to Adamsky. "Your interrogation lasted for thirteen hours without a recess for lunch and supper. This is a violation of the law. Why didn't you demand—"

"I reject your question," interrupted the judge, who promptly dismissed the witness. I called out a demand that Adamsky be summoned to the open session.

Soon they brought in Zakharov, the custodian who "found" all the material from Bob's office. He was a short, thin, and almost colorless man, although one could glimpse in him the soul of a predator. In his dullness, his indifference, and his self-confidence, he reminded me of my tails. Calmly and without rushing, he described how he found these papers near the garbage pail, how from the text he understood that they were about people who had recently been mentioned as spies in *Izvestia,* and how he had turned the material over to the reception office of the KGB.

There was no point in entering into a conversation with Za-kharov, as he wasn't the one who interpreted these papers in a way that suited the KGB. His business was merely to sign a document that legitimized their theft of these papers. Nevertheless, the temptation to point out their crude methods was enormous, and I asked Zakharov, "On what date did you turn over the documents to the KGB?"

"I found them on the fourteenth of April and brought them in on the fifteenth."

He smiled derisively, or did it merely seem that way? Yes, I had prepared him for that answer with my big mouth. I cursed myself and continued: "And why is the date March 15 on all the documents?"

"That's their business," he replied. "I don't look at the dates."

The judge intervened. "This was the secretary's mistake. Any further questions?"

"Yes. You say you noticed that these papers mentioned the same people who were in the *Izvestia* article. . . . I ask the court to give the text of the article to the witness. Let him read it aloud and translate from English those passages that evoked his suspicions."

I knew very well that a KGB worker at Zakharov's level couldn't read English. Zakharov calmly looked at the judge, who reacted immediately: "I reject the question. You, Sharansky, are the defendant, and not the expert who is called in to verify matters. Witness, you are free."

There were several other witnesses whose testimony wasn't especially interesting. When the session was over, the judge announced that the following day would also begin with a closed session. I asked the judge, "How long will the closed sessions last? And how many days is the trial supposed to go?"

"You'll know in time," he replied.

On the way back to Lefortovo I waited for the opportunity to glimpse a tiny piece of the outside world through the crack, but either the door was closed more tightly this time or the curves were not as steep, for I was surrounded by complete darkness up to the moment the car drove into the courtyard of the prison. But neither this minor disappointment nor my fatigue could spoil my good mood. At first I didn't understand what was making me happy. Yesterday I saw my brother and the world learned the truth about my case. But what good thing happened today?

Then I understood: today a succession of people filed by, each with his own character, his own life, and his own role, but the KGB found it difficult, even at a closed court session, to maintain the same "reality" they had tried to construct during their investigative interrogations of the various witnesses.

Day three. The closed session continued. The procurator and the defense (myself) both submitted written questions to two experts who were brought in. One was a specialist on secrecy for the Academy of Sciences, and the other was in some ministry—electronics, I believe.

The procurator asked, "Are the lists of refuseniks prepared by Sharansky and his accomplices secret?" The experts repeated their formulation: as a whole they were secret, and in aggregate they comprised state secrets.

I asked, "What is the meaning of the phrase 'as a whole and in aggregate'? Does it mean that there are secrets as a whole, but that each separate piece of information relating to an individual refusenik is not secret?"

"No, it doesn't mean that. The list contains specific information constituting a state secret."

"Can you show me the line that contains information that is secret?"

"No, we can't, for reasons of state security."

"Can a person who gives information about himself for a list of refuseniks, in particular about the place where he was formerly employed, fail to realize that this information is secret?"

"No, he can't. In accordance with the law, each person who leaves work that is classified signs a note that he won't reveal the corresponding information."

I therefore petitioned the court to summon any one of the refuseniks about whom, in the opinion of the experts, there was classified information in the list. I proposed to show the refusenik the signed note the experts had spoken about which confirmed that this information was truly secret, and then to cross-examine both him and myself in order to ascertain how this information could wind up in the lists. This would be an entirely logical way for the investigation and the court to establish the truth, which is why I knew my request would be rejected.

I had long ago concluded that the only way there could be any secrets in our list was that they had been inserted by the KGB. And the KGB certainly didn't want to attract the attention of any refusenik for whom this was true. My confidence was reinforced by the fact that the few refuseniks to whom the lists were shown at interrogations had categorically declared, "The information about me is not secret."

The judge didn't ponder the matter for long. A look to the left and the right: two nods. The petition was rejected.

The key witness in today's session was Vladimir Riabsky, a large, sporty man of around forty. Riabsky, whom I didn't know, had previously given false and menacing testimony about Richard Pipes, a Harvard professor who he claimed was an agent of the American government. On a visit to Moscow in 1975 Pipes had met with a few of us at Vitaly Rubin's apartment. This much was true, but Riabsky also claimed that Pipes had specifically recommended that we use the Helsinki Final Act to unite the Zionists and the dissidents in the Helsinki Watch Group.

When Solonchenko had read me Riabsky's testimony, something hadn't made sense, until I realized that our meeting with Pipes had taken place a month *before* the Helsinki conference, when it wasn't even clear whether such a conference would even take place. Recalling my mistake in pointing out the error in Zakharov's report, I had decided to save this one for the trial.

Riabsky testified in an even, confident voice, calmly shifting his glance from the judge to the procurator, then to me, and then back to the judge. He said he was Jewish, and that friends had begun to invite him to the home of Rubin and those of other dissidents and refuseniks. At Rubin's apartment he had expected the discussion would be about philosophy and history, but it turned out that Rubin (an internationally known expert on ancient Chinese philosophy) "knows as much about Chinese philosophy as I do about Chinese grammar." Here Riabsky paused, as if to say, Enjoy my joke. Finally, he came to the only concrete episode in his repertoire—the meeting with Pipes.

I hesitated before rushing in with my questions. Riabsky's testimony was related not to the espionage charge but to the charge of assisting foreign states, which meant he could be interrogated at the open session. I didn't want to reveal my surprise now, so I asked the judge whether Riabsky would be summoned to the open session.

"We shall decide this question later," he replied. "Are there any questions now?"

In case this was Riabsky's only appearance, I decided to go ahead.

"You say that Pipes appealed to us to unite with the dissidents, utilizing the Helsinki Final Act. Was he familiar with the text of this act?"

"Of course! It was lying right there on the table."

"According to your testimony, the meeting took place on July 4, 1975. Is that correct?"

"Yes, I remember it well. It was the American Independence Day, and that was mentioned, too."

"Correct. I also remember that. But the Helsinki Final Act came in August 1975. A month before that it wasn't even clear whether the conference would take place. Yet Rubin already had the text and Pipes was suggesting that we utilize it. How do you explain this?"

I hadn't managed to finish my question when Riabsky's expression quickly began to lose its confidence. He frowned, hesitated, and finally muttered, "Yes, yes, well, yes, apparently I simply made a mistake. The meeting with Pipes took place not in 1975, but on July 4, 1976."

It was easy to prove him wrong. In July of 1976 not only was Pipes not in Moscow but Rubin was already living in Israel. However, I merely asked the court secretary to record Riabsky's answer—that the meeting took place in 1976. I would be sure to mention this in open court.

The closed sessions were finally over. After the recess I again returned to the courtroom, which was now full of spectators. My brother was sitting toward the middle, with his guard next to him, and another escort on the other side. We exchanged joyous smiles. He was holding a notebook and pen in his hands. Right—he must record everything! Even if they took away his notes, he'd absorb it better this way.

The first witness was Abramov, a Tat from Derbent. The Tats are Jews who came to the northern Caucasus from Persia many centuries ago, and they constitute a significant percentage of the inhabitants of Derbent. Despite their limited education, they are less alienated from their Jewishness than many Ashkenazic Jews. Many of them took an active part in the struggle for emigration to Israel, and in time there were proportionately more refuseniks from Derbent than from anywhere else. When the authorities began harassing them, the Tats acquired their own Prisoners of Zion.

We often wrote about Derbent in our documents describing Soviet Jews, but Abramov's name was unknown to us. At the trial he was described as the director of a school and a member of the Party.

"What can you say about the situation of the Tats in Daghestan?" asked the judge.

Abramov described how well they lived, how there was no discrimination, how they all condemned Zionist propaganda, and so on. I asked him whether it was possible to study the Tat language in school.

"The parents don't want their children to study it."

"Are you aware that there are Jews in Derbent who aren't permitted to emigrate to Israel?"

"To me they're traitors, and I don't want to know anything about them."

"Are you aware that in Derbent they don't let people study Hebrew?"

"We don't need that language."

"Do you attend the synagogue?"

"Religion is a vestige of capitalism," said Abramov, but the judge interrupted him.

"I disallow that question. In the USSR there is freedom of conscience and a person cannot be asked such questions in court."

In the court's verdict this scene would be described as follows: "The testimony of the witness Abramov refutes the slanderous fabrications about Soviet reality contained in the documents that were prepared and sent to the West by Sharansky and his accomplices."

The next witnesses were two doctors who had been brought in to repudiate statements by the Helsinki Watch Group on the terrible conditions suffered by political prisoners. One of these women worked in the labor camp for political prisoners in Mordovia, the other in Vladimir Prison. Each described the fine sanitary conditions in prisons and camps: the food was nutritious, the punishment cells were warm, and "the medical service is better than in many places in the outside world." Moreover, a prisoner's family could always receive complete information about his state of health.

It was difficult to dispute general assertions, although my few days in a punishment cell were clearly at odds with the witnesses' testimony. I asked specific questions about Yakov Suslensky, a Prisoner of Zion who had lost consciousness in the punishment cell of Vladimir Prison and had to spend several months in the prison hospital. At Ida Nudel's request I had passed myself off as Suslensky's cousin and had once made the rounds of all the highest official levels, trying without success to learn about his health.

Dr. Sukhachev answered me calmly, "These are all lies. No one can lose consciousness or become ill in the punishment cell. A prisoner can be taken there only with the doctor's permission, and we check his health every day."

After a recess, the judge declared that my petition had been partially granted, and that Riabsky, Tsypin, and Lipavsky would be summoned to the open court session.

In the meantime a witness named Platonov entered the room. He was a small, pasty-looking man of around forty, a librarian from Leningrad.

"What can you tell us about the case of Sharansky?" asked the judge.

"Nothing. . . . I'm not familiar with this case," replied the witness timidly.

The judge paused. "Well, tell us about yourself."

The witness explained that he had served time in a political camp together with Alexander Ginzburg from the late 1960s to the early 1970s. Ginzburg, he said, behaved badly, pushing his fellow prisoners into a hunger strike and sending slanderous information to the outside world. Platonov added that he, Platonov, had realized his errors and had repented, and was now satisfied with everything.

There was another long pause. Finally, Solonin said, "Well, now, explain to the defendant"—he nodded at me—"that he is following a false path, that the truth lies not with Ginzburg but with us."

Platonov looked at me mournfully and sadly, and said, "Yes, young man, I'm telling you the truth. . . ."

I found this whole scene very funny. I didn't know that Ginzburg's trial was taking place in Kaluga, about a hundred and fifty kilometers from Moscow, concurrently with my own, and that this poor fellow, presumably the victim of a bureaucratic error, had ended up in the wrong courtroom. But assuming something like this had happened, I asked him, "Tell me, did you ever see me or hear anything about me? Do you know anything at all about my case?"

In his first and only emphatic gesture, Platonov vigorously shook his head. "No," he said, "I don't know you or your case."

"Thank you. I have no further questions."

I sat down with a smirk. The procurator and the judge looked angry, but the expression on the faces of the two assessors remained as serene and attentive as always.

Now Riabsky, appearing for the second time today. I immediately regretted that I had pointed out the contradictions in his testimony, for he had had several hours to prepare a new version.

Riabsky repeated his early account almost word for word, including the crack about Rubin's limited understanding of Chinese philosophy. But when he described the meeting with Richard Pipes, he said nothing about Helsinki.

When I repeated my earlier question about the discrepancy in the dates, Riabsky answered without hesitating, "I already said this morning that I made a mistake, and that the meeting took place on July 4, 1976, rather than 1975."

So three hours of recess wasn't enough time to think up something better? Or did they consider this episode too important to exclude it? Now there was no need to hold back.

"When did Vitaly Rubin leave?"

"I don't remember," said Riabsky.

"He left in June 1976. On July 4, 1976, neither Pipes nor Rubin was in Moscow. The meeting with Pipes really did take place in 1975."

The judge swiftly intervened: "Defendant, are you asking questions or answering them? Witness, you are free."

Tsypin. While approaching the stand he suddenly turned toward me and I saw his frightened expression for the first time, but only for a moment. His testimony was frankly boring. The banal facts he cited contrasted sharply with the scope and seriousness of the charges against me. This was exactly what I wanted to demonstrate when I insisted that he and Lipavsky appear in the open court session. I limited myself to a single question: "You assert that you saw me meet secretly with correspondents, conspiratorially and not publicly. Can you name at least one place where such meetings took place?"

He thought for a minute and said, "The café on Kutuzov Boulevard."

I did meet with correspondents there. "You mean the café opposite the store Russian Souvenir?"

"Yes."

This was a glass-front café adjacent to the building where foreign correspondents lived and worked. Police units guarded their peace and quiet around the clock. One could just as easily speak about a conspiratorial meeting with a correspondent in the reception room of the Central Committee during one of our sit-ins there.

Lipavsky again. Approaching the witness stand, he, too, cast a quick glance in my direction. What was this? I wondered. Were Tsypin and Lipavsky given instructions to look at me first in order to calm down? I could imagine a KGB psychologist telling them,

"Sharansky is a failure, you've got nothing to fear, so take a good look at him and you'll feel better."

This time Lipavsky spoke without notes, listing the correspondents and diplomats with whom I met and through whom I sent information to the West. He explained that the entire operation was organized in the West, and that he himself had been recruited by the CIA. Then, turning to me with his entire body and switching to a hysterical tone, he suddenly cried out, "We Soviet Jews, patriots of our motherland, are now ashamed to appear on the streets when you, Sharansky, have trampled our good name in the mud! No, your mathematical memory for dates won't save you from the anger of the people!"

During this strange outburst Lipavsky's crazy, widened eyes seemed to bulge out of their sockets and were looking somewhere above me. This performance was obviously prepared in advance, but it seemed as if Lipavsky had to exert enormous effort just to keep his head and his body turned toward me. As soon as he completed his tirade he returned to his former position as if jerked back by a string.

I decided to check Lipavsky's own memory. "You claim that we acted on orders from the West, but the only episode confirming this is our statement in support of the Jackson Amendment from February 1976. You claim that Senator Edward Brooke of Massachusetts brought the rough draft and gave it to me, and that I organized the collecting of signatures and returned the statement to him. During the interrogation in the spring of 1977 you indicated that Brooke did this in your presence. But at your second interrogation in the fall of 1977 you said that you knew this from Rubin. When were you telling the truth?"

Lipavsky thought for a moment and, addressing the judge, declared vigorously, "I always speak the truth. During his visit to Moscow, Brooke met with many refuseniks in many homes. I saw him only once, Rubin saw him several times, but you accompanied him all the time. In my presence Brooke instructed you to collect signatures under this letter, and from Rubin I learned that you carried out this assignment."

In fact, during his brief visit to Moscow, Brooke appeared among us for only an hour at Slepak's apartment. Since Lipavsky wasn't there, I knew for sure that he didn't see the senator. But how could I prove it? I wondered if Lipavsky knew that Senator Brooke was black.

I asked, "Does this senator differ from all the others whom you happened to see?"

Lipavsky shrugged his shoulders in bewilderment, but the judge disallowed the question.

I then asked, "What party does Brooke belong to?"

Lipavsky shrugged. Someone yelled from the audience, "What difference does it make? Why do they let Sharansky ask such questions?"

The judge quickly disallowed this question, too, and dismissed the witness. As Lipavsky left I realized I would probably never see him again. But he must have been very relieved to know he would also never have to see me again—or any of the other people he had deceived all these years. I remembered what Peter Osnos had said to me on the telephone after the *Izvestia* article appeared—that Lipavsky would have to live with this all his life.

14

The Verdict

ANOTHER recess. My head was burning, probably from the stuffiness. I turned to the prison doctor who traveled with me each day. When she gave me a pill for my headache, I asked, "Couldn't a nurse do this? Why do you need to be at the trial?"

She replied with a smirk, "And what if they give you the death sentence? You'll collapse in a faint, and then you'll see why I'm here."

The next witness was Sofia Gaskov, the daughter of Colonel Yefim Davidovich, the leading refusenik in Minsk. I went to visit him in 1974, when he was dying a slow, drawn-out death, one heart attack after another. He sent telegram after telegram to the Soviet leadership, asking only that he be allowed to die in Israel. We in Moscow did our best to support him, but the authorities remained true to form.

His funeral in April 1976 developed into one of the most emotional demonstrations in the history of our movement, with dozens of refuseniks coming in from Moscow and many other cities. Vitaly Rubin and Lev Ovsischer—who, like Davidovich, was a Red Army colonel—delivered eulogies at the grave. Maria Karpovna, the widow, who was overcome with grief, condemned the authorities for their cruelty and called on everyone to follow her husband's example.

Then came the next act in this tragedy. Maria was determined to bring the casket with her husband's body to Israel, where he could be buried. She received an exit visa, and together with her daughter,

Sofia, and Sofia's young son, she traveled to Israel with her husband's remains. But she was a Russian woman, and soon began to yearn for her motherland. This is where things stood when I was arrested. A year later I learned what had happened next.

The letters Maria Karpovna wrote from Israel, which were appended to my file, were full of sadness. How could she get used to a land with no snow, a land with a foreign language and alien customs? While her husband was alive she had lived only for him—his health, his concerns, his struggle. But now she was filled with longing for her own world.

In December 1977 Maria and Sofia were permitted to return, but before their citizenship was reinstated, they were interrogated for my case. They were pressured to testify that their husband and father was actually a victim of the Zionists, who used his name and even his death for their anti-Soviet goals, and that his demise was caused not by constant KGB harassment, as we all knew, but by our visits. Although I wasn't mentioned by name in this testimony, the KGB had evidently decided to parade Sofia at my trial to squeeze additional propaganda value out of her return to the Soviet Union.

I had last seen her two years ago at the funeral, looking pale, thin, and sad. Now she seemed even paler, thinner, and sadder. When the judge asked her to testify, she was silent, then whispered something.

"Louder!" they yelled from the audience.

"Louder!" repeated the judge.

"I don't know what to say. It's better if you ask a question."

The judge paused, and then read aloud from her testimony at the preliminary investigation.

"Is this correct?" he asked.

She nodded silently, although all this was the crudest violation of the law.

When it was my turn to ask questions, I said, "If you don't want to answer, then say so right away. Did you read your father's book, *A Jew in the Soviet Army?* And do you think he expressed his own thoughts—or were they imposed on him by other people?"

"I don't want to answer that question," she said softly, blushing.

"Do you have any grounds whatsoever to believe that my friends and I forced your father to make statements in support of Israel and against Soviet emigration policy?"

"I don't want to answer that question," she said in an even softer voice.

My last question was a cruel one, but it was necessary because the KGB had accused us of making a political demonstration out of Davidovich's death against the wishes of his family.

"Do you remember your mother's speech at your father's funeral?"

Her words—which were no longer words, but simply a gesture and a tearful whisper—coincided with the judge's peremptory shout: "Why are you asking such questions?"

How touching. The regime which tormented Davidovich for so many years, which allowed Sofia Gaskov to return only after she signed testimony that she couldn't even bring herself to repeat in court, and which then used this testimony to charge me with treason—this regime was indignant about *my* heartlessness! Still, for a long time I felt embarrassed because I had to ask Sofia these questions. Immediately after her departure they declared a five-minute recess. In the final text of my sentence there was no mention of Sofia's testimony.

Next, the witness Irina Musikhin. She shared a communal apartment with Lida Voronin, and was therefore my neighbor during the time that Lida let me use her room. In her preliminary testimony she said that with the help of Lida I had prepared lists of refuseniks and transmitted them to Robert Toth. She also testified that I received items from abroad and was messy in household matters.

Irina was a large, blond woman of about twenty-five with a striking dark suntan, which reminded me that this was summer. She timidly approached the witness stand and looked at me bashfully and, it seemed, with an apologetic smile. Surprisingly, she quickly replied that she knew nothing of Sharansky's crimes.

"But you gave testimony?"

"That was a long time ago. Now I no longer remember. Ask me a specific question."

I expected that the judge would begin reading her previous testimony, as he did with Sofia Gaskov, but apparently during the recess somebody explained to him that this simply wasn't allowed, and that witnesses must testify voluntarily and without threats. "Fine," he said. "You lived in the same apartment as Sharansky for a long time. What can you say about him?"

"That he was a good neighbor—smart, intellectual, quiet."

The procurator quickly interrupted: "But at the investigation you also spoke about his negative qualities."

Poor Irina turned beet-red, her tanned face becoming even darker. Burning with embarrassment, she replied, "Well, yes, as a medical worker I couldn't help noticing that he wasn't always neat."

Seeing the look of disappointment on the procurator's face, I wanted to laugh. Irina spoke the truth; sometimes in the bathroom I had used her soap, and occasionally left a dirty pot on the stove. But the KGB hadn't expended all this effort on a witness and selected her from among three hundred others to hear this sort of exposé!

"And what did you know about Sharansky's Zionist activities?"

"Nothing."

"But the lists of refuseniks . . ."

Before the procurator could finish the question, Irina said, "I learned what lists of refuseniks were only at the investigation!"

The procurator stopped short, for it was clearly dangerous to pursue this topic. Then he asked, "Did you ever see Robert Toth?"

"Yes, sometimes he visited Sharansky. When Sharansky wasn't home, Toth left his card with me and wrote a few words on it. He was very polite and good-natured."

"But you saw Sharansky giving material to Toth—"

Again the shy Irina interrupted him. "Once, as I was passing by an open door, I happened to see Sharansky give Toth some paper. Perhaps it was only a blank sheet. How should I know?"

I could imagine how annoyed the judge and the procurator must be that they hadn't summoned this witness to the closed session! Then the judge could have shouted at her, called her to the table, shown her the signature under the text where she had testified that she saw me give Toth the lists of refuseniks typed by Voronin, and forced her to remember "better." But now he was powerless. After I exchanged a friendly smile with Irina and said that I had no questions for her, the judge had no choice but to dismiss her.

The judge called the next witness: Ida Petrovna Milgrom. Mama!

My brother stood up and declared, "Our mother is standing outside the entrance and demands that she be permitted into the courtroom. She refuses to be a witness against her own son. Summoning her as a witness is only a pretext not to permit her into the courtroom."

The judge warned Lenya that he could be removed for interfering in the proceedings of the court. Five minutes passed in agonizing expectation. My heart was thumping—perhaps now I would see Mama? But, no, she must not agree. I could imagine how badly she wanted to enter the courtroom, but she was demanding to be admitted for the entire court session and not for just a few minutes as a witness. Mama darling, I said to myself, don't give in. But I said it without conviction.

The court usher returned and said, "The witness Milgrom refuses to appear in court to testify."

The judge paused, turned, immediately received two nods from the left and the right, and said, "Of course we could bring the witness by force, but taking into consideration that she is a mother, and given her age, we won't insist on it. The court session is ended."

Immediately after my return to Lefortovo, Leonid and I were taken to the exercise yard, where I described each witness to him. As we talked I was both happy and amazed. For almost a year and a half the KGB had concocted its case. Prior to my arrest they had spent years recruiting and infiltrating agents and weaving cunning nets of provocation that resulted in the indictment exposing an "international Zionist conspiracy." The formulation sounded very menacing, and I could see that the reading of the text made an impression not only on the public but also on my brother. And even I, who knew perfectly well how flimsy the case was, couldn't shake the heavy feeling of hopelessness when I heard the indictment in court.

And yet how frivolous and fragile, how simply absurd, were the arguments and proofs that the KGB had finally managed to bring to court! The accusations of the squealers hadn't held up against the most elementary logic. The same witnesses who were terrorized during their interrogations had all tried to jump off the train, and the list of witnesses was exhausted. "Is this really the end of the trial?" I asked Leonid. He had three or four trials behind him, but had never been involved in a political case, which made it difficult for him to answer.

"Probably they must read in court the documents they alluded to in the charge," he said uncertainly.

Good, that would give me at least a few days to expose their working methods and to show that the slander was not in our documents but in theirs.

The following day really did begin with a presentation of documents. But first I was led into the still-empty room, with only the procurator, my guard, and the court secretary. Solonin hobbled up to me and said, with his malicious smile, "Sharansky! The Soviet regime expended so much effort on you. It nurtured you, raised you, and gave you an education, and you turned all this against it. Don't you understand that our patience has its limits? How can I walk on the same ground as you and breathe the same air when you're an enemy of all that is dear to me? It's still not too late—think it over!"

Was this their final attempt to intimidate me? "Look," I said, "I don't want to walk on the same ground as you, either, but you won't let me go to Israel!"

Half a year later, in Chistopol Prison, I recalled his words when I came across an obituary in *Izvestia* about the sudden death of the meritorious figure of justice, the head of the department of the procurator's office of the USSR, Solonin, P. N. He got his wish, I thought, for now we were no longer walking on the same ground and breathing the same air.

But now, still full of energy, Solonin asked the court to append an "important document" to the case, that during the years 1974–77 I received from abroad material aid in the form of monetary remittances and clothing packages valued at approximately eight hundred dollars. "There it is," he said. "Payment for treachery."

The Soviet correspondents quickly recorded this in their notebooks. Then the court showed the two Granada films, *A Calculated Risk* and *The Man Who Went Too Far.* In the second one I again saw Avital leading the demonstration—only, this time she was coming right at me into the courtroom! They didn't want to let my relatives in, but Avital had broken through! My joy and shock were quickly interrupted when shouts began to ring out in the courtroom: "This is brazen slander! Death to the traitor!"

One of the spectators burst forward to the barrier. Lightly restrained by the sergeants, he screamed, brandishing his fists directly in my face: "Sharansky! We will never tolerate traitors like you!"

Apparently, according to the plan, this moment marked the climax, the "spontaneous outburst of popular anger" in the trial. But I replied to this festival of rage with a self-confident smile, for I was guarded not by the sergeants but by Avital.

When the noise died down, Solonin asked me a question: "You claimed you did not engage in clandestine slanderous activity. But now we have all seen how you gave an underground interview and slandered the Soviet Union. What can you say about this?"

I replied, "All the information I transmitted to the West was exclusively for open use. The fact that I gave an interview for Western television is the best proof of that. The fact that those who filmed this interview had to conceal it until they brought the film out of the USSR says nothing about the closed nature of our activity, but says much about the closed nature of Soviet society. Moreover, not one of my statements in the film is slanderous. I discussed specific facts concerning demonstrations of Jews who are trying to emigrate and Germans who are seeking to be repatriated."

After I said a little more about German emigration, the judge unexpectedly declared a one-hour recess "so that the procurator and the defendant may prepare their speeches."

"What speeches?" I cried out.

"The speeches for the prosecution and for the defense."

Well, that was a surprise! I had assumed there were a few days left, as even a simple enumeration of the documents used against me would take up several court sessions.

During the recess I tried to concentrate on preparing my speech. But it was impossible, as my thoughts jumped from fact to fact, from document to document. What a fool I was. For a year and a half I prepared for the trial, and for three and half months I studied the evidence. But in all that time I didn't write a defense speech. Should I tell them I wasn't ready today because I wasn't informed about this, and that I would speak tomorrow? No, that wouldn't do, for what if they didn't admit Lenya into the courtroom? I was calmed by the fact that my brother was here, and that I could now tell him a great deal about my case. What did I really need to prepare for? I knew the material better than anyone else, and I could talk about the essentials.

The procurator would speak first. Then, in my own speech, I could analyze and refute his arguments. But instead of an analysis of my criminal file I was forced to listen to a lecture about the Soviet perspective on the world. With a glass of water and about a hundred pages of text in front of him, Solonin solemnly began to read for an hour and a half. He described the persecution of blacks in the United States and South Africa, the Irish in England, and the Arabs in Israel. Throughout the world, capitalism propagated unemployment, drugs, and prostitution, and tried to defend itself by wars—hot wars in Vietnam and the Middle East, and cold wars, too, such as the propaganda campaign against the Soviet Union. There was operation Solzhenitsyn. There was operation Sakharov. Now there was operation Sharansky. Well, I thought, at least I landed in good company.

After speaking about subversive operations by Western intelligence services in general, Solonin came to the specific provocations of world Zionism. Israel, he said, was not a country but an armed camp. The economy lay in ruins, and religious terror was unbearable. The Sabbath was a silent period of mourning that stretched for twenty-four hours. Israel required cannon fodder in order to oppress other peoples and conquer new territories, which explained why international Zionism was in league with the Soviet Jewry movement.

Moving to the USSR, Solonin spoke at length about the advantages of life under socialism. But when he finally came to my case, he simply read the same indictment that was presented to me before the trial. There was no reference to documents or to the testimony of witnesses, and no response to the lies I had exposed in the testimony of Lipavsky, Riabsky, and others. It was as if the trial had never taken place.

Solonin then returned to the international situation and the criminal links between the imperialist secret services, the Zionist organizations, and their accomplices in the USSR. In the course of his lecture he quoted Lenin and Dzerzhinsky, Brezhnev, and Martin Luther King, Jr. Near the end of his remarks he quoted Benjamin Franklin: "Before pointing your finger at me, wash it off!"—and pointed his finger at me. I burst out laughing.

I listened carefully to Solonin's remarks and took notes, but today, as I try to reconstruct his speech, I can't recall anything substantial from it. It sounded as if he had taken a propagandistic article from a Soviet newspaper and read it over and over for an hour and a half.

Finally he came to the point: "For his criminal activity, Sharansky undoubtedly deserves capital punishment. But considering his age, and the fact that he has not been tried before, the state prosecution is asking to sentence him to fifteen years—the first three to be served in prison." (The other twelve, it was understood, would be served in a labor camp.)

"That's not enough," shouted one of the spectators. "He should get life. *Life!*"

The judge declared a twenty-minute recess.

How should I respond? Should I introduce a historical perspective or should I speak directly about the charges against me? No matter how weak the procurator's speech was, it did give the case a certain historical dimension, and I felt obliged to take up the challenge.

I reentered the courtroom without knowing how I would start, but when I caught my brother's glance I immediately calmed down. I had to speak for him, for Mama, for Avital, for my friends and my people.

I began: "I am faced with a seemingly hopeless task. It would seem pointless in a court where everything has been decided in advance, about a case where even before my arrest I was charged with espionage by the official state organ, *Izvestia,* to speak before a specially selected audience—"

Cries were heard from the audience: "Slander! Lies!"

I paused and looked sternly at the judge, who reacted quickly: "Stop the noise in the room!"

I repeated, "—to speak before a specially selected audience who came with special passes, and whose sole function is to greet the predetermined sentence with applause." (This sentence was suggested to me by the press report of Yuri Orlov's trial: "The spectators greeted the court decision with applause.")

"But the charge made against me today, which extends to all Jewish activists in the Soviet Union, and, in some ways, to our entire people, is so serious that I have no right to let it go unanswered. Yes, in today's world, as the procurator indicated, there is a struggle between two social systems. But not everything can be reduced to this dichotomy, for there is also the struggle of peoples for their national liberation, for the right to live in accordance with their own national culture and religious traditions, and for the right to live in their own state."

I briefly summarized the history of Zionism—how Theodor Herzl, influenced by the Dreyfus case, concluded that it was necessary to create a Jewish state, and how Jews from various countries, including Russia, participated in the struggle for this goal. I mentioned that the Doctors' Plot, which was trumped up by Stalin just before his death, was another reminder that the Jews could not feel secure here. And I spoke of the Six-Day War in 1967, when Israel defended its right to exist, and how that event led to a rise in the national consciousness of Soviet Jews.

Arriving at the present, I abruptly changed the perspective: "I could spend hours discussing where human rights are violated more—in the USSR or in America, England or Israel, but this is not the essence of the charge against me. I am charged with 'aiding capitalist states in conducting hostile activity against the USSR.' Our open activity in informing world public opinion has been presented as clandestine and conspiratorial, and organized and coordinated from abroad.

"Let us examine where our movement was directed from. In all the episodes where guilt is ascribed to me, there are only two where we allegedly acted in accordance with instructions from abroad. One is when Senator Brooke—according to Lipavsky's testimony— brought to Moscow at the request of Senator Jackson the draft of a letter in support of his amendment. Senator Jackson needed this for his primary campaign prior to the presidential election of 1976. I allegedly carried out Jackson's request, gathered signatures, and returned the letter to Brooke."

I then analyzed the contradictions in Lipavsky's testimony on this episode—contradictions that were chronological, factual, and even political. Why would Jackson, a Democrat, choose Brooke, a Republican, to help in his primary campaign? I emphasized, however, that our statement in support of the Jackson Amendment was real, as were all the other statements mentioned in the charge. Not only did I not deny my authorship; I was proud of it. But I stressed that these statements were written not upon orders from abroad but as a direct result of Soviet emigration policy, the policy of state anti-Semitism.

The other episode where I allegedly acted in accordance with instructions from the West was the meeting with Richard Pipes in Vitaly Rubin's apartment, when Pipes allegedly appealed to Rubin and me to "unite with the dissidents under the flag of the Helsinki Final Act." The entire proof was based on the testimony of Riabsky, and I reminded the court how I caught him in a blatant lie with regard to the dates.

"But no matter how distorted are the facts of our activity in this part of the charge," I said, fearing I'd be interrupted at any moment, "the charges of espionage are even more sinister." I continued to speak quickly, without stopping, trying to tell my brother as much as possible before they stopped me.

"First," I said, "all the basic documents of proof—the instructional letter to Lipavsky from abroad, the questionnaire with questions 'of an espionage nature,' the list found by the janitor Zakharov, and others—I saw for the first time only at the investigation. And the Russian text of Toth's testimony differs from the English version just enough so that one can deduce from it that, in addition to the information for the articles, I also gave him other information about refuseniks."

"But your petition was granted," said the judge. "The text was corrected."

"Yes, that's true, after all my protests it was finally corrected. But the mistake was restored in the indictment as if nothing had happened."

The judge stopped short, and, embarrassed, he leafed through the pages of the charge. But this embarrassment didn't prevent him from reading the sentence in the same uncorrected form the following day. There was no time to dwell on details, however, and I hastened to present the essence of my defense, using whatever I had obtained in the closed session.

The judge made no effort to stop me, but I could see that Lenya, unfortunately, was unable to catch it all. And no wonder! I had been stewing in this kettle for a year and a half, but he had to understand everything at once. It would be another two years before I'd have the opportunity to tell him in detail about my case.

The final "slanderous" document in my charge was our statement with regard to the Soviet-made film *Traders in Souls,* which was shown on Moscow television a few weeks before my arrest. This officially "anti-Zionist" work was actually a flagrantly anti-Semitic production designed to "expose" an international conspiracy of imperialism and world Jewry against the USSR. Together with Slepak, Begun, and Yuly Kosharovsky, I had even tried to bring a suit against the filmmakers. To confirm the charge that we slandered the Soviet regime and Soviet television in accusing them of pandering to anti-Semitism, the KGB followed the natural path for a Soviet organization: they asked the producers of the film to send them responses received from Soviet citizens, which were added to my file. Now, with great pleasure, I quoted one of these people, a Soviet teacher from a village school, who wrote as follows: "Having viewed this film, I want to thank those who made it for once again reminding us that at the same time as we, the Russian people, are building Communism together with other peoples of the USSR, the Jews are doing the only thing that their nation is capable of—living at the expense of other people."

"Isn't this anti-Semitism in the purest form?" I asked. "These are the kinds of feelings that the producers of so-called anti-Zionist material want to arouse in the people." And here I gestured in the direction of the Soviet journalists sitting in the front row.

I felt tired. I realized that my brother was also tired, and that it was probably becoming increasingly difficult for him to absorb new material. Although there were still many episodes I wanted to speak about, I asked, "Do I understand correctly that I'll have the right to a final statement?"

"Yes," the judge replied.

"In that case, I shall end with this today. I declare once more that all the charges presented against me are false and absurd."

Back to Lefortovo. Leonid and I were taken to the exercise yard, where I described my duel with Solonin. Although I was satisfied that Lenya now had a clear picture of the case, I regretted having omitted many important details, including the comedy with the dates of Zakharov's "discoveries" and the attempts to repudiate the testimony of the two telephone women. Every few minutes I recalled an additional point that I could have mentioned, and they all seemed important. Why hadn't I prepared a speech in advance? I asked myself.

I seemed to have forgotten completely that only a few days ago I hadn't had the slightest notion of how the trial would proceed, who would be present, and what I could say. Back then my only goal was to attain an open trial. The idea of writing a speech in advance would have seemed ridiculous.

Back in the cell, Leonid said, "Calm down. There's still the last sprint—your final statement—where you can say everything you forgot to say earlier."

Everything? Well, no. All my experience as a spokesman for refuseniks and dissidents indicated otherwise. I recalled my rule: Only secondary statements can be long. The important ones should be no more than a page, and the most important half a page.

"You also have the right of reply," Leonid reminded me.

True, if the procurator wished to respond to my arguments, then he had the right of reply, in which case I, too, had that right, which could be worked into a new speech.

I decided to prepare a list of fifteen points in case I received the right of reply. But first, the final statement. I sat with a clean sheet of paper and concentrated for a long time, trying to distill the essence of my case.

I didn't know how to begin. Eventually, a sentence came into my head that I would use in the middle of the speech: "I hope that the false and absurd but terribly serious charges made today against me—and the entire Jewish people—will not impede the process of the national revival of the Jews of Russia, as the KGB has assured me they would, but will actually provide a new impulse, as has often happened in our history."

Then something strange happened: I wrote without stopping or correcting a single word. I wrote quickly, but I could barely keep up with the words. I soon reached the end: "Next year in Jerusalem!" Then I took a breath and returned to the beginning. Now I knew how to begin—with a description of how wonderful my years of freedom had been, despite the threats, despite prison, despite the investigation. This time the opening proceeded so naturally to the middle that I practically didn't have to edit a word.

I read the speech to my cell mate.

"It's strong," he said. "Read it again."

When I began, "From the very beginning of my case, Colonel Volodin and the other KGB investigators—" Leonid interrupted me: "Stop. That's the part I don't like. You write a speech that condemns the entire system, and suddenly, 'Volodin.' Who the hell is he? Why even mention him?"

I agreed; I was no longer struggling against Volodin. But this was the only correction I made. When I awoke the next morning I didn't even need to read my speech. It was already part of me, and I knew it by heart.

I felt remarkably well, with no tiredness and no regret that I didn't say this or that. Still, I put the list of fifteen points for a reply in my left pocket, and in the right the text of my final speech and Avital's picture. Because I had been going without a jacket, I had kept the picture in the pocket of my pants, where it had become noticeably crumpled. Sorry, I told the picture, you'll have to suffer one more day.

Lenya was already in his seat when I entered the courtroom. Solonin had no papers in front of him, which meant that there would be no reply from the procurator. (He hadn't said a word without paper in front of him.) I was irritated and disappointed that they didn't even want to discuss the arguments I presented at the trial. Perhaps I should add a few points to my speech, after all? The procurator, in reply to the judge's question, said that he had no remarks. The judge solemnly turned to me. "Defendant! What would you like to say to the court in your final statement?"

I—to the court? Well, no, I had nothing to say to them. I almost told him this, but I caught myself in time. I would mention it at the end—yes, they had just given me my ending.

Now I would speak, but not to them. I rose, turned demonstratively toward my brother, and began to dictate my final speech. I spoke slowly, and only after making sure that Lenya had written down each sentence did I proceed to the next one. (Not until I was writing this book did I learn that by the last day of the trial the KGB had confiscated his notebook. He continued taking notes on the palm of his hand, but still he retained 95 percent of my final speech. In fact, the only sentence lost was the one I had written first.)

I recited my text like a commander dictating a report to headquarters about a victorious operation, which was how I felt. From time to time I put my hand in my pocket and squeezed Avital's picture. At one point my hand trembled and the edge of the photograph tore; to this day, that tear remains as a memento of that moment.

I began: "From the start of my investigation, the heads of the

KGB told me often that given my position with regard to this case, I would receive either capital punishment or, at best, fifteen years of imprisonment. They promised that if I changed my mind and cooperated with them in their struggle against Jewish activists and dissidents, I would receive a short, symbolic sentence and the opportunity to join my wife in Israel. But I did not change my position either during the investigation or at the trial, and yesterday the prosecution demanded that I be sentenced to a term of fifteen years.

"Five years ago I applied for an exit visa to emigrate from the USSR to Israel. Today I am further than ever from my goal. This would seem to be a cause for regret, but that is not the case. These five years were the best of my life. I am happy that I have been able to live them honestly and at peace with my conscience. I have said only what I believed, and have not violated my conscience even when my life was in danger.

"I am also happy to have been able to help many people who needed help and who turned to me. I am proud that I came to know and work with such people as Andrei Sakharov, Yuri Orlov, and Alexander Ginzburg, who are carrying on the best traditions of the Russian intelligentsia. But most of all, I feel part of a marvelous historical process—the process of the national revival of Soviet Jewry and its return to the homeland, to Israel. I hope that the false and absurd but terribly serious charges made today against me—and the entire Jewish people—will not impede the process of the national revival of the Jews of Russia, as the KGB has assured me they would, but will actually provide a new impulse, as has often happened in our history.

"My relatives and friends know how strong was my desire to join my wife in Israel, and with what joy at any moment I would have exchanged my so-called fame as a Jewish activist—for which the charge asserts I was striving—for a visa to Israel. For two thousand years the Jewish people, my people, have been dispersed all over the world and seemingly deprived of any hope of returning. But still, each year Jews have stubbornly, and apparently without reason, said to each other, *Leshana haba'a b'Yerushalayim* (Next year in Jerusalem)! And today, when I am further than ever from my dream, from my people, and from my Avital, and when many difficult years of prisons and camps lie ahead of me, I say to my wife and to my people, *Leshana haba'a b'Yerushalayim.*"

Now I turned to the judge and replied to his question, "And to the court, which has only to read a sentence that was prepared long ago—to you I have nothing to say."

I sat. There was a long silence. Then, "The court is retiring to confer," and I was led away. I spent several hours on a bench in the holding cell, half sitting and half lying. The tension gradually left me, but the satisfaction remained. I looked at Avital's picture, and the feeling that now we were together, that we had broken through all the walls and all the barriers, became increasingly strong.

Lunch. No, I refused the food. I didn't seem to require anything earthly now.

Four hours later, when they led me back to the courtroom, Captain Minaev said, "Neaten yourself up." I felt I was neat enough, but then I realized that now they would be taking my picture. Indeed, the courtroom was full of TV cameramen and photographers. As the judge began to read the verdict they divided their attention between him and me. They shot me for a long time from various angles. At first I looked at the cameras and sneered, but I soon turned to my brother and we stared at each other until the end.

Lenya was calm and serious, and it felt as if we had never understood each other so well. Sixteen months ago, when I disappeared into Lefortovo, he was a loyal Soviet citizen with a family and a job, far from my life and my interests. How would he conduct himself? Would he repudiate his younger brother? I knew he wouldn't, but perhaps he would agree to the role of a silent observer, accepting the KGB's terms—Don't bother us and we won't bother you. But now I saw him standing among the KGB men, boldly ignoring their looks and gestures, taking notes, and linking me by his gaze to family and friends, to the entire world. We smiled joyfully at each other. "Take care of Mama," I told him mentally.

The reading of my sentence was over: thirteen years. After my final statement I had completely forgotten that they still had to impose a sentence. Fifteen, thirteen, what's the difference? It made no impression on me. Just before they took me out of the courtroom, my brother suddenly cried out, "Tolya! The whole world is with you!"

Someone grabbed him. I wanted to cry out, Take care of Mama! but an elbow pressed my throat and some unknown force grabbed me, rushed me along the corridors and stairs and threw me into the van. They locked me in the pencil box, switched on the siren, and drove off. In five minutes I was back in my cell at Lefortovo. I barely managed to say "Thirteen years" to my cell mate before they took us to the exercise yard.

As I caught my breath Leonid congratulated me. Why?

"First, they're not going to shoot you. And second, such a marvelous sentence—thirteen years!"

"Why is it marvelous?"

"Why? Among us swindlers thirteen is considered the luckiest number. Look." He took off his shirt and on his right shoulder was a tattoo of the number 13.

Just then Leonid pricked up his ears to catch the sound of a radio from the fourth floor. The radio was far away, but it was turned up as loud as possible. I began to make out the words "Sharansky, Filatov, CIA, traitors."

"They're talking about you!" said Leonid rapturously.

But I felt only anger. The swine! Now they'll scream to the entire world that Sharansky and Filatov are spies. Never mind, I told myself, you said your piece, that's the main thing.

Tomorrow we would read in *Pravda* the article that they had already broadcast over the radio, an analysis of the trials of the spies Sharansky and Filatov. Today, only a few minutes after the reading of the verdict, the article was already completed. Normally it takes several days before such broadcasts are officially approved and edited for the public.

But why was I angry? Didn't I know better than anyone else that everything connected with my trial was prepared in advance?

When we returned from our exercise, I continued pacing back and forth in the cell. The joy of victory didn't want to give way to fatigue. I took the slightly torn picture of Avital from my pocket. "Do you mind if I put this on the table?" I asked Leonid. He quickly consented and lay down on his cot so as not to interfere with my pacing.

Three steps forward, I looked at Avital. Turn, three steps to the door. Turn, I looked at Avital. I began to recite my prayer. The feeling of joy and victory was still with me. And suddenly, a lump, which had already formed several times in my throat, took my breath away. A gasp—and I began to weep.

Book Two

July 15, 1978—February 11, 1986

The World of
the Gulag

15

O N July 15, 1978, the morning after the trial, I woke up in the same prison where I had spent the past sixteen months. "Exactly sixteen months," I said aloud. I was still in Lefortovo, of course, but it was a different Lefortovo from the one I had come to. This was no longer the building where they had coerced me, deprived me of my freedom and threatened to kill me. Now it was the place where I had emerged victorious, defended my freedom, retained my spiritual independence against the kingdom of lies, and reinforced my connection with Israel and with Avital.

Sixteen months ago I had set myself three goals: not to help the KGB in its investigation; to study its methods; and, finally, to expose it during the trial. I had now achieved the last of these objectives. The world would soon learn that the entire case against me was a sham, and it seemed as if everybody and everything in Lefortovo was a witness to my victory—my cell mates, the guards, and even the cell itself and all the objects in it. I wanted to embrace and kiss them all. I had been through a real war—and what a difficult one! It *was* possible to struggle against this enemy, I exclaimed to myself.

From here on, I thought, it should be easy. Now that the trial was over, according to the law, to *their* law, I was entitled to a meeting with my family, which I saw as an initial reward for our victory. And then—who could say? Somehow the fact of my thirteen-year sentence had not quite sunk in, as I was still overjoyed that the prosecution had produced no terrible surprises at the trial. For who knew what I could have found? Certainly the KGB could have presented *something* unexpected. But, no, the evidence at the trial was as weak as the material they had shown me during the investigation. Just as I thought, their damaging accusations had been based on lies.

The aura of victory overshadowed everything else, and brought another feeling in its wake—that I would soon and inevitably be released. The intense feeling of being together with Avital that I experienced in the courtroom only yesterday was surely a harbinger that soon, very soon, we would truly be together.

The following days sobered me up somewhat and diluted these feelings. But it took a whole year of my new life before my expectation of a speedy release was fully replaced by a stern determination to follow my path to the end, no matter how long it took.

Four days after my trial, at four in the afternoon, they brought me to a transit cell, searched me carefully, and sat me at a table opposite the door. Two KGB colonels came in. "Now you will have a meeting with your mother," one of them said. "But if you utter a single non-Russian word we will immediately terminate the visit!"

"In what other language could I speak with her?" I asked.

"Well, we don't want any 'Shalom Avital's!' "

I smirked nervously, without tearing my eyes away from the door. Someone came in. Mama? She had grown thinner, older, and very small—or did it only seem that way? Was I actually remembering her as she used to be, years ago?

Without even looking at me, Mama immediately turned to Colonel Povarenkov and addressed him angrily: "Why are they detaining me for so many hours and not allowing me to see my son? I have the judge's permission. And why did they take away the food I brought him?"

As if in a trance, I did not interfere.

"Here is your son," said Povarenkov. "But he may eat only our food."

Mama turned to me; we both cried out. But as soon as she sat down on the other side of the table, she turned back to Povarenkov: "I brought some strawberries for my son. Why can't he have them?"

At this point not only Povarenkov but I, too, became impatient. "Mama! Forget about the strawberries! How is Papa? Natasha? How are all of you?"

I no longer remember the specific details of our conversation, but

Mama held up excellently, with no tears or lamentations. She told me Papa had suffered a heart attack and was quite ill. I was afraid he had died, but Mama said, "Didn't you see his handwriting on the food lists?" Tomorrow they were bringing him to Lefortovo to see me, for instead of one family meeting the judge had permitted three separate meetings—with Mama, Papa, and Lenya.

I also learned that during the trial Natasha was on the phone with the family almost every day, that she was traveling a great deal, and that they had occasionally heard her voice on shortwave radio broadcasts.

"Speak about family!" said the other colonel.

"This *is* family," we replied with one voice.

Mama quickly delivered greetings from many friends. I remember asking only one question: "The charges of espionage didn't fool anyone, did they?"

"Don't be ridiculous," said Mama. She began repeating a string of compliments from friends, acquaintances, and people I didn't even know, but the colonel quickly stopped her. She told me the joyful news that Dina Beilin had left for Israel. But there were also sad tidings—Slepak and Ida Nudel had recently been arrested.

Suddenly Povarenkov announced that the meeting was over.

"How can that be?" I demanded. "We are permitted a minimum of one hour!"

"Yes, but you will be having three meetings, so each one will be twenty minutes."

Mama and I quickly made arrangements with Povarenkov for my meeting with Papa. "Tomorrow at the same time," he said.

As our meeting ended we reached out to each other across the table and managed to embrace. Nobody tried to stop us, but we were rushed with cries of "That's enough, it's over."

Mama whispered something to me, but I was unable to catch the words. I held her more tightly, and only now did her tears start to flow. "Soon you will be released," she cried, but was this real information or merely a wish? Looking back, I'm not even sure if she spoke those words at all.

We said farewell—until tomorrow and my meeting with Papa.

After the meeting I was so excited that I didn't even open the copy of my sentence delivered that evening, which was supposed to remain with me throughout my term. All I could think of was Papa. How was he doing? How could I encourage him? What messages should I pass on to Avital? I fell asleep with these thoughts in my head.

The next morning brought a rude shock. An hour earlier than usual I was awakened by a new command: "Get your things. You're leaving!" How could this be? What about the meetings with my father and brother? I refused to leave the prison and demanded that they summon Povarenkov. But two low-ranking officers grabbed me by the arms and dragged me to the prison yard, where I was turned over to a unit of Interior Ministry forces.

Officially, the KGB would have nothing more to do with me, as I was now under the jurisdiction of the Interior Ministry, which controlled the Gulag. The officers put me in a police van and piled in the possessions I had accumulated over the past sixteen months— except for my notes, which were confiscated. I wouldn't need any of these items, mainly clothing, in prison or in camp. A prisoner's family normally retrieves his possessions after he leaves, but evidently the KGB was eager to leave no trace of my stay in Lefortovo.

When you're taken on a transport from one prison to another, you're never told where you're going. I assumed I was headed for Vladimir, where many political prisoners were kept, and that assumption proved correct. When the police van arrived at the train station, I saw for the first time a scene I had seen before only in films, but which would eventually become familiar: rows of submachine gunners, German shepherds, and a column of zeks. I was placed at the head of the line, and for the first time I heard the standard warning: "A step to the left or the right will be viewed as an attempt to escape. We shall use arms."

I had trouble lifting my belongings. I should have thrown them away, but I hadn't yet come to my senses. All I knew was that they had brazenly deceived me, and that I would not be seeing Papa today.

"Which regime?" asked the guard when I reached the train. All Soviet prisoners are separated into four regimes, or levels of punishment: normal, and then—in increasing order of severity—reinforced, strict, and special. Political prisoners are either strict or special.

"All are strict regime except the first one," replied one of the convoy guards. (Technically, I, too, was on strict regime, but "politicals," known officially as "particularly dangerous state criminals," constitute a separate category.) The guards pushed me into the train and cursed me for carrying so much stuff. They crammed me into a compartment cell that was bursting with zeks, who cursed and shouted indignantly, "What, another one?"

The soldiers demanded that they make room, and somehow I squeezed in. Seeing all my possessions, the zeks immediately began to yell, "What kind of a bourgeois did they send us?"

My fellow zeks in the cell were all criminals who carried small bags. The grating slammed shut behind me, and I was pressed against it by an angry crowd. There was no time to be afraid, but I was embarrassed. "Sorry, guys, for taking up so much room."

"Who are you?" a voice demanded. "What article?"

Like it or not, this was my new home and I had to introduce myself.

"Sharansky. Article 64."

"What? You're the one they've been talking about all week on the radio?"

"Yes."

"A *politik*. A spy!" These exclamations contained a mixture of amazement and admiration.

"Really?" somebody shouted out from above. "All my life I've wanted to talk with one of them." He was on the top bunk, with far more space than the others. I wondered if he was the *pakhan*, the ringleader of a gang of thieves.

"Hey, give the *politik* more room! What's your name? Care for a bite?"

"Tolya. . . . Only I'm not a spy. I—"

But before I could explain, the grating opened and a guard angrily pulled me out, cursing heavily. "Why the hell didn't you say you were a *politik?*"

An officer standing next to him interrupted: "And where were *you* when this mistake occurred?"

The zeks, who only moments ago had expressed indignation at my arrival, began protesting our speedy separation. But it's forbidden to let a particularly dangerous state criminal, a *politik*, mix with the criminals, so I was led to the far end of the car into an empty "threesome"—a small compartment with three bunks stacked up, which happened to be unoccupied. I threw my things on the floor, stretched out my legs, and sat down on the bunk.

Just then someone asked me a question. I turned around and saw a young lieutenant. "What?"

He repeated his question. Either it was too noisy in the train or he was speaking quietly, but I couldn't make out what he was saying. I went right up to the grating and he whispered, "Are you the one they're making such a fuss about now in the West?"

"Well, yes, I don't know. . . . Perhaps. Yes, probably."

Just then another officer appeared at the far end of the corridor, and my lieutenant hastily whispered, "Well, hang on to the finish line, and good luck!" Then, in a completely different voice, as he moved along the corridor: "No smoking! No loud talking!"

There was something deeply comforting about his message of encouragement. At the time, I didn't appreciate how valuable it was, how rare and unique. But during all the years that followed, I would never again hear anything like it from an officer of the Gulag.

I dozed off. After a few hours the grating clanged again as it opened. I left my overcoat, jacket, and some other things in the train, as I would not be needing them. I was put into the pencil box of a police van for the drive to Vladimir Prison.

When we arrived I was taken to a cell with a hole in the cement floor that served as a toilet. I walked up to it and then stepped back in astonishment. Could it be that human voices were coming out of it? Yes—some of the criminals were having a lively conversation. I had no idea that by leaning over this hole I could have called to Yosef Mendelevich, a veteran Prisoner of Zion and one of several defendants from the Leningrad Trial in 1970, whose cell was two floors above mine. But I was still in a daze and unable to show any initiative. I wanted only to rest, to get my bearings, and to think over what had happened.

It was not until the next morning that I returned to my senses. A prison officer summoned me to fill out some documents, and after dismissing the guard so that we could be alone, he closed the door and said, quietly and conspiratorially, "Yesterday I had an argument with a friend. The newspapers don't say which secret service you worked for. Isn't it true you worked for the Japanese?"

I burst out laughing. "I don't know, but one of the correspondents mentioned in the case was Japanese, so probably it was for them, too!"

The stupidity of his question snapped me out of my daze. Although the trial was over, the farce was continuing. The world of evil continued to present itself in all its absurdity, and, as before, I could view it from a distance. The sweet sound of my victory, which had been drowned out by the barking of the dogs and the cursing of the guards, echoed in me again. I knew that my captors had lost, that they were angry, and that they were now taking their revenge on me and on my family. The only shadow was the premonition that I had lost my last chance to see Papa.

In theory, I knew quite a bit about Vladimir Prison before I arrived there. I was aware that it was a huge place with thousands of prisoners, although fewer than a hundred were politicals. I had heard that the punishment cells were terrible, and that sometimes the prison authorities didn't permit you to correspond with your family for many months. But it took years before I fully understood how the KGB machine worked in a consistent and deliberate way to break a man's spirit in prison.

In the larger zone, as the zeks cynically refer to the rest of the country where people are theoretically free, Soviet citizens are divided by a host of invisible barriers that determine what they can read, where they can shop, which countries they can visit, and where they can be buried. In the smaller zone of the Gulag, the divisions are even more elaborate. There are eighteen nutritional norms, from 1A through 9B, each with a specific number of calories—from 2,200 to 900—and its own selection of foods. Some prisoners may spend as much as five rubles a month in the prison store (which sells bread, margarine, candies, jam, and other items), while others have lost that privilege entirely. The length of your exercise period can also vary, from two hours all the way down to nothing. You can send two letters a month, or one every two months, or none at all. (In theory, you can receive an unlimited number of letters, so long as they're not anti-Soviet, supportive of criminal activities, or helpful to a zek who wishes to escape. But in fact very few letters get through.) Technically you're allowed two meetings a year with your family, but years can pass without your seeing them at all.

If you want to continue being the same person you once were, if you want to maintain your religious, political, and national convictions, if you hope to remain a human and decent person who cares about his cell mate, if you intend to know what is happening around you, or if you try to attempt to contact another cell, you will be punished for it. You will receive less food, less clothing, less fresh air, fewer letters. Like a laboratory rat's, your reflexes will be conditioned: a step in one direction means less food; a step in the other means more. Your stomach becomes your guide. As Comrade Marx declared, "Material life precedes spiritual life."

There is an elaborate system of power in the prison: guards, sergeants, the block commander, duty officers, deputy heads, prison head, and, above them all, officials from the "corrective labor" institutions. There are procurators at various levels, and you can complain to them, but you soon understand that they're all part of the same system. In the end, all decisions are made by the organization that put you here—the KGB. Although their representatives in the prisons and the camps have no official function, they summon zeks and talk with them informally, and everything depends on these conversations.

The KGB representative holds all the strings, and his aim is to control your body, your tongue, and your thoughts, as if you were a marionette. The KGB must now achieve what it was unable to attain in the outside world or during your investigation. And when you tire of this miserable life, when you show the first signs of weakness or indecisiveness, or, better yet, fear, the KGB will be the first to know—perhaps even before you know it yourself.

They will invite you for a talk. You think nothing depends on you? On the contrary: they will explain that *everything* depends on you. "Do you like tea, coffee, meat? Would you like to go with me to a restaurant? Why not? We'll dress you in civilian clothes and we'll go. If we see you're on the road to rehabilitation, that you're prepared to help us—

"What? You don't want to squeal on your friends? But what does it mean to squeal? And on what friends? This Russian [or Jew, or Ukrainian, depending on the situation] who's serving time with you, don't you realize what kind of nationalist he is? Don't you know how much he hates you Ukrainians [or Russians, or Jews]? Why, he once told so-and-so . . .

"Incidentally, soon you'll have a meeting with your family. How long has it been since you've seen them? A year? Yes, but right here we have a report that you didn't get up on time, that you were talking after lights out. The administration is supposed to deprive you of your next meeting, but perhaps we can speak with the boss?"

It may be primitive, but it works. It affects some zeks after a month, others after a year, and still others after five years. It works, but not on everyone, and you have to see the desperate persistence with which the KGB fights year after year for each "unsaved" soul.

But why? Why is it so important for the KGB to destroy each individual? Why is it that even if he has spent years in prison and represents no danger to it, the KGB still wants him to confess? There are several reasons. Every prisoner who recants is a potential influence on other zeks to do likewise. And each one who breaks undermines support in the West for human rights. But beyond these self-evident reasons, there is something larger at work here, some kind of psychological imperative, as though the KGB is so lacking in confidence that it has to prove itself again and again, as though even a single holdout undermines everything it stands for and makes a mockery of its intentions.

When I arrived in Vladimir, I had only a vague understanding of this. But I was fortunate, as the KGB soon showed me one of its finished products. After the quarantine section took away all my civilian clothing and gave me a black zek's outfit with my name printed across the chest, they led me to a narrow cell where I saw a shriveled old man with darting eyes and an expression that was both malicious and servile.

"Viktor Anisimov," he introduced himself. I was startled, for Anisimov was one of those zeks whose testimony about conditions in the camps had been used in my case to refute the Helsinki Group reports on camp conditions. I decided to set everything straight right away: "Yes, I know, I read your testimony."

He merely sighed and said, "Yes, they brought me to Orlov's trial, but I shall explain everything later," as he bustled around to help me get settled.

Anisimov had been a thief from his youth and had served several years in criminal camps. I never learned what led him to become a "parachutist," that is, one who moves deliberately from the criminal to the political zone. It could have been a huge gambling debt, or some other serious act, for which, according to the harsh laws of the criminal zone, he could have been murdered, crippled, or raped and turned into a "girl" who must satisfy the desires of any zek who wants him. (Such a person loses the right to sit at the same table with the other zeks in his cell, and must sleep near the toilet.) In these cases the victim sometimes commits a political crime, such as writing and distributing anti-Soviet leaflets in the camp. The prisoner is then immediately sentenced under Article 70 and sent to the political zone, the only place in the entire Gulag where the offender's brethren cannot reach him.

Anisimov had received an additional term in Vladimir Prison for an escape attempt, and when I met him he had already spent about ten years there. About a year earlier investigators had arrived from Moscow and promised to move him to a labor camp if he cooperated. He gave them the testimony they needed, and when he traveled to the trial about ten months later, a KGB worker dropped by to freshen his memory.

When I met Anisimov he was awaiting two verdicts—one to be transferred to a camp and another to restore his paternal rights. (Although he had rarely seen his son, he was very upset when a court decree deprived him of his legal status as a father.) This was a hook on which the KGB kept him dangling, but I soon realized it wasn't the main one.

The main hook for Anisimov was tea, which he received regularly in a variety of ways. Sometimes he was summoned to talks with the local KGB officer, who gave it to him. Sometimes he was taken to see the doctor and "along the way"—or so he claimed—an officer acquaintance gave him "a loan." Occasionally, when a meal was being distributed, a packet would sail through the food trap, and Anisimov would explain that he had dealings with the guard who brought the food.

At first I believed my cell mate's explanations, but I soon noticed that he received two or three of these packets a day, and was dependent on them. When a tea packet arrived, he would hold a mug of water over the toilet bowl with a spoon and heat it over a flame, burning one sheet of paper after another. When the water was boiling he would add half a packet of tea. The result was a cup of *chifir*, an incredibly strong brew with a massive dose of caffeine.

He offered me a taste. I took a small gulp; it was very bitter, and my heart began to pound. Anisimov drank slowly, one swallow at a time, and in the process he would become cheerful, talkative, and animated. At night, however, his feet and head would ache and he would experience chest pains, which caused him to get up and pace back and forth. In the morning he would ask for pills, which they didn't give him. He would begin shouting, and only the next packet of tea would end his suffering.

I had already heard that tea was the local currency in the prisons and camps of the Gulag. Unless you lost the right to buy goods in the prison store because of "bad conduct," you could purchase one packet of tea per month; the rest had to be "earned" by cooperating with the authorities. I was shocked that they could exercise such control over a zek's behavior, and as I witnessed this painful spectacle I was disgusted by those who used *chifir* to reduce this pathetic man to such a state.

Several days later I had my own opportunity to deal with the KGB. I was brought to a room opposite our cell, where a man who seemed to be neat, affable, and intelligent—especially compared with the guards—introduced himself as Obrubov, a representative of the Committee for State Security. I immediately cut him off: "The KGB is a criminal organization that persecutes people for their beliefs. I want nothing to do with you or anyone else from the KGB."

He quickly changed his tone and began to warn me that my life would become a lot worse, but I simply stood up and returned to my cell. I had had enough of the KGB in Lefortovo. Back then, during the investigation, there were things I had still hoped to learn. But now, when I was feeling victorious from the trial, I had no interest in talking with them. I knew that physically my life would now become more difficult, but I hoped that psychologically it would be easier.

At the time, I couldn't imagine what an important step I had just taken, or how favorably it would influence my life and my relations with other zeks in the years ahead. My commitment to have nothing to do with the KGB turned out to be the most serious and most principled decision that I made in the Gulag.

. . .

In Vladimir, the political prisoners' cells were surrounded by the criminals' cells. This arrangement was supposed to hinder contact among the politicals, but it actually made communication easier. The criminals talked with one another every day in the workshops, where they performed "corrective labor," such as processing metal and making shoes. So the guards barely reacted to communication between *their* cells, preferring to devote their energies to keeping the politicals isolated. And the service staff, which consisted of criminals on a more lenient regime who distributed food, washed the floors, and performed other tasks, constantly engaged in business dealings with their fellow prisoners and delivered messages, tobacco, food, and other items from cell to cell. They didn't do this for nothing, of course; the other zeks would pay them with fountain pens, 3-D postcards, nylon stockings, and other items they received in packages from home, which could be resold on the outside by the guards. Although there were plenty of informers among both the service staff and the other criminals, information circulated regularly among the cells of political prisoners.

Two weeks after my arrival in Vladimir a zek slipped me a message along with the miserable portion of daily soup. "Read it so your partner doesn't notice," he whispered.

It was a note from Hillel Butman! I knew from the criminals that two of our Prisoners of Zion, Yosef Mendelevich and Hillel Butman, were in Vladimir, and the idea thrilled me. After all, the Leningrad hijackers' trial of 1970 had provided the impulse for the start of the massive demand for Jewish emigration to Israel, and the names of the first victims were part of our history. For years we had spoken about them in press conferences, arranged hunger strikes in solidarity with them, and demonstrated in their behalf. For me they were more like symbols than real people—and now I was reading a message from one of them!

In his note, Butman told me about himself and the other politicals in Vladimir. Assuming that I was stunned by the length of my sentence, he told me the old joke about the king's servant who was given seven years to teach the king's donkey how to speak. If the servant failed, he would be put to death. The poor man consoled himself with the thought that seven years was a long time. By then, he reasoned, either the king would be dead, or the donkey, or himself. Butman inquired about my trial, and asked why he hadn't heard from Ida Nudel for so long. Not knowing which languages I spoke, he offered me a choice of Russian, English, or Hebrew.

I chose Hebrew. Selecting the words with difficulty, I wrote about myself, my case, and the Soviet Jewry movement in the Soviet Union and the United States. I also had the unpleasant task of informing him that Ida Nudel had been arrested.

And so began an extended correspondence. Soon Yosef Mendelevich was moved to Hillel's cell from the neighboring block, and the exchanges among the three of us became even more interesting. Yosef's Hebrew was rich, like the language of the Bible, and I wasn't even insulted by the reprimand in his first note, where he asked why I had written a letter on the Sabbath. On the contrary: after so many months of isolation, I was delighted that I had once more rejoined *our* life, and was dealing with *our* problems.

I don't mean to imply that communicating between cells was easy. The guard who delivered the first note from Hillel soon disappeared, and we had to find a new form of communication. By using a floor rag to pump the water out of the toilet bowl and then leaning over and sticking your head deep in the toilet and whispering, it was possible to converse with the zeks in the adjacent cell. But you had to be exceedingly careful, as you could easily be seen or heard by a guard and end up in the punishment cell.

Through the toilet telephone I communicated with criminals, and at the workshops they passed on messages about mutual friends and the outside world to other zeks whose cell was within toilet range of Hillel and Yosef.

On the way to the exercise yard, when circumstances permitted, I would throw a small message at a designated spot, or would attach it to a door with a tiny magnet that one of the criminals had given me. Hillel and Yosef's neighbors would pick it up and lower it by a thread from their window to the window of the cell below, where Hillel and Yosef would catch it. This operation was both complicated and dangerous, and sometimes two or three weeks would pass between one message and the next. But such was the communal life of our tiny "Israeli" team that the many obstacles to our discourse only made our lives richer and more interesting.

As important as these links were, from the moment I arrived at

Vladimir I waited with growing impatience for the opportunity to meet with my family and to receive mail. According to the law, every six months I was entitled to a meeting lasting between two and four hours. I was aware that these could be canceled at any time and for any reason, and I knew that some prisoners had gone for years without being allowed to see their families. "Until they give you a meeting," advised my cell mate Anisimov, "sit tight and don't break the rules."

But I refused to listen. I had chosen a certain path, and I wouldn't allow any outside circumstances to influence it. Moreover, if the KGB believed I would act differently in anticipation of a meeting, it would give them leverage over me. I was caught several times while conversing through the toilet bowl; reports were drawn up and I fully expected to be punished. But two weeks after my arrival at Vladimir I was led to a meeting.

Lenya and Mama sat about four meters from me across a table. A female guard was present, who warned that we could speak only about family matters, without a word about politics or prison. We talked about the family and about all the changes that had occurred during the long sixteen months of separation. We discussed Papa's illness and Avital's struggle and her travels. Every time Avital's activities were mentioned the guard interrupted us, so our conversation went in circles but kept returning to the same topic. As the meeting drew to a close I quickly mentioned all those who, judging from the evidence in my case, were in the greatest danger: Slepak, Lerner, Brailovsky, Ulanovsky, Ovsischer, and Nudel.

When the guard announced that our time was up, Lenya stood and said, "Tolya, your name is written on your outfit, right? Look, I also have something written on mine!" He suddenly pulled open his shirt, which he had unobtrusively unbuttoned. Underneath he was wearing a T-shirt with a picture of my face and the words, in English, "Free Anatoly Sharansky!" As I laughed in delight the startled guard pounced on Lenya and pushed Mama and him out of the room.

The officer who came to take me back to my cell said, "Well, now, you're alone for six months. That's tough."

"My sentence will end someday," I replied. "But what about yours? You're spending your whole life in jail."

As I walked back to my block along the sunlit yard I felt intoxicated by the dark green of the trees and the grass. Another six months, I thought, until I see Mama and Lenya again. But what was six months after the sixteen I had spent in isolation at Lefortovo? As things turned out, I had to wait another full year before our next meeting. Still, from the perspective of my new life, it was *only* a year.

From the day I arrived at Vladimir I began to anticipate letters. The knowledge that, at least in theory, I could receive mail that very evening from my parents, my brother, my friends, and perhaps even from Avital completely changed the psychological environment and destroyed my feeling of isolation from the outside world. It soon became obvious, however, that the impatience with which you wait for mail can be dangerous, as the KGB controls whether to give you a letter, confiscate it, or simply conceal it. You must control yourself so that your desire to receive letters doesn't grow into a dependence on the KGB.

The first letters began to arrive a few days after the meeting with my family. Not all of them reached me; for every letter I received, two were confiscated, and many more were simply not reported. And those that did reach me usually had several lines blacked out—including references to the many people in Moscow and abroad who were writing to me. But even this could not conceal the feeling that emerged in the letters from my family—the joy of victory and their hopes for a speedy release.

I was allowed to write home once a month, and the administration was required to inform me within three days whether or not my letter had been confiscated. In August I wrote a letter and waited two weeks to learn whether it had been sent. Yes, it had. I asked for a receipt but was told it wasn't permitted. Two weeks passed without a reply to my letter, then two more weeks. Moreover, letters also stopped arriving from home. I wrote a protest to the post office, to the procurator's office, and to the Interior Ministry. Finally, in mid-September, I was summoned for a talk with the KGB worker.

"I already told you I have nothing to say to you," I said.

"What, you don't want to receive any letters from home?"

I left without answering. So this was the KGB's first test of strength in my new life. In response, I immediately wrote to the procurator general demanding an end to these provocations. I insisted that my correspondence with my family be restored, and threatened to begin a hunger strike. A few days later I was summoned by a prison officer, who dryly informed me that a mistake had been made, and that they had forgotten to inform me that my August letter had been confiscated.

"They didn't forget, they deceived me!"

"Fine, let's not argue about it. You are therefore permitted to write two letters at once instead of one—for August and for September. Normally, this is against the rules, as August has already passed. By the way, your family is worried about you, so let them know you're alive and well."

Everything became clear. In the first confrontation with our family the KGB had retreated. But the surprises did not end there. In the next few days they gave me not only several letters from Moscow but one from Vitaly Rubin in Israel—and two from Avital! During my trial she had seen me every day in her dreams, and many of her friends had also seen me in *their* dreams. She described our apartment in Jerusalem, where you could walk on the roof and look out over the Judaean desert. "When you come," she wrote, "we'll sit up there with our guests." For the next few years I kept that image in my mind. Avital also mentioned that strangers were stopping her in the street and on the bus, and giving her words of support. The final paragraph was blacked out by the censor.

The good life is beginning, I thought, but unfortunately this burst of mail proved to be the exception, not the rule. During the next seven and a half years of imprisonment I received only seven letters directly from Avital, although she wrote twice a week. (Sometimes her letters were passed on through Mama.) And I received no mail at all from my friends outside the Soviet Union, except for two letters from Vitaly Rubin in Israel.

Later, after my release, I learned that tens of thousands of people all around the world had written to me during my imprisonment. None of these letters ever reached me, and I was never informed about their existence. In all probability they were burned.

But although I never received them, it was extremely important that these letters were sent. To the regime, they served as a constant reminder that people all over the world knew about me and cared about my fate. This was why the authorities sometimes retreated, and it probably explains why they kept me alive during my prolonged hunger strike in 1982. The moment the KGB feels that interest in a prisoner is declining it immediately increases the pressure. So these many letters, which themselves did not survive, nonetheless helped to save my life.

16

The Marathon Begins

ALTHOUGH I was sent to Vladimir for twenty months (my sixteen months in Lefortovo counted toward the three-year prison part of my sentence), I was actually there only a few weeks. For on October 8, 1978, all the politicals in Vladimir were shipped off to another, more isolated site. Before I was arrested, it had been relatively easy for us to find out what was happening in Vladimir, as it was relatively close to Moscow, and criminals who were released would often bring information to families of political prisoners. But the more interest the West showed in Soviet political prisoners, the more the regime tried to isolate them. Most of the political camps had been moved from Mordovia to the Urals, and now it was the turn of Vladimir Prison.

"They're moving the politicals!" The word was passed from cell to cell as they began to lead us out into the prison yard and onto the vans. The entire prison shook with the noise of thousands of zeks banging on the doors and shouting encouragement to us. I hadn't realized we enjoyed such love there.

We were taken to a train. Yosef and Hillel were at the opposite end of the car, and ignoring the threats of the guards, we shouted a few Hebrew sentences to each other. We agreed to fight to have them put the three of us in the same cell, but when we arrived at Chistopol Prison, our struggle to live together was brief and unsuccessful.

In the next compartment was Victoras Piatkus, the leader of the Lithuanian Helsinki Group, whom I had once met when our Moscow group organized a press conference for them. Piatkus had been tried the same week as I, and was given ten years of imprisonment and five more of exile for "anti-Soviet agitation and propaganda." This was the third time he had been convicted on the same charge, which made him a "recidivist." So instead of being on a "strict" regime, as I was, he was on a "special" regime—the most severe of all.

In the language of the zeks, Piatkus was a "tiger," as the recidivists wore striped outfits instead of the black ones issued to most political prisoners. This meant we would never meet in the Gulag, for the law stipulates that, like liquids of different densities, prisoners on different regimes do not mix. For the KGB, however, nothing is impossible, and two months later, in Chistopol Prison, the guards led a large, plump, older man in a striped outfit into my cell. His face seemed familiar.

"Victoras?"

"Yes!"

We hugged in joy and disbelief. Although the authorities refused to put me with Mendelevich and Butman, they were also reluctant to place me with other political prisoners because I had, in their words, "a bad influence on the others."

Why did the KGB take the unusual and even illegal step of uniting two zeks on different regimes? Even if I hadn't known how rare this was, I saw how long it took for the guards to grow used to the sight of black and striped zeks in the same cell; their immediate reaction was to correct the mistake of the previous shift and to separate us back into our "own" cells. One possible explanation is that the authorities didn't want us to influence other prisoners. Victoras and I knew each other from the outside world, we were both activists and in the Helsinki Group, and we were both "incorrigible" anti-Soviets. Let them influence each other. This hypothesis seemed to be confirmed by the fact that we remained together for the next sixteen months, until the end of my prison term and my departure for camp. Other prisoners were moved from cell to cell, but only ours remained a fixed point in this constantly changing world.

Among zeks, every deviation from the normal routine is analyzed from the perspective of what is going on in the outside world. In addition, the mind naturally seeks reasons for optimism. Many zeks believed that the authorities were thinking of releasing or exchanging some or all members of the Helsinki Group, especially when we learned that two Soviet spies had been arrested in America. According to this theory, the authorities had separated out Piatkus and Sharansky as likely candidates for an exchange. The two of us were not completely immune to such speculation, especially during our first few days together. But his many years of prison experience, combined with my own psychological independence, saved us from this widespread prison disease.

Chistopol Prison is in the Tatar Republic, 140 kilometers east of Kazan. There were approximately three hundred zeks here, with the politicals grouped together on the second floor of a three-story building. The prisoners worked in their cells at a variety of jobs, including sewing sacks, making shoes, and assembling watches.

Here, as in Lefortovo, the daylight was blocked by iron shutters on the window. The only natural light we saw was in the exercise yard, but in the winter we were often taken out first thing in the morning, when it was still dark, so you could go for months without seeing the sun. The food consisted mostly of watery soup, bread, and porridge.

At Vladimir we had been mixed together with the criminals; at Chistopol we never saw them. But among ourselves there was intense intercell communication. The toilets were the most effective means, but it took a lot of work to remove the water, and the toilets were near the door, where the guards could see you. We also communicated through the radiators. You would press your mug against the heating pipe and speak into it; to listen, you'd turn your mug upside down. A third method was tapping to the next cell in Morse code, and a fourth involved throwing a note into the next exercise yard. A zek caught using any of these methods could be sentenced to the punishment cell or deprived of his next family meeting.

In Lefortovo the zeks were preoccupied with the details of their many interrogations. But in Chistopol, with its inferior library and no interrogations, cell mates had far more contact with each other. There were from two to five zeks in each cell who had to sleep together, work together (in our case, the work was sewing bags), eat together, talk to each other, and use the toilet in front of one another. In a communal cell the closest you can come to privacy is to lie on your cot and turn toward the wall. But then a vigilant guard, looking through the peephole, opens the food trap and yells, "Sharansky! Why are you lying down? It's not bedtime yet!"

Each man was under severe KGB pressure, and all of us suffered from being separated from our loved ones. In other ways, however, we were very different: A loved to smoke while B choked without fresh air. C went crazy from the silence and wanted to sing all the time, but D couldn't bear anything but absolute silence. E was a veteran zek who used the toilet twice a day—you could set your clock by him—while F went whenever the need arose, even while his cell mates were eating dinner.

Moreover, each cell mate had his own convictions, usually very firm ones, for which he had been jailed. One might be a Ukrainian nationalist; another, an activist in the Russian Orthodox Church. Although you shared the same enemy, you couldn't help noticing that you reacted differently to events. Take, for example, the issue of Soviet troops in Afghanistan. "I'm in favor of the Russian influence prevailing in that region, but of course, not by such methods!" said the advocate of Great Russia. "After all, this is an old and historic quarrel."

"All you Russians are the same," replied his cell mate. "You never have enough influence!" Then a real storm broke out in the cell.

When the French Communists joined Mitterrand's government, the Eurocommunist was delighted. He had been jailed for his beliefs, and now he felt vindicated.

"All Communists are swine!" responded an Estonian, "and your Eurocommunists are no better. They issue hypocritical statements about human rights in the USSR, but they're only helping the Soviets worm their way into Europe, just as our Communists did in 1940."

These discussions and arguments were often sparked by news reports in the newspapers or on the radio. Zeks could subscribe to officially permitted newspapers, and there was a radio loudspeaker in each cell. Sometimes it was tuned to Radio Moscow, but there were also special prison programs dealing with corrective labor, or with a competition (always among the nonpoliticals) as to who was the most productive worker. Back in Lefortovo, radios were forbidden, and whenever I entered an office the investigator would quickly shut it off. In Vladimir and Chistopol, for the first time in my life I actually enjoyed listening to the Voice of Moscow, for no matter what was said, it was still the latest news.

Now, a radio is fine if you're alone in a cell, but what if there are several zeks and each has his own idea of what's worth listening to? Then it can be a real time bomb.

Here's an extreme example. Two men shared a cell, and one of them, with whom I later became friendly, used to analyze Soviet propaganda in samizdat publications. He called himself a "nonsens-ologist," and for him, listening to radio broadcasts was a way of continuing his profession. His cell mate, however, had spent a life-time trying to escape from the Soviet regime. For him, listening to the hateful sounds of Radio Moscow was real torture. Both men firmly opposed the KGB—and each other. In the best of circum-stances they would ask the guard to separate them, and he would, with one of them landing in the punishment cell. But sometimes they'd fight, in which case both would end up in the punishment cell and be threatened with an additional term for "hooliganism."

I've heard it said that when astronauts are selected for a long space flight, they are given special tests to determine their psychological compatibility. In the Gulag, I often had the impression that the KGB conducted its own tests and selected cell mates on the basis of incompatibility. This is not merely a matter of sadism, for such an arrangement can also help the KGB break a man. It can intensify his desire to get out at any price, and can turn him into a squealer. It helps the KGB incite national and religious discord between zeks, which can be useful not only at the time but also in the future, when these men are eventually released.

I don't know whether the KGB was thinking along these lines when they placed Victoras Piatkus and me in the same cell, but it would have been difficult to select two more different individuals. Victoras was around fifty, a Catholic from a Lithuanian peasant family who was first imprisoned under Stalin and given six years for "nationalism." He was sent away a second time under Khrushchev for the same crime, this time for eight years. Now he was serving a third term for the creation of the Lithuanian Helsinki Group. His vision of freedom was pre-1939 Lithuania, before the Baltic states became the victims of Stalin's pact with Hitler, and he judged the

West against this ideal. And so, for example, he hated the fact that Western nations allowed the Communists to operate freely in their societies.

Victoras related to people in terms of their age. Since I was considerably younger, and was also serving my first term, he thought I should simply accept his opinions without arguing. But ever since childhood I had dealt with people older than myself, with whom I sometimes disagreed. Fortunately, Victoras's many years in camps had made him open to new information and new ideas.

For Victoras Christianity wasn't a dogma; it was the moral basis for social behavior. During the war his father had hidden two Jews on his farm. Although thirty-five years had passed since then, Victoras told me with pain and anger about the mass murder of Jews by the Germans and the Lithuanians who collaborated with them. "They shot them not far from our home," he recalled. "My aunt prayed and counted prayer beads. She said, 'You pray, too, children, for those innocent souls.'"

At the same time, Piatkus was deeply prejudiced against the Jews who supported the Soviet regime when the Soviets occupied Lithuania and those who helped the KGB in their reprisals against the Lithuanian people. It was a prejudice that was reinforced by years of life in the camps, where many zeks, particularly those who had served time in the 1930s, regarded the Soviet government as "a regime of Zhids."

I told Piatkus about Jewish history. I explained the blood libels in Russia and the Dreyfus Affair in France. I described the Pale of Settlement and the quota system. I taught him about Zionism. I even paraphrased an article by the Zionist theorist Jabotinsky, who wrote that we Jews have had enough of justifying ourselves for every criminal in our midst. Just like any other people, he declared, we have the right to both our heroes and our criminals. Our mission is to build our own country, which is the best contribution we can make both to ourselves and to the world.

Victoras listened attentively. He was an appreciative listener who wasn't afraid of the truth. He was also sympathetic to the struggle to create a Jewish state, which seemed to give him hope for his own people—just as Jabotinsky had predicted. In return, Victoras taught me about the history of Lithuania, its struggle against the Crusaders in alliance with Poland, and its resistance to Russia. He told me about Lithuania's struggle for a national culture, and proudly described the ancient Vilna University.

Almost without noticing it, we would distance ourselves from explosive topics. The following day, however, we would return to them, and each time we understood each other better. I had the feeling that through our conversations we were somehow bringing our two peoples a little closer together.

Before long, Hillel and Yosef were moved into the cell next to ours. Now we could communicate directly through the toilet bowl. When the guard was far from the cell or his attention was distracted, we would exchange prearranged taps and quickly pump the water out of the toilets in both cells with a floor rag. Victoras would stand by the door, protecting me from the peephole and listening for the guard.

We had to speak quickly, of course, usually no more than a minute or two, although on a few occasions we could talk for five minutes without interruption. We spoke in Hebrew, not only because it would be more difficult for the KGB to listen in, but also because using our own language here, in Chistopol Prison, had a special meaning for us. I would practice for the next conversation like a student preparing for his lesson. I worked on simplifying my sentences as much as possible in order to convey with my modest vocabulary everything I wanted to say. The sentences I heard in reply contained not only information but material for the next lesson—new words, expressions, and phrases. I would spend a lot of time repeating each new sentence that reached me from the toilet bowl. I studied the new words, writing them down as soon the conversation ended. To this day there are several Hebrew words, such as *yozmah* (initiative) or *minzar* (monastery), that I use with special pleasure, as they instantly evoke memories of my "lessons" in Chistopol.

These brief moments of conversation were clearly inadequate, so we soon set up a channel for written messages. We used the shower room, where zeks were taken once a week. Hillel or Yosef would stick a piece of soap on the bottom of the bench in the shower room with a message in it, and I would pick it up and leave my reply. A week later they would receive my message. This continued for several weeks until we were caught.

I came out of the shower room as usual, put my soap dish on the bench and had slowly begun drying myself with a towel when the guard suddenly swooped down. There was nothing I could do; he grabbed the soap dish and ran off. He returned a minute later, but now my soap dish held a new piece of soap. "Your soap was handed over for inspection," he informed me curtly.

I didn't have to wait long for the results: an hour later I was summoned to the prison director and given ten days in the punishment cell. When I yelled out this news to my neighbors, the guards added on another day for the yell.

The punishment-cell diet in Chistopol consisted of norm 9B, with bread and water on alternate days. The bread—450 grams of inferior dark bread—was brought to you in the morning, and the three cups of hot water came at intervals during the day. Unfortunately, the water wasn't always hot by the time it reached the punishment cell.

On the "full" days, in addition to the bread and water, they brought you tiny salted sprats in the morning, and you often found yourself eating the whole fish, including the head, tail and fins. The noon feeding consisted of sour cabbage boiled in water, and in the evening they brought a tiny amount of poor-quality cereal. In short, it didn't take long before you started feeling hungry.

Once again I kept busy by singing and by thinking about the past. I also solved chess problems in my head. In Lefortovo, I had seen a few chess magazines, and following an old habit, I memorized some of the problems without solving them. Now, with time on my hands and nothing else to do, I started working on the solutions.

One day I received a visit from Lieutenant Colonel Malofeev, the head of the prison. "You must behave better," he told me, "or we'll keep you here in the punishment cell."

"What's wrong with the punishment cell?" I said. "Someday I'll go to Israel, and people will ask me about the punishment cell in Chistopol. I must be able to answer them."

"That's exactly why we must keep you in prison," he replied. "You're always thinking of bad things to say about us to the West."

"What bad things?" I said. "Are you saying that conditions in Soviet prisons are bad? That sounds like slander!"

"It's impossible to talk with you people," he said, terminating the conversation. Malofeev was used to dealing only with criminals, but when the politicals from Vladimir were sent to Chistopol, he had to be more careful.

When I left the punishment cell, Yosef, Hillel, and I found a new means of communicating. We exercised in adjoining yards, and I discovered two small holes in the two-layered wooden fence that separated us. The boards were approximately twenty centimeters apart and the holes were not at the same height, so it was practically impossible to push through a piece of paper. But if I fastened several pen refills together, I could push them through both holes and wrap a letter around them. All of this was extremely risky, of course, since the guard was watching everyone from above during the exercise period. But except for my stay in the punishment cell, our communication was practically uninterrupted until the middle of April.

One Sunday evening, about an hour before bedtime, the lock clanged in the next cell and I heard the guard say, "Butman, with your things!"

Was he being transferred to another cell? But why so late? Hillel assumed he was being taken to the punishment cell. "Shalom," he called out to Yosef in Hebrew. "I'll probably be back in fifteen days."

That's logical, I thought. After all, he recently tried to send me another note via the shower, and again the guards found it. But to my surprise, Hillel was taken to an empty cell. Early in the morning they sent him on a transport.

"Shalom Yosef, Shalom Natan!" was all he managed to yell out.

What could this mean? Where was he going? From time to time political prisoners were taken away for "prophylactic measures"—to the nearest regional prison or even to their native city, where the KGB "worked" with them. They might arrange a walk around the city or even a meeting with the zek's family. There was even a case where they took a political home on his birthday and told him he could stay there if he was willing to condemn his own views and those of his colleagues.

These scenarios were possible, but I preferred to believe that Hillel was being released. And why not? He had hardly more than a year left of his ten-year term, so perhaps the regime intended to trade him for something or someone.

Victoras and I discussed this situation at length. Knowing how easy it was for people in our situation to believe in illusions, we tried to restrain our imagination. But when we heard over the radio that Carter and Brezhnev had agreed to meet in June in Vienna, our hopes soared. We recalled Carter's statements at the beginning of his presidency in support of Jewish activists and members of the Helsinki Group. At the meeting with my brother I had found out that Carter had defended Soviet human rights activists after we were arrested. I told Victoras that it was impossible for Carter and Brezhnev to meet without some change in our fate.

Victoras disagreed. "It's dangerous to count on the West," he said. "In the Baltic we waited for their support throughout the postwar years as they kept saying, 'Just a little longer.' Hundreds of thousands of people fought in the forests, waiting for help. People would listen to the radio and say, 'The Americans will intervene in a few days.' They called on us to continue the struggle, but they never delivered. This went on for years until the Russians slaughtered us all."

I knew the analogy was flawed and that his charges against the West were not wholly justified. And yet there was something to what he was saying. When it came to dealing with the Soviets, the difference between the rhetoric and the actions of Western governments was often astonishing.

In the meantime, Israel's Independence Day arrived, which is preceded by Memorial Day for the martyrs and the heroes of the Holocaust. In the morning Yosef contacted me through the toilet to say that in a few hours there would be a moment of silence in Israel, and he would signal me when it arrived. At the appointed hour I rose, put on my cap, and turned toward the southeast, toward Jerusalem. I recited my prayer, and Yosef stood close by. I couldn't see him behind the cell wall, of course, but what did a wall matter when at that moment I could sense the beating of hearts even in Jerusalem?

Seven years later I greeted this same moment in Jerusalem. The sirens began to howl, and all cars and pedestrians froze. The Old City was visible from the balcony of my apartment and I gazed at it, but what I saw was Chistopol Prison, and what I heard were the heartbeats of the men who were still there.

We still hadn't learned what had become of Hillel, but in May I received another sign that something unusual was going on, as the authorities began to confiscate all my incoming mail. Letters had been confiscated before, of course, but suddenly all contact was cut off. Almost every day I received a notice about the confiscation of letters because of "coded messages in the text."

The same was true for Victoras, Yosef, and other political prisoners. We comforted one another with the thought that if there was something they didn't want us to know, it was probably good news. But it was difficult to suppress our anger and frustration after each notice of confiscation. After all, a letter was our sole opportunity to feel the warmth of home, the love of dear ones, and the concern of friends.

The next time I wrote to my parents, I reported on the mass confiscation of letters. But the censor refused to let my letter go through. "Don't mention the confiscations," he said.

"Do you affirm that they are legal?"

"Yes."

"Then why is it forbidden to mention this?"

"No one mentions it. Why should you have better conditions than the others?"

I wrote a statement to the procurator, warning that if in fifteen days I did not receive confirmation from home about the arrival of my letter, I would begin a hunger strike. A few days later they informed me that my letter had been sent, and a week after that I received confirmation from home that my letter had arrived. Perhaps now the situation with letters would improve?

At the same time I took another "provocative" step and signed up for a meeting with the head of the prison. (All zeks have the right to request such a meeting, although they don't always get it.) Malofeev was a simple peasant and a poor liar, which was a serious flaw for a man in his position. (Not surprisingly, he soon left for other work.)

I began the conversation about some mundane topic and then suddenly asked, "Incidentally, how long will this scandal with the mail continue? After all, it's not our fault that Butman was released!"

Malofeev blushed with embarrassment and confusion. "I don't know," he stammered, "I don't deal with letters."

There was no astonishment, no attempt to deny that Butman was free! I returned to the cell and waited impatiently for the next opportunity to contact Yosef. When I told him about my conversation with Malofeev, we both rejoiced but were afraid to believe it. As for Victoras, my skeptical cell mate insisted that this was all nonsense, that it was stupid to talk that way with the head of the prison. In a few days, however, the dam burst, and they gave me two letters from home and one from refusenik friends. Many lines were crossed out, but enough remained for me to realize that Hillel was really free.

Moreover, Mama wrote in one of her letters that "I must find time to say farewell to Arina, or else she'll go to her husband and we may not see each other again." Arina was the wife of Alexander Ginzburg, who was tried at the same time as I. Did that mean he was already in the West? The desire to believe waged a fierce battle in my heart with the fear of being deceived.

It took several months before we learned for certain, through a family meeting, that five political prisoners had been exchanged for the two Soviet spies who were arrested in America. A few days earlier, in the framework of the same deal, Butman and four other Prisoners of Zion from the Leningrad Trial, who had only one year left in their terms, were released early. In order to create a favorable atmosphere during the summit talks, the Soviets ransomed their spies, paying in dissidents. I found out much later that President Carter had tried to include Yuri Orlov and me in the deal, but the Soviets had refused. Our terms were longer, our price was higher, and our time hadn't yet arrived. The KGB are experienced merchants who know how to bargain with the West over live goods.

As the summit approached our impatience mounted by the day. The release of our friends was a good omen, and we all awaited the next moves. Were the Soviets planning to sign the SALT II agreement with the Americans? Could America really consent to any serious accords after what happened with the Helsinki Final Act? Would Carter back down from his demands that the Soviets release members of the Helsinki Group who were arrested as American agents? He couldn't, I told myself.

"Don't be naive," said Victoras. "The West can do anything it wants." But he, too, waited eagerly to see what would happen.

The summit took place as scheduled, and the prison loudspeaker reported that Carter and Brezhnev embraced after signing the SALT II agreement. We were astounded. Did this embrace mean a speedy release? The loss of hope? A week passed and then another, with no change in our situation. In the showers, where some zeks thought there was less chance of being overheard, Piatkus delivered the verdict: "Now we must wait at least five years until the entire Politburo dies off."

I couldn't agree with this analysis. The ratification of SALT II lay ahead, and the Soviets would need the vote of every senator. And I knew that our supporters wouldn't stop their struggle for a moment.

I often turned out to be right in my disputes with Victoras, as his ideas about the Western press and Western democracy were far removed from reality. But at other times his experiences as a dissident and as a zek during the Stalin years enabled him to draw the correct conclusion when my own heart was full of deceptive hopes.

Although I wasn't released in the summer of 1979, it turned out to be an exceptionally important period for the remainder of my prison years, as it helped me strengthen myself psychologically before new problems descended on me. In my concluding remarks at the trial I had ended with the phrase "Next year in Jerusalem." I felt that Avital and I had defeated the KGB, that our bond had turned out to be stronger than their absurd logic, and that we were now entitled to a reward for this—a speedy reunion in Jerusalem. My hope was so concrete and so strong that it seemed as if no developments within the prison or in the international arena could shake it.

When this expectation reached its limit after the summit and then quickly declined, something inside me obligingly suggested new reasons for optimism. I found these reasons everywhere, and in the end this frightened me, for you didn't have to look far to see what such a state could lead to. In one of the neighboring cells sat X, a loyal and faithful friend who continually tried to guess what was happening in the outside world. Every day he made new calculations about the significance of some change in the prison routine. Once, during the exercise period, at the risk of landing in the punishment cell, he called out, "For several days now they have been feeding us better, and they conducted a medical examination!

One of the doctors was obviously a KGB man, so it seems they are preparing the dissidents for release."

The next day, however, it seemed to him that the duty officers spoke to him more rudely than to the others, which apparently meant that he was not among the candidates for release.

An even more drastic example was the zek in the corner cell, a former Soviet officer who was arrested for attempted espionage and sentenced to fifteen years. He lived with the certainty that in another day or two they'd exchange him for some Soviet spy in the West. He wasn't affected by arguments such as "But they don't even know you over there! After all, you didn't manage to make contact with them; you only *planned* to spy." He perceived reality very poorly, and spent every day waiting to leave.

These were, I repeat, extreme cases. Still, there were many zeks who slowly, step by step, moved toward this extreme as their world of illusory hopes shielded them from the brutal reality. As their minds became focused on scenarios of freedom they degenerated both intellectually and spiritually.

Hearing stories about such people and eventually observing them up close, I both mocked and pitied them. In the summer of 1979, however, having myself experienced high hopes followed by major disappointments, I realized with horror that I, too, could become the slave of such illusions or, even worse, of external circumstances that didn't depend on me.

During the course of the investigation and the trial I had prepared myself for death and had emerged victorious. No matter how long those sixteen months dragged on, they were one long merciless duel. Now, I told myself, I must become used to another rhythm, the rhythm of a marathon. I had to accustom myself to the thought that this period could last all thirteen years, or more—and possibly even my entire life.

As in Lefortovo, I returned to my memory journeys, recalling all the best and most precious times of my life. Now, however, the goal was different—to feel that I was continuing that life, that I had no other way, that this was the life of a free man rather than of the slave I used to be before I joined the aliyah movement.

While the hope of "Next year in Jerusalem" didn't leave me for a moment, it gradually changed from a denial of my current life to a justification of it. Only now did I understand the full meaning of my final statement at the trial. There was a reason I had felt that I wasn't writing those lines myself, and that some higher force had been guiding my hand.

When I walked in the exercise yard, only the wire grating, the patrolling guard, and the sky were above me. I would sometimes hear the hum of a distant plane, and my eyes would automatically look up and search for it.

"Don't get your hopes up, it's not for you!" the guard, who was familiar with the fantasies of prisoners, would call out.

I knew, of course, that the plane had not come for me. I was free of such illusions and protected against false hopes. In the first letter I received from Avital, however, while I was still in Vladimir, she wrote, "The attitude toward our subject [toward us, in other words] is hot, like that toward Entebbe." The sound of a plane would always remind me of Yoni and his friends, who flew thousands of kilometers to the aid of their people. Each time I heard it hope and faith would well up in me with a new vitality, and I would think: Avital is with me, Israel is with me. Why should I be afraid?

"Iɴ prison, the important thing is to guard your strength and maintain your health." This was the advice I received from a friend a few days before my arrest, and at first I agreed with it. But as a zek I soon came to understand an important principle: if you want to remain the same free man you were before your arrest, if you don't want to wind up in the ranks of the loyal Soviet citizens—those slaves who don't dare express their own opinions, who justify themselves with such simplistic arguments as "I'm just a little man, nothing depends on me," "You can't chop wood with a penknife," or "Why beat your head against the wall"—and if you don't want to become a laboratory rat in the hands of the KGB, *you must resist!*

Does this mean you should disobey the orders of the guards, or that you shouldn't let them cut your hair? Or that you should refuse to cooperate during a search? A tiny number of zeks did resist in this way, and I never condemned them for it. If that's what you must do to maintain your dignity, go ahead. Every man must draw his own line.

But I preferred to adhere to a principle I heard from a fellow Jewish activist during my first demonstration: "We don't fight with the infantry; we fight with the generals." In other words, we wouldn't physically resist the police when they detained us. In prison, I stayed away from arguments with the noncommissioned officers, but I never allowed the officials to influence me. I made it clear that I didn't accept their world and their values, and that my determination to protest their illegal actions was as strong as ever.

It's not widely known that Soviet political prisoners observe their own holidays: October 30 is the Day of the Political Prisoner; December 10 is United Nations International Human Rights Day; and December 24, which marks the anniversary of the Leningrad Trial, is Prisoner of Zion Day. How can these days be commemorated in prison? Usually by a twenty-four-hour hunger strike and a written protest to the Soviet leadership. The KGB will warn, threaten, and punish, but the harsher the threats and the punishments, the more important it is not to give in.

Solidarity with people whose rights have been violated is the natural desire of a free man, which is why the prison rules are designed to suppress it. Contact between cells is categorically forbidden, as are collective letters and statements in defense of other prisoners. But if you want to remain a free man, you must ignore all these prohibitions. You *must* have contact with other zeks. You *must* speak and write to each other. And when something terrible happens to a fellow prisoner, you must immediately support him with a work strike or a hunger strike. Your solidarity won't always help your neighbor, but it will surely help *you* in your opposition to the KGB.

They summoned Victoras after he wrote a declaration protesting the fact that the millions of Soviet Tatars were unable to receive higher education in their native language.

The KGB worker expressed surprise: Did Victoras really want this letter to be sent?

"Yes, of course."

"But you wrote it under someone else's influence!"

Victoras was highly insulted. Who and what could influence *him*, a veteran zek who had served fifteen years in prisons and labor camps? Nevertheless, I was labeled as having "an exceptionally harmful influence on others because of anti-Soviet views and actions," a description that stayed with me in official reports and conversations with the authorities throughout my years of imprisonment.

Although the KGB worker didn't summon me, he once dropped in on our cell and inquired amiably, "How are things, Anatoly Borisovich?"

"Where's the tea?" I replied.

"What tea?" he asked in surprise.

"What do you mean, 'What tea?' Black! Preferably Indian."

"But black tea is prohibited in the prison!"

"It is? But in Vladimir you gave my cell mate three packets a day! All your power is maintained by tea, and you want to talk with me just like that? And what's the legal basis for your presence in the cell? So either hand over the tea or get out!" I said this loudly and rudely, openly mocking him.

My visitor looked fearfully from me to Piatkus and made a hasty retreat. I never saw him again.

Around that time an extraordinary event occurred: a prison officer struck Misha Kazachkov, a political prisoner and a physicist from Leningrad. The nonpoliticals were often beaten, and sometimes their cries, and the protests of their neighbors, reached us from the other end of the corridor. Of course we never actually *saw* these beatings, so the facts couldn't be "confirmed" for the procurator, as we didn't know the names or the cell numbers of the victims. (Officially there was no difference in the rules governing the treatment of criminals and politicals, but with us the authorities were far more careful.)

Nikolaev, the deputy head of the prison, once asked me, "Do you really think we permit ourselves to beat people?" Like a character in a bad film, he liked to walk around in white gloves with a haughty look. Later, during a transport, I was told by the nonpoliticals that in his presence the guards would beat the zeks with particular frenzy. They knew how much he enjoyed it, and sometimes he even joined in.

"What? He takes the club from the guards?" I asked incredulously.

"No—the boss likes to hit only with his fist!"

In 1981, when I returned to Chistopol for the second time, I learned that Nikolaev had deliberately hanged himself, apparently while drunk. The criminals celebrated his death with triumphant slogans on the walls of the exercise yards and the shower room.

Sometimes we politicals saw clubs in the hands of the guards. They were never used in our presence, although I'm sure it wasn't easy for the guards to hold back. On one side of the corridor they spoke with vulgar curses and used their fists and clubs, but when they crossed to our side they were supposed to stop cursing and to address us politely. Although they didn't always succeed, at least they would catch themselves and apologize. We knew that if we ever permitted them to overstep their bounds and address us as they did the criminals, it would be very bad.

To return to Misha Kazachkov: we heard his cries and those of Vladimir Balakhanov, his cell mate. Kazachkov yelled out that the prison official had seriously injured him. Balakhanov yelled that we must demand a doctor to establish whether there was any evidence of the beating. A few weeks earlier Kazachkov had begun a hunger strike when he wasn't permitted to send a letter to his mother. They force-fed him every few days, and as the weeks passed he grew increasingly weaker. We wrote protest statements and called for the procurator, but to no avail. And now the authorities had decided to increase the pressure.

In response to his cries, Victoras and I began to kick the steel door of our cell, yelling, "Call the procurator and a doctor!" One after another, the other cells joined in. Soon the head of the prison and the procurator came to every cell to explain that Kazachkov's complaints were merely a provocation. Naturally, they refused to call a doctor for a medical opinion, and refused to let us see Kazachkov.

Victoras and I decided that to allow the prison administration to get away with this incident could set a dangerous precedent, so we made contact with the neighboring cells and suggested that in three days we all start a hunger strike in solidarity with Kazachkov. We calculated that it would take that long to contact all the cells.

Yosef Mendelevich's cell was at the end of the corridor, but the adjacent cell was empty, which made it impossible to communicate with him directly through the toilet bowl or the radiator. There was another, more dangerous way to communicate—by throwing a note over the wall during the exercise period.

This was on a Saturday, however, and I remembered how unhappy Yosef had been when I had once violated our Sabbath. I decided to wait one more day, which infuriated Victoras.

"And if there's a war, then you won't fight?"

"We would fight, but now we can wait. We have another two days in reserve."

"And what if tomorrow something goes wrong? Can you really risk it?"

"Nothing will go wrong," I replied, hoping it was true. On the following day I managed to send the note to Yosef by dropping it in his garbage pail on the way to the exercise yard, and he joined us. But an hour before we were ready to begin the hunger strike, we had still not managed to contact the cells opposite us. I decided to take extreme measures.

I called out in English to Kazachkov, and told him of our plans and demands. Although the guards tried to drown out our voices by banging on the doors, Misha managed to hear me and passed the message on to his neighbors. The guards drew up a report against me and a punishment was supposed to follow. In an hour, however, our hunger strike began and the authorities were busy with other problems.

On a hunger strike, when they brought you meals, you would refuse to take the bowl and would tell the guard that you were refusing food. (To stay alive, zeks on a hunger strike continued to drink water.) Later, the guards were instructed to bring the food in anyway, to make the experience more difficult. This was the first collective hunger strike of political prisoners in Chistopol with concrete demands made to the authorities; previously there had been twenty-four-hour hunger strikes during our "holidays."

By evening a procurator arrived from Kazan. He entered our cell and threatened us with an additional new term for organizing disturbances in the prison, but we refused to speak to him and demanded a representative from Moscow. For several days various prison officials came to speak with us, alternating between exhortations and threats.

Then the authorities began to yield. Officially, nothing changed, but suddenly we began to receive a few letters from home. Lucky Yosef was given eighteen letters from Israel all at once, which was more than I received from abroad during my entire nine years of imprisonment.

A few days later they brought me a huge pile of books, for zeks have the right to order books from Soviet bookstores. Of course, all of this was done under careful KGB supervision, for even in the larger zone it's difficult to find good books. So there was no hope in asking for Bulgakov or Mandelstam. I had requested hundreds of books on mathematics, the history of religion, and other specialized topics. In a year, not one of them had arrived, but now, in the midst of the hunger strike, they brought me twenty-eight books all at once, with a vague explanation that they had only now been approved.

(There was no question of ordering a Hebrew textbook, so for years I tried to get hold of an Arabic primer so that I could study the second official language of Israel. It didn't arrive until 1984, at which time I drove my cell mates crazy trying to pronounce the various guttural sounds. Although the alphabet is different, some of the Arabic roots are similar to those in Hebrew, which added to my enjoyment. I was able to learn the grammar, but, of course, there was no way of knowing if my pronunciation was correct.)

Finally the administration entered into talks with Kazachkov. They allowed him to reestablish communication with his mother, which enabled him to stop his hunger strike. They also promised that the officer who had struck him would not reappear in the political wing of the prison.

Our hunger strike had lasted for eleven days. Formally, our demand to see a representative of the procurator general's office was never met, but our action accomplished several things: it enabled Kazachkov to end his long hunger strike; it helped us, at least temporarily, to solve a number of minor problems; and, most important, it showed the KGB that there were limits beyond which we would not permit them to go.

About three weeks later I was again sent to the punishment cell. I don't remember the official pretext, but Nikolaev didn't hide the true reason—"for yelling to Kazachkov in a foreign language and organizing the hunger strike." The length of my punishment was also unambiguous—eleven days, to correspond to the eleven days of the hunger strike. But by prison standards this was not an especially high price.

During 1979 I had to switch over to a new pace—the pace of a marathon. The expectation that I would soon cross the finish line was gradually replaced by the realization that I still had a great distance to go. When you suddenly shift gears in a car, the engine reacts with an angry shriek; my body responded in a similar way. In Lefortovo, where I was engaged in a daily struggle against the KGB, I felt fine, but in Chistopol my body seemed to have lost its equilibrium. For several months I suffered from almost constant chills. My heart began thumping and I was tormented by headaches. And yet from the point of view of punishment it wasn't a difficult year, as I was in the punishment cell only twice, and spent the rest of the time on a normal prison diet.

I should point out that the "normal" prison diet includes no milk products, fruit, fresh vegetables, or eggs. We were supposed to receive seventy grams of fish a day, plus twenty grams of sugar, and 450 grams of bread. They were also supposed to give us forty grams of meat, but I never saw any, although it was clear that the soup they handed out at lunch had been cooked with meat. We continually protested that we wanted our meat served separately. Most days the soup included one or two dead flies, and one zek even submitted a complaint about this: In the future, he said, he wanted his flies served separately.

The fish were tiny salted sprats. The vegetables consisted of sour cabbage in the soup and boiled potatoes in the morning that were simply dumped on our plates. The black bread and the sugar, however, were genuine. Still, I continually lost weight. Over the year I lost about ten kilos—approximately 20 percent of my entire body weight. And this was on a "normal" prison diet. Victoras, a large, plump man, lost thirty-six kilos!

In later years, after I had grown accustomed to prison conditions and had spent many months on a reduced diet that officially included no meat or sugar, I was amazed that I could feel hungry and lose weight on a "normal" prison diet. By then, however, I was on a different level of existence, when I weighed less and possessed fewer reserves of energy. In 1979 my body was still making the transition to this new level, which it strongly resisted.

During the summer I developed a serious problem with my eyes, which reacted painfully to any tension. I had only to read for a few minutes when I began to feel a sharp pain in my eyes and then in my head. In prison, of course, losing the ability to read creates a tremendous problem.

I was filled with anxiety and tried to get an examination by a specialist. I wrote home about it, and after several months of effort an ophthalmologist appeared in the prison. His diagnosis was that my eye muscles had grown weak because of a lack of vitamins A,

B, and C. He prescribed some drops but they didn't help at all. Mama sent me a special course of exercises to strengthen the eye muscles. After a month of exercises, which I continued even in the punishment cell, the situation improved slightly and I was able to read for twenty or thirty minutes without a break. But a real improvement came only later, when I was transferred to the camp zone and was finally able to see the sun. A month of natural light was the best cure, but the moment I was back in prison the problem started all over again.

Around this time I received a postcard from Avital, a colorful photograph of Eilat. Every single word had been crossed out by the censor, except for "Dear Tolya," and "Kiss you, Avital." I remember thinking how considerate it was of the KGB to protect my eyes in this way.

In July I also received a letter from Papa, who noted that July had become a time both of joy and of sadness in our family, because it was in that month that Avital and I were married, and that I was convicted in court. Then he wrote about Avital: "I'll never forget how shy and vulnerable she seemed when I first met her. I was actually irritated by her soft speech, and I asked her, 'Why do you speak so softly? I once had a boss who spoke that way so that we would give him respect, but why do you do it?'

"Poor girl, she became embarrassed and blushed, and I felt ashamed for speaking so harshly to such a delicate soul. With time, I can see how mistaken I was. How loudly she can speak when it is needed, and with what excitement people everywhere listen to her."

I grinned as I read these words, which were an obvious reference to Avital's international efforts to call attention to my situation. By some miracle, this particular letter was not confiscated, and none of it was crossed out by the censor. Papa continued: "She appears to be an exceptional woman, reminding me of our biblical grandmother Judith. As a child, I read a beautifully printed book called *Kol Aggadot Yisrael* [The Legends of the Jews]. But now this book is clearly outdated, for it lacks a chapter on Avital."

One winter morning Victoras and I were taken to the exercise yard as usual. But the snow was so deep that it was practically impossible to move. We told the guard to either give us a shovel or have somebody else clear the snow. Just then, as the guard led us back to the cell, another zek came toward me.

"Natan!" he cried.

It was Yosef! He recognized me from photographs that Ida Nudel had sent him in back in 1975. I had never seen his face, but I knew the voice.

We immediately embraced, and the guards had to drag us apart. But neither of us was punished, as it was the guards' mistake in allowing the incident to happen, and they had to keep quiet about it to avoid being disciplined. (The next time I saw Yosef was in 1986, when I landed in Israel. At first I didn't recognize him because he had a beard on his face and a little boy on his shoulders.)

On January 20, 1980, my birthday, I was impatiently waiting for a congratulatory telegram from home. Nothing arrived that day, but I knew that the authorities could always hold a telegram for examination or even confiscate it. But for some reason I felt anxious. I decided to start writing my February letter home, but after a few lines I had to put down the pen because some mysterious force seemed to be preventing me from concentrating. I found myself pacing back and forth in the cell, unable to write.

The next day I received an unexpected surprise—a real birthday gift!—when the official in charge of storing the prisoners' belongings brought me a tiny book with a black binding, my Book of Psalms! I had received it a few days before my arrest, in a letter from Avital that was delivered by a tourist. "I've had this little book a long time," she wrote. "I feel it's time to send it to you."

I had put the tiny Psalm book on the table, and then it had disappeared along with my other belongings after a search by the KGB. At the end of the investigation period it was "returned" to me, but because prisoners were forbidden to have reading matter that was printed abroad, the book was kept in the prison's storeroom.

During the transport from Vladimir to Chistopol, when I was briefly able to get at my things, I had performed a simple "circumcision" on the Psalm book by tearing out the line in English that said the book had been published in Tel Aviv. After all, not every prison guard or KGB worker knew that no Jewish literature was published in the Soviet Union. And since it was entirely in Hebrew, I could pretend that it wasn't a religious work at all. Even so, they didn't return my Psalm book right away. A year passed, and I tried again to obtain it from the storeroom by submitting a request that I be given my collection of Jewish folk songs. And now, suddenly, my—no—*our* Book of Psalms was in my hands.

On the evening of the next day the food trap opened and I noticed a telegram in the hands of Captain Mavrin, head of the political section of Chistopol. But before I could rejoice, he said, "Sharansky, I have a very unpleasant telegram for you."

I immediately understood everything, although I didn't want to believe it. No, I told myself, Mavrin didn't say anything, it only seemed that he did. I took the telegram with trembling hands.

> My dearest son! Yesterday, on January 20, Papa passed away. Please bear this sorrow as bravely as I did. Natasha and I are well, and are with you all the time. I kiss you affectionately. Mama.

It can't be true—it's a KGB provocation! But no matter what I told myself, I knew I no longer had a father. By some miracle I managed to control myself, and in a strange, hoarse, and dead voice, I asked, "May I send a telegram to my mother?"

I heard the standard reply: "Write a request to the head of the prison and we'll see."

I went to my bed, turned toward the wall, and cried silently—for the second and last time since my arrest. The first time was after the trial, but those were tears of relief, while these were the tears of a helpless child. I suddenly felt alone, that nobody and nothing was protecting me. The days that followed were perhaps the most difficult of all my years in the Gulag.

By this time Yosef had been moved to a cell across from mine and we devised yet another means of communication: while pretending to sing Hebrew prayers, we were able to send brief messages to each other. The day after I received Mama's telegram, Yosef sang me belated birthday greetings. But instead of singing back, I simply said *Avi met* (My father died).

A few days later we were walking in adjoining exercise yards when Yosef tried to throw a message over the wall. It hit the fence and fell back. He tried again the next day, without success. On the third day he tried once more, and this time I picked up a tiny rolled-up note, which contained the words to the Kaddish, the Jewish memorial prayer. Yosef had taken a considerable risk, but he knew how important it was for me to be part of our people at this time.

Three weeks later, still immersed in sadness, I wrote to my mother:

It's never easy to pass such terrible landmarks in life, and it's all the more difficult when I am so isolated from you. I have managed to live thirty-two years, day by day, without losing any of the people who were especially close and dear to me, and now I must become accustomed to this completely new situation. I have been severely jolted. It's so painful to touch the open wound and to recall everything connected to Papa—which includes virtually my entire life, starting with childhood, which was so full of his stories. From now on, my birthday will no longer be a happy occasion.

In the daily bustle of life, we don't always realize that the values we hold dear are actually a vessel, filled by our parents and our ancestors. In my case, that vessel was filled not by empty words but by our family's view of the world, with its good-natured optimism and humor, its curiosity about people and events, and its constant readiness to face life's more difficult moments.

Lenya and I were children of your later years, and you and Papa were always afraid that you wouldn't be able to raise us. You took out life insurance to provide for us in case you died, and you continued doing so until they stopped insuring you because of age. But you succeeded in raising us and in transmitting what no insurance could bestow upon us. You used to be sure you wouldn't live to see your grandchildren, but in his last letter Papa jokingly complained that Sasha was already taller than his grandparents, who were clearly no match for him.

Finally, Mama, imagine how much more difficult it would have been if Papa hadn't survived until the summer of 1978 and hadn't found out anything about me. Papa not only lived his seventy-five years in a worthy manner, but he also saw the fruits of his labor and of his life. And this is not granted to everyone.

By the time I wrote this letter I was feeling much stronger and more confident than when I first heard the news. One thing that helped me was a short telegram from Avital that said, simply, "I am with you." Most important of all, however, was the pocket Psalm book, which I had received so fortuitously in my cell. I didn't want to do anything on the day I received the telegram, nor on the following day, but then I remembered the Psalm book. I opened it and immediately decided that I must read all 150 of the Psalms—not sometime in the future, but starting today.

The print was very tiny and my eyes began to hurt as soon as I looked at the text. Ignoring the pain, I began to copy the Psalms in large letters onto a sheet of paper, which took at least an hour for each one. After giving my eyes a long rest, I began translating.

At first I couldn't see a thing. The problem wasn't just with the words, for I knew many of the roots and could guess at many more. But it was sometimes difficult to understand where one sentence ended and the next one began. I was also unfamiliar with many of the Hebrew forms and expressions, but I pressed on to the next Psalm, where I found certain words that had appeared in the previous one, whereupon I compared and analyzed them.

I can't say that I understood the Psalms completely, but I sensed their spirit and felt both the joy and the suffering of King David, their author. His words lifted me above the mundane and directed me toward the Eternal. I especially liked Psalm 23:

> *Though I walk through the valley of the shadow of death*
> *I will fear no evil*
> *For thou art with me . . .*

Who was "thou"? Avital? Israel? God? I didn't try to narrow it down.

And Psalm 27 was a particular comfort to me:

> *Do not forsake me, do not abandon me,*
> *O God, my deliverer.*
> *Though my father and mother abandon me,*
> *The Lord will take me in. . . .*

As a child, as soon as I opened my eyes in the morning I saw a brown statue of a naked man, whose foot was resting on an enormous black head. I didn't know who he was—I knew only that Lenya thought somebody ought to make him a pair of pants. Later,

Papa explained that this was David, standing on the head of Goliath. He explained who these people were, which was my first lesson in Jewish history, religion, and Zionism. And now, in my cell, King David had come to my aid.

Following the Jewish custom of mourning, I refused to shave, and the guards did not insist on it. The guard in charge of shaving and haircuts, a malicious Tatar, showed an unexpected respect for an alien tradition, a tradition about which I knew only slightly more than he did.

For forty days I copied the Psalms and read them. For one thing, it was intense work, which left me almost no time for sad thoughts and painful recollections. For another, the project helped me study Hebrew and fill one of the many gaps in my Jewish education. Finally, through reading these Psalms I thought continually about Papa, Mama, and Avital, about the past and the future, and about the fate of our family. Day after day I reconciled myself with the past, and my feelings of grief and loss were gradually replaced by sweet sorrow and fond hopes.

Although I could not visit my father's grave, I knew I would think of him whenever I came across these marvelous Psalms. They were a memorial in my heart that would stay with me forever.

A few months later Mama wrote to seek my advice about the inscription on Papa's gravestone. Not surprisingly, I turned to the Psalms—in particular, to Psalm 25, with its prophetic reference to Israel, to my father, and to his imprisoned but hopeful son. The verse read: "His soul will rest in peace, for his seed shall inherit the Land."

18

Camp

On March 15, 1980, exactly three years after my arrest, I was scheduled (according to the terms of my sentence) to be transferred from prison to camp. "After prison," Victoras promised me, "camp is like being free. There's fresh air, you see other people, and you can walk around without a guard."

Of course I looked forward to camp, but after three years in prison I even looked forward to the transport. The voyage from one island of the Gulag to another offers a unique opportunity to catch a glimpse of freedom, to come into contact with zeks from various parts of the country, and to hear news and gossip from the entire population of the Gulag, which is large enough to constitute a separate country. If you're lucky, sometimes it's even possible to send a letter to the outside world through one of the nonpoliticals or the soldiers along the way, although here, of course, there's always the risk of a provocation. In any case, after the long, gray years of prison routine, a transport is a real carnival.

Or so it seemed to me. I knew that it could also be a terrible ordeal, with many zeks squeezed into small compartments, with herring and bread to eat and almost nothing to drink, and few opportunities to relieve yourself. But I was prepared to suffer some physical inconvenience in return for the opportunity to see a little of the world.

As I left the cell Victoras and I said a warm farewell. Would we ever see each other again? In the Gulag every parting can be final, and all the more so in our case because he was a striped zek and was therefore sent to a stricter camp. As it happened, I received a greeting from Victoras only once in the following years, from a zek who was in the camp hospital with him. But I was unable to send a message back.

The guards gave me a new set of clothes and put me in the pencil box of a police van, whose common cell was occupied by ten or so criminals. We were driving to Kazan, four hours away, and we would be crossing the frozen Kama reservoir. When they gave me a pair of felt boots, I was pleased by this unexpected generosity. My response was premature, however, as not even the boots could protect me from the forty-below temperatures in the metal pencil box. My feet froze, and it was so tight in there that I couldn't move my hands or feet.

Two soldiers with submachine guns rode with us, along with several officers. They warned the other zeks and me not to talk to one another, but naturally we ignored their orders. When they heard my name, they yelled to me, "Hey, we just heard a whole lecture about you, that you're an American spy!"

"Well, did you believe them?"

They answered evasively: "No, we realized right away that you're a good person."

The sympathy in their voices was obvious, but it was hard to know whether they considered me a spy. Hearing that I knew Andrei Sakharov, they bombarded me with questions: Was he planning to carry out a revolution? What did he intend to do with the camps when he came to power? And what about the Communists— would he shoot them or put them in camps?

They were clearly disappointed when I shouted over the engine noise that Sakharov was opposed to violence, and that he stood for democratic reforms, human rights, and the rights of zeks. Their reaction was "Well, then, he's not serious." But they were eager to know what I meant by "the rights of zeks."

"For example," I replied, "it's forbidden to beat prisoners. Did they ever beat you?"

They all started talking at once. This was when I learned about the sadistic Nikolaev, the deputy head of Chistopol, and about the systematic beating of criminals in punishment cells.

"Do you politicals have pressure cells?" they asked me.

I had heard about pressure cells from friends who had served time among nonpoliticals, but to keep the conversation going I asked these zeks what they meant by this term, and they explained in great detail.

How do the authorities keep several thousand people in submission? And how do they persuade them to give the necessary testimony at an investigation or a trial? There's a simple method: in one of the cells the administration keeps a group of specially selected "bitches," who have turned against their own group of murderers and bandits and have begun working for the authorities. If a zek gets out of line, they transfer him to the "pressure cell," and it's not the authorities' responsibility if the prisoner is then beaten half to death or raped, depending on the orders from above.

In these situations rape has a special meaning. According to the unwritten code of the criminals, a ringleader who is raped, even if he was unconscious at the time, becomes an outcast. He may no longer sit at the zeks' common table in the camp or be a full member of their community. Naturally, the authorities take full advantage of this situation.

I once asked a criminal, "Why are you so unfair to a rape victim? If you were beaten until you lost consciousness and were then raped, what would *you* do?"

He answered without hesitation: "I'd kill the scum who did it and then I'd kill myself."

My traveling companions also told me how the authorities used pressure cells during an investigation. The police might have an unsolved case, which could be a problem because if they didn't solve enough of their cases they would lose their bonuses. The investigators would then check as to whether any of the men arrested in other cases could take the rap for this one, too. Then they would summon the designated candidate and offer him a deal—Plead guilty to this one, too, and we'll send you to an "easy" camp zone. (Not all the camps are in Siberia; there are camps in Georgia, too.) Or they might permit him an additional food package from home, which is often an effective inducement because it's something concrete. As a last resort, they would threaten him with the pressure cell.

Eventually, our conversation returned to politics. "Yes," one of them said, "there are no more men like Stalin."

I was astonished to hear this, for in Stalin's time the Gulag was many times larger.

"Don't you know that after Stalin won the war with the help of the zeks, he wanted to close all the camps?" one of my fellow passengers explained. "But he died before he could arrange this, and they hid his will from the people."

I knew, of course, that Stalin had won the war "with the help of the zeks." I also knew that the zeks were taken from prison and thrown into the most dangerous positions. If they tried to retreat, their own troops would fire on them. Although the men riding with me were young, their comments contained an echo of the ancient and inveterate faith of the Russian people in a benevolent, patriarchal czar—a faith that was apparently even stronger than the memory of the tens of millions who were tortured and killed by Stalin.

In Kazan I spent several days in a local prison while waiting for the transport to the Perm region in the Urals. When they finally came to take me from the prison to the train station, the duty officer cursed and berated his subordinates because there wasn't enough room in the van. "We're supposed to put you in the pencil box," he explained, "but both of them are occupied by women. So you can either wait for the next transport or let me put you in with the others. You'll be near the door, and the soldiers will see to it that the criminals leave you alone."

I quickly replied that I had nothing against this plan. In fact I was longing to travel like a regular zek so that I could talk to my fellow prisoners. But I rejected the soldiers' protection, as I already knew that I had nothing to fear from the criminals so long as the authorities didn't try to turn them against me by giving me special attention.

They stuffed me in last. When the van arrived at the train station, to the accompaniment of the barking of dogs and the shouting of guards, we were quickly led past the astonished crowd of civilians and locked into a railway car. The soldiers on the train were unaware that I was entitled to a separate compartment, but I had no intention of pointing this out.

Twenty-eight zeks and all our possessions were locked into a single cell. The air was stuffy and it was impossible to move. "Soon we'll take the roll call and separate you," we were promised. An hour passed, then another, and a third, as we were given an assortment of excuses for the delay. Meanwhile, I struck up a lively conversation with my neighbors. Some of them knew my name, and again there were questions about Sakharov and Solzhenitsyn, and comments about the good Stalin and the bad Brezhnev.

During this transport, for the first time in my life I began to feel I was no longer a young man. At thirty-two, I was one of the oldest prisoners in my compartment; most of the others were in their early twenties. Two of the zeks were especially young—fifteen and thirteen. The older one had been convicted of robbery, while the younger was in for the murder and rape of a nineteen-year-old student.

"I know your town," somebody said to him. "That place is full of whores! Why did you need to rape her?"

"I wanted fresh pussy," he replied.

"But why did you kill her?"

"So she wouldn't talk," he said, without a drop of regret. He received the maximum sentence for his age—eight years. "My youth is gone," he said with a broad grin, as if he were rejoicing at the start of a new, picaresque stage in his life.

Finally the search began. One after another the zeks were led to the platform at the end of the corridor, and there, under the pretext of a search, they were robbed. You may wonder what can be found on a zek, but the soldiers managed to find plenty. They took a good scarf from this one and a cigarette case from that one. The zeks cursed, but they submitted.

"Why are they going along?" I asked my neighbor indignantly.

"Who knows what else is hidden on them?" he replied. "They take obvious things, but they're not about to cut up books in search of money. They have the power, so it's best not to argue with them."

Finally, it was my turn. The soldiers were pleased because I was carrying several bags and they would make a good profit from me. One of them, a very young fellow who looked no more than sixteen, pushed me toward the platform. He seemed not to be totally corrupted yet, as he pushed me only when his commanding officer was watching. His two friends, however, were more energetic and began to rummage through my belongings.

"I like this scarf," one of them said. Then he spotted the American pen that Mama had sent me (a pen is one of the few things that can be sent to a zek in his semiannual package from home), and added, "And you'll give me this pen, won't you?" Without even looking at me, he put the pen in his pocket.

A few minutes earlier I had decided to play the role of a loyal nonpolitical as long as possible so that I wouldn't be separated from the other zeks. But I failed my first test when I snatched the pen out of his pocket and put it back in my own. "I also like it," I said.

He seemed surprised, and grabbed my knapsack with a brusque laugh. "What have you here? Aha, books! Let's see what you're hiding in the covers." He turned to his companion: "Give me a knife."

I had gone to great lengths to obtain these books, and he was planning to rip them apart. My Psalm book was on top. "That's enough!" I yelled, covering the books with my hand. "If you don't want problems, call the duty officer immediately."

"What, what?" The master sergeant reached for his club.

I was trying to decide whether or not to tell him that I was a political, but the young private solved my dilemma by whispering into the master sergeant's ear. The master sergeant frowned, put down his club, and asked me, "Are you the one whose thick file they brought in? What's your name?" Here he switched from the familiar form of address used with criminals to the more formal *vy*.

"Sharansky."

My name meant nothing to him, but again the young private whispered something in his ear, and without saying a word, the master sergeant ran for the boss.

Twenty minutes later a sleepy and not entirely sober lieutenant arrived. Apparently he had already looked over the first page of my file and had determined that I was a political.

"Are you the one who's a pal of Solzhenitsyn?" he asked.

I didn't want to disillusion him and admit that I didn't know Solzhenitsyn. "Solzhenitsyn or Sakharov, what's the difference? You've been asleep, and you don't know how your subordinates are carrying on."

"Oh, but we're supposed to hold you separately," he said nervously.

"I'm not asking for that. There's not much room and I'm willing to ride with the other zeks. But why are the soldiers allowed to rob us?"

He looked at my things and turned to one of the soldiers: "What does he have here?" Seeing my books, he yelled, "What do you know about books? Can't you see he's a serious person and not some hooligan? Take his things to a threesome."

As we passed by the cell with the criminals I felt guilty that I hadn't held out and couldn't remain with them. "Guys," I called out, "if anyone starts robbing you, call me. I'll write to the procurator general about this!"

But the search was not continued. The soldiers simply took a roll call and distributed the zeks in the various compartments.

The next morning I woke up to the sound of women singing—apparently there were female zeks in the next compartment, who had boarded the train during the night. But what cursing! Soon they were exchanging curses, and then compliments, with the men in the next compartment. Within a few minutes amorous conversations began. The participants couldn't see each other, so they introduced themselves by describing their appearance, then their interests, and finally their personalities. Several couples were carrying on parallel conversations, but gradually they all dropped out until only one couple remained. Eventually they made the transition from love talk to "love" itself, as they each described how they were undressing each other, caressing each other, and so on. In the end, their words (and perhaps their deeds) apparently brought them and their listeners to orgasm.

When we arrived in Perm they put us in a van without a pencil box, so during the short ride to the local prison I was once again in the company of the criminals, where I witnessed another unforgettable scene. As soon as the van started moving, one of the soldiers who were sitting in front of the cell held up a small container of eau de cologne through the grating and said, "I'll give it to you for a quarter." Twenty-five rubles, in another words. In the outside world this item would cost only three or four rubles, but the Gulag has its own prices. Many of the zeks eyed it greedily, but the two young ones were the first to respond. After some noisy bargaining they agreed on twenty rubles. They rummaged through their clothing, trying to conceal the exact location of their hiding places (zeks are forbidden to carry money in the Gulag). Finally, each one pulled out ten rubles.

But the soldier was afraid of being blackmailed, and wouldn't hand over the bottle. "Give me a mug," he said, "and I'll pour it in."

Suddenly the other zeks yelled out, reminding the two of special favors owed to them. First one youngster drank, and then the other, the young rapist and murderer, took a gulp. Several other zeks managed to get a few drops each.

When the drinking spree was over, the soldier tossed in a pack of cigarettes so that the smoke would eliminate any trace of the eau de cologne. By now the young rapist was not only drunk but terribly pleased with himself.

I don't know how all this ended, because as soon as we arrived at the Perm prison they separated me from the criminals. I did, however, manage to speak to some of them later, while we traveled from Perm to Zone 35, where I was supposed to spend the next ten years. These were all zeks who had served time in various zones in the Perm region, which gave me an opportunity to discuss one of the greatest secrets in the Soviet Union: the number of zeks in the USSR.

Although it's impossible to know the answer, those who spend years in the Gulag, especially if they're not as isolated as we politicals, are often able to make some kind of conjecture. During the few hours that I traveled around the Perm region, I calculated that there were over fifty thousand prisoners in the various zones where my traveling companions had served time. It was clear, however, that the number was considerably higher in the Perm region as a whole.

For years I tried to make my own estimates, during which time I encountered several approaches. Some people drew up totals by zones, while others calculated approximately how many had been arrested in their village and the neighboring one, and tried to generalize for the entire Soviet population. I was always amazed by the enormous discrepancy in the results obtained by the two methods: the first estimate was in the range of five million, while the second method yielded an answer on the order of fifteen million.

Not until shortly before my release did I learn of the figure cited by a former senior member of the Supreme Soviet, in camp for bribery, who explained this discrepancy. According to his calculation, there were about five million zeks in Soviet prisons and camps, another two million in investigative prisons awaiting trial or review of their cases, and about six million "chemists."

Our train to the camp arrived late at night in the middle of a raging snowstorm. As usual, a detachment of submachine gunners with dogs had taken up positions around the train. I was the first one off, and an officer, who had arrived especially for me, said, "Go ahead alongside the train."

"Sit!" yelled a soldier from the detachment.

The officer, however, repeated his command: "Go, go."

Stumbling in the deep snow, I barely managed to drag my things a few steps before a soldier lunged at me, brandishing a submachine gun. "Fuck you! Weren't you told to sit?"

As the gun fell on my knapsack and the soldier was about to kick me, the officer yelled, "Leave him alone, he's with me!"

Thank God! The soldier turned away, still cursing. Walking in front of the officer, I saw a line of criminals seated in the snow. A police van was waiting for me, and although the larger cell was empty, they put me in the pencil box and closed the door. An officer, a soldier, and a huge German shepherd were there to guard me. But the lock on the pencil box was broken, and the door flew open as we rounded a turn. The dog immediately lunged at me and pinned me to the wall: his paws were on my shoulders, his bark was deafening, and his clammy jaw was touching my face. The soldier quickly pulled him back. Startled, I began shouting, "What's the matter, you need two guns and a dog for one man? You sadists, call off the dog!"

The soldier was about to reply, but the officer interrupted him. "You sit over there," he said, pointing to the communal cage. The soldier and the dog moved to the cage and the officer closed the door after them. He didn't even attempt to lock my door again, and tried to relieve the tension by saying, "You're right, we also have slip-ups." Meanwhile, I was calmed by the thought that ahead of me was the political zone—the camp—with all kinds of interesting people, perhaps even friends and acquaintances.

They brought me past several rows of barbed wire and into a building that didn't seem much like a prison. "This is the camp hospital," I was told. "You'll spend a few days here in quarantine before you're allowed into the camp."

"After prison," Victoras had said, "camp is like being free." I recalled his words as I fell asleep between two sheets on a comfortable spring bed. After three years of prison, where I had slept, curled up inside a coarse sack, on a bed made of iron rods, two sheets and a set of springs felt like freedom.

When I awoke, it took a long time to realize where I was. I recalled the transport, the screaming and the cursing, and I could still feel the panting of the dog on my face. Although I knew that my life as a zek was continuing, I also had the sensation of some kind of strange and long-forgotten calm, of peace and a sweet Sunday rest. What was going on?

I lay quietly, staring at the ceiling and not moving, afraid of driving away this wonderful feeling. Then I slowly turned my head and understood everything: through the windowpane and the fine wires of the grating the sun was shining into the cell and flooding it with light! For three years I had been living in cells where the only illumination was an electric bulb burning day and night.

I went to the window and gazed out at the bright sun and the blinding white snow. My eyes hurt, but still, what a delight to see the landscape and the noble green pines. How wonderful, I thought. All over the world, bars on a window are a symbol of prison, but for me, accustomed to steel shutters, they symbolized freedom. Even the rows of barbed wire a few meters away did not remind me of imprisonment. They, too, were covered with snow and looked like festive wreaths.

During my ten days in the hospital, Major Osin, the head of Perm 35, and all his subordinates came to lecture me on how to behave. "Let's not waste time," I said. "Why don't you just tell me how to escape?" I joked with them all, except for Major Balabanov, the KGB representative. I simply refused to talk to him.

In the zone, dressed in a new zek's outfit, I moved uncertainly among the snow-covered buildings. There was no guard with me. About three hundred meters away, of course, guards with submachine guns stood on the watchtower, and the entire camp was surrounded by barbed wire. Even so, after prison this area seemed very large.

Perm 35 was no more than a small clearing in the woods, approximately five hundred meters by five hundred meters, surrounded by numerous fences, rows of barbed wire, and electronic warning devices. Rising above it was the "birdhouse," a booth where the duty officer sat with a unit of noncommissioned officers. Unlike the criminal camps, the political zones were quite small. Whereas Perm 10, only a few hundred meters away, contained about three thousand zeks, Perm 35 held between seventy and eighty. After prison, however, this seemed like an entire country. We all slept in the same barracks, stood for roll call in the morning, went to work together, and took our meals in the same dining room. In the evening you could spend your free hour or two over a cup of tea, talking or strolling.

At six each morning a siren rang and you woke up to the call "Get up." In a few minutes the guard passed through the barracks, and anyone still in bed would be reprimanded or punished. Then you washed, dressed, made your bed, and went outside for roll call. After that it was off to the dining room to gulp down the morning swill. Still, camp food was better than prison food, and there was more of it, too. Here, at least, you could see the meat, and whenever a zek returned from the punishment cell, his friends made sure there was extra food for him.

After breakfast we had half an hour of free time before work. Some people dozed, some read (there was a modest camp library), and some drank tea with their friends. In the first few weeks after my arrival from Chistopol I did only one thing: I walked along the narrow path that had been dug out of the deep snow, and enjoyed the low northern sun crawling along the tops of the pines and the watchtowers, which seemed like a natural part of the landscape. I would hear the rustling of the forest and the occasional bark of a guard dog, but mostly I would greedily drink in the fresh air.

In the beginning of May the snow began to melt rapidly. The camp was on a height, and for three or four days the streams gurgled and then green grass appeared. In another month or so the mushrooms would sprout. In the large zone, of course, nobody would touch most of these mushrooms, but in camp they were a real delicacy.

The summers were quite warm, and you could even tan yourself. If you were seen without a shirt, you could be punished for a clothing violation, but an experienced zek would always manage to steal at least a few minutes to expose part of his body to the sun. I strolled on the green grass, breathing in the pure air and strengthening my eyes in the sunlight.

To return to the daily routine. At seven-thirty we went to work. My job was at the lathe, where I turned the cutter. For the first three months I was an apprentice, so they didn't demand quotas from me. But I could see that I wouldn't be able to fulfill the norms, as I had neither the ability nor the strength. They gave me a ladder to make the work easier, and hung an enormous red poster in front of me: GLORY TO LABOR! It didn't help. I still couldn't manage to fulfill the quota, and I decided not even to try. I didn't plan to follow the "path to rehabilitation" in any event.

Officially, we were working for the Sverdlovsk instrument factory. Once, when the deputy for political affairs wanted to arouse our enthusiasm, he showed us a chart indicating where the products of the Sverdlovsk instrument factory were sent—to Bulgaria, Yugoslavia, Egypt, Cuba, and France. I wondered, Does the French worker know that some of the instruments he uses were prepared by the prison labor of, say, Orlov the physicist, Koryagin the psychiatrist, or Kovalev the biologist?

In addition to the lathe shops, there was also a sewing workshop where old men sewed sleeves from morning to evening, as well as a workshop that produced special souvenir chess sets with inlaid pictures and chiseled pieces. I once saw such chess sets in a Moscow store for tourists. Here they were being produced both "for the plan," that is, for such stores, and also "on the side"—for the officers and KGB officials who ordered such souvenirs for themselves and paid with tea. In the camp I once saw a chessboard with a portrait of some KGB colonel instead of the standard inlaid picture. His subordinates had ordered this gift for their boss's birthday, and they paid the zeks with fine Indian tea.

In the evening after work there was another inspection. Then, after supper, you could read a book, look at newspapers, or read letters from home, if you were fortunate enough to receive any. You could also play chess, billiards, or table tennis. Twice a week there were political-instruction classes, but like most of the "anti-Soviet" prisoners, I refused to attend.

Sunday was a holiday, with a cutlet at dinner, which was followed by a film. Sometimes they showed foreign films, and I once saw an excellent French movie, *Deux Hommes dans la Ville* (Two Men in Town), about a criminal who is released for good behavior and ends up killing a policeman. But most of the films were primitive and patriotic, like the war movies I had once mentioned to Solonchenko. Once a year there was a special dinner for the best workers, who then received two cutlets and got to watch an additional film.

In a word, it was just like the large zone. The only difference was that here the officers continually roamed around and picked on people, and occasionally sent them to the punishment cell. Even this, however, did not represent a major deviation from the norms of Soviet life.

Another enormous difference between camp and prison was that here you were entitled to an annual *private* meeting of up to three days with your family. (Officially, these were known as "extended" meetings.) During the entire period of the visit you actually lived with your family in a special room with a kitchen. Naturally, you could always be denied a meeting for "poor behavior," but after three years of prison the authorities decided to act humanely toward me.

On April 26, when the duty officer picked me up from the dining room in the evening and led me to the buildings set aside for meetings, my heart began to thump. Now could I hug Mama and Lenya? The guards undressed me and carefully searched me. Alik Ataev, one of the most meticulous officers in the camp, showed an unusual interest in my rear end.

"Don't confuse us," I joked with him. "I keep all *my* information in my head!" He laughed amiably, as if rejoicing with me on this special occasion. They gave me special clothing, which they would take away again after the meeting, and led me to the room were Lenya and Mama were already waiting.

Finally, after three years—and what years!—we were really together. Before the meeting began, however, the officer informed us that we had only twenty-four hours.

"What do you mean?" I protested. "According to the law it's supposed to be three days!"

"No, the law says between one and three days. It's not clear how long the building will be free."

Mama interrupted: "Major Osin promised us that he would extend it if possible. He simply doesn't know yet."

"So let him extend it if he wants. In the meantime, it's twenty-four hours," said the officer as he left.

Mama continued to argue with him, but I knew the battle was lost. "Let's not waste time," I said. "Let's talk."

"But you must also eat," said Mama.

The meeting took place in a kind of apartment, and in the kitchen Mama had spread out all the foods whose tastes I had forgotten: red and black caviar, onions, cucumbers, parsley, sunflower oil, oranges, lemons, strudel baked by Lenya's wife, Raya, milk, tea, chicken, and much more. Although we weren't allowed to bring letters, books, newspapers, paper, pencil, or pens to the meeting (lest we write messages to avoid the bugging), almost any kind of food was permitted. But you couldn't stuff yourself for a whole year, or even for more than a day or two, so this policy did not affect the KGB's opportunities to manipulate your behavior.

I sat down to eat, but didn't know where to begin. I wanted to sample everything, but most of all I wanted to talk. I began by describing the investigation, and tried to recall all the material that the KGB had gathered about other refuseniks. I then repeated the verdict, which after all these years I had learned by heart. I suspected that one of the witnesses in my case was an informer, but I wasn't sure, and I didn't want the KGB to hear, so I traced the letters of his name on Lenya's hand with my finger.

Now, finally, I was able to speak about every document, to clarify every episode. Not that our conversation was logical or consistent. I interrupted myself constantly, asking questions about Avital, friends, and relatives. Mama ran back and forth from the stove to the table, as she was constantly remembering "something very important." As a result, our conversation progressed rather slowly.

I proposed to Lenya that we stay up all night. Mama, tired but happy, fell asleep in my arms, but my brother and I kept talking, and he told me what had been going on in the world during the three years since my arrest. Among other things, I learned that back in 1977 President Carter had declared that I was never a CIA spy, which was an important statement because American presidents normally don't comment on such matters. Lenya told me that a public tribunal on my case was about to begin in Amsterdam, and I decided to send a greeting. Because nothing could be written down, Lenya repeated the message to himself several times. Here, too, I had no secrets from the KGB.

In the morning, Mama began trying to summon Major Osin, but

the officer on duty replied that nobody was around. I knew it was useless to try to extend the meeting, but Mama had a hard time accepting it. As time started running out, the atmosphere became increasingly tense. This was our last opportunity for normal conversation until—who knew when?

Lenya and I spoke about Papa, and recalled our childhood. Then we skipped to current matters—what to tell Avital and our friends. Soon the duty officer came in and informed us that the meeting was over.

"What? We have another two hours!"

"No," he repeated, pointing to his watch, "your time is up."

The clock in the room had stopped, and we hadn't even noticed. Yes, the meeting was really over, and we embraced for the last time. Mama tried to give me some food—she had brought enough for three days—but it was forbidden. I grabbed the largest apple of the bunch, took a bite, and left with it. In the next room they searched me again, gave me back my other clothes, and allowed me to finish eating the apple there. It was forbidden to bring anything into the zone.

I left the meeting exhausted and burdened by the thousands of questions I had forgotten to ask, which now whirled around in my head. When would our next private meeting be? In theory it was only a year off, but in fact I waited for another five years.

My Fellow Prisoners

19

W HEN I first arrived in camp, approximately half the zeks consisted of *politsai*, or collaborators—men accused of working with the enemy during World War II, either by serving in the German army or by assisting the Nazis in other ways. They had been arrested long after the war was over and sentenced to terms of between ten and fifteen years. One had gone over to the German side in a POW camp, where he was racked by hunger, illness, and the knowledge that his motherland considered him, as a prisoner of war, an "enemy of the people" in any case. Another had been mobilized by the occupying authorities when he was eighteen. A third had been summoned to testify against other collaborators, and eventually they arrested him, too.

Every one of the *politsai* now zealously served and feared his new masters just as he had once served and feared the Germans. In return, the authorities generally trusted the collaborators. Gavriliuk, for example, had once served in the German headquarters. Then, after the war, he worked in his village council. In camp he continued his "staff" duty: he sat in the office, where he drew up work assignments, summoned people to see the boss, and so on.

The collaborators held most of the easy jobs—in the dining room, the hospital, the library, and the storeroom, and in production, although some were too old and sick to work. (There was no retirement age in the camp, and only severe invalids were excused from work.) These older men would wander around the camp and warm themselves in the sun, seemingly with nothing to do. But this apparent idleness was deceptive, and I soon learned that each one had his own particular area of surveillance. As a result, it was almost as difficult to hide or to be alone with somebody in the camp—which seemed so huge after prison—as it had been in the closely watched and bugged cells of Chistopol.

These old men competed fiercely for information, and it was often hard to keep from laughing when I saw one of them scurrying ahead of his comrades so that he could be the first to inform the authorities, for example, that dissidents X, Y, and Z had isolated themselves and were whispering suspiciously in the library. It was difficult to predict what would come of this—whether the duty officer would send his subordinate to disperse the gathering or would order a search of the participants, or whether the KGB would tell the officer not to interfere because they had planned this meeting. But whatever happened, the informer would be rewarded with a package of tea.

Just as the status of an official in the large zone is defined by the level of the special store where he can acquire goods, so, too, the kind of tea a collaborator drank in the camp revealed a lot about him. Second-rate Georgian or Krasnodarsk tea came from the noncommissioned or duty officer; first-rate Georgian tea came from the Godfather (the director for discipline and operative work) or from the head of the operative department; Indian or Ceylonese tea generally came from the KGB.

Another way the collaborators were encouraged was by allowing them to receive extra packages from home. According to the law, after a zek has served half his term he is permitted to receive one five-kilo package of food per year. Naturally, you can lose this privilege for "bad behavior," and in nine years I received only one such package. But for "good behavior" you could be given the right to an additional package. And while the list of products allowed in these packages was strictly delineated, if the KGB gave the order the medical sector would request and the camp director would permit— "for reasons of health"—honey, chocolate, coffee, tea, and cans of meat from home. It all depended on your behavior.

But it wasn't really a matter of the tea or the honey itself, as many of the *politsai* ate very little because of their health, and some couldn't drink the strong tea because of their ulcers. What mattered was the mere *possession* of these items, which were unavailable to the other zeks and made the collaborators feel the regime was treating them well.

There were, however, definite limits to their good fortune. In a burst of frankness one of the collaborators once said to me, "You dissidents have it good. People make noise about you in the West, but the KGB could do anything to us and nobody would say a word in our behalf."

Although the collaborators enjoyed certain material benefits, they couldn't count on anything more. When Prikhvatilo, another *polit-sai* who occupied one of the "privileged" positions in the camp, suffered a stroke and half his body was paralyzed, he lay in the infirmary for two weeks waiting for a doctor from Perm. The doctor never arrived, and Prikhvatilo died without receiving any help from the masters he had served so zealously.

"What, he died?" I asked one of his fellow collaborators.

"He didn't just die, he croaked like a beast!" he replied. The zek who told me this was happy because he had envied Prikhvatilo, who had enjoyed a better position in the camp.

Incidentally, when a dissident dies in a political camp, his family is not permitted to claim the body, which is buried in a grave marked only with an untraceable number. The authorities like to say that his time isn't up, that the corpse cannot be returned because the man's term has not been completed. (Anatoly Marchenko was an exception; because he was internationally known, when he died in Chistopol the authorities allowed his burial in a civil cemetery near the prison.) And before a corpse is taken from the camp, a guard jabs at it with a sharp object to make sure the prisoner is really dead.

Another advantage we dissidents enjoyed over the collaborators was that if one of us was willing to be released at any price, he generally had the opportunity to do so. He could recant, by agreeing to write—or, more accurately, to sign—a letter to a newspaper, or he could renounce his views (or his friends) in a press conference while condemning the harmful influences of "Western secret services." And no matter how many "sins" he had committed, or how often he had been punished for disciplinary violations, if he was willing to recant properly and sling mud at his friends, the regime would pardon him as a father forgives a prodigal son.

A collaborator, however, had no such options. In the camp he could enjoy the best job and the best conditions. He could share secrets with the guards, and sometimes even secretly share a little vodka with them. But he could never be pardoned.

When I arrived in Perm 35, the names of some collaborators were familiar: they were the witnesses for the prosecution who had testified in my case, and who had claimed that conditions in the camps and prisons were fine and that the documents of the Helsinki Group on this issue were slanderous. I remembered the name Udartsev, because he had also been mentioned in the testimony as a victim of the Zionists; Hillel Butman and Israel Zalmanson had allegedly insulted him on his road to rehabilitation.

Udartsev was a large, flabby, gloomy, and perpetually irritable peasant. He had once retreated with the Germans and remained in France, but had later returned, trusting the Soviet amnesty. He was always ready to vent his constant anger, particularly on those who were more intellectual than he—which included almost everybody. His anti-Semitism would erupt in every line he uttered, and the distance from words to fist was always short.

But the camp authorities gave Udartsev excellent references, first, because the KGB always needs a man like him to provoke conflicts, and, second, because as a lathe operator he seemed willing to stand by his machine twenty-four hours a day. Without leaving the lathe for a moment he would lift an enormous quantity of pig iron—sixty kilos at a time—place it on the lathe and go to work. He would go to lunch without removing his dirty apron; he merely lifted his lathe goggles to his forehead. He gobbled down the camp swill and was back at the lathe without having used even half of his thirty-minute lunch break. He usually fulfilled the work quota by 160 or 170 percent.

When I met him, Udartsev had served three quarters of his fifteen-year term. By law, at least in theory, he could count on a so-called provisional early release, as his references were uniformly excellent. But collaborators were never released early, so the authorities needed an excuse to keep him in the camp. They conveniently remembered his anti-Semitism. "You still carry with you a vestige of capitalism—anti-Semitism," he was told by the head of the political section, "whereas our Party follows a policy of internationalism. Your release would have a harmful effect on the Soviet people."

When Udartsev returned to work after hearing this, he was crushed. Once again the Soviet regime had deceived him. His fellow *politsai* didn't hide their malice, as if to say, That's what you get for trying.

Suddenly he turned to me, of all people, for sympathy. "How could they deceive me like that?" he asked.

"You're such a good worker they couldn't stand letting you go," I replied. It was all I could think of to say.

I don't know whether he caught my irony, but he suddenly shouted, "Well, enough! From now on I won't work above the norm!"

The next day a crushed Udartsev stood near the lathe, barely moving his arms. Gradually, however, his movements became faster, and in a few days he was furiously tossing off one finished sheet of pig iron after another, and then running off to the dining room and rushing back to the lathe.

Aside from the collaborators, there were other old men in the camp—Ukrainian nationalists, and Lithuanian and Estonian "forest brothers," who had fled to the woods with their weapons to defend their land from the Soviet occupiers. Many of these zeks were now weak and ill but, unlike the collaborators, they rarely assisted the KGB. Tovkach, one of the few exceptions, had fought in the Ukrainian Insurgent Army and had also been director of the district security service. After hiding for many years he was arrested, broken, and, according to his former companions in the camp, had informed on many people. Now he held a particularly trusted post—that of hospital orderly. Unlike the camp infirmary, the hospital served several zones, and zeks from different camps were kept in isolated compartments to prevent information being leaked from one camp to the next. (Although camp was more open than prison, here, too, the KGB wanted the zeks to know as little as possible.) The hospital orderly, then, was in a unique position, as he met with zeks from different zones. Naturally, this offered special opportunities for informing to the camp authorities.

When I first arrived in the zone, Tovkach became involved in an incident that was the talk of the entire camp. The wife of Captain Kuznetsov, the camp Godfather, worked as a nurse in the hospital, and Tovkach started an affair with her. The zeks who knew about it, and who hated both Tovkach and Kuznetsov, made sure it became public knowledge. A scandal developed, and in the end the Godfather had to resign and leave for another region, while Tovkach was transferred from his hospital job to a position that was only a slight demotion—that of camp barber. Apparently he was more valuable to the KGB than the Godfather himself. But for a nationalist to behave like one of the *politsai* was very unusual.

Harold Kivilio was an Estonian whose cot was next to mine in the barracks. When the secret police came to his farm in the late 1940s to transport the entire family to Siberia, he and his brothers managed to join the partisans, but the KGB sent his parents and sister into exile. One after another, his brothers and friends were killed, and Harold remained alone in the forest. For years he lived with his girlfriend in a bunker. When she became seriously ill, he sent her to friends in the city. When troops combed the forest and surrounded it, he kept moving from one spot to another.

He had become a beekeeper, and each time he moved he carried the beehives on his shoulders. In 1957, when capital punishment was abolished for a brief time, he was one of the last to come out of hiding. He was given twenty-five years of camp and was serving the last two years when I met him. He served with dignity.

Each afternoon when Harold returned from work he would read his two favorite magazines, *Floriculture* and *Beekeeping*. They even permitted him to tend a small flower bed, and although it was forbidden to cultivate any food products in the camp, Kivilio managed to plant grasses that were high in vitamins, which he surreptitiously fed to me and other starved dissidents who had arrived from prison or the camp lockup. Without attracting attention, Kivilio shared his enormous camp experience with me, telling me who could be trusted, how the system of informers worked, and so on.

Years later an eyewitness described Harold's release when his twenty-five years were up. He was met by his sister, his sole surviving relative. As they drove away she began to explain that her children knew nothing about why Harold had served time, and she asked him not to involve her family in politics.

"Stop the car," Harold ordered. As he got out he added, "You don't know me and I don't know you. Good-bye." Refused permission to settle in Estonia, he finally went to a Latvian village and returned to his occupation, beekeeping.

Harold Kivilio belonged to the older generation of "anti-Soviets," but the KGB was more interested in the younger generation of dissidents from the 1970s. These zeks, who were here exclusively because of their political, religious, or national convictions, actively defended their right to these beliefs in the camp as well. They wrote declarations and conducted hunger strikes and work strikes, protesting against the arbitrariness of the authorities or the violation of prisoners' rights.

I knew some of their names from Helsinki Group documents I had given to foreign correspondents in Moscow, and when I arrived in Perm 35 I was eager to meet them. But many of the most active dissidents were transferred to other camps just before I arrived, while others were in the small camp prison, where a zek could be sent for up to six months for "bad behavior," at which point it became virtually impossible to contact him.

About six months after I arrived in Perm 35, several new dissidents appeared in the camp, including Vladimir Poresh, a Russian Christian who became one of my closest friends in the Gulag. Tall and emaciated, and a year younger than I, Poresh was a philologist from Leningrad and an expert in Russian and French literary history. In the late 1970s he had become active in the dissident seminars of the Christian revival in the Soviet Union. He began to publish a magazine and was arrested.

At one point during the investigation he vacillated; apparently he was weighed down by the notion that all authority emanates from God and it is therefore sinful to oppose it—an idea that the KGB forcefully exploits in its work with Christian dissidents. Of course, when a man is afraid and accedes to fear, he will always find arguments to justify his own surrender. But Poresh took himself in hand. In an attempt to soften him up again, the KGB took the unprecedented step of permitting him to meet with a priest to take the sacrament.

The priest arrived with a copy of *Izvestia* that contained a letter of recantation from the well-known dissident priest Dudko, which was written from prison and brought Dudko a speedy release. "Render unto God what is God's, and unto Caesar what is Caesar's," the priest reminded Poresh.

"But if Caesar encroaches on what is God's, then it's forbidden to agree to this," Volodia objected.

The court's sentence was five years of imprisonment plus three years of exile.

The meeting with the priest was not the only example of the KGB's "humanity" to Poresh. During the investigation they permitted his wife to bring him a Bible, and at the trial the procurator used this fact as yet another proof of religious freedom in the USSR. When the trial ended, however, so did religious freedom. They took away Poresh's Bible and he went on a hunger strike. After thirty days they finally gave it back and admitted him to the camp. This was why he was so frightfully thin when I met him.

Presumably, the KGB didn't expect that the two of us would become friendly. The circles Poresh moved in were rather suspicious of Jews, while I had never shown much interest in Russian nationalists. At first I was shocked by the depth of his prejudices.

We were discussing the number of Jews in the Soviet Union; according to official statistics, there are fewer than two million, although the real number is thought to be between two and three million. "There are probably about ten million," said Poresh, half asking, half telling, as he repeated the old line about how all the cozy spots in Russian society were occupied by Jews. He regarded *Kontinent,* the dissident émigré journal of the democratic movement, as a Zionist journal. (So did official Soviet propaganda.) Finally, and most shockingly, he believed that there might be some element of historical truth to the blood libels—an ancient anti-Semitic canard that the Jews made their Passover wine and matzoh from the blood of Christian children.

What on earth could I have in common with such a man? But it was amazing to see how quickly and easily his prejudices disappeared as soon as Volodia found himself in a new environment. This wasn't because he adapted himself to this milieu or lacked firm convictions; Poresh was ready to pay the highest price for his principles. But his natural kindness, together with his faith in mankind, made him open to the world and receptive to new people and new ideas. He seemed genuinely pleased to be rid of his perverse views.

"If I ever publish another magazine for Christian youth," he once told me, "I'm going to include a translation of your Passover Haggadah. You can't imagine what a revelation it will be. Many people think Passover is a festival of sacrificing Christ, and it turns out to be a remarkable hymn to freedom!" In a country where the majority of *Jews* have never read the Passover Haggadah, what could you expect from Christians?

Volodia clearly admired the simplicity of my relations with the KGB and the clarity of my position. He himself was involved in torturous searches: Where exactly is the line between the struggle against evil and the beginning of pride? Where is the line between humility before God and humility before the executioner? Is it moral to lie to the KGB? Is it moral to be kind to a squealer? During his investigation, Volodia suffered greatly from his brief vacillations because of the possible harm he could have caused his friends. In my opinion, however, what really made him suffer was the realization that he was insufficiently prepared for his encounter with evil. Poresh lived with the belief that his every step, his every act, was being weighed and measured above. This quality, together with his kindness and his utmost sincerity, won me over to him.

Vladimir Poresh immediately became a regular member of our "kibbutz," a small group of dissidents who sat together at meals, discussed poetry and literature, and pooled our few possessions, mostly food. Another member of our group was Iura Butchenko, a member of a rock group who had daringly tried to contact the American consulate in Leningrad to discuss the idea of a propaganda campaign via rock music. He was sentenced to eight years for attempted espionage.

One of our frequent guests was Zhanes Skudra, a modest Latvian peasant who had spent several years traveling around the Baltic countries and photographing former churches, cathedrals, and synagogues that had been destroyed or turned into warehouses. He sent the photographs abroad, where an old school friend published them in the form of a diary of occupation. As a result, Skudra was given twelve years for "treason." He was a quiet, timid-looking man who looked as if he would break if anyone so much as yelled at him. He submissively followed orders, but when he was required to attend political lectures, or to participate in a day of voluntary labor, he refused. Quietly, but with dignity, he would reply, "I cannot serve two gods at once, mine and Lenin."

Once, when we were discussing a fellow zek, he said, "I cannot trust him completely; he doesn't seem to believe in God."

I cannot complete this brief survey without mentioning one of the saddest stories I witnessed in all my years in the Gulag. In the camp prison I again met Mark Morozov, the Moscow dissident who, shortly before my arrest, had fed us information from the KGB. Among other things, he had told me that one of my associates was an informer, and that the KGB had recorded one of my conversations with Robert Toth.

In the fall of 1978 Morozov was arrested for disseminating leaflets in defense of imprisoned members of the Helsinki Group. He was brought to Lefortovo and interrogated by Solonchenko and Gubinsky. The investigation was supervised by Volodin.

Morozov had convinced himself that if he was released he could perform such valuable services for the movement that he was completely justified in recanting if it would lead to his freedom. He told his interrogators that he was willing to condemn his former activities, but would say nothing against his fellow dissidents. In return, they promised to release him directly from the courtroom.

To simplify a complicated story, Morozov recanted at his trial. The judge's final question was "Tell us about the activities of your accomplices."

"No," Morozov replied firmly. "That goes against my ethics."

The sentence was five years of exile.

When Mark was led back to prison, he told me, he screamed like a madman, breaking the funereal silence of Lefortovo: "Fakers! Bastards!"

"Mark Aronovich," said Volodin. "Five years of exile for Article 70 is a very light sentence!"

"But you promised me! Now I'll lose my residence permit for Moscow, I'll lose my apartment, I won't be able to live with my daughter, I'll be sent to heavy labor in Siberia—"

"Well, Mark Aronovich, not everything depends on the KGB, you know. If only you had answered the judge's final question, things would have turned out fine. But I promise that you'll live in very good conditions in exile, and that you'll be able to return to Moscow at the first opportunity."

Mark's conditions in exile really did turn out to be exceptionally good, for instead of being sent to some desolate village in Siberia he ended up in a large northern city where he was given work in his specialty area. Even so, Mark felt that since they had deceived him, he was free of any obligations to the KGB.

And so, in spite of his promises to the KGB, he sent information to Moscow about Viktor Orekhov, his secret source in the KGB, who really did exist and who had been uncovered and secretly brought to trial. The news that a KGB agent had apparently been arrested for helping dissidents reached the foreign correspondents, and one of the radio stations—I think it was the BBC—broadcast this information to listeners in the Soviet Union. Even worse, Morozov tried to send an article to the *New York Times.*

The KGB did not forgive him for this transgression, and he was soon rearrested and given an eight-year sentence. In prison he was treated very harshly, and after a particularly fierce beating he completely lost his hearing in one ear.

While we were together in the camp prison Morozov met with the KGB almost every day in an attempt to trade additional information for his own freedom. (He kept hinting to the KGB that he had learned some particularly important secrets from his friend in the agency, while assuring me it was all fluff.) "I won't survive eight years in prison," he told me in writing to avoid the bugging. "My health isn't good enough. But if I can get out, imagine how useful I can be."

"Don't you realize," I wrote back, "that before they release you they'll make you pay up? They won't be satisfied with hints. They'll want real information, or at least a public condemnation of dissidents. You won't agree to that, will you?" I asked hopefully. I was choked with pity and anger.

"Of course not!" he said loudly. "What do you take me for?" Then he continued writing: "Don't you think I can fool them? If I get out, you can't imagine what valuable information I'll have." He was writing to me, but I could see that he was really trying to convince himself.

Then he tried another tack: "I can also report how they're humiliating you. Isn't that important?"

When I replied that no, it wasn't worth selling his soul for, Mark changed his tune again. A few days later he told me that during his exile he had made notes on the location of certain missile bases, and that if he was released he could transmit this information to the

Americans. I wrote back: "In no way should a dissident be linked with espionage. I don't want to know anything about this, and I advise you to forget about it as well."

The next day he came up with yet another reason for being released: "You're right, we must not be connected with espionage, so it's important to destroy the papers I told you about yesterday. I'm the only one who can do this."

And so on. I fear I'm unable to convey the full drama of this man whose sickly appearance couldn't help evoking pity and empathy. Here was a man who was filled with the kindest feelings toward me, and who would willingly give up his own food if he thought I was going hungry. But he was also a man who was feverishly and fanatically seeking to justify his own treachery. Returning from his talks with Balabanov, he would always want to outline some new pretext to explain why he could permit himself what others could not allow themselves. As he tried to defend himself he strayed further and further from reality—or at least the reality in which I was living.

Watching him, I clearly understood what I had sensed intuitively in Lefortovo—that without firm moral principles it was impossible to withstand the pressure of the KGB. If you're a captive of your own fear, you'll not only believe any nonsense, but you'll even invent nonsense of your own in order to justify your behavior. When Mark recounted his conversations with the KGB, it was difficult to know how true his stories were—not because he consciously lied to me, but because there was an enormous gap between what he did and how he perceived his actions. Moreover, from other prisoners I learned that he wasn't reporting everything he told the KGB, and that he was also providing information about his fellow zeks.

Certainly he sought my consent, if not my approval, for his meetings with the KGB. Realizing that the very fact that I knew about these meetings served to make them more legitimate in his eyes, I finally gave him a simple choice: "Mark, either you stop your games with the KGB or we stop communicating with each other."

He was highly insulted. "You don't trust me," he said. "If it was only a matter of my own life, I wouldn't consider it. But the fate of many people depends upon my release, so I must continue."

He really believed this, and thereafter I had nothing to do with him. After further conversations with the KGB, Mark recanted in a written statement. Actually, "recanted" is not the right word, for he condemned not himself but other dissidents, getting even with those who, according to the KGB, had spoken out against him. His physical condition soon improved noticeably, but later his relations with the KGB went through further ups and downs.

By the time he arrived in Chistopol Prison in 1984 his health was completely ruined. He was given a nourishing "hospital" diet, but by then it was of little help. He met with the KGB every few days and often asked his cell mates if they wished him to help them procure a hospital diet also. But nobody wanted his patronage.

In September of 1986, half a year after my release, I flew from Tel Aviv to Paris. The stewardess gave out copies of the *Jerusalem Post*, and I opened the newspaper and read: "The dissident Mark Morozov, who at one point was in prison with Natan Sharansky, died recently in Chistopol Prison."

My heart sank and the blood rushed to my temples as I heard the echo of his voice: "I won't survive eight years in prison; my health isn't good enough." He was right. Had I been fair to him? If I could have played the whole thing over from the beginning, would I have behaved any differently toward Mark? But when I returned in my mind to the reality of the Gulag, I knew there had been no other choice.

20

Oh, Hot Water!

THE summer of 1980 was both the first and the last summer I spent at large in the camp zone, a time when, despite the rules against such things, my diet was supplemented by mushrooms and grasses that defiantly grew wild in the zone. But most of all I enjoyed the sunshine and the fresh air. Although I didn't gain weight, I did grow noticeably stronger and my eyes stopped hurting.

Two things, however, kept me from enjoying life: first, I felt a constant anxiety about Mama and Avital; second, I felt a deep embarrassment, almost shame, with regard to those zeks who were serving time in the camp prison—I was obsessed with the idea of making some contact with them, of sending a greeting, a note, or food, but I found no way to do this.

The authorities were clearly in no hurry to place me in either the camp prison or the punishment cell. On August 1, in connection with the fifth anniversary of the signing of the Helsinki Final Act, I wrote a declaration to Brezhnev demanding free emigration and immediate amnesty for political prisoners. To my surprise, not only did they not punish me for this letter but they even told me it had been sent on to the addressee. Naturally, there was no reply.

On another occasion, several other dissidents and I wrote a series of declarations demanding immediate medical aid for Mikola Matusevich, a member of the Ukrainian Helsinki Group who was in the camp prison. I was accused of organizing "illegal protests," but I was merely deprived of my privileges in the camp store.

In the meantime the camp prison began to empty out. One zek

was sent back to prison, another was transferred to a different zone, and a third was released back into the camp. In early September the KGB remembered me and I was summoned to see Major Balabanov. When I declared, as usual, that I would have nothing to do with his criminal organization, he said, "It's no use, Anatoly Borisovich. So far the administration has been very tolerant of you, but all this can change. The punishment cells are free, and so is the camp prison. What's the matter, are you bored with the sunshine? Do you want to go back to prison?"

How crude he is, I thought, while looking at this large, athletically built peasant with a simple, open, but unkind face. A few days later I was sent to work in the "forbidden zone" to help clean it up. The camp zone was surrounded by many rows of barbed wire. Then there was a strip about six meters wide, and beyond that another fence of barbed wire. This strip was the so-called forbidden zone, and was brightly lit twenty-four hours a day. When there was no snow, it was plowed up so that any footprints would be detected. The guards on the watchtowers kept a vigilant eye on the forbidden zone, and any zek who appeared there was regarded as an escapee. They would yell at him to stop, and if he didn't, they would shoot. Whenever it was necessary to dig a ditch or string up some new wire in the forbidden zone, the guard was told in advance how many people were going in and for how long.

During the time I served in the camp, construction was going on constantly in and behind the forbidden zone. The administration was continually putting up new and stronger fences, new varieties of barbed wire, and more modern security devices. To me all this activity was a fitting symbol for the larger Soviet system, which never stops strengthening its barriers.

There is an unwritten rule among prisoners, dating back to Stalinist times, that no self-respecting zek will enter the forbidden zone. There are two explanations. In Stalin's day, when the authorities wanted to take revenge against a zek, they would send him to the forbidden zone and then kill him under the pretext of halting an escape. This practice had been discontinued, but who knew when it might be revived? The other explanation is moral and ethical: working in the forbidden zone would mean cooperating with the authorities in constructing our own prison.

I didn't think they wanted to kill me, but I expected to suffer some kind of humiliation. Indeed, not long ago one of the old men who went into the forbidden zone to collect some kind of garbage found himself the victim of a "bureaucratic mistake," and stood under the gun for two hours while the camp guard and the administration tried to clear things up. I refused to enter the forbidden zone, and was punished, predictably, by being denied the right to the next meeting with my family.

A few days later they again told me to work in the forbidden zone, and when I refused they sent me to the camp punishment cell. But here I was pleasantly surprised. For one thing, the floors were wood rather than cement, and therefore not as cold. For another, there were no shutters on the barred windows, so daylight flooded in. This is a punishment cell? I wondered joyfully. Moreover, the political zeks, utilizing a vague formulation of the law, had recently obtained the right to read books in the punishment cells, which completely changed the rhythm of time. Of course, it was still a punishment cell, where they tortured you with hunger and cold, took away all your warm clothing, and gave you hot food only every other day. But the possibility of seeing the sun in the mornings and of reading books made it incomparably better than the punishment cells in Lefortovo and Chistopol.

Unfortunately, these improvements didn't last long. Official instructions soon arrived from Moscow: "For the purpose of enforcing strict discipline in the penalty isolator and intensifying its educational effects, convicts are not to be given books or newspapers." And five years later, when I returned to Perm 35, they had installed shutters on the windows.

The punishment cells in Perm 35 were not in the basement, as in Chistopol and Lefortovo. But this had some serious disadvantages, as there were dozens of cracks in the building, and when my cell was on the windy side it was practically impossible to warm up. Pressing a hot mug of water to various parts of my body wasn't much help when I was facing gusts of wind. Fortunately, although the winds in the Urals are strong, they frequently change direction, and after two or three days of being chilled by wind there would be a period of relative calm when I could rest while lying on the wooden floor.

When only a few hours remained before I was supposed to leave the punishment cell, Major Osin, the head of the camp, came to see me. "Sharansky, don't you want to talk to Balabanov?" When I refused, he said, "You're making your own life more difficult, and ours, too."

Then the duty officer appeared and read a new decree: "Sharansky violated discipline by lying down on the floor. Another eleven days of punishment cell."

I wrote a very sharp declaration to the procurator's office, and about ten days later a district procurator came to see me in the punishment cell. I asked him whether the law obligated me, a prisoner, to communicate with the KGB.

"There is no such law."

"Does the KGB have the right to influence the actions of the camp administration?"

"No."

"Nevertheless, neither the KGB nor the administration hides the fact that they're punishing me for refusing to have anything to do with Balabanov."

"You misunderstood something," said the procurator. "The decree on punishment indicates other reasons. You refused to work, and you also violated the discipline of the punishment cell."

"If the KGB's blackmail with the help of the administration does not stop," I said, "I shall be forced to begin a hunger strike."

The procurator left. When I returned to the zone after twenty-six days in the punishment cell, it was November, and deep snow covered the ground. My friends had saved food for me. Also, a number of new dissidents, including Poresh, had come into the camp.

The holiday of Hanukkah was approaching. At the time, I was the only Jew in the zone, but when I explained that Hanukkah was a holiday of national freedom, of returning to one's own culture in the face of forced assimilation, my friends in our kibbutz decided to celebrate it with me. They even made me a wooden menorah—a candelabrum—decorated it, and found some candles.

In the evening I lit the first candle and recited a prayer that I had composed for this occasion. Tea was poured, and I began to describe the heroic struggle of the Maccabees to save their people from slavery. For each zek who was listening, this story had its own personal meaning. At one point the duty officer appeared in the barracks. He made a list of all those present, but did not interfere.

On each of the subsequent evenings of Hanukkah I took out my menorah, lit the candles, and recited the appropriate blessing. Then I blew out the candles, as I didn't have any extras. Gavriliuk, the collaborator whose bunk was across from mine, watched and occasionally grumbled, "Look at him, he made himself a synagogue. And what if there's a fire?"

On the sixth night of Hanukkah the authorities confiscated my menorah with all my candles. I ran to the duty officer to find out what had happened.

"The candlesticks were made from state materials; this is illegal. You could be punished for this alone. And the other prisoners are complaining. They're afraid you'll start a fire."

I began to insist. "In two days Hanukkah will be over and then I'll return this 'state property' to you. Now, however, this looks like an attempt to deny me the opportunity of celebrating Jewish holidays."

The duty officer began hesitating. Then he phoned Balabanov and got his answer: "A camp is not a synagogue. We won't permit Sharansky to pray here."

I was surprised by the bluntness of that remark, and immediately declared a hunger strike. In a statement to the procurator general I protested against the violation of my national and religious rights, and against KGB interference in my personal life.

When you begin an unlimited hunger strike, you never know when or how it will end. Are the authorities interested at that moment in putting a swift end to it, or don't they give a damn? In a few weeks a commission from Moscow was due to arrive in the camp. I didn't know this at the time, but the authorities, presumably, were very aware of it, which probably explains why I was summoned to Major Osin's office two days later, in the evening.

Osin was an enormous, flabby man of around fifty, with small eyes and puffy eyelids, who seemed to have long ago lost interest in everything but food. But he was a master of intrigue who had successfully overtaken many of his colleagues on the road to advancement. During my brief time in the camp he had weathered several scandals and had always managed to pass the buck to his subordinates. I could see that he enjoyed his power over the zeks and liked to see them suffer. But he never forgot that the zeks were, above all, a means for advancing his career, and he knew how to back off in a crisis.

Osin pulled a benevolent smile over his face as he tried to talk me out of my hunger strike. He explained that the duty officer should not have called Balabanov, but that it had happened in the evening when none of the camp officials were at work. Osin promised to see to it personally that in the future nobody would hinder me from praying, and that this should not be a concern of the KGB.

"Then what's the problem?" I said. "Give me back the menorah, as tonight is the last evening of Hanukkah. Let me celebrate it now, and taking into account your assurances for the future, I shall end the hunger strike."

"What's a menorah?"

"Candlesticks."

But a protocol for its confiscation had already been drawn up, and Osin couldn't back down in front of the entire camp. As I looked at this predator, sitting at an elegant polished table and wearing a benevolent smile, I was seized by an amusing idea.

"Listen," I said, "I'm sure you have the menorah somewhere. It's very important to me to celebrate the last night of Hanukkah. Why not let me do it here and now, together with you? You'll give me the menorah, I'll light the candles and say the prayer, and if all goes well I'll end the hunger strike."

Osin thought it over and promptly the confiscated menorah appeared from his desk. He summoned Gavriliuk, who was on duty in the office, to bring in a large candle.

"I need eight candles," I said. (In fact I needed nine, but when it came to Jewish rituals I was still a novice.) Gavriliuk took out a knife and began to cut the candle into several smaller ones. But it didn't come out right; apparently the knife was too dull. Then Osin took out a handsome inlaid pocketknife and deftly cut me eight candles.

"Go, I'll call you later," he said to Gavriliuk. Gavriliuk simply obeyed orders. He was a fierce, gloomy man, and this sight must have infuriated him.

I arranged the candles and went to the coatrack for my hat, explaining to Osin that "during the prayer you must stand with your head covered and at the end say 'Amen.'" He put on his major's hat and stood. I lit the candles and recited my own prayer in Hebrew, which went something like this: "Blessed are You, Adonai, for allowing me to rejoice on this day of Hanukkah, the holiday of our liberation, the holiday of our return to the way of our fathers. Blessed are You, Adonai, for allowing me to light these candles. May you allow me to light the Hanukkah candles many times in your city, Jerusalem, with my wife, Avital, and my family and friends."

Then I repeated the prayer I had composed long ago in Lefortovo. This time, however, inspired by the sight of Osin standing meekly at attention, I added: "And may the day come when all our enemies, who today are planning our destruction, will stand before us and hear our prayers and say 'Amen.'"

"Amen," Osin echoed back. He sighed with relief, sat down and removed his hat. For some time we looked silently at the burning candles. They quickly melted, and the hot wax spread pleasantly over the glass surface of the table. Then Osin caught himself, summoned Gavriliuk, and brusquely ordered him to clean it up.

I returned to the barracks in a state of elation, and our kibbutz made tea and merrily celebrated the end of Hanukkah. Naturally, I told them about Osin's "conversion," and it soon became the talk of the camp. I realized that revenge was inevitable, but I also knew they had plenty of other reasons to punish me.

Several days later, as I was returning from the work zone, the duty officer informed me: "Sharansky! Starting tomorrow you will be transferred to a new job. You'll be a sanitation worker."

On the way to the dining room I wondered with amazement what this could mean. I was working as a lathe operator, which was considered one of the more difficult jobs in the camp. Some of the lathes were even idle, as there weren't enough operators. Workers were also needed in the furnace room and the joiners' shop. Sanitation work, however, was one of the cushiest jobs. You had to make sure the toilets in the zone were working, and, if necessary, you repaired them. If snow had fallen, you had to clear a path to the toilets. That was all; you worked two or three hours a day, and then you strolled around the camp or sat in a special booth to wait for a summons. Usually this job was given to one of the collaborators or to a sick old man with trembling hands who could no longer be put at the lathe or even the sewing machines. The position was currently held by an older man named Ostrovsky.

When I returned to the barracks it was buzzing like an agitated beehive. The old men were clumped together and whispering about something, and looking angrily at me. I soon found out what they were saying: What can you expect from a Jew? He made himself a hero here, he wouldn't talk with the KGB, but he set up poor Ostrovsky. You don't get such a job for having nice eyes.

I went up to Ostrovsky, who was lying down and crying. He had been transferred to a normal, more difficult position.

"Don't worry," I said. "I won't take your job."

I wrote a declaration explaining that I couldn't view my new assignment as anything other than a provocation, and I refused to start as a sanitation worker.

For two days they waited to see whether I would begin cleaning the toilets. I took advantage of the occasion to wander from morning to evening, breathing in the fresh, cold air and enjoying the sun, which clambered along the pine crests. But I knew that my "freedom" was coming to an end. When the two days were up, they sent me to the punishment cell for fifteen days for "refusing to work," and I disappeared into prison cells for years.

The prison and punishment cells were isolated from the rest of the camp by barbed wire and a fence. The barracks contained six cells—four punishment cells and two ordinary prison cells. According to law, a zek can spend no more than fifteen consecutive days in the punishment cell, but I had already learned how casually this law was observed, so I wasn't surprised when the first fifteen days were followed by another fifteen. Then, because I still hadn't started on the path to rehabilitation, I was transferred to six months in the camp prison.

What did this entail? To begin with, I was now in a larger cell. (Actually, it seemed large only because it came after the punishment cell and was intended for four people, while I was alone.) There was a table and a bench, and I was permitted to bring in a jacket, warm underwear, and five books. I was allowed to write one letter every two months. (In the punishment cell I couldn't write any, and in the camp the limit was two a month.)

I was fed every day, and although the norm was lower than in the camp, it was considerably higher than in the punishment cell. I was supposed to receive thirty grams of meat and ten grams of sugar per day (as opposed to fifty of meat and twenty of sugar in the camp, and none of either in the punishment cell), which is known as norm 9A. But I could receive the 9A diet only if I fulfilled the work quota. Every morning I was taken to the adjacent work cell, which contained a sewing machine. The quota was the same as in the zone. If I gave them 345 bags a day I would be given a 9A diet; otherwise, a 9B. Fortunately, since I had never worked on a sewing machine, I was an apprentice for the first month and they fed me "normally." But as soon as this period was over, the meat and the sugar disappeared completely from my rations. My new diet consisted of salted fish in the morning, soup from sour cabbage and a few potatoes at noon, and either oats or barley gruel in the evening. But at least I didn't suffer from starvation.

There were no other zeks in the camp prison or punishment cells, but I didn't suffer from loneliness, especially when there were books. Once, when I was eating lunch, I almost broke a tooth on a raw potato. I was furious, until I sensed that in my mouth was—a message! The guard was watching me just then, and I could hardly wait until he left.

I recognized the handwriting and saw that the note was from Iura Butchenko, a member of our kibbutz, with the latest news from the zone—mostly who had arrived and who had left. Iura had managed to land the job of potato peeler in the kitchen for a few days and had immediately tried to establish contact with me. Unfortunately, this was his first and last successful try. When Butchenko was sent to Chistopol a few months later, the KGB showed him some of the notes he had tried to send me.

In early February 1981 I was invited to talk with a "fellow townsman," a KGB worker who had come from Moscow to see me. He said he brought greetings from many friends.

"We have no friends in common," I said, and went back to my cell.

At the end of February they took away my Psalm book. In reply to my protests a representative appeared from the Perm region's procurator's office, who said, "It is the duty of the state to guard you in prison from harmful influences, so your religious literature has been confiscated with our consent."

I realized that this was serious. I declared a work strike, refusing to enter the work cell until they returned my Psalm book. It turned out that I wasn't the only victim of the struggle against "harmful religious influences." They again took away Poresh's Bible, the same Bible that at his trial had served as proof of religious freedom in the USSR. Volodia declared a hunger strike. He kept it up for seventy days, but they still didn't return his Bible.

In my case they began by denying me meetings with my family for the next two years. Three days later they put me in the punishment cell for fifteen days. When my time was up, they brought me back to my cell in the camp prison.

"Are you going to work?"

"Only when you return my Psalm book."

They added on another fifteen days. One day they gave me norm 9B, and on the next, the off-day, only black bread and a glass of hot water three times a day. It's a good thing that the punishment-cell robe and pants were too big, for by letting down the sleeves I could hide in the arms, draw the robe over my head, and breathe into this shelter of warm air. But with each off-day I felt weaker and weaker. The cell was increasingly cold, especially at night, and I had less and less energy to do exercises or warm myself up. In time I felt a constant weakness, chills, and light dizziness. Again my eyes hurt and I had chest pains. I didn't even pay attention to such trifles as bleeding gums. And so the days passed: thirty, forty, fifty, sixty, seventy-five. To stay within the law, every fifteen days they took me out for an hour.

I had long ago stopped listening to the guards' orders of "Don't lie on the floor!" I tried to assume a position where it was easiest to relax and to mentally escape as far away as possible. Naturally, I thought about my family, but it would be difficult to pinpoint the moment when my memories turned into reveries or even a brief sleep. In effect, my entire struggle for the Psalm book was an attempt to maintain a connection to what was dear to me—Avital, my father, Israel. At the same time, my sleepy mind was increasingly occupied with chess.

Once, in a student chess competition, I lost a game to a professional, a chessmaster who represented Moscow State University. Playing black, I had used a rare and risky variation of the Spanish Opening, which was a favorite of mine during my school years. My opponent responded with a completely new line of play, and when the game was over he told me he had found it in a Swedish chess magazine. I had long ago stopped reading chess literature, even in Russian. Still, it seemed to me that the Swedish innovation was flimsy and there had to be some way of countering it.

Until now, I had never had the time or the desire to think about it seriously. But as I paced in a half-stupor around the punishment cell, trying to sit on the tiny cement stump or lying on the floor, my thoughts often returned to this particular variation. When I thought I had finally discovered a refutation, the following day I found a way to reinforce white's position. Again and again I played one variation after another, analyzing it for ten, twenty, thirty, even forty moves. I don't know how many games I played, but I did finally find a refutation. Of course, that wasn't the important gain; what chess did was help preserve my sanity.

After seventy-five days in the punishment cell, when I was overwhelmed by weakness, the authorities slowed down the pace and began adding on only five days at a time.

"Are you going to work?"

"Only when you return my Psalm book."

"Five days in the punishment cell."

Around this time, after many days of silence, I suddenly began to hear voices, protests, and the opening and closing of doors in the punishment cell farthest from my own. I hesitated for a moment about whether to signal to my new neighbor, as communicating between cells was immediately punished. I myself had little to lose, but why get someone else in trouble? But my ethical dilemma was irrelevant, for as soon as he settled into his new spot my neighbor immediately called out, "Is anyone here?"

Naturally, I answered right away, and learned that the new arrival was Vazif Meilanov. Born in Makhachkala, in the Caucasus, he, being half Lezghian and half Kumyk, belonged to two ethnic

minorities. He was brought up, however, on Russian culture, literature, and history. Although he graduated from the mechanical mathematics division of Moscow State University and was a highly
qualified mathematician, he was equally at home in the humanities.
He had a keen critical mind and a journalistic flair, and some of his
writings had been circulated in samizdat.

In 1980, immediately after Andrei Sakharov's arrest and exile to
Gorky, Meilanov felt that he could no longer remain silent. He went
out to the central square in Makhachkala, where he stood for half
an hour opposite the provincial Party committee with a placard
demanding the release of Sakharov and respect for human rights in
the Soviet Union. This was an unprecedented event in Makhachkala, and at first neither the police nor the authorities knew how to
react. Finally, they invited Vazif into the Party office "to talk." As
a result of this talk he was sentenced to seven years of imprisonment
and two of exile.

Soon after his arrival in the zone, Meilanov declared, "I am not
a slave. As long as there is forced labor in the camp, I shall not
work."

Almost as soon as he entered the camp he was sent to the punishment cell. During the first months of his struggle hardly anyone
believed that Meilanov would stick to such a position.

"We've broken others better than him," declared his guards.

"And we've seen bigger heroes," said those zeks who were unwilling to take such a step themselves but couldn't forgive someone
else for doing so. Four years later the two of us shared a cell, and
he kept just as firmly to his position as in the beginning. Behind him
were years of punishment cells. His health had been ruined, and not
much remained of his former athletic build. In spirit, however, he
was as strong as he had ever been.

Although there were many courageous dissidents in the camps,
Meilanov stood out for his unflinching stubbornness. Vazif made
few friends in the Gulag, and my own policy of being tough with
the authorities but conciliatory with my cell mates was unacceptable
to him. He was demanding of himself, but no less demanding of
others, and he didn't forgive weakness in anyone. He was also
unable and unwilling to conceal his feelings. In short, he was not

an easy cell mate, and the authorities skillfully used this fact in order to provoke conflicts.

But Meilanov and I never had any arguments. Perhaps this is because I have always had a lightning rod in reserve—chess. When I played against him with a one-pawn handicap, we were about equally matched and could get lost in a game for hours.

But now, ignoring the yells of the guards, we began to get acquainted and soon discovered that the best way of communicating was through the top windows of our cells. Overcoming my weakness, I would climb up to the windowsill, grab on to the window with my arms, and hang on for as long as possible. Our conversations lasted for hours, which drove the guards crazy. Unable to stop us by shouting, they hammered on the metal door and created their own jamming. Meilanov and I would keep quiet until they grew tired, at which point we would continue our conversation. We never saw each other, of course, but given Meilanov's temperament I expected to be spending a lot of time with him in the future, which turned out to be the case.

Unfortunately, Vazif could not play mental chess, so as we hung on to the windows of our punishment cells, we kept ourselves busy with mathematical puzzles. Soon we were joined by yet another fan of mathematics and logic when a third punishment cell was occupied by Mark Morozov.

The number of days I'd spent in the punishment cell after the confiscation of my Psalm book was approaching one hundred, and my weakness was becoming more and more pronounced. One morning, after hearing Vazif's voice, I dragged myself to the windowsill. Suddenly everything went blank. I think I yelled something and sat down. I heard a roar in my ears like the sound of the ocean in a seashell. I don't remember anything else.

When I regained consciousness I was lying on the floor. The guard, looking fearfully through the food trap, called my name. Seeing that I had opened my eyes, he said, "The doctor is coming. I called him."

According to the rules, the guard couldn't open the door by himself—he could do it only with a partner. He therefore merely watched me through the food trap until the doctor arrived with an officer. This was fine with me, for it was the first time I was lying on the floor of the punishment cell without breaking the rules. But my head was buzzing and spots were swimming in front of my eyes.

The doctor took my blood pressure and said curtly, "He must lie down."

They opened my "cot," the wooden plank I lay on at night.

"This is forbidden in a punishment cell," insisted the guard.

After several telephone calls, however, they brought me a mattress, pillow, and blanket. But these were the final concessions. Today was an off-day, so for lunch they brought me assorted medicines and a glass of hot water. (Bread was distributed only in the morning.)

Vazif Meilanov burst out, "How can you treat a man and not feed him!"

"He isn't entitled to food today," the guard replied.

"Medical attention is being given only in order to facilitate the process of destroying Sharansky's health," wrote Vazif in his next sharp statement to the procurator, for which he was given still more time in the punishment cell. I lay down, enjoying the comfort of my bed and recalling the testimony of the doctors at my trial: "The assertion that a prisoner can lose consciousness in the punishment cell is a lie. We maintain constant medical supervision over the state of prisoners' health and we don't permit the administration to put sick people in the punishment cell."

I lay in the punishment cell for several days, until the doctor returned and took my blood pressure. I was now "healthy," so they took away the bed. A day passed and again I felt sick. My feet gave way, my head felt heavy, I was dizzy, and worst of all, my heart began to pound like a jerky machine gun. The doctor arrived and was clearly not pleased with my heart and my blood pressure.

"Vegeto-vascular distonia in the form of a crisis," he said. "When there's room in the hospital, we'll put you in. Until then you'll have to be patient."

Fortunately, the next round of five days in the punishment cell ended, and I was moved to the camp prison. Although here, too, the bed was locked up during the day, at least there was a bench, and I lay on it from morning until evening. My heart continued to beat in jerky rounds.

Finally, after a few more weeks, they took me to the hospital.

Until then I just lay on the bench without getting up. When I finally left the camp prison, the fresh air completely intoxicated me, and I began to sway. The noncom grabbed me and called his partner, and the two of them half carried me into the hospital.

The hospital treatment was vigorous: shots for strengthening the heart; a painful injection for lowering blood pressure; shots of vitamins, and, of course, the sumptuous hospital diet—a glass of milk and one hundred grams of meat daily, twenty grams of butter, forty grams of sugar, and two hundred grams of white bread. Moreover, on a hospital regime you are permitted a two-hour walk. During the first week, however, I barely got out of bed. I then began to walk for fifteen or twenty minutes. It took close to three weeks before I began to use the full time that was allotted to me. First my heart stopped jerking and then the chest pains ended.

At the end of my stay in the hospital, a doctor came in and took an EKG. My condition, apparently, was still unstable, with intermittent arrhythmia. The doctor cursed and took one reading after another until it yielded the desired result. "See how well we treated you?" he said. "Your heart is working like a clock! And your mother is making a commotion and complaining. Write to her how we are treating you and how you feel *now*."

Naturally, I wrote home not only about how they were treating me in the hospital, but also about how I had lost consciousness, although I knew that any mention of the punishment cell would automatically lead to the confiscation of the letter, the first one I had written in months.

Meanwhile, they transferred me out of the hospital and back to the punishment cell.

"Will you go to work?"

"Not until you give me back my Psalm book."

"Another fifteen days."

And so on. It was amazing how fast my body shed everything it had gained in the hospital. In a few days the chills returned, and then the weakness, followed by stabbing chest pains and arrhythmia.

Meilanov was now in the adjacent cell, and we were soon joined by Vladimir Poresh. Each of us tried to fight the hunger in his own way. Poresh, who was worn out from lengthy hunger strikes as he tried to regain his Bible, seemed to suffer the most, and would devise clever ways of extracting the maximum benefit from what little food they gave us. He would rip the heads off the sprats and drop them into the mug of hot water, forming a mock cod liver oil. Vazif, by contrast, would consume his food as quickly as possible so as not to think about it. He would eat his bread ration, which arrived at seven in the morning, and survived on water the rest of the time.

My own approach was to divide my food equally between the off-days and the "normal" ones. I soon lost the feeling of hunger, which had returned after the hospital, but I felt my strength ebbing away day after day. Our main weapons against the tortures of hunger and cold were the conversations, arguments, and discussions we held constantly, ignoring the cries of the enraged guards. Each of us would be hanging on to his own window, but because of our declining strength we no longer attempted to shout over the guards. Instead, we spoke during the pauses between their yells.

Meilanov and Poresh were both extremely well versed in literature, and during one of these conversations they got into a debate: Does it really affect the influence of a book if, in his personal life, the author lives out the ideals he writes about? Meilanov was particularly angry at the semidissident Soviet writers. Although their books showed some originality and courage, these authors were continually making compromises with the authorities. They also failed to speak out in behalf of political prisoners. Meilanov maintained that it was important that the lives of these authors conform to the principles of their writing, and he believed the value of their books was diminished by their shameful behavior.

Nonsense, argued Poresh. The world of literature has its own values, which often have nothing to do with the writer's own life. Look at Goethe, who wrote in *Faust* that the only people who really deserved life and freedom were those who struggled for them every day, and yet he served as the Duke's prime minister and dedicated his books to the ruling authorities.

The argument soon became arcane, as both Meilanov and Poresh introduced writers I had never heard of. Although I was emotionally sympathetic to Meilanov's position, I had to agree with Poresh, and pointed out that we knew nothing at all about Homer, while there were still arguments about Shakespeare's identity. In the final analysis, an author's words had to stand on their own. It was an amazing scene: three men, dying of hunger, hanging on to their windows while deeply engaged in a discussion about literary values and the guards doing everything possible to disrupt our conversation.

We also told each other stories, and, like starving men everywhere, one of our favorite subjects was food. I once described how back in October 1976, before my arrest, a group of us were jailed after protesting the beating of fellow refuseniks after a sit-in at the Supreme Soviet. I was taken to a facility near Moscow and detained for fifteen days in a large holding cell with about thirty other men.

Most of my fellow prisoners had been charged with drunkenness and wife-beating, but I became friendly with a swindler named Alosha, who worked in an exotic-food shop and was arrested for selling goods on the sidewalk at inflated prices. Alosha begged me to visit his store after we were released. "Please come," he said, "and I'll give you the best stuff we've got."

I had no real intention of going, but shortly after I was released I happened to be in the center of town, not far from where he worked. When I popped in to say hello, Alosha tried to give me a bag of pomegranates, which were very scarce in Moscow. But I insisted on paying, and explained to Alosha that ever since I applied for my visa I was taking no chances with the law. I wouldn't even cross the street on a red light.

A few days later Joe Pressel from the American embassy came to see me, and I gave him the pomegranates. That weekend I attended a dinner party at Joe's apartment, where his wife served a compote made of Alosha's fruit. Such a dish did not go unnoticed, and one of the guests asked our hostess how she had managed to find pomegranates in Moscow. "It was Tolya," she replied, whereupon I regaled the group with the story of Alosha. "Only in Russia," somebody said. "If an American diplomat wants to serve pomegranates at dinner, he must be friendly with a dissident who shared a jail cell with a swindler."

My friends among the foreign press were continually amazed at how hard it was to find fresh fruits and vegetables. They had traveled and lived all over the world, and they found it incredible that a city as important as Moscow could experience such shortages. Deborah Shipler, whose husband, David, was Moscow bureau chief of the *New York Times,* once said to me, "My kids used to be normal; they cried for ice cream and sweets. But here they go around saying, 'Oh, a cucumber! Oh, a tomato!' "

When I told this story to my two comrades, Meilanov laughed. "Cucumbers? Tomatoes? Here it's 'Oh, hot water!' The phrase quickly became a running joke among us, and three times on each off-day we would cry out, "Oh, hot water!"

When a month had passed since my return from the hospital, I realized that I would soon have to be taken back for treatment. In order not to sit back idly and wait for my next fainting spell, I demanded paper and pen and wrote another sharp declaration to the procurator general of the Soviet Union. This was one of hundreds of declarations and statements that I wrote during my imprisonment, none of which made any difference, except that some resulted in further punishments. But such declarations have a calming effect on a zek; they give him the feeling that his struggle is continuing. Every time you write a statement in which you insist on your views, defend your actions, and accuse the authorities of criminal behavior, you're taking a risk that your situation will become even worse. And so each statement is a way of proving to yourself that you haven't surrendered to fear, and that you, and not they, are the master of your fate.

Surprisingly, this particular statement turned out to be the only effective one I wrote during my entire imprisonment. After writing a draft, I climbed onto the windowsill to read it to Meilanov and Poresh. As usual, Z., the noncom on duty, yelled, "Stop talking!" He then went outside and stood under my window in order to hear better.

This is approximately what I read:

> During my trial in 1978, among those who appeared as witnesses were camp doctors. They testified that punishments given to prisoners could not damage their health, and that the cases mentioned in the documents of our Helsinki Group about prisoners who lost consciousness or suffered heart attacks in punishment cells were pure fantasy. They maintained that such things could never occur in view of the system of medical supervision in the prisons and camps. The same argument was made in documents presented by the Ministry of the Interior and the Health Ministry of the USSR. [I then de-

scribed everything that had happened to me during the past few months.] The punishment cells, which are described in these documents as a special measure that is limited to periods of fifteen days and is necessary to "pacify" particularly dangerous and "rebellious" criminals, are really used systematically to destroy the health of the regime's ideological opponents. My own personal experience proves that the truth lies in our documents, which were declared slanderous, and not in the documents presented by the investigation.

Will my prosecutors declare even now that no such thing ever happened, and could never have happened?

"Of course they will!" said Vazif, laughing. "Look, just imagine that they ask Z., 'Is it true that you starve people in the punishment cells? Is it true that they lose consciousness there? Is it true that you not only don't give them camp food, but that you don't even let them have their own private food, which is located in the adjacent storeroom cell?' What will he answer? That it didn't happen and it can't happen! Isn't that true, Z.?"

The three of us began laughing, and Z. suddenly joined in. "Of course it didn't happen! I didn't notice a thing!"

I couldn't see his face through the bars, but his voice was cheerful, as if to say, Fine, I accept your joke. Imagine my astonishment when about ten minutes later the food trap in the door of my cell opened quietly and Z. pushed in a note: "Where are your provisions in the storeroom and what should I give you from them?"

Ten months earlier, when I moved from the camp zone to the camp prison, all my food provisions, such as sugar and jam, had been taken away. According to the rules, the provisions you received in one regime could not be used in another regime with a lower dietary norm, for that would destroy the "educative effect" of the hunger. But it's forbidden to confiscate these items, which are stored away until the end of your stay in the camp prison.

Z. made his inquiry in writing because he was afraid of being overheard, and while I read the note he didn't let go of it. It was, after all, material evidence of his crime. I wrote an answer on the same slip of paper, which he immediately burned. A few minutes later he returned with a piece of bread (his own, presumably), covered with a thick layer of jam. He also poured several spoonfuls of sugar into a cup of boiling water. With a gesture he indicated that

I should eat before anybody came. I, too, made a gesture—that he should also feed my friends. And so Poresh and Meilanov received the same delicious treat.

For the next two weeks, whenever Z. was on duty we would receive this supplemental nutrition from my reserves. I soon left for another term in Chistopol, but years later, when I returned to camp, I learned that Z. had moved to another city to become a factory worker. That made sense, I thought. Anyone who was capable of violating the rules to give a starving man a piece of bread was obviously not suited for this kind of work.

21

Friends and Companions

A T the end of October 1981, when I was finally let out of the punishment cell, the ground was already covered with snow and the sun was shining cheerfully. I felt pleasantly dizzy from the fresh air. They led me toward the building where a year and a half ago I had my daylong meeting with Mama and Lenya, and I began to hope fiercely. Could it be? No chance! This was no meeting, but a trial—a simplified trial with a judge, two nodders, a procurator. There was nobody to represent the defense. A representative of the camp testified that I had not started on the path to rehabilitation or repented of my crime, and that my behavior was a bad influence on the other prisoners. Twenty minutes later they delivered the expected verdict: three years in prison. This sentence concluded my year of struggle for the Psalm book. In the past twelve months I had spent 186 days in the punishment cell.

This time the transport was very brief, and by November 4 I was back in Chistopol Prison, where for the next three years the shutters on the windows blocked the sunlight from reaching me. A few days after I arrived they brought me thick nylon thread and a loom to weave bags that were used in carrying vegetables.

"Start working."

"What about my Psalm book?"

In another few days they returned my Psalm book. Without rushing, I began to study the simple art of weaving nets.

During the year and a half that I had been away, certain changes had occurred in Chistopol. Malofeev, the director, had retired, and Nikolaev, his deputy, was dead. The real boss—the KGB man in charge of political prisoners—was new, and he instigated a complete change in how they dealt with us.

Previously, the KGB had tried to limit communication among zeks as much as possible, so prisoners were not transferred from one cell to another without a clear reason. But now we were constantly shuffled around, and almost every day somebody was pulled out of one cell and thrown into another. Zeks became acquainted and sometimes separated forever without having managed to spend even a week together. To be sure, this made the monotonous prison life far more interesting, for now, as in the camp, there was an opportunity to meet many more people and to hear their stories.

On the other hand, each move from one cell to another required a major psychological adjustment. A cell is a tiny society whose inhabitants work out a routine where they try to take into consideration each other's habits and weaknesses. They know what topics can be discussed and which ones are best avoided. And suddenly, when you don't expect it, they move you to a new cell. At the other place your cell mate liked to keep the radio blaring; here he can't stand it at all. There he was an outspoken nationalist; here he's a cosmopolitan. There you heard that X was a squealer while Y was a terrific fellow; here you're given equally compelling evidence that it's the reverse.

As a result of the KGB's tactic of moving people around, much more information was transmitted—both among the zeks and to the KGB. Galkin, the KGB representative, used to summon zeks for conversations where he would feel them out, ask how he could help, and offer them the opportunity to enjoy some extra comforts. Then, if the zek tried to hide any or all of the conversation from his cell mates, Galkin would invariably try to press his success, using the fact that he and this zek now shared a secret. If the "negotiations" were successful, the zek's diet improved and so did his ties with home. If they came to a standstill or the zek turned his back, there were always the punishment cells and a reduced diet to help bring him around.

Even if you didn't agree to any compromises with the KGB, the very fact that you talked to them at all made their job easier. Let's say that Galkin summoned a zek and talked with him for two hours.

"What did you discuss?" his cell mates would ask.

"Nothing, really. He told me what films were being shown in the outside world."

A would believe him, B would pretend to believe him, and C would be distrustful. Two days later, in a conversation with C, Galkin would let slip something as if he had learned it from A, which was one way the KGB sowed distrust and doubt among the zeks. If a zek didn't trust his cell mates, he would experience a heightened sense of loneliness and impotence, and would be more inclined to depend on the KGB.

This was when I fully realized what great benefits I derived from my position—not only morally but also in practical terms. Everyone knew that for years I had been refusing to have anything to do with the KGB. Although I was sometimes punished for this position, no matter whom I shared a cell with or how complicated the relationships were between cell mates, I was always above suspicion, which imparted a clarity and a trust to our friendship.

One of the redeeming aspects of prison life is the continuing education it provides in human nature. I met Arkady Tsurkov, or Arkasha, as we called him, while still on a transport. When the police van was taking me from the camp to the train station, we picked up a zek from Perm 37. He was very young (about twenty) and very tall, and wore glasses with thick lenses. He had trouble making his way into the van, and he started losing things that spilled out of his broken suitcase.

"A political?" I exclaimed when I saw that they didn't separate us. After the long months of solitude in the punishment cell and hospital, I was overjoyed at the opportunity to have a direct conversation without having to shout over the yells of the guards.

"Yes, Arkady Tsurkov," he said. As he gave me his hand he stepped on my foot with his huge shoe.

"Sharansky," I replied, wincing at the pain.

"Sharansky? Anatoly?" He began to smile, and as he wiped the lenses of his glasses his expression turned to disbelief. Suddenly he threw himself on me. I thought he was trying to embrace me, but, no, he wanted to read the name on the side of my jacket.

"It's really you!" he said, and then we embraced. Twenty minutes later, when we had already begun addressing each other informally, I offered him the choice of calling me either Anatoly or Natan. He immediately chose Natan.

"Why did you look at my name tag?" I asked.

"I know your face very well. I saw your picture many times, and I even traveled to Moscow to your trial. When they arrested me, I was holding a copy of *Time* magazine with your picture on the cover. But now you look so thin, with bags under your eyes, and I wondered if this was really Sharansky. Oy, what have they done to you?"

"What if it's not me? If they could put you in with a counterfeit zek, they could certainly arrange to give him a jacket with Sharansky's name on it!"

"Yes, that's true," he said. A moment later he burst out laughing.

Tsurkov was a Jewish kid from Leningrad with a talent for mathematics and a complete contempt for literature and other "nonserious" subjects. By the age of sixteen he had become a dissident. Like his closest friends in school, Arkasha was critical of the adult world in general and the Soviet world in particular. By the age of eighteen this criticism inspired them to publish a samizdat magazine where they proclaimed their political credo. The state in its present form, they said, had not justified itself: the economy was on the edge of collapse, and various political and economic reforms were necessary.

Tsurkov regarded Marxism as the basis for his views, and believed that Eurocommunism was the true continuation of Marxist ideology. The articles that Tsurkov and his friends typed up did not call for any violent actions; they merely presented the political views of a group of teenage philosophers. Still, the kids were arrested.

Some recanted and were released immediately; others got out later. But Arkady Tsurkov turned out to be a tough nut for the KGB to crack, and his childish stubbornness was stronger than the adult machinations of the KGB "educators." His own mother condemned him, but his faithful girlfriend from school arranged to marry him after his arrest, which gave him a great deal of support. He was sentenced to five years of camp and three of exile.

In the camp Arkasha was given relatively easy work in the laundry because of his poor health and his exceptionally poor vision, which bordered on blindness. But his stubborn character and his honesty quickly brought him to the camp prison and then to Chistopol. In the camp prison he had shared a cell with Yuri Orlov, and I listened with interest and agitation to the news of my friend, who was desperately trying to continue his scientific research in the camp. From time to time Arkasha would interrupt himself and exclaim with childish rapture, "Wow! I'm the only one who was ever in jail with both Orlov and Sharansky!"

When we arrived in Chistopol we were put in the same cell, and both were given an especially strict regime because of "poor behavior in camp." This meant shorter exercise periods, fewer letters, no meetings, and, most important, a less nutritious ration. For a big young fellow like Tsurkov, who had starved in the punishment cell and the camp prison, this wasn't easy, but our conversations and mathematical studies helped distract him from thoughts of food.

In addition to his poor coordination, Arkasha had trouble seeing where he was going and what he was stepping on. The table, the bench, and the cots were all solidly nailed to the floor, but when Arkasha walked around the cell, everything thundered and shook, and things would fall and sometimes break. Whenever he got up I would scramble onto my cot to get out of the way. I took some consolation in the fact that perhaps I wasn't the world's clumsiest person after all, despite what my friends had been saying all my life.

This was one of the very few times I ever shared a cell with another Jew, and naturally we talked a great deal about Israel, Zionism, and Jewish history and traditions. Arkasha knew little about these subjects and was eager to learn more. But although he was proud of his Jewishness, he believed the Jews should seek universal formulas of a happy life for everyone, and not lock themselves into a narrow, nationalistic framework. Marxism, "unspoiled by Bolshevism," seemed to him like such a formula.

We were separated after two months, but in the years ahead we kept in touch by tapping and by speaking through the toilet bowl and the radiators. Tsurkov's views displeased many of the politicals, as Marxism in any form was highly unpopular in the Gulag, but Arkasha stubbornly followed his own path. He was practically the only zek to make use of the miserable prison library, which consisted mostly of the works of Marx and Lenin. In 1983, however, they confiscated all his notes on Marx. After several unsuccessful attempts to get them back, Tsurkov began a hunger strike. In his statement to the procurator he wrote that a Soviet prison is apparently the only place in the world where you can't keep your own notes on the works of Karl Marx.

After several days on a hunger strike Arkasha began to lose his sight and the authorities decided to back down. By order of the procurator, his notes were returned to him. By this time, Arkasha was nearing the end of his prison term and the start of his exile. Normally in these cases, zeks were taken early to exile, as the transport to the far east or the north could take at least a month. But Arkasha was kept in his cell until the very end of his term. Moreover, almost every day they added on new penalties for "poor behavior," and only five days before his scheduled departure he was given two months of strict regime. They had recently read us a new law that gave the authorities permission to extend prison terms almost automatically. Would Arkady be the first victim?

As the tension mounted he became increasingly anxious. On the day he was supposed to be released—I believe it was October 31, 1983—his agitation could be felt even through the prison wall by those of us in the adjacent cell. Every half hour Arkasha would pound on the door, demanding, "Why am I still here? My term is already over!"

Along with the others, I supported his demand to summon the head of the prison, but I also took my mug and called Arkasha to the radiator. "Calm down," I said. "At the last moment there can be all kinds of provocations."

When they finally took him out of the cell, they once again confiscated his notes on Marx. I found out later that Arkasha began to resist and tried to tear away his notes, but the guards grabbed him and dragged him to the police van. His glasses flew off as he helplessly jerked his arms and legs. They took him to Kazan, the first stop on the transport, where he was sentenced to another two years of camp for resistance to authorities—this time, to a camp with criminals. Earlier, his wife—they had married in prison—had received three years of camp for distributing money to families of political prisoners. Not until the end of 1985 did Arkasha leave camp for exile, where his wife joined him.

Whereas Arkady Tsurkov became a dissident at the age of sixteen, Bogdan Klymchak hated the Soviet regime since early childhood, and with good reason. He was a native of the western Ukraine, and before the war his village belonged to Poland. After the war it went first to Poland but then, after an additional "partition," it became

Soviet. This decided Bogdan's fate, for in front of him was a border he was destined not to cross.

Nationalists throughout the entire western Ukraine resisted the Soviet regime, but slowly, step by step, the Red Army and the NKVD suppressed this resistance. Bogdan was too young to participate in this struggle, but when a monument to some Soviet leader was blown up in the next town, his oldest brother was among those arrested. His entire family, along with other "enemies of the people," was transported to Siberia.

Bogdan remembered this move as the most terrible nightmare of his life. An enormous train car was packed full of women, children, and old men. They spent a month in this car: here they ate, relieved themselves, died (the corpses were stacked in a corner), and gave birth (the women would tear their shirts to make diapers for the babies).

The families were brought to a distant forest and thrown off into the snow. Nearby were barracks, saws, and axes. "Cut down the trees," they were told, "deliver them to the state, receive money for your labor, search for subsistence." In other words, fight for your life.

Some died; others, including Bogdan's family, survived. Several years later, during the Khrushchev thaw, his brother was released from camp. The authorities agreed he had been arrested by mistake, which meant that his family could now return to the Ukraine. But by then Bogdan was starting a local technical school, so he delayed his departure. His anti-Soviet feelings soon became known, however, and he was arrested and sentenced to six years in political camps.

In the 1960s Klymchak finally returned to the Ukraine. He dreamed of settling on his own farm, but there were no longer any private plots and he despised the idea of a Soviet collective farm. He was driven to fury by the Russian language, which was increasingly driving out Ukrainian, and he began to hatch the idea of escaping, the farther the better—to Canada or America, where he could grow his own vegetables, raise cattle, and write. Although he was the son of a peasant, with no pretensions as an intellectual, Klymchak wrote science-fiction stories in Ukrainian.

For many years Bogdan harbored his plans for escape. He went on scouting trips to the borders of the Soviet empire, studied maps, and became familiar with train schedules and the movements of border patrols. Finally, at a distant station in Central Asia, he left the train and walked for two days in the desert toward the Iranian border. (Actually, he walked for two nights, for during the day he dug into the sand like a lizard so that he wouldn't be visible from the air.) When he reached the first barrier, he simply pulled apart two rows of barbed wire and crawled between them. The poor fool didn't know that an electronic signal was transmitted immediately to the nearest border post.

"Another fox jumped over," said the officer at the post as he turned off the alarm. (Klymchak learned this later, at his trial.)

After walking another five kilometers, Bogdan cut through the final rows of barbed wire with wire cutters and landed in Iran. At last! For forty years he had lived in slavery and now he was free! He went to the first village and asked to see the police. "I fled the USSR for political reasons," he told them. "Help me get to the American embassy in Tehran."

They brought him to Tabriz and put him in jail, where a representative of the Shah's police began to talk with him. Meanwhile, the Soviets, having learned about him through an informer, sent a telegram to Iran: "A dangerous criminal and murderer has crossed your border. We demand his extradition."

Because the Shah didn't want to spoil relations with the Soviets, the police took Bogdan to the border and handed him over to the Soviet authorities. Bogdan couldn't believe it—Iran, the friend of America! The free world was betraying him? His simple peasant mind simply couldn't understand it, and at the border he began screaming hysterically. He turned to the Iranian officer and spit in his face. "Damn you," he said in Ukrainian, "damn your land, damn your people!"

He was given the maximum possible punishment (other than death) for treason—fifteen years of imprisonment plus five of exile. When we were together in Chistopol and heard the news over the radio about massive reprisals by Khomeini's followers against both the right and the left, Moslems and atheists, officers and politicians, Klymchak gloated: "Look, my curse is working!"

In general, however, he couldn't stand the radio, with its Russian

language and Soviet propaganda, and he cringed in pain whenever
it was on. In the cell, he had two favorite projects. One was to design
a house on paper with all the necessities—a cow shed, pigsty, and
vegetable garden. What he couldn't build in life he created on paper.
Sometimes, throwing down a book or rising from his cot, he would
grab his plans and rearrange something—the bedroom wouldn't be
here, but there.

Klymchak's second project was to compile a dictionary of syno-
nyms in Ukrainian. Until now, he told me, no such work had ever
been published. Searching through his memory and going through
every text on the Ukrainian language he could get his hands on,
Bogdan would copy each new word in his notebook. In the end he
filled up several notebooks, made copies, and tried without success
to send them to Ukrainians in other cells. When he was supposed
to leave for camp, he tried to take a copy with him. I warned him,
"Bogdan, don't repeat Arkasha's mistake! Don't let them provoke
you into a fight!"

He agreed, and notified the authorities in advance that he was
taking his dictionary. They let him out of Chistopol with all his
things, but when he arrived in camp they took away his dictionary
for inspection. Several months passed before Klymchak received the
reason: "Confiscated because it was not permissible to keep."

I learned all this later, when I returned to Perm 35. There I found
Bogdan Klymchak working as an orderly in the workshop, where
he moved with ferocity and persistence. He would cut into the pile
of metallic shavings with a sharp shovel and dig into it as if he were
fighting both the KGB and the Iranian police.

Like Klymchak, Mikhail Slobodian grew up in the western
Ukraine with no love for the Soviet authorities. He worked as a
policeman during the day, but at night he and his friends secretly
put up Ukrainian flags in the public squares. For years the KGB
tried to identify the guilty parties, and as a loyal policeman,
Slobodian helped them look for the offenders.

He was also the organizer of the election campaign, and he told
me that when he and his co-workers found something "wrong" on
a ballot, they would replace that ballot with one from a pile of
"correct" ones.

"But wait," I said, "we're always told that the election results are
ninety-nine percent."

"True," he replied, "but that's the responsibility of the higher-ups. We're supposed to deliver one hundred percent."

Slobodian was friendly with a regional KGB officer who hated his bosses. He gave Slobodian a list of KGB informers, and Mikhail sent copies of the list to the village officers. This became a major scandal and several KGB men were fired, which was exactly what Slobodian's friend wanted. When Slobodian's activity was finally discovered, he was arrested under Article 70 and sentenced to a total of eleven years.

Chistopol Prison filled up with politicals in two ways. Some were arrested on the outside and immediately sentenced to prison terms, while others were sent to prison from camp, as I was in 1981, for "bad behavior." About a year after I returned to Chistopol, my friends Poresh and Meilanov were brought in from Camp 35, Balakhanov and Kazachkov from Camp 36, and Anatoly Koryagin from Camp 37.

Koryagin, a psychiatrist, had worked closely with the Moscow Helsinki Group in exposing psychiatric abuses, and even in prison he felt obliged to use all available means to continue the struggle against torture. On December 10, 1982, International Human Rights Day, he wrote a statement asserting that the reduced dietary norm 9B represented torture by starvation. As a doctor he considered himself required to protest by the only method available: every time he was put on the 9B diet he declared a hunger strike until he was assured of a normal diet that would guarantee the restoration of his strength and health. As a result, he spent years on hunger strikes.

You hear a lot of stories in prison, and, of course, I told some stories of my own—about the Jewish emigration movement, about my trial, and many other topics. My fellow prisoners were especially interested in hearing about my experiences with KGB tails, and in learning more about Andrei Sakharov.

The story of how I had once ordered my tails out of the Institute for Oil and Gas on November 7 was a great favorite among my fellow zeks. Another one I enjoyed telling was how I could tell if I was being followed. Sometimes my tails would simply vanish, and it wasn't always clear whether they had temporarily disappeared or had merely become more circumspect. I didn't like guessing, so I'd go down into the subway, get on a train, and discreetly stick my foot in the doorway. All the doors would close—except mine. It used to be that you could actually escape from your tails by this method, but they quickly learned all our tricks. And before long they, too, would be standing with their foot in the door, usually in the next car. You'd step out at the last minute, and they'd step out too, and suddenly you were alone with them on the empty platform and you'd greet them with a cheerful wave. Now you knew you were being followed, and you could continue on your way with a feeling of security.

Almost every political prisoner wanted to know more about Sakharov, and I was happy to satisfy their curiosity. Whenever a dissident was on trial, Sakharov would be standing outside the courtroom with the rest of us, and his very presence would draw attention to the trial in the Western press. When Mama came to see me just before I left Lefortovo, I asked her if she had met Sakharov. "Met him?" she replied. "Who do you think was standing with me every day?"

I once had to collect some documents from Sakharov to bring to the foreign correspondents in Moscow. He was ill at the time and was recovering at his dacha, just a few kilometers from Moscow. He had an especially nice one, which the regime had given him after his work on the hydrogen bomb. The authorities tried to take it away when he became a dissident, but it turned out that the certificate had been signed by Stalin, so what could they do?

Normally I would make the trip by train, but I was in a rush, so I hailed a taxi. It took us a while to negotiate a price; the driver wanted a high fee and in the end I agreed to pay it. He promised to drive both ways, and to wait for me while I ran in for a few minutes. But I didn't mention that the man I was going to see was Sakharov.

When we got there, Elena Bonner gave me something to eat and drink, and I quickly gulped it down. Opposite Sakharov's dacha was the dacha of Kirilian, a leading Soviet academician, and when I came back out I noticed that my taxi driver was chatting with the driver of Kirilian's limousine. Kirilian's driver must have mentioned Sakharov, because on the way back to Moscow my driver, who had been quite talkative on the first part of the trip, was afraid to open his mouth. I had more than enough work to do, so I didn't press the issue. When we returned I paid him the sum we had agreed upon and got out of the car.

A moment later he, too, got out of the car and handed me the money. "Take it," he said. "I can't accept payment from you. I wish you all the success in the world." After his tough bargaining, this could only have been a demonstration of his great respect for Sakharov.

I, too, was full of admiration for this great man. During my days as an activist I was often asked by Jewish organizations in America, or by my fellow refuseniks in Moscow, if I could get Sakharov to write a letter, sign a statement, or make an appearance in behalf of our movement. Although he was one of the busiest men in Moscow and the whole world was beating down his door, he never once refused us.

22

Hunger Strike

ON January 4, 1982, if all went well, I had the right to a two-hour meeting with my family. That morning, following the exercise period, they took me into the familiar room, where I sat on one side of the glass, with Lenya and Mama on the other. Two officers sat off to the side.

It had been eighteen months since I last saw them. Mama looked very tired, but she brightened up when she saw me. Lenya was businesslike and tense, and kept a watch in front of him to keep track of the time. Before I could even open my mouth, Mama began to complain loudly: What had they done to me? How thin and pale I had grown since our last meeting!

As usual, I had been warned not to say a word about what was going on in prison. It seemed, however, that they didn't care what I said about the camp, which fell under a different jurisdiction. I described my struggle for the Psalm book and my 186 days in the camp punishment cell, but all efforts to speak about my fellow prisoners, both in Chistopol and in Perm 35, were resolutely checked by the officers.

In a few choppy sentences, Lenya was able to hint that a Soviet spy had been caught in South Africa, and that Avital fervently hoped that in the near future I might be exchanged for him. Both Lenya and Mama were clearly excited by this possibility, but I couldn't allow myself to live with illusory hopes. I explained this, and while they nodded in reply, they clearly didn't want to agree with me.

Mama answered all questions about herself by saying, "I'm completely fine, don't worry," and quickly switched the conversation to other topics. Not wanting to waste our valuable time or to divert attention to herself, she didn't tell me what had preceded our meeting. Later, from her letters, I learned that after arriving in Kazan, Lenya and Mama had discovered that bus traffic across the Kama reservoir was temporarily suspended. But Mama refused to wait, for what if suddenly, on the next day, they deprived me of the meeting? And so in freezing cold weather (minus 40 degrees Celsius), Lenya and my seventy-three-year-old mother trudged through the night across the reservoir. The trip was long—seven kilometers—and on the other side Lenya literally had to carry her onto the bus. They arrived in Chistopol, warmed up with a glass of hot tea, and went straight to the prison.

We agreed that in January I would write a letter directly to Avital in Jerusalem, and that in the beginning of February I would write to Mama. During these years Mama rewrote all my letters and sent them on to Avital. Avital would also call Leonid, who would read my letters over the phone.

"Write to Avital right away," said Lenya. "I'll tell her by telephone. She's dying for your letters!"

It didn't occur to us to discuss what to do if they didn't allow my letter to go through. After all, they had just let me talk freely about everything that happened in camp! But I was quickly sobered when my letter to Avital was not sent. Instead of being confiscated, it was simply returned to me. "You are a citizen of the USSR," I was told. "Therefore you have no need to write abroad."

"What's this, a new law? Show it to me."

"We have our instructions. We are not obliged to be accountable to you."

Next, my letter to Mama was confiscated because of "coded signals in the text."

"Show me where," I demanded.

And again the same answer: "We don't have to explain anything to you."

Soon after this they denied me the right to the next meeting with my family, which was supposed to take place in six months. So even under the best of circumstances I wouldn't see them for at least another year. The official reason was my failure to fulfill the work norm, but the authorities didn't hide the real reason: "You abused our kindness; you used the meeting for slander."

They were cutting me off from my family. Month after month went by, and I submitted one letter after another, but the results were always the same: "Confiscated because of coded signals in the text." Mama didn't understand what had happened, and I could see from her letters, some of which I was still receiving, that she had become anxious and upset. Why hadn't she heard from me? "Is my son alive?" she was asking the authorities. The anxiety made her blood pressure jump, and she began to experience dizzy spells. Hoping to calm her down, I shortened my once-lengthy letters to two brief pages. I wrote only about my health and included a list of letters that I had received. But this one, too, was confiscated.

Sometime in the spring Captain Romanov, the new head of Chistopol Prison, summoned me for a talk. He was a short, thin, sullen man, and to judge by the bags under his eyes he was also a drunk. He showed neither the cunning of Osin nor the artlessness of Malofeev—only maliciousness. But another feature of his character soon showed itself: an acute inferiority complex. He always thought that zeks weren't sufficiently respectful to him, didn't look at him right, or didn't smile properly.

"What are you smirking about?" he said. "You're not performing before the faculty at your institute! You're not hobnobbing with foreigners here! You're a criminal and I'm your boss, and you'll do as I tell you. If you want your mother to receive your letters, then sit down and write: 'I'm alive and well and provided with work. There's no need to worry about me.' And that's all, period! I won't permit anything else."

"Perhaps it's possible to add a greeting to my brother?" I asked with an ironic smile.

Romanov became even more fired up. "Didn't I tell you to stop smirking? No greetings to your Aunt Mania or your Uncle Pete! Write only to your mother, and don't you dare mention anyone else."

"And what about my wife in Israel?"

"Forget about Israel!" he exploded. "We didn't put you in prison so that you could carry on a foreign correspondence. And you don't have any wife there!"

Apparently the KGB had decided to turn my letters into an echo of the official communications that Mama received from the Interior Ministry. I protested, of course, but the replies from the procurator's office and the Ministry of Internal Affairs proclaimed, "No violation of the law was discovered in the acts of the administration." In private conversations, however, I was told, "If you really feel sorry for your mother, then write what you're told—that you're alive and well and she doesn't need to worry about you."

I wondered whether perhaps I really *was* acting cruelly toward my family, and whether I ought to forgo my pride and write what I was told. At least Mama would calm down for a while. Wasn't that the main thing, when her health, and perhaps even her life, were in danger? But Mama would hardly calm down if her son's letters began to sound like official replies. No, she would become even more agitated. I also knew that if I gave in even once, and renounced my right to send normal letters to Jerusalem or Moscow, then it would become far more difficult to win back this right after they had broken the last remaining thread that connected me to my world.

Should I take the offensive and declare a hunger strike? The word "hunger strike" had been on the tip of my tongue from the moment the prison authorities halted my correspondence with my family, and during my conversation with Romanov I had barely refrained from declaring one on the spot in response to his humiliating demands. What stopped me?

This time it was clear that they were serious. This was not an initiative of the local KGB, like the confiscation of the menorah in the camp. No, all the higher-ups were supporting this patent illegality. If I started a hunger strike, it would be a long one. Either the authorities would back down, or . . .

Every man has to draw his own line, and mine was the mail. If I accepted this final restriction, I would be giving up my freedom. You can protest all you want by writing statements, but there comes a time when you have to go beyond that, when you must make the ultimate protest. I knew that a hunger strike was a tool of last resort, and that I might die in the process. But at this point there was no other choice.

In order for my hunger strike to be effective, the outside world had to learn about it in advance. Then Avital and my friends would do everything they could to mobilize international support. For in addition to making a statement to the KGB, I was determined to expose the hypocrisy and harshness of the Soviet system to the entire world.

But how could the world be informed? The only channel I could think of was Iura Butchenko, who was scheduled to end his prison sentence at the end of August. My old camp friend was now only a few cells away from me, and if I could somehow communicate with him . . .

I waited impatiently for an opportunity to contact Butchenko without attracting attention. Month after month went by, and my letters continued to be confiscated. The tension was growing, but there was still no way to implement my plan. April passed, then May and June. In a few more weeks Iura would be leaving. Finally, on June 25, I was lucky: they put me in the punishment cell for fifteen days. Butchenko's cell was now directly above me.

I found a stone on the floor and quickly began to signal him through the radiators in Morse code: "This is Natan, this is Natan." Iura answered back with the usual questions—how many (that is, how many days was I in for), for what reason, and so forth. We both assumed that they were listening in on us, for what could be easier to overhear than tapping on the radiator? Perhaps that was even why they put me here, in order to overhear my requests to the outside world. But he and I had already worked out our own language and special codes in the cell. "If nothing will move," I tapped, "then from January 17 I shall celebrate to the limit." In other words, if the situation with my letters did not change, on September 27 I would begin a hunger strike.

I had chosen this date deliberately: from Mama's letters I knew that September 27 was Yom Kippur, a day of reckoning and of making decisions about the future, a day when I would start my own Yom Kippur War against the KGB. I paced back and forth in the cold, damp punishment cell, trying to improve my circulation, but it was stimulated more by the awareness that I had now crossed the Rubicon. Once Butchenko left, it would be too late to back down or make any adjustments to my plans.

(I later learned that Iura contacted my family as soon as he arrived home in Siberia. Lenya flew out to talk with him, and then, through foreigners, he passed information to Avital about my impending hunger strike.)

On July 4, the eighth anniversary of our *chuppah*, I signaled to Iura through the radiator: "Send Avital my greetings and don't let her think of celebrating together with me; she has enough to deal with."

The decision was made and the date set, but during the next three months I still cherished the hope that my plan could be averted. Every ten or fifteen days I submitted another letter. The text was always the same; I had shortened it as much as possible, leaving only the minimum that would distinguish a letter of a son and husband from an official Soviet document. But I continued to receive the standard answer: "The letter was confiscated because of coded signals in the text." I was greatly disappointed and full of angry resolve to prevail in this struggle.

On the morning of September 27 I submitted yet another letter home. I also sent a short statement to Romanov, announcing the start of a hunger strike. And I wrote to the procurator general explaining the reasons for my hunger strike, and declared that I wouldn't stop until I could send letters to my wife in Israel and my mother and brother in Moscow.

I thus began an open-ended hunger strike with the clear understanding that it would be very difficult to get my demands granted. Nevertheless, I had firmly resolved not to give in.

Beginning a hunger strike is like starting out to cross the ocean in a small boat. The future is completely unknown. Would I survive? And if so, would I attain my goal or back down?

As soon as I announced my hunger strike I got rid of the feeling of despair and helplessness, and the humiliation at being forced to tolerate the KGB's tyranny—not to mention the severe mental torture to which they were subjecting my family. The bitterness and angry determination that had been building up during the past nine months now gave way to a kind of strange relief; at long last I was actively defending myself and my world from *them*.

After three days they isolated me from the other prisoners. On the little table in the small cell at the end of the corridor where they kept me for the next six weeks I placed four photographs: one of Papa, one of Lenya and Mama, and two of Avital—the one from Lefortovo and a new one that Mama had recently sent me of Avital near the waterfall of Ein Gedi in Israel. I arranged the pictures where I could see them even while I lay on my cot, so at any moment I could find support by a glance.

When Avital and I lived together on Kaliaevsky Street, she would sometimes toss a few coins into a box or even under the rug. Later, when we were desperately trying to figure out where our next ruble was coming from, she would "find" these coins, and it was a truly joyous discovery. In much the same way I would dig into my memory and invariably come up with a scene or sometimes merely a phrase from the past that would quickly bind us together.

The beginning of my hunger strike was unexpectedly difficult, apparently as the result of the weakening of my body during the preceding years and of my own mistakes. After two days my blood pressure dropped, my head began to ache, and my heart started pounding. I lay down, trying to conserve my strength, but this was a mistake. From the very beginning I should have tried to overcome my weakness by walking, doing exercises, and massaging my muscles. I should have mobilized my body, but instead I speeded up its deterioration. As a result, after about ten days I lacked the strength to get up. I felt dizzy and nauseated. Since I was eating nothing and drinking only water, the constant urge to throw up was particularly surprising.

Below my cell was the very same punishment cell where three months ago I had sent a message to Butchenko about my impending hunger strike. Now Vazif Meilanov was down there for another round. I knew what it meant to be able to communicate with a friend while you were in the punishment cell, so I overcame my dizziness, sat up on the bench, and began to tap to him.

I described my dizziness and nausea. He thought a moment and tapped back: "Stick it out a few more days, until Monday, and then stop the hunger strike."

"No," I replied immediately. "My family knows I shall fast as long as they don't get my letters. I won't back down."

"That's just what I wanted to hear from you," Vazif tapped in reply. I did not complain further.

After about twenty days I was literally pinned to the bed with weakness. I now had severe chest pains, but the heavy feeling of time dragging out endlessly had disappeared. I gazed at the pictures of my family, wandered mentally into the past, and recalled Avital's old letters. Several times a day I recited my prayer. Day was imperceptibly replaced by night.

Finally, as I had expected, my "saviors" appeared in the cell—a doctor, a nurse, and several officers and master sergeants. The nurse carried a deep dish with some kind of liquid; in the other hand she held a rubber tube. After asking, "Will you eat?" they sat me on the bench and lifted the tube to my face. I grabbed it with my hands. They twisted my hands behind me and handcuffed them. I began to shake my head. One of the guards grabbed the back of my head, another held me by the shoulders, and a third by the feet. When I clenched my teeth, they squeezed my nose in the hope that I would be forced to open my mouth. Then they tried to open it with a spoon.

"Let's try through the nose," said the doctor, and someone began poking the tube first in one nostril and then in the other. But the tube was either too thick, or my slightly crooked bridge was in the way (a reminder of my sole fight when, at the age of fourteen, I had to respond to the anti-Semitic attacks of a neighborhood bully). My "providers" did not succeed in attaining their goal.

"O.K. Let's try through his butt," said the doctor.

They put me on the cot, pulled down my pants, and forced in the "life-giving" mixture in the form of an enema. I don't know what the specialists in penal medicine were counting on, but the effect was exactly the same as an ordinary enema. For the first time in weeks I was purged. For a few hours, the taste in my mouth was not toxic or bitter. (It's no accident that doctors recommend giving an enema as part of fasting. Here, of course, I had no access to a water enema. Fine, I told myself, we'll use this instead.)

I didn't feel in the least humiliated, but neither did I gain any strength. Mostly I was indifferent. In another three days the procedure was repeated, and in a few more days, when my pulse could hardly be measured, the same team arrived in my cell with more reliable weapons.

"That's enough of playing the fool! We'll feed you anyway," said the doctor as the handcuffs were clicked on and the guards held me by the feet, head, and shoulders. Somebody pressed pincers on my cheeks where the two rows of teeth begin, pushing down very painfully while rotating the pincers up and down. It felt as if my teeth were cracking, and as soon as my mouth opened slightly, a metal plate was inserted between my teeth.

"Turn the mouth opener," said the doctor.

From the turning of the screw, onto which two plates were attached, the plates began to separate, which made my mouth open wider and wider. The complicated task of introducing a tube into the mouth had been successfully completed.

I no longer resisted. On the contrary, I relaxed, hoping that my torturers would finish their "body-saving" mission as quickly as possible. But suddenly my throat began to resist, and when the doctor tried to push the tube deeper into the stomach, I responded with convulsive spasms. When the doctor continued to poke the tube back and forth, I started choking. This continued for an agonizingly long time, perhaps half an hour or more. I had almost lost consciousness by the time the tube landed in the stomach and the liquid began to flow into me.

I don't know why this procedure turned out to be so painful for me. (From other zeks I learned that it was much easier for many of them.) I convulsively drew in air through my nose; my heart was pounding fast and hard, and my stomach felt so heavy that I thought it was about to burst.

When they finally jerked the tube out of my throat, a stream of the liquid gushed up like a fountain, leaving traces on the ceiling, the wall, and the table. A few drops even landed on my photographs. Today, the picture of Avital that Papa took on the eve of her departure for Israel still bears the traces of my former battles: the tear on top is a reminder of the trial, and the stain on the side is a souvenir of the hunger strike.

My visitors held me down for a while before they finally left. I lay on the cot and frantically gulped in air through my mouth. My heart was thumping madly and my temples were pounding. The image of the cell before my eyes was jerking strangely, and it seemed as if my intestines were bursting. At least an hour passed before the tension began to ease, and in another hour or so I felt better. My strength had returned, and although my chest still hurt, my heart seemed to be normal. I got up from the cot and slowly walked around the cell a few times. Good—I didn't seem to be dizzy. I sat down at the table and wrote another brief letter home—an exact copy of the previous ones that had been confiscated. This one, too, was confiscated, but every two or three weeks I continued submitting a new copy. It was my way of reminding them that I didn't intend to give up.

On the following day I woke up with considerably less energy. Once again I felt dizzy while walking around the cell, and I started blanking out at any abrupt movement. By the end of the day I was already lying down. The following day was more difficult; I lost strength with every hour, and my pulse grew weaker until it could not be felt at all. I fixed my gaze on the photographs as I imagined what Avital was doing at that moment. When the imagination began to fail and the only feeling left was stubborn indifference, the doctor and the guards came to pour in another liter of the mixture. The whole process began all over again.

The worst part of this three-day cycle was the violent swings from one extreme to the other—from an almost unconscious condition to a state of extreme agitation, followed by a slow three-day decline, and then another extreme jump. After each of the feedings my chest pains grew stronger. It would have been easier on my system, of course, if my saviors had divided the mixture into three parts and poured some in every day; salvation was now indistinguishable from torture. The forced feeding was intended to save my body, the torture to save my soul.

To conserve my strength, I almost never turned off the loudspeaker in the cell, as I couldn't even sit up to turn the switch without starting to black out. Under "normal" conditions, of course, I would have found it intolerable to hear lectures about the Communist morality of prison educators and news about new labor victories in Moscow. Now, however, the radio was simply a background that helped me know I was still alive and aware of what day it was.

On the morning of November 10, 1982, on the forty-fifth day of my hunger strike, I was waiting for the next round of forced feeding. As usual at the end of the three-day cycle, I was on the border between sleep and reality, and the soft, solemn music that wafted to my ears seemed most appropriate. Then my nurturers arrived and poured in my fuel, and I experienced the usual hour of stomach shock as I began to return to reality.

The sounds I heard were thoroughly familiar. Their time and place were fixed—when the food traps were supposed to bang, when the door of the cell was supposed to open. Today, however, something unusual was happening. I heard—or did it only seem that way?—some kind of commotion and bustle by my door. It appeared as if someone was looking through the peephole and talking quietly, but I couldn't really see from my cot. Suddenly, from the opposite end of the corridor I heard the barking of German shepherds, who were then silenced by the shout of a guard. What kind of nonsense was this? Weren't there enough dogs surrounding the prison? Why did they let them inside? The strangest thing, however, was that the soft, solemn music echoing in my ears did not disappear after the forced feeding. Could it be real? And suddenly, "Moscow speaking, Moscow speaking— After a serious illness—" Kirilenko? Chernenko? Tikhonov?—the possibilities rushed through my head. "—Leonid Ilich Brezhnev has passed away."

Brezhnev? On the forty-fifth day of *my* hunger strike *his* heart didn't hold up? The attempt to deflate my excitement with irony was natural, but this was more than irony. For no matter how I tried to restrain my pride and to view my struggle realistically, without letting myself succumb to the prison syndrome of exaggerating the significance of one's captivity, I couldn't shake off the feeling that I had embarked on a struggle against the entire Soviet system. This feeling intensified a thousandfold during my hunger strike. While listening and not listening to the various prison officials and procurators who tried to persuade me to stop my hunger strike, I knew that my struggle was not against them personally. The portraits of the leaders in the newspapers personified the evil I was trying to oppose. And look, their top leader had fallen at the very height of the duel! Fate was sending me a clear sign: Hold on and you will win.

"Hooray!" the cries of joy burst forth from the adjacent cell and were taken up by other political cells as the cheers resounded throughout the prison. The guards responded by banging their clubs on the metal cell doors. Then they began to open one cell after another.

An officer entered my cell followed by two noncoms with clubs; behind them was a soldier with a German shepherd. It was the first time I had ever seen clubs or a dog in my cell. "We're warning you—you shall be severely punished for any anti-Soviet cries," declared the officer. As if I had the strength to cry out!

I lay on the bed, ignoring the order "Get up!" and gloating. What fears grip the rulers of this country! Their leader dies and they don't inform the people for days in order to prepare for possible disorder, and they fill the prison corridors with guards and dogs. What are they afraid of?

When the guards left I remembered that I hadn't done my duty as a zek. In the basement, in the punishment cell beneath me, was Robert Nazarian, a member of the Armenian Helsinki Group. Naturally there was no loudspeaker in the punishment cell, so I was the only one who could dispel his dreary gloom with these joyful tidings. I got up from bed and sat at the table, pretending to read. Listening carefully, I heard a suspicious rustling on the other side of the door. But what have I got to lose? I asked myself. While continuing to look at the book, I started tapping on the radiator.

I had barely managed to tap out the word "Brezhnev" when the locks on the door began to clang. I tapped out "died" as the door opened. A triumphal drum roll of tapping from below mixed with the yelling of the guards. They grabbed me by the arms, dragged me away from the table, and began to frisk me.

"Where's the note?"

"What note?"

"That was on the table! You were tapping it out!"

I laughed. A new zek who was still learning Morse code might use a note, but why would I? But in order to tease the guards, I gave a conspicuous swallow. One of them grabbed me by the throat. "He swallowed it!" said his partner.

"Why aren't you at a memorial meeting?" I asked cheerfully.

They drew up a report, and a few hours later I was led to another cell at the opposite end of the corridor. This one was separated from the other cells by a special room where representatives of the administration would meet with the zeks.

After my tiny cell this one was very large; it was meant for six people, although I was alone. Under other circumstances, being brought to such a cell would have been a real gift, but I didn't require much room. It was also colder here, and during my hunger strike I was always freezing. I would gladly have exchanged this cell for my smaller one. Unfortunately, I would be here for a long time.

Brezhnev was replaced by Andropov, the former head of the KGB, a persecutor of dissidents and the man who had signed the first document of my criminal case. What good could be expected from him? On the other hand, perhaps it was important for him, of all people, to show the West that he wasn't "that kind," and to cleanse himself of his past. Perhaps he, a full-fledged ruler of the KGB, could do more easily what Brezhnev could not?

These thoughts didn't stay with me for long. Not only was I trying to guess as little as possible, but the cycles of forced feeding left me less and less strength for contemplation. I felt continually weaker, and the pains in my chest grew stronger with each feeding. It seemed to me that my heart could not withstand yet another leap of my pulse from a sinking state to 250 beats a minute. On the second and third day after the feeding I would lie flat, trying to listen to the sounds of the loudspeaker, which was my only opportunity to be in contact with reality. But more and more I began to tune out, and when the sounds of the radio reached me again it seemed that an hour or two had passed. I don't know whether I dozed off or lost consciousness, but I recall that I often spent those hours with Avital, both in memories of the past and in dreams of the future. I was haunted by visions of my release and my arrival in Israel, and of meeting my wife. I also had visions of sitting on the roof of our Jerusalem apartment, of visiting the waterfall of Ein Gedi, and of lying in the sand in Eilat and swimming in the blue waters of the Red Sea.

About three months after the start of the hunger strike, when the periods I was tuned out became too long, they began to pour in the feeding mixture every two days. But this was of little help, as I was rational for only two or three hours after my body handled the shock. My benefactors—security officers, procurators, and doctors—would appear during that time. Their ranks kept growing and their voices were heard more frequently. They had long ago given up on the crude tone of their earlier visits, where they had said things like "We've broken better men than you." But the essence remained the same: "Write a letter home as the head of the prison tells you and then we will permit you to write more extensively. Then you'll be able to write to Moscow and to Jerusalem, wherever you want." My tormentors, who had so cruelly broken my ties with my family, actually appealed to my filial sentiments: "If you really love your mother, then have mercy on her, reassure her, don't make a seventy-five-year-old woman the victim of your stubborn pride."

After a long interval, for the first time during my hunger strike they began to bring me postcards from Mama. Of course they didn't bring them all, but brought only those that were full of anxiety, pain, and suffering. "How are you, my dear, are you alive?"

"I am alive, well, and provided with work," Captain Romanov would prompt me. I knew from the postcards that Mama was suffering from nervous tension and was losing her balance—she couldn't walk without help. "Do you see what you've done to your mother?" Romanov told me.

Compassion toward my mother and hatred toward my would-be executioners struggled against each other in my heart. Was it humane to subject Mama to such torture? Was it worth it for the sake of a letter to gamble on her life and mine? I had to remind myself again and again that this was war, and that if I surrendered, my ties with home might never be restored. Would Mama and Avital really feel better if my letters read like official notices? No, this would mean the end of my struggle. It would convince our enemies that they were omnipotent, that they could erect barriers between us and make me reinforce them with my own hands.

No, I decided, my hunger strike is a continuation of the same struggle I have been engaged in from the moment they arrested me, a struggle to remain in the world of my friends and family. If I gave in, I would lose more than the right to send letters home; I would also be losing that marvelous spiritual connection with Avital, which had given me strength all these years and had become even stronger during my hunger strike. In short, I understood now, just as I had previously realized when I was facing the threat of *rasstrel* in Lefortovo, that giving in meant returning to that servile soulless life I had once led and no longer wanted any part of.

I had declared an open-ended hunger strike, but the human mind has trouble perceiving infinity. Even the greatest dreamer, lost in the clouds of the distant future, makes concrete plans in his daily life and links his actions to specific time periods. When I began my hunger strike in late September, I decided to count down until January 4, when I was entitled to my next meeting. Clearly they would not let me see my family while I was still on a hunger strike, which meant that they would deny me this meeting, just as they had denied me the previous one. I told myself that the denial of a second meeting, when not one letter had arrived from me for an entire year, was a clear signal to the outside world that I was continuing the struggle, and that the authorities had something to hide.

January 4 was also convenient for another reason, as it marked the one hundredth day of the hunger strike. I didn't calculate the days or weeks, but each day I told myself that n days of hunger strike had passed, and only 100 minus n remained until January 4. As the days passed my anticipation grew stronger, as they had still not deprived me of the meeting. What was going on? Obviously the KGB could not have my family see me in this shape, but although they usually denied me a meeting with great ease, this time, apparently, they couldn't make up their minds. What was forcing them to hesitate and delay? Was it pressure from the West? I tried not to let my imagination run wild.

On the evening of January 3, not even my weakness could hide my agitation. The prison administration's working day was already over, and tomorrow Mama and Lenya would presumably arrive at the prison. Before bedtime, at nine in the evening, the lock clanged and the door opened. I was lying with my back to the door and didn't see who came in, but everything was clear to me. My agitation vanished, giving way to a deadening weakness. With my eyes closed, feeling tired and indifferent, I heard the head of the special division reading me a decree. My chest pains seemed more severe than usual as he spoke: "The convict Sharansky, A. B., over such and such a period of time has refused to take food, which is a pretext for refusing to work. Sharansky, A. B., is deprived of the next meeting for violation of prison discipline as expressed in the refusal to take food and the refusal to work."

Nothing had changed, I told myself. Now that a hundred days of my hunger strike had passed, what new marking point could I set? I decided on January 20—my birthday and the anniversary of my father's death. Then I would see. But I lacked my former strength and soon lost count of the time.

Days of almost complete lack of consciousness were followed by several hours of "enlightenment," but even during those moments of awareness, after another infusion of the mixture, it seemed that my heart would split from the pain as it leaped from a sinking state to barely beating and then to a feverish throb. I still resisted the feedings, but I had so little strength that by now my resistance was merely symbolic.

A week or ten days passed, and Captain Romanov appeared in my cell. Once again he adopted a very crude, aggressive tone as he tried to convince me that my struggle was ridiculous and hopeless.

"What do you think, that you're stronger than the entire country? Everyone told you it's impossible! You're going to die, and we'll bury you anonymously. Nobody will even know where your grave is," he said, switching back to the familiar form of address.

I had neither the strength nor the desire to fight with him. He left, but appeared again the following day, this time a few hours after my feeding, when I was full of strength and energy. Now I was sitting up and ready to argue if necessary. But Romanov's opening words, which were now polite and more formal, astonished me.

"Your mother is here, Anatoly Borisovich. She begs you to stop your hunger strike."

Before I could say that I didn't believe him, I noticed some kind of note in his hand.

"She wrote you a letter," he said. "But in addition, she asked to tell you orally: 'Stop the hunger strike, stop torturing yourself and our family!' "

"Yes, of course, orally!" I snickered gleefully and impatiently reached for the letter.

My eyes devoured in an instant the little page with Mama's handwriting. Then I began to read each word slowly. I didn't know that this note was the result of many hours of struggle between Mama and Romanov and Galkin, the KGB officer, over every word, and that several earlier versions had been rejected. But all my experience told me that behind this note were months of an enormous struggle by many people, especially Mama and Avital. Yes, Mama asked that I stop the hunger strike, but only on the condition that it would lead to an immediate renewal of our correspondence. She wrote of guarantees that she received.

"We are meeting you halfway," said Romanov. "You can write a note to your mother that you are stopping the hunger strike and I'll give it to her immediately. Let her be reassured, and we won't even count this note as your next letter. In another ten days you can write in more detail to your mother and your wife." He spoke tenderly, with concern, and I could see that it was not easy for him to adopt this tone.

"Why wait ten days?" I said. "I'll write a letter now, the same one I was writing all these months, and you can give it to her."

Romanov exploded: "What am I, your delivery man?" Then he calmed down. "I'm very busy and I can't wait long. Write two or three sentences and I'll give it to her."

He tried to hurry me and kept looking at his watch, pretending he was about to leave. I took a sheet of paper and briefly informed my mother of everything they hadn't let me tell her: that I had heard nothing from Avital, that a majority of Mama's and all my letters home had been confiscated on a pretext, and that I had started my hunger strike for this reason. I wrote that I was prepared to resume eating as soon as I received confirmation that she had read this letter, and that I would write the next one in ten days. I also explained that if the situation recurred, my hunger strike would be automatically renewed in the future.

While I was writing, Romanov kept circling around me, glancing at my letter and saying, "Really, is such a long one possible? I permitted you only two or three sentences!" He kept grabbing his cap, saying, "Well, that's enough! I'm leaving."

All this activity prevented me from concentrating. "Fine," I said, "if you're so busy, then leave. You're disturbing me and I can't think. When I finish, I'll give this note to the duty officer."

"That's what it's worth to be nice to you!" he screamed, returning to his usual tone. "Go ahead and croak, if that's what you want." He rushed toward the cell door, but at the last moment he turned around and said, "Well, O.K., it's not you, it's your mother I feel sorry for. Give me the note quickly."

Yes, it was obvious that Romanov was being pressured to end my hunger strike today, which only reinforced my resolve to make my message to Mama as informative as possible. When I finally finished, Romanov grabbed the paper from my hands and said, "So now I can tell them to bring you food?"

"First bring me a note from my mother that she has read my note. Only then will I eat."

"Are you making fun of me? I, the director of the prison, have nothing better to do than deliver letters for you?"

Romanov was clearly not suited for the role of peacemaker that had been assigned to him. He started in again with his threats: "Stop the hunger strike immediately or you'll die!"

There was no point in arguing with him, and I was exhausted. The note from Mama, the unexpected opportunity to end the hunger strike successfully, and, above all, a sense of returning to life at the very moment when I had reconciled myself to the prospect of death—all this had brought me out of my somnambulistic state and led me to forget about my physical weakness. But now it overcame me again.

I lay down, almost falling onto the cot, and turned toward the wall. Romanov said something and left. An hour or two passed; my heart was thumping but I had no energy. I didn't even have the strength (or the desire?) to turn around and check whether Romanov had taken my note to Mama. When the door of the cell began to clang, however, I sat up on the bed and turned toward Romanov to see what was in his hand. He was carrying a note but—no!—it was in my handwriting.

"Anatoly Borisovich, you were permitted to write only two or three sentences about stopping your hunger strike. But you wrote a whole letter. We're willing to meet you halfway again—look, just copy it over now, only without these two paragraphs."

He pointed to the sections where I wrote about the outrageous state of our correspondence, where I said that not one of Avital's letters and only a few of Mama's had reached me. It also included the part where I explained my conditions for terminating the strike and for renewing it in the future if these same problems occurred again.

"Otherwise we won't give her the note," Romanov said.

"Then I'm continuing the hunger strike," I said, and turned toward the wall.

"So you don't have pity on your mother?" Suddenly Romanov switched to a kind of berserk screech: "I'm the head of the prison here, not some kid! You want to make fun of me?" Then he began cursing in the most vulgar manner. A mug of water flew off the table and the cell door slammed. From the corridor I heard Romanov's furious voice as he bumped into a zek from the cleaning staff and vented all his wrath on him.

An hour later the duty officer brought me a note from Mama that she had read my message, that she would now wait two weeks for my letter with a description of how I ended the hunger strike, and would continue her efforts to prevent any further disruptions in our communication. Below was the date, January 14, 1983. This was the one hundred tenth day of my hunger strike. For a long time I sat on the bed with the note in my hand. Slowly the realization that I would live took possession of me—my head, my heart, my entire body. The weight of impending death was leaving me. That feeling, which had possessed me for months, gave way to another, a triumphant one that *we* had won, that again we had breached the wall behind which the KGB had been trying to entomb me forever.

I took my Psalm book and for days on end, with the photographs of my dear ones in front of me, I recited all one hundred and fifty of King David's Psalms, syllable by syllable.

The Interconnection of Souls

23

O N the day of my arrest I weighed sixty-five kilos. When I began my hunger strike I weighed a little over fifty, and by the time it was finally over I was down to thirty-five. As soon as I stopped the hunger strike they immediately began a repair job on me, and the very next day I was moved to a "hospital cell" at the other end of the corridor. Slowly, barely shuffling my feet, and staggering under the weight of the mattress and pillow, I dragged myself past the doors of the seemingly identical cells. But they were different in that various types and amounts of food passed through the food traps of these doors, depending on the behavior of the occupants.

My cell was the most fortunate of all because such rare items as milk, meat, and butter came through the food trap every day. I was also given vitamins in the form of pills and shots. I gained strength daily, and before long I was able to go out for exercise. But it took at least two weeks before I could utilize the entire two hours that were allocated on a hospital regime.

"You have dystrophy of the myocardium—a weakening of the heart muscle," the doctor told me. "It could take months before it goes away."

In reality, it took years before I could lie on my left side. Even now, as I write these words fifteen months after my release, any slightly increased physical activity, such as running or swimming, reminds me of my hunger strike in Chistopol.

"Don't fool around with your heart like that again," warned the doctor. "You shouldn't go even one day without eating."

Perhaps he was right. In the future, even during a twenty-four-hour hunger strike my chest hurt as if I had been fasting for two months. But the doctor's concern had nothing to do with my health. He was merely conveying the standard KGB message: Stop being a troublemaker.

Despite these warnings I did undertake other hunger strikes. A little over a month after my hunger strike had ended, I heard Anatoly Koryagin scream from the corridor that he had been beaten while being taken to the punishment cell. Our demand that the incident be investigated immediately was rejected, so I joined a group of zeks who carried out a week-long hunger strike as a sign of solidarity with Koryagin.

And what became of my correspondence? As I promised in my note to Mama, ten days after the end of my hunger strike I wrote my first letter, about fifteen pages. A week later I was informed that it was confiscated. This time, it's true, they didn't demand that I reduce everything to a few predetermined words; they merely suggested that I mention nothing about my health. But I knew this was only the beginning, and that once again they were testing my resolve. They undoubtedly assumed that it wouldn't be easy for me to start a new hunger strike now that I had begun to regain my strength and to taste life once more.

Without hesitating, I wrote to the procurator declaring that unless my letter was sent I would renew my hunger strike. A few days later it was sent to Moscow, which initiated a remarkable period of a year and a half when virtually all my letters reached home and their size gradually increased from a few pages to forty. (There were never any specific limits on length, but the longer your letter, the less chance it had of going through.) In these letters I analyzed my entire prison experience, discussed topics that had agitated me over the years, and explained, sometimes allegorically, the reasons for certain decisions I had made. My link with home, with my family in Moscow and Jerusalem, had never been so valuable and so deep as during these months when we reaped the fruits of our victory.

After the hunger strike was over, I was visited by a series of procurators and inspectors. But now they were prepared to admit that mistakes had been made in the past. They even indicated the source of these mistakes—Romanov. The general procurator of the

Tatar Republic told me that only someone who was ignorant of Soviet law could demand that a zek reduce his letter to one sentence, and he added that I had every right to send letters abroad.

The most remarkable thing of all was that this was said in the presence of Romanov himself, who sat to the side and sullenly looked downward. His days are numbered, I thought, as they assured me that in the future there would be no problems with mail. The authorities also hinted that justice would soon prevail in the case of Koryagin, who had been conducting a hunger strike for several months after his beating.

By May the word was out that Romanov had been fired, and in another few weeks we learned that he had committed suicide. The Andropov purge had swept him away, too. As usual in these cases, when they decide to get rid of someone, they blame him for everything. Among other things, Romanov was blamed for driving me to a hunger strike, although here, as in so many other areas, he was merely the obedient executor of the KGB's will.

In early March the KGB brought me to a special room where Galkin usually talked with political zeks. But today somebody else was behind the desk, a large man with an affable smile. "Hello, Anatoly Borisovich," he said. "I've come from KGB Headquarters in Moscow at your mother's request. I spoke with her at length only yesterday over a cup of tea." He walked toward me and offered his hand.

Naturally, I didn't take his hand. Instead I sat down and said, "I'm listening."

Why didn't I simply turn around and leave as I had been doing all these years? Was I intrigued by his mention of Mama, or was it simply that after my hunger strike I was eager to learn what was going on in the outside world, just as in Lefortovo? It was probably both reasons.

The KGB man sat behind the desk and reached for a package of Validol pills. He put one on his tongue and said something about his heart ailment. Then, showing the sympathy and solidarity of one sick man to another, he switched to the topic of my own heart problems. He told me how anxious and distressed Mama was about me, how she had cried in his office and had begged the KGB to help her obtain a meeting with her son.

"You were deprived of your January meeting," he said, "and the next one is in July. So far it hasn't been canceled. The KGB, however, is willing to be accommodating toward your mother's request and to ask the prison administration for an earlier meeting. Moreover, this year you will complete half of your term, and the Presidium of the Supreme Soviet may review the question of a pardon. This would depend exclusively on your behavior."

He continued: "Why not show some compassion toward yourself? I can understand that you were upset about the lack of correspondence with your mother and your wife, but why must you interfere in the relations between the administration and other prisoners? [This was a clear reference to our recent week-long hunger strike in support of Koryagin.] Why should you care about them? Your term is much longer than theirs and your case is more serious; you should think about your health and your family. Besides, they aren't serious people; they're vain, and their only concern is how to use your fame to their own advantage. The KGB is willing to meet you halfway; what guarantees can you give us?"

All of this was banal and very familiar—the references to family attachments, the attempts to play on my self-esteem, the disparaging references to my fellow zeks, the reminder that I could be deprived of my next meeting. I rose and walked toward the door, telling him, "I have nothing to say to you."

My new companion in heart ailments called after me: "If you change your mind, write, and I'll come to you right away."

Had Mama really turned to him? Had she wept in his office and begged? They're lying as usual, I told myself, but there was a bitter aftertaste that wouldn't go away. I had no way of knowing, of course, that Mama had been forcibly brought to the KGB, that they had tried to persuade her to send me a letter and a food package through them, and that she had categorically refused to cooperate. I didn't know any of this, but I hoped this was what had happened. I hoped and I feared.

The visit of this KGB man from Moscow, the new "liberal" attitude toward me on the part of the prison officials, who stopped throwing me into the punishment cell or subjecting me to other harassments even though my conduct hadn't changed at all; the attempts by the procurators and the Interior Ministry to blame

Romanov for all previous violations—all this and much more told me that after my hunger strike the ice around me had started to melt. Some kind of game was in the works, but I resolved not to give in to idle fantasies, and used the opportunity to write long and detailed letters home.

The mystery was cleared up on July 5, 1983, at the next two-hour meeting with Mama and Lenya, our first meeting in a year and a half. It had been six months since my hunger strike and I had grown noticeably stronger, but even so, Mama was horrified at how thin I was. And while I tried to put on a good front and not complain about my health, I gave myself away by my habit of lightly massaging my chest with my right hand, which seemed to alleviate the constant chest pains. But not even my health could distract Mama and Lenya from the main piece of information they brought me, which was undoubtedly why our meeting had not been canceled.

"During your hunger strike there were many protests," said Lenya, speaking quickly in case they stopped him. "Some were by heads of state and Party leaders. On January 21, Andropov replied personally to an appeal from Georges Marchais in France, and it was clear that in doing so he was simultaneously replying to all the other leaders as well. He let it be known that you could be released soon, and after that our correspondence was restored."

Lenya continued: "The Helsinki Review Conference is now drawing to a close in Madrid, and the Americans made it clear that they won't sign the final document without a resolution of your problem. The head of the Soviet delegation has informed Max Kampelman, the head of the American delegation, and Kampelman told Avital, that if you sign a statement requesting a release for reasons of health, the request will be granted. In Moscow, the KGB told us the same thing. Kampelman thinks the Soviets are serious, and that this is a major concession. They aren't asking you to admit guilt, or to recant, or to condemn anyone else. Elena Georgievna [Bonner], in the name of herself and her husband [that is, Sakharov], asked me to tell you that in their opinion it's possible to accept this proposal."

I interrupted Lenya: "And what about Natasha? Did Natasha ask me to do it?"

"No, she asked nothing," he said. I sighed with relief, for otherwise it would be the first time I had to disagree with Avital since my arrest, which would have been a terrible blow to our spiritual unity.

"Mama and I won't advise you what to do," said Lenya, "but I must convey your answer to the American embassy in Moscow. They're waiting for it. So think about it and let us know by the end of the meeting."

"I can tell you now," I replied. "I committed no crimes. The crimes were committed by the people who arrested me and are keeping me in prison. Therefore the only appeal I can address to the Presidium is a demand for my immediate release and the punishment of those who are truly guilty. Asking the authorities to show humanity means acknowledging that they represent a legitimate force that administers justice."

Neither of them tried to contradict me, but I could see how Mama's face had fallen. She and Lenya continually brought up Natasha's name, trying to tell me about her tireless struggle, but the guards stopped them every time. At the end of the meeting Mama said timidly, "Well, Tolya, perhaps you'll think about this proposal again anyway?"

My poor old mother! How hard it was to disappoint her. I shook my head, for there was nothing to think about. We agreed that I would send my next letter, the July one, directly to Avital in Jerusalem. We had agreed on exactly the same point at our previous meeting, a year and a half ago, which had led to my hunger strike.

At the end of the meeting the guards demonstrated yet another sign of the Andropovian "thaw" as they allowed me to hug and kiss Mama.

"And now my brother," I said, tearing myself away from my weeping mother.

"No, that's already too much!" The duty officer reacted indignantly to my impudence, and two noncoms grabbed me by the arms and quickly took me to my cell.

The meeting had not been easy. As always, everything became confused in my head and questions emerged from this chaos almost by chance. And with each question, another, unasked question: Is this item worth spending precious minutes of a two-hour visit, a visit whose price was a year and a half of my life?

As soon as the meeting was over, I began the usual calculation of credits and debts—this I said, that I knew, something else I forgot or didn't understand, and so on. Inevitably, I was flooded with thousands of questions that I hadn't been able to ask. I recalled dozens of people I hadn't managed to ask about, and whom I might not learn about for years. The few details I was able to grasp invariably opened up an enormous window to the world, and for months I would review this information. Seeing my family for fleeting moments every year or two was a vivid reminder that time wasn't standing still, that life continued to rush on, that the people I cared about were changing, maturing, growing older. I had to make a continual effort to live my life with these dear, beloved people. This time, however, in addition to everything else there was also Mama's sad face and her half-hoping question "Perhaps, after all?"

I had rejected the KGB's offer outright, without even trying to explain the reason to Mama. But was it really possible to explain such a thing during a brief meeting? And were the reasons impelling me to say no completely clear and comprehensible even to myself? Avital, of course, would understand. But how could she explain rationally what I myself could not?

In Lefortovo they had demanded that I recant and condemn my "accomplices." In exchange they had promised me a speedy release and the possibility that later, in Israel, I could take back my confession. At the time, I formulated three reasons why I couldn't do this: it would weaken the resolve of my comrades; it would sabotage our support in the West; and it would help the KGB prepare new reprisals against dissidents and Jewish activists.

Even then I realized that these rational arguments were only partial answers, and that embedded deep within me was a commitment to resistance that automatically gave a negative answer to every KGB offer. I knew that if I began to bargain with them, to "understand" them, I would inevitably return to that former servile state of doublethink in which I had spent the first twenty-odd years of my life. In an effort to uphold my commitment and to remain beyond the reaches of the KGB, day after day, month after month, I mentally reinforced the bonds with my world, my family, Israel, and Avital.

"We need each other," I had once told her, and after my arrest our interdependence had increased a thousandfold. "The time has come for this little book to be with you," Avital had written on the eve of my arrest, and later I spent many long months in the punishment cell so that our Psalm book really would stay with me. There, in the cold and dark punishment cell, I heard not only Avital's voice but also the singing of King David.

And had King David not expressed himself on this very matter of the KGB's offer? I recalled Psalm 39:

I resolved I would watch my step
Lest I offend by my speech;
I would keep my mouth muzzled
While the wicked man was in my presence.
I was dumb, silent;
I held my peace
While my pain was intense.

Back in Lefortovo, Socrates and Don Quixote, Ulysses and Gargantua, Oedipus and Hamlet, had rushed to my aid. I felt a spiritual bond with these figures; their struggles reverberated with my own, their laughter with mine. They accompanied me through prisons and camps, through cells and transports.

At some point I began to feel a curious reverse connection: not only was it important to me how these characters behaved in various circumstances, but it was also important to *them*, who had been created many centuries ago, to know how I was acting today. And just as they had influenced the conduct of individuals in many lands and over many centuries, so I, too, with my decisions and choices had the power to inspire or disenchant those who had existed in the past as well as those who would come in the future.

This mystical feeling of the interconnection of human souls was forged in the gloomy prison-camp world when our zeks' solidarity was the one weapon we had to oppose the world of evil, and when the defeat of any of us had an immediate and painful effect on the others. It was tempered in the punishment cells, where the supportive voices of my friends reached me only if I summoned them through a mental effort and only if our hearts were tuned to the same frequency. This feeling of our great unity and solidarity that knew neither temporal nor spatial limits crystallized during my hunger strike when the voices from *their* world, the voices of the guards, the doctor, or the radio, hailed me only in order to pour in another portion of the mixture or to remind me it was still not too late to join them. With each round, however, I lingered with them less and less. My eyes would indifferently scan the drab cell, lingering over the picture of Avital at the waterfall of Ein Gedi, and I would happily follow her into *our* world.

"The time is out of joint," says Hamlet in a moment of despair when he encounters villainy face-to-face. But now I was restoring temporal connections by entering into a fraternal union with those who helped me defend dignity—not my own personal dignity but the dignity of Man, created in God's image and likeness.

Of course the world in which I was immersed was not black and white, or good and evil. In order to divide the entire world into two distinct camps, one had to pass through a long zone of fear, vacillations, and doubts. And there were many people, both real and fictional, who tried to reinforce my doubts.

Above all, there was Galileo, whose name had come up in a conversation with Timofeev, my cell mate in Lefortovo. "Now, there was a smart man," he said. "He recanted to the Inquisition and was able to continue his scientific research with so much benefit to mankind. And at the end of his life, he uttered the eternal words [referring, of course, to the earth], 'And yet it moves,' restoring the truth." Once it was brought up, Galileo's name didn't leave my mind. The authority of that great scientist pressed upon me no less than the arguments of my own inquisitors. In the end, I stood up to debate with Galileo as well, and he and I ended up on opposite sides of the fence.

For me, Galileo was one of the few true giants in history, a scientific pioneer who, among other achievements, discovered the principle of inertia. And yet his very fame undoubtedly multiplied the number of individuals in various times and places who cited his great name in order to justify their own moral failure, caused by an inertia of fear, and who argued that what they told the authorities was less important than the fact that "it moves."

Although Galileo recanted to the Inquisition three and a half centuries earlier, his capitulation was pressing on me, trying to push me into doing likewise. But if I accepted the KGB's proposal, in addition to betraying myself I would be adding to the evil in the world. For perhaps at some future date my own decision would be a harmful influence on some other prisoner.

As I recalled my disputes and conversations with friends and opponents, both real and imaginary, as I thought about those who inspired me in this struggle and inspired me by their very existence, I formulated for myself a new law: the law of universal attraction, interconnection, and interdependence of human souls. I discussed it in a letter to Avital, although from prison, of course, I could explain my position only allegorically: "In addition to Newton's law of the universal gravitational pull of objects, there is also a universal gravitational pull of souls, of the bond between them and the influence of one soul on the other. With each word we speak and each step we take, we touch other souls and have an impact on them. Why should I put this sin on my soul? If I have already succeeded once in tearing the spider's web, breaking with the difficult life of doublethink and closing the gap between thought and word, how is it now possible to take even one step backward toward the previous state?"

A few days after I sent this letter, it was returned to me with words that ominously recalled the terrible events of the previous year: "You are a citizen of the USSR and there is no reason for you to write letters abroad."

Romanov, of course, had said exactly the same thing after my last meeting with my family, and I had then embarked on a long struggle that led to the hunger strike. The procurators had blamed Romanov for this situation, but Romanov was dead. Now what? After all that had happened, I had no intention of submitting complaints all over again. I immediately began another hunger strike.

But my heart was clearly unprepared, and within a day I suffered chest pains like those I had experienced in the second month of my longer hunger strike. On the third day the procurator appeared, and I reminded him of all the assurances that he and his superiors had given me.

"You're right, it's scandalous," he said. "I will immediately order them to accept your letter, and you will stop your hunger strike."

"No, first of all, explain to the administration in my presence that they are violating the law. Let them take the letter and show me it was sent, and then I'll stop the hunger strike."

The procurator summoned the censor, and I gave him my letter to Avital. The procurator explained that I had the right to send a letter to Israel, and that he was speaking in the name of the procurator general of the Tatar Autonomous Republic.

"You have your boss," the censor replied, "and I have mine. I have orders not to accept the letter."

I stood up and laughed, saying, "Well, now we can see who wields the real power—the KGB or the procurator's office."

I returned to my cell, leaving the letter with the procurator and the censor. The next morning they brought me a confirmation that my letter had been sent to Israel. I stopped my hunger strike, but it took another three weeks before Mama informed me in a telegram that Avital had received my letter.

After my long hunger strike, the restoration of my correspondence home was the most significant feature of my life in prison, but it wasn't the only change. During a sixteen-month period I wasn't punished even once, nor was I deprived of any meetings. My behavior hadn't changed at all: I maintained intercell communication, continued to write "slanderous statements," and participated in solidarity hunger strikes with other prisoners. As before, the prison officials regularly drew up reports about disciplinary violations, which were normally the harbingers of punishment. I would be caught talking through the radiator or the toilet bowl, and my companions would be punished, but not I. Or we would declare a hunger strike in solidarity with a friend, and my fellow zeks would be deprived of a meeting and switched to a less nutritious diet, while the authorities would pretend not to notice me.

The reader might rationally assume that the policy was related to my health. True, I was plagued by constant chest pains, which intensified with sudden motions and turned me into an invalid in the months following my hunger strike. But anyone who is familiar with the Gulag will understand the absurdity of this assumption. The authorities had their own reasons for being lenient. In response to the wave of protests over my hunger strike, Andropov had promised that I would be released for "good behavior," and apparently he was determined to prove that I had genuinely started on the road to "rehabilitation," no matter how I actually behaved. This hypothesis was confirmed by the fact that my punishments were resumed a few weeks after Andropov's death in February 1984.

Whereas 1983 was a year of "thaw" for me, this wasn't the case for the other politicals in Chistopol. Many zeks waited tensely for the results of the Madrid conference, where, based on the meager reports in the newspaper, we assumed that a struggle was taking place around the issue of human rights. The prison held members of the Moscow, Ukrainian, Lithuanian, and Armenian Helsinki groups, men who had sacrificed their freedom trying to test the willingness of the Soviet Union to observe the agreements it had signed in Helsinki. What would the West do now, when, eight years after Helsinki, the Soviet Union had moved even further along the road of repressions against any citizen who took those agreements seriously? Fragmentary information that reached us during family meetings confirmed that the West was pressuring the Soviets, demanding the release of political prisoners and freedom of emigration. But in the highly isolated environment of prison, encouraging words spoken at international forums were often inflated into significant hints, or even incontestable indications, that there would soon be a change for the better.

The Madrid conference ended, the next declaration was signed, and *Pravda* printed a condensed version of the text. We read it carefully, how all sides obligated themselves, made promises, and so on—just as at Helsinki. So what had the West attained during this period? Prison is the most sensitive barometer of change, and in prison nothing had changed. The politicals did not conceal their disappointment, and one of them began to circulate a new curse: "Madrid, you motherfucker." In Russian the two words are almost identical.

In October 1983, only three weeks after Madrid, the prison bosses went from cell to cell and announced the adoption of a new law, Article 188.3, which stated that the terms of prisoners who violated discipline in prisons and camps could routinely be extended by a court. In the case of politicals, up to five years could be added at once. In other words, if you continued to insist on your views or to protest injustice, they could now give you an additional prison term just as if you had committed a new "crime."

And why not? After all, we were imprisoned in the first place because of our views, so why should the authorities release us if those views hadn't changed? Previously, however, they'd had to invent some kind of provocation to justify their logic, whereas now the law made their job much easier. Rumors about the new law had been circulating for months, but apparently the authorities had waited until after Madrid to avoid giving critics in the West something more to use at the conference.

It is human nature to hope for the best, and after a few months the more optimistic zeks said, "Look, they adopted the law, but they aren't in a rush to apply it." Unfortunately, even these hopes proved idle.

When the news came of Andropov's death, I was writing my next letter. As with Brezhnev's death, shouts of joy rang out in the cells, and prison officers and soldiers with German shepherds began making the rounds. I decided not to interrupt my letter. On the one hand, of course, I couldn't be indifferent to the death of a dictator who had headed the KGB for many years and had directed the fabrication of charges against me. On the other hand, I didn't want to think about the possible consequences of Andropov's death—either positive or negative, for the country in general or for me personally—at the very moment I was concentrating on communicating with my family.

In March my letter to Avital was confiscated. In April they put me in the punishment cell for throwing a note to another zek in the exercise cell. Punishment is inevitable in such cases, but during the past sixteen months I had gotten away with much more. And so I would have to spend Passover in the punishment cell—the first Passover when I was to have matzoh!

Arkady Tsurkov had received a package of matzoh from home. He divided it into two parts, and for a long time sought an opportunity to send it to me and another Jewish zek. "I don't need it," he said. "After all, I'm going to be released." But instead of release he earned another two years of camp, and he greeted Passover, the holiday of freedom, somewhere far away, among criminals. And now, I, too, at the last moment had lost the opportunity to use Arkasha's matzoh, which I received from a zek who was transferred to my cell. Well, so what? The salted sprats would be my *maror*, the bitter herb, and for the *charoset*, the sweet mixture of nuts, apples, and wine, I would use my cup of hot water. What could be sweeter in the punishment cell? I tried to recall everything I could from the

Passover Haggadah, starting with my favorite lines: "In every generation a person should feel as though he, personally, went out of
Egypt" and "Today we are slaves, tomorrow we shall be free men.
Today we are here; tomorrow in Jerusalem." The thaw was over,
the future was fraught with new tribulations, and I hurried to steel
myself with the words of the Haggadah.

My mood improved markedly when I left the punishment cell
and learned that my April letter had successfully reached home.
Good, at least I didn't have to start another hunger strike. I had put
a lot of effort into that letter; each one that arrived home was like
another part of my life that was saved from imprisonment.

But the KGB was eager to show me that the period of liberalization was over. I soon spent another term in the punishment cell,
which was followed by six months of strict regime. In response I
increased the length of my letters, bringing them up to forty, even
forty-five pages. Still they passed the censor. Evidently the authorities didn't want me to start another hunger strike.

On the strict regime I again wound up with my old camp friend
Volodia Poresh. He had gone through work strikes and hunger
strikes to get back his Bible, so our astonishment and rapture knew
no bounds when, toward the end of 1983, he suddenly received it.
What was going on here? Was the KGB playing new games with
Poresh? Or had there been a change in attitude at the highest levels?

It was impossible to know, but in any case I decided not to let the
occasion pass without trying to obtain a Bible of my own. My efforts
were fruitless, but I was still able to enjoy reading the Bible with my
Christian friend Volodia.

Every morning after returning from the exercise yard, we began
our Bible study. Volodia did the actual reading, as my eyes were
again failing me and I couldn't follow a printed text for more than
five or ten minutes without pain. Although we knew they could take
the Bible away from us at any time, we made no effort to hurry. We
decided to read both from the Old Testament and the New, and to
discuss what we had read.

We called our sessions "Reaganite readings," first, because President Reagan had declared either this year or the preceding one (it
wasn't exactly clear from the Soviet press) the Year of the Bible, and,
second, because we realized that even the slightest improvement in

our situation could be related only to a firm position on human rights by the West, especially by America, and we mentally urged Reagan to demonstrate such resolve.

As a child I knew almost nothing about the Bible other than Papa's stories about David and Goliath, Samson and Delilah, and Joseph and his brothers. And in the heat of my struggle to become a free person, almost no time was left for contemplating why the biblical tales, which were full of miracles that my skeptical mind refused to believe and accounts that I perceived only as a poetic rendering of history, had such an enormous moral influence on me.

My arrest changed everything. When the prison gates closed behind me, the huge world that had opened before me in recent years as the arena of an all-encompassing struggle between good and evil was suddenly narrowed down to the dimensions of a prison cell and my interrogator's office. I had to take everything that was dear to me, everything that had meaning in my life, with me to prison. The world I re-created in my head turned out to be more powerful and more real than the world of Lefortovo Prison; my bond with Avital was stronger than my isolation, and my inner freedom more powerful than the external bondage. Mysticism turned into reality, and through my prayers I seemed to admit the power of an external force that my rational mind had denied.

The Psalm book was the sole material evidence of my mystical tie with Avital. What impelled her to send it to me on the eve of my arrest? And how did it happen that I received it on the day of my father's death? The reading of the Psalms not only reinforced our bond but also demystified their author. King David now appeared before me not as a fabled hero or a mystical superman but as a live, indomitable soul—tormented by doubts, rising against evil, and suffering from the thought of his own sins. He was proud, daring, and resolute, but in order to be bold in combat with his enemies, he had to be humble before the Lord. The fear of God guided David when he entered the valley of death.

When I first came across the concept of *yir'at shamayim* (the fear of God), I automatically understood it as referring to the fear of God's punishment for our sins. But as I read the Psalms it became harder to maintain this narrow, utilitarian understanding of these words. Why had I refused to enter into any discussions with the

KGB after my trial? Why was I prepared to die unless they sent my letters? Why did I refuse to ask for a release for reasons of health? Why was it so important for me not to take one step back toward that servile life I had once led? In time I began to understand that *yir'at shamayim* includes both an admiration of the grand divine design and worship of the divine might, as well as man's instinctive fear of being unworthy of his lofty role.

"The fear of the Lord is the beginning of knowledge," Poresh read aloud from the words of King Solomon in the Book of Proverbs, and for me these words seemed to be a natural summation of long years of spiritual search. I wrote in my next letter home:

> Perhaps this feeling is a necessary prerequisite for man's achieving inner freedom, and is also the prerequisite for spiritual resolve. Perhaps the fear of the Lord is the only thing that can conquer human fear, and all that remains for us is to repeat after King Solomon, "The fear of the Lord is the beginning of knowledge."
>
> And if you want my opinion on the origin of this fear of God, whether it was bequeathed from on high or was cultivated by man himself through the course of history, this is essentially a question about the source of religion—that is, a question to which there will never be an answer. And while I am well aware how much blood has been spilled over this question and how important it is to so many people, for me it's immaterial. Having realized there is no answer, I am not even searching for it. Does it really matter where this religious feeling stems from, whether man in some fashion was able to rise above his physical nature, or whether he was created that way? For me, the important thing is that this feeling really exists, that I sense its force and power over me, that it influences my deeds and my life, and that for ten years it has linked me with Avital more concretely than any letters.

Yes, we were bound to each other not merely by memories of the past, or by photographs or a few letters, but precisely by that elevated feeling of freedom from human evil and bondage to God's covenant that lifted us above earthly reality. Volodia read how God's angel instructed the prophet Elijah on how he would hear the divine voice: first there will be a storm that will crush the rocks, but God will not be in it; then an earthquake, but God will not be there; then a fire, but He is not there, either; and finally, a quiet wind—and there you will hear Him. Having passed through the storm of my struggle against the KGB for the right to emigrate, having undergone the earthquake of my arrest and the fire of cold punishment cells, I listened to the words of the Bible and through them Avital and I both heard and understood each other.

Volodia and I normally read a book of the Old Testament and a short chapter of the New Testament, but I perceived these texts in different ways. Although I was responsive to the New Testament's concern with not losing the meaning or the spirit of the ritual in the letter of the law, I could not detach myself from its historical context. When my companion read me the parts where the Jews scream, "Let him die! His blood will be on us and our children," I couldn't help thinking how many bloody crimes against my people, how many millions of murders and other violent deeds, had been justified by these words.

Volodia was also aware of it. Tearing himself away from his reading, he suddenly said to me, "You know, I feel like"—and here he named some unfamiliar French Christian philosopher—"who said that persecuting Jews in the name of Christianity is the same as murdering one's parents for the sake of affirming a 'new truth.' There can be no justification for this."

His voice was trembling, and I already knew Volodia well enough to realize that he was speaking from the bottom of his heart.

This marvelous reading continued for an entire month until they put us in different cells, and during that month the feeling grew stronger that no matter how different our paths, or how different our prayers, we were praying to the same God, who instructed us to fear no evil as we entered the valley of death.

Half a year later, in July 1984, I wound up in the same cell as Volodia for the last time, as his five years of imprisonment were due to end on August 1. But would he really be released? In recent months the situation had changed for the worse. New orders had come out, making the conditions in the punishment cell even harsher "with the purpose of intensifying its educative effect." And if you began a hunger strike they put you in the punishment cell immediately.

The main thing, however, was that the authorities began to apply the new law that enabled them to extend a prison term almost automatically for disciplinary violations. Recently, one of the political prisoners, Nikolai Ilishkin, was separated from us and put in the end cell in anticipation of a trial under Article 188.3. In this context, it seemed particularly ominous that in the past two months the prison administration had punished Volodia as often as possible—the punishment cell, followed by strict regime, followed by another term in the punishment cell—and were probably doing this to justify the application of Article 188.3. It looked as if the KGB was unwilling to accept that yet another zek—especially one who had seemed like easy prey at the time of his arrest—could leave the kingdom of the Gulag undefeated.

Volodia had two lovely daughters. When he was arrested, one was two years old and the other had just been born. Poresh followed their lives through occasional photographs, but the girls lacked even this connection to their father. Their only link to him was through their mother's stories and the reading of his infrequent letters from prison. I remember how long Volodia would sit over each letter, slowly choosing the words to send to his little girls, words that had to take the place of a paternal caress and a father's smile. The last time Volodia had seen his wife was two years earlier, in their native Leningrad, where he had been brought for so-called prophylactic work. The KGB had pressured him and threatened him and suggested that he influence his wife; he had refused. They had pressured his wife, suggesting that she influence her husband; she had refused. They took him to Chistopol and he hadn't seen his wife again. Four times in a row they had denied him his next meeting.

As his final weeks of imprisonment came and went the tension mounted by the day. Would they release him or not? His mail showed that the tension on the outside among Volodia's family and close friends was just as great. In one recent letter from his wife, Tatiana, describing the girls' playfulness, she had written that the time had come for them to have a father: "They need you so much, Volodia. . . ." It was as if she were trying to influence fate.

Volodia's name day—the day of his patron saint—was four or five days before his scheduled release. It was also the name day of our third cell mate, Volodia Balakhanov, whom I had first met back in 1978. His twelve-year term was also coming to an end; only half a year remained. In the current situation, however, given his record of "bad behavior," who knew what awaited him? In order not to give in to anxious thoughts, we decided to use the opportune excuse of the double holiday to enjoy ourselves a little. We decided to hold a feast and to prepare a torte for it.

I had long ago heard tales about prison tortes, but as with the fabulous exotic delicacies of the East, I had never actually eaten one. In order to prepare such a torte you had to accumulate a fair amount of various foods, which was possible only under certain conditions. First, you had to have been on a "normal" diet for a long time; second, you or your cell mates had to acquire an additional three rubles' worth of food products in the prison shop; and third, nobody in your cell could be in such terrible health that it would be immoral to hoard food without feeding him.

All three of us were far from the dietary norm, but our desire to hold a memorable evening before our separation was so powerful that we decided to hoard food anyway. Over the course of two weeks we piled up about two hundred grams of sugar and two kilos of rolls. Moreover, Balakhanov, who had not lost his store privileges, acquired a package of margarine and some candy and a packet of green tea. On the morning of July 27, we began with pomp and ceremony to prepare the torte.

With the help of bowls and mugs we ground up the rolls—that was our flour. A glass of water into which all the candies had been melted was poured over it and the mixture was stirred; this was our sweet dough. The package of margarine was mixed with the sugar and whipped up—this was the frosting. Now we had only to stick in the matches with their heads up in the shape of the letter V. In the evening an appropriate speech was delivered, and we lifted up our mugs of tea and lit the end match. The flame raced forward, and then we ate.

I ate my portion over three days, as I simply couldn't manage more than two spoonfuls at a time of such a filling, delectable treat. In the end I even shared my portion with my friends, who managed to finish their portions more rapidly. To call the result "tasty" is to demean it. The very word "tasty" seems insipid with regard to this celestial dish.

Before we sat at the festive table, Volodia took out the photograph of his dear ones and put it on the little bedstand together with postcards from home of biblical scenes painted by Raphael and Rembrandt that he used as icons, and he began to pray. He did this every evening, but this time he prayed for an unusually long time and with special passion. An experienced zek respects the right of his cell mate to a personal life, and doesn't violate the temporal and physical bounds that are reserved for his neighbor. I was lying on my cot, engrossed in a book, but when I accidentally turned toward Volodia I saw that he was looking at the photograph of his wife and little girls and his eyes were full of tears. He was praying to God for mercy. His position toward the KGB was like reinforced concrete, but in order to be strong in this world he had to be humble before God.

That evening was also the start of the Sabbath, so when Volodia had finished praying, I sat at the table and began reciting the Psalms. I had long ago become accustomed to reciting twenty or thirty Psalms on the Sabbath, but because they had taken away all the large-print Psalms that I had copied out, I had to read the microscopic text of my tiny Psalm book while ignoring the pain in my eyes. I was reading to myself when I heard a sigh from Volodia Balakhanov, who was pensively squatting and smoking near the cell door.

"O Lord," he said, "give us the strength to preserve the purity of this life in the future!" What awaited us in the future? Volodia Poresh's fate would be decided in a few days, and Balakhanov's in a few months. But what about mine?

On the morning of August first, the final day of Poresh's five-year term, they took us out for exercise. For the last time I repeated to Volodia the messages I wanted him to convey when he was released. I didn't want to mention other possibilities, but Volodia sensed my unspoken question.

"Don't worry, I'm ready for any possibility."

When we returned to the cell, the duty officer said, "Poresh, with your things!"

"Can the bedstand be left with us?" I asked.

"No, let him take everything. Ten minutes to collect your things."

"Everything will be fine, I'm sure," Volodia Balakhanov kept repeating.

I kept silent. I had asked about the bedstand because if they were really taking Poresh out of prison, then he wouldn't need it. This looked like a bad sign, but maybe they were simply playing games with us.

The final embraces. We blessed each other, each with the words of his own prayer. Volodia left, the cell door slammed. I glued myself to the door, and it looked as if they had taken Volodia into the opposite cell, where the administration usually talked with prisoners. The minutes dragged ever so slowly, and a funereal silence reigned in the cell. Finally the door of the opposite cell opened and I heard a hoarse voice, "So, now I'll be with Kolya."

Was that really Volodia's voice? Yes, he was informing us that they were taking him to the end cell, with Nikolai Ilishkin, where he would await a new trial. Soon he received another three years of imprisonment under Article 188.3 for "malicious violation of prison discipline." His violation consisted of the fact that he somehow slept in the cell during the daytime, that on another occasion he didn't sleep at night, and that he was also caught in an attempt to throw a note to a neighboring yard during the exercise period.

For several days I was preoccupied with Poresh's rearrest. Why did this incident have such an effect on me? Hadn't many dramas unfolded in front of me during these years? I wasn't thinking of Volodia, however. I knew that he wouldn't break, and although it would be very difficult for him, he would take himself in hand. No, I was thinking about his wife and children. How would they bear this blow?

You choose your own path of struggle in this world, but in making choices for yourself you also make them for your family. Do I have the right to do this? I asked myself. The KGB often tried to play on these feelings: "If you don't have compassion on yourself, then have compassion on your mother!" I had long ago learned to reject their conclusions and not to allow their words to enter my heart, but now I couldn't help thinking of Volodia's family—and also of mine.

Shortly before these events, another prisoner gave me a gift of some ragged little pages that had been torn out of a journal many years ago by a zek, and had been passed from hand to hand ever since. It was an excerpt from Camus's essay "The Myth of Sisyphus."

> The gods had condemned Sisyphus to ceaselessly rolling a rock to the top of a mountain, whence the stone would fall back of its own weight. They had thought with some reason that there is no more dreadful punishment than futile and hopeless labor. . . . At the very end of his long effort measured by skyless space and time without depth, the purpose is achieved. Then Sisyphus watches the stone rush down in a few moments toward that lower world whence he will have to push it up again toward the summit. . . . It is during that return, that pause, that Sisyphus interests me. . . . I see that man going back down with a heavy yet measured step toward the torment of which he will never know the end. . . . At each of these moments when he leaves the heights and gradually sinks toward the lairs of the gods, he is superior to his fate. . . . Again I fancy Sisyphus returning toward his rock, and the sorrow was in the beginning. When the images of earth cling too tightly to memory, when the call of happiness becomes too insistent, it happens that melancholy rises in man's heart: this is the rock's victory, this is the rock itself. The boundless grief is too heavy to bear. . . . But crushing truths perish from being acknowledged. . . .

I read and perceived these words as if each sentence had been written about us zeks. For wasn't this the way we traversed the circles of the Gulag, and having finished one term, began another? Didn't we suffer when "images of earth" became too strong? But what did "too strong" mean? Did feeling pain over loved ones mean we were permitting the victory of the stone?

In my next letter home I wrote:

> I felt long ago that the meaning of life can be discovered only when you challenge fate and destiny, when you tear yourself away from the numbing iron embraces of "social," "historical," and other necessities. In time I also understood what a cunning and deadly enemy even hope can be. . . . If you don't see the meaning of the life you are leading this very minute, if it appears only when you live on the hope of rapid changes, then you are in constant danger.
>
> It is difficult enough for man to reconcile himself to infinity and to meaninglessness, but it is totally impossible to adjust to infinite meaninglessness. Therefore, if his life today seems meaningless, man

inevitably makes himself see the end of it on a near horizon. All you must do is drag the stone one more time to the summit. But in the end, deceptive hope poisons the soul and weakens the spirit.

During these years I have met people who have been weakened from constant disappointments. They continually create new hopes for themselves, and as a result they betray themselves. Others live in the world of illusions, hastily and incessantly building and rebuilding their world in order to prevent real life from ultimately destroying it.

What, then, is the solution? The only answer is to find the meaning of your current life. It's best if you are left with only one hope— the hope of remaining yourself no matter what happens. *Don't fear, don't believe, and don't hope. Don't believe words from the outside; believe your own heart. Believe in that meaning which was revealed to you in this life, and hope that you will succeed in guarding it.*

In Camus's essay, Sisyphus looks calmly at the stone rolling down. Although he has no control over the stone, he is calm. He descends not as a slave but as a man who has risen above his fate. But what if his mother, his wife, and his children are in the way of the stone? That is the real problem here. Simply rising above this suffering means making all your efforts meaningless. If you are going to suffer, then how can you suffer and not flinch? How can you suffer and not be broken by the desire to defend your loved ones from suffering?

There is, of course, one solution—in the complete mingling of two fates into one—together we roll the rock up the mountain, and together we stand under it, like Avital and me.

I thus shared my gloomy thoughts from prison without being able to explain what evoked them. When the opportunity finally arose, and I told Avital about my doubts, she said, "I don't understand the problem. Had you betrayed yourself for my sake, you would have betrayed me as well."

24

The Call of the
Shofar

I N the spring of 1984, a few weeks before our tenth anniversary, I had the following dream: I saw Avital in what was apparently our Jerusalem apartment, although she looked as she had in Moscow, with long hair down to her shoulders. She had just come back from the market with two full bags, a detail that clearly wasn't part of our Moscow life, where we never had full bags of food except at our wedding. We joyfully rushed toward each other, and for some reason Avital asked me anxiously, "Do you know me? Haven't I changed?"

I was astonished. "How long has it been since I've seen you?" I asked. "An hour or two?"

We looked at each other and said, as if to ourselves but out loud, "Ten years."

These words clapped like thunder, and I awoke. Lying there, under the burden of ten years, I realized again what a piece of life had been cut off. Our youth had gone by and we couldn't deceive each other that our life was just beginning. But what were the days, weeks, and even months that still separated us, compared with the time when we would finally be together in Israel?

My second term in Chistopol came to an end in the fall of 1984. Now I faced another transport to the camp, and then, if all went well, another private meeting with my family.

I looked forward to new encounters along the way, to amusing and informative conversations with criminals, but this time I was disappointed. I traveled with a special convoy, and there was no

chance of being mistakenly thrust into a compartment with criminals because my personal bodyguard would not permit it. I acquired
a companion only on the last segment of the journey, but I shall
describe him later.

I arrived in Perm 35 at night. The pitch-darkness was broken up
by the brightly lit snowy strips of the forbidden zone. If they took
me straight ahead, I was going to the zone; a right turn meant the
punishment cell, a left turn the hospital. As they did five years ago,
they took me to the hospital. But this time, instead of ten days, I was
there for two months.

These were undoubtedly my two healthiest months since my
arrest seven and a half years earlier. In addition to hospital food, I
received as much meat soup and kasha as I wanted, and very soon
I began to gain weight.

A medical examination confirmed the old diagnosis of myocardial
dysfunction. They began to treat me with injections, pills, and
vitamins, and my heart grew stronger by the day as I was flooded
with new energy. I went out for two hours a day of exercise, but
instead of being confined to stone prison yards, I now had the
opportunity to walk among pines and birches, which were drown-
ing in deep snow. Although barbed wire surrounded a tiny segment
of the winter forest, it didn't fence me off from the sun that hung
above the trees, the pure frosty air, or the gorgeous northern sunsets.
It seemed like such a marvelous change in my fate, but as I soon
discovered, this change also had its dark side.

When I first returned to the camp I had demanded a meeting with
my family, the private meeting I was entitled to once a year on the
camp regime but which hadn't taken place for five years. My old
friend Osin, with whom I had once celebrated Hanukkah, explained
with an affable smile, "I can't give you a meeting while you're in
the hospital. The doctor says you need treatment. What if you
suddenly had a heart attack in the middle of the meeting?"

They also confiscated all my letters home, so I couldn't inform
my family that I was in the hospital and our meeting was delayed.
Even when I reduced my letter to the brief notice that I had safely
reached the camp from prison, it didn't pass the censor.

I learned later that my family and friends were sick with worry,
as I had left the prison on a transport and had seemingly disap-

peared. If I was in camp, why were there no letters—not even an official confirmation that I had arrived, as required by law? As the tension mounted, my supporters turned to international organizations, including the Red Cross. One inquiry followed another, but to no avail.

This went on for two months. I was on the verge of declaring a new hunger strike when the duty officer came to the hospital and led me to the guardhouse, into the room for meetings. This time, too, I was searched by Alik Ataev, who once again showed a great interest in my rear end. Suddenly I was in the embrace of Mama and Lenya! This time our meeting would be forty-eight hours instead of twenty-four. "You'll see," I joked. "In another five years they'll give us three days."

Mama and Lenya looked at me in disbelief. They had feared for my life, but now I looked so much better than when they saw me through the glass in Chistopol. I explained that I had just spent two months in the hospital.

Quickly, the picture became clear. At that very moment, another two-day meeting was taking place—in Geneva, between Secretary of State Shultz and Foreign Minister Gromyko. Before it began, Avital held a press conference for the foreign press. The following day a representative of the Soviet Foreign Ministry, who was also in Geneva, declared that soon I would be given a meeting with my family. After two months of anxiety about my whereabouts, everyone breathed a sigh of relief. The Soviets had made another of their "goodwill" gestures, and the American State Department responded that they viewed this as a positive development.

And what if I hadn't disappeared for two months? What if they had given us the meeting as soon as I arrived in camp, as prescribed by Soviet law? My family would not have been tormented by uncertainty, but then the Soviet Union would not have reaped political dividends for its "flexibility." "Yes," I told my brother, "the KGB knows how to work. This way they can present not only each meeting but each letter home as a magnanimous gesture. Why release a man? That's only a one-time concession, whereas if you keep him in jail, you can concede to the West any number of times."

The atmosphere at this second private meeting differed from the one five years earlier as maturity differs from youth. Back then we had forgone sleep in a hopeless attempt to make up for lost time and to fill each other in on the mountains of information that had accumulated over the years. But now, in unhurried conversation, we enjoyed each minute, recalling not only the past five years but our entire lives, from childhood on. Lenya even told me the latest jokes from Moscow, and sang some songs of the late Volodia Visotsky, the fantastically popular songwriter and performer, that had appeared after my arrest.

Most of all we talked about Avital's travels and her meetings with Shultz, Reagan, Thatcher, and Mitterrand. She had been almost everywhere, and had complained to Lenya that Italy was the worst, for each time she arrived in Rome there was a different prime minister.

Not wanting to become a prisoner of my own optimism, I moderated my delight. Poor darling! I thought. Yes, we are together all the time, but how much harder it is for you than for me! I was doing all I could, but as long as I was a prisoner, Avital would feel she wasn't doing enough. I did what I could, but at least my choices were clear; hers were far more complicated. But she didn't like it when I wrote along these lines. "Aren't we together?" she replied. "Please don't separate me from you."

Although I knew some of the surface details, I simply couldn't imagine the enormous scale and depth of the nonstop campaign that Avital was waging with thousands of friends and supporters around the world. I understood this only after my release, and even then it took many months.

The recent photographs of Avital showed her wearing a kerchief. Mama was obviously concerned that Avital had become more religiously observant, but for me this wasn't a problem. I knew that her growing involvement with Judaism was giving her strength, and that even if there were some differences in our respective paths, these changes were only adding to her spirituality, which was the one way we could be together.

Despite the unhurried, smooth tone of our talks during these two days, I managed to tell my family a great deal about life in Chistopol Prison, including details I couldn't write in letters and couldn't mention in the shorter meetings where the guards listened to every word. Among other things, I described how my fellow prisoners were treated, giving names, dates, and sparing no details of brutality.

The KGB, of course, was listening to everything we said. Their office was right above the room where zeks met their families, and from the zone you could see that during these meetings the lights in that office burned around the clock.

Osin himself came in toward the end of our meeting. (If the meeting hadn't been a deliberate concession by the Soviets to the Americans, we would have been interrupted much earlier.) He looked unusually upset, and choosing his words carefully, he turned to Mama: "You will return to Moscow, and there you will not—uh, will not talk about what you heard here. Otherwise, you know that, well, it won't be good for your son."

I don't know what surprised me more: Osin's stupid attempt at blackmail or his naive hope that it might work. Mama reacted quickly: "You can rest assured that I won't give out any slanderous information. I'll tell only the truth."

Although Osin was clearly displeased by Mama's response, he made a goodwill gesture and permitted me to take back into the zone five kilos of food she had brought to the meeting—an improvement over last time, when they didn't let me bring back a half-eaten apple. Although the KGB was unhappy with our conversation, in sending Osin they were trying to play the good cop.

Mama saw this gesture as cause for hope, but I remembered all too well how things had often changed immediately after a meeting, so I didn't jump to conclusions. After the farewell embraces and the traditional words of hope for a speedy release, I finally returned to the zone I had left four years ago, where it turned out that miracles hadn't ceased.

This time I was given the job of barracks orderly, or, in camp slang, "busybody." My duties consisted of washing the floors in the barracks when everyone went out to work, dusting, bringing the bed linen to the laundry once a week, shoveling the snow near the entrance to the barracks, and so on. All of this was much easier than working at the lathe or in the boiler room, and as a rule the authorities gave this job to their own people. How had I come to deserve such an honor? Perhaps, like last time, they had kicked out some old guy to turn the other zeks against me? No, this time the position was truly open. I assumed they wanted to present me as a "promising" zek, if not one who had actually started down the road to rehabilitation. Well, I decided, the position won't determine my conduct.

The zone had visibly changed in the past four years, between 1981 and 1985. Some of the older collaborators had died, others had been released, and those who remained hadn't grown any younger. Now the softer jobs were occupied by younger people—including failed spies, unsuccessful border violators, and even penitent dissidents. Unfortunately for me, most of the active zeks (including Anatoly Marchenko, my colleague on the Moscow Helsinki Group) had either been transferred to other zones or were sitting in the camp prison or punishment cell. The punishment-cell records established by Poresh, Meilanov, and me in 1981 had long ago been broken as the KGB tried to demonstrate that resistance was pointless. Since I was last here, Ivan Kovalev and Valery Senderov had spent an entire *year* in the punishment cell.

Several other dissidents who agreed to ask for a pardon had been released with great pomp. Formerly the KGB had said: Win our favor through good behavior and then apply for a pardon, which we will support. But now they were urging zeks to request a pardon without any preconditions. Then, when the matter was being considered, when the hopes of a zek's family and his friends had been raised, and everybody was pressing on the zek to compromise, they would impose their conditions: Do this, tell us about that. I had to admit that in some cases their success was evident.

The newcomers to the zone were considerably better educated than the older residents. Many knew several foreign languages and held advanced degrees. As a rule, they did not come out of the tradition of common resistance, so it was no longer possible to organize a collective work or hunger strike, or even a campaign of protest letters in support of those who were locked in the punishment cell.

"It's senseless."

"What good does it do?"

"I'm not well enough to sit in the punishment cell."

These were the arguments I now heard.

Not every active dissident had been removed from the zone. By leaving two or three recalcitrants, the authorities, with the help of informers, could carefully monitor how the other zeks responded to these people. After all, it's much easier to study people in a dynamic, heterogeneous environment than in a world that's amorphous and static.

I immediately became friendly with Boris Grezin, a Russian of about thirty-five. He had spent his life in Latvia, married a Latvian woman, and preferred to speak Latvian. Boris had worked as an electrician on a fishing boat, which enabled him to travel to Europe, Africa, and Latin America. Naturally the sailors had to be let ashore, which subjected them to the risk of infection by the germs of capitalist ideology. As a result, the men were permitted to leave the boat only in groups of between two and five. (It was difficult to keep an eye on more than five men at a time.) Each group included one person whom the KGB especially trusted, although, understandably, all seamen who sail abroad must receive special approval.

But no matter how strict the rules, people always find ways around them, and on several occasions Boris managed to detach himself from his group. His aim was not to remain abroad, as he had a wife and daughter waiting for him in Riga. But he wrote poetry, and he sent his poems to Western radio stations that broadcast in Russian to the Soviet Union. His poems were critical of the Soviet regime, and although Boris supplied neither his name nor his return address, the KGB tracked him down. When the crew returned home, he was arrested. They showed him copies of his letters and gave him a very mild sentence for the Gulag—five years.

His dissident activity, which had been secret until his arrest, became open here in the zone, and he offered quiet but stubborn resistance to all KGB efforts to "reeducate" him. But you could count on the fingers of one hand the number of such people in the zone.

Zakharov, the KGB worker, was a large man with small, malicious eyes and the cold look of a murderer, who would talk with each zek alone at great length, calling him into his office in front of all the others. The camp tradition of immediately revealing to one's fellow zeks everything that was said in these meetings had apparently disappeared, and the result was an atmosphere of universal distrust—a sorry picture that was remarkably similar to life in the large zone.

Some of the newer zeks knew almost nothing about my case, and even those who did had only a vague notion about it. But they were all aware that I didn't deal with the KGB, which they found far more interesting than the details of my "espionage" for the benefit of international Zionism.

As soon as I arrived in the zone, rumors began circulating—their source was obvious—that I had begun playing games with the KGB. Naturally, the KGB did everything possible to ensure that these rumors would correspond to reality. First, they gave me an easy job. Then they granted me the right "because of conscientious work" to purchase additional items in the camp store. In January both of my letters passed the censor and flew to Moscow. Osin and Bukin, his deputy, kept hinting that my case would soon be reviewed. In short, at the height of a severe winter in the Urals, another thaw began for me.

Osin and Bukin alternated their hints about impending changes in my fate with appeals to stop my anti-Soviet remarks and my public criticism of KGB workers. "You're not a kid who enjoys teasing adults," said Bukin. "Why curse the KGB in public? Nobody's asking you to love them, but why must you advertise your feelings? I'm telling you clearly that the KGB won't bother you if you don't hinder their work." He apparently believed it would be difficult for me to reject such a generous offer.

To all external appearances I really did act like a kid waving a red flag in front of a bull. My target was opportune, as Zakharov was a petty and conceited peasant who turned red at any gibe, real or imagined. He even looked like a bull. To give him his due, unlike most KGB officers he didn't shun dirty work. He showed up in the factory workshops and in the barracks, where we'd see him slinking along the walls, keeping an eye on everyone. If he noticed any kind of "violation"—leaving the lathe during work hours or lying on one's cot before bedtime—he personally ordered the noncom to punish the offender. When he appeared in my fiefdom, from my position as orderly I usually noticed him first and signaled the others that he was coming.

"Why do you do this?" Osin asked me.

"That's how I understand my duties," I replied. "To look after the zeks in the barracks."

Once, when Zakharov came up to me and affectionately inquired, "How's your health, Anatoly Borisovich? How's your heart?" I replied rudely, "What do you care about my heart? You're a specialist in brain transplants, and my brains are clearly beyond your competence."

Then, turning away, I began to discuss loudly how the shortage of goods in the country was finally having a negative effect on the KGB. Whereas they used to pay off informers with Indian tea, they now used the inferior Georgian stuff.

Was Bukin right? Weren't these childish games I was playing? To some extent, yes. Even after ten years of intensive contact with the KGB, I preferred to be a kid who couldn't take them too seriously. In Moscow, then in Lefortovo, then in Chistopol, and now here, I felt that if I became too earnest with the KGB I would no longer feel in control. But this wasn't the only reason for my behavior. My refusing to deal with them was especially important in this new setting, as I had no desire to be part of the pious atmosphere of fear and submission they had created in the zone. And from their perspective my privileged position of orderly was supposed to reinforce that atmosphere. Before long, my recalcitrance began to yield remarkable fruit.

A few days after my arrival in the zone, R., a young zek, stopped me in the toilet and whispered that he wanted to talk to me without attracting attention. I have already explained that this was extremely difficult in the zone, as all the buildings as well as the outside spaces were watched—either by noncoms or by informers. You could conceal the contents of a conversation, but you couldn't hide whom you were talking with.

But R. wanted even the fact of our contact to remain secret. From time to time, in the early mornings, after rising before daybreak, as I was rushing to the toilet or to the hospital—one of my duties was to canvass prisoners to see who was sick—I would slip off to the side for a few minutes, away from the bright searchlights. In that setting, R. told me how the KGB had recruited him after his trial, why he had agreed, what assignments he had received, under what name he wrote reports, and where he was supposed to leave them. Initially he had refused, but then he decided to play along without working for them seriously. He had told all of this to Anatoly Marchenko when Marchenko was here, and now he was telling me.

"Why not tell others?"

"How do I know they won't tell the KGB?"

Although there were many decent, honest zeks in the zone, in the current atmosphere of universal distrust R. felt perceptible relief that there was someone who knew his secret, and to whom he could confess.

R. was only a harbinger. By the end of my first month in the zone I was regularly receiving reports from no less than four different KGB informers, not to mention several others who were vacillating. Of course it was possible that one or more of them had actually been ordered to approach me, but I had nothing to hide and no fear of provocation. I gave each one my standard advice: Don't try to outwit the KGB. If you have the strength, break away entirely. Otherwise, cooperate with them as little as possible. If they've entered into a game with you, don't assume they will leave you alone after your release. This relationship is permanent. And the further you go in these games, the higher the price you will have to pay later, when you finally break with them.

Several of my confidants offered to plant misinformation with the KGB that might be useful to me, but despite the temptation I resolutely rejected the idea. Among other things, I would be justifying their connection with the KGB and would be encouraging them to continue this contact, which couldn't result in any good for them.

I mentioned earlier that I met only one zek on the transport between Chistopol and Perm 35. Viktor Poliektov was a twenty-year-old kid with an open, almost childish Russian face, whose athletic build only highlighted his essential shyness and tendency to be easily embarrassed. He had been part of a group of young people who rebelled against the drabness of Soviet life; they had formed a secret society and exchanged letters outlining their views. The kids were arrested and recanted in court, and Viktor's sentence, in keeping with his age, was four years.

"What happens now?" he asked. "What should I be prepared for?"

"You'll be in quarantine for about ten days, and the KGB will probably talk with you."

"What, they talk with everybody?" he asked hastily and blushed.

Was this fear, I wondered, or something else? The fact that they had put me in with a new zek who had just recanted could be suspicious. But my principle was to act the same way with everyone, and not to allow suspicion to drive a wedge between us.

"Yes," I replied, "they probe everyone to discover his weaknesses. They will promise you a pardon after half a term in exchange for your cooperation. If you don't cooperate, they'll threaten to make your life difficult."

"What does cooperation mean? What do they ask you to do?"

"Squeal on your comrades."

"No, I'll never do that." He shook his head firmly, but I could see he was afraid. What would happen when he was alone with them?

"I myself have nothing to do with them," I said, "but each person must define his own position and must understand how far he is willing to go. I advise you to begin by telling them honestly, 'I want to live with you in peace, but you should know that for moral reasons I can't be an informer.' They won't leave you alone, of course, but when you enter the zone and see how different zeks behave, you'll make your own choices. But once you give in to them, it's for your whole life."

"It's really for your whole life?" Viktor asked fearfully, and—or did it only seem that he did?—he blushed again.

When I entered the zone after two months in the hospital, Viktor, or Vitia, as he was called, had completely mastered his new camp life. He worked in the boiler room with Boris Grezin, who would look after "the little kid," as we called him. We often sat with him in the evening over a cup of tea, and Vitia seemed to take in all the old zeks' experience. But his childish gaiety was frequently replaced by attacks of deep anguish, and it seemed that something was bothering him and preventing him from being completely open with us. As a result of my contacts with informers, I knew a lot about the KGB's work in the zone. When my sources confided that Boris, Vitia's co-worker, was a special object of KGB attention, the suspicion that Vitia was hiding something grew even stronger.

So what? At worst he was one more squealer in a society full of informers. But I felt sorry for the kid and genuinely wanted to help him get out of his deadly despair. Boris and I and a couple of other zeks began to tell Vitia various instructive stories about the KGB and its squealers, how easy it was to fall into their snares, and how difficult to extricate yourself. Vitia listened avidly, asked questions, and became even more gloomy. Finally, near the end of February, I asked him directly: "Vitia, I see that something is tormenting you. If you really have a secret that is weighing you down, then you'll have to live with it all your life. Is it worth it? If I'm wrong, please forgive me."

This last line wasn't necessary, for his quivering lips and tearful eyes spoke for him. With a trembling voice he told me, "It's good that you yourself asked. I've wanted to tell for a long time. And I'll do it publicly."

The following day a small crew gathered during work time in the barracks—several stokers on the off-shift and I, the orderly. Vitia told us that during the investigation and after the trial the KGB convinced him that everyone had renounced him and that his friends, whom he had trusted, had testified against him. Feeling betrayed by the entire world, Vitia started out on a transport. Zakharov came to meet him at the Perm Prison, shortly before Viktor and I met. Several hours of talks with Zakharov ended with Vitia's writing and signing a statement in which he agreed to help the KGB. He was put in the compartment with me just after this happened, and then was attached to Boris in the hope that Boris would reveal the location of some documents that the zeks had allegedly hidden in the boiler room.

Vitia told us in detail about his relations with the KGB in the camp, and how he submitted information under the code name "Zabelin," his grandfather. He described a suitcase full of special foods that was kept for him outside the zone, but said he somehow couldn't bring himself to eat them. Most of all, however, he talked about his doubts and anguish during these four months, his attempts to avoid carrying out the KGB's orders without angering Zakharov, how ashamed he had been to sit at the same table with us, and how happy he was that all of this was now behind him. He wept with relief and joy, and my own feelings were similar.

I brought out the remains of my former wealth—food that I was allowed to take back to the zone after the meeting with my family—and five or six of us brewed tea and happily held a wake for "Zabelin." I was only sorry that Zakharov didn't come by to see how this food, which the KGB had allowed me to keep in the hope that I'd be more cooperative with them, was really being used.

"I feel as if I'd been reborn," Vitia told me the following day as he ran around the zone laughing and butting like a young bull. I had never seen him so cheerful.

I was quickly punished, of course. The next day I was switched to the lathe workshop, and during the following week they wrote a dozen reports about me: "He left the lathe for five minutes"; "He talked at the lathe with X." They deprived me of meetings for a year in advance; one letter after another was confiscated, and it was clear that my days in the zone were numbered. I knew they were taking me to the punishment cell the day before I was told, as two of my informers warned me that the KGB had entrusted them with watching the reaction of zeks to my disappearance: who reacted indignantly, who proposed a protest, and so on.

That evening was the Jewish holiday of Purim. The night before, I had received my semiannual one-kilo food package from home, with candies and homemade cake. I assembled my friends, brewed tea, and shared the sweets. I told them about the holiday of Purim, and how the fate of the entire Jewish population of Persia had changed in one night. I recalled the Purim of 1977, when a single article in *Izvestia* had changed my own fate. I knew that on this Purim, too, my fate would change, that tomorrow I would be in the punishment cell, although I couldn't mention this to anyone.

Where will I be next Purim? I wondered wistfully. Still in the camp prison or back in Chistopol?

I celebrated the next Purim in Jerusalem.

The following evening after work they summoned me to the guardhouse and read a report: I had kept underwear under my pillow before sending it to the laundry. The punishment was four days in the punishment cell. The interesting part, however, is that I had put the underwear under my pillow twenty hours *after* I learned from my sources that I would be taken to the punishment cell. So much for the KGB's logic, I laughed to myself, as I left the zone forever under the guard of two noncoms.

The four days in the punishment cell were followed by fifteen days, and then another fifteen. Then I was transferred to the camp prison for being a "harmful influence" on my fellow zeks. Well, I thought with satisfaction, recalling the wake for "Zabelin" and my contact with other reluctant informers, at least this time the charge is well founded.

Boris Grezin was sent to the camp prison around the same time as a man named Valery Smirnov, with whom I spent seven months. Smirnov was a software specialist who had defected during a trip to Norway and had settled in America. He found work in his field, but he soon yearned for his wife and daughter. Living in a free society, he said, you quickly forget what the Soviet Union is really like. Incredibly, Valery decided to go back home to try to bring out his family.

Despite assurances that he wouldn't be arrested, Valery was met at the Moscow airport by a black Volga sedan. Without even seeing his wife and child, he was driven directly to Lefortovo and sentenced to ten years of strict camp regime.

The work in the camp prison was the same as four years ago: sewing sacks, with a quota of 345 units a day. The rules hadn't changed: if you made the quota, then on the following day you were fed according to norm 9A; otherwise, norm 9B. I hadn't become any more nimble over the past four years, and I didn't even try to fulfill the norm. Valery, however, was amazingly fast on the sewing machine. He suggested that we divide up the work conveyor-belt style; he would undertake the more complicated operations while I would handle the simpler ones. As a result we both received a 9A diet, and although this was considerably worse than the good life in the zone, it was still better than the punishment cell and the especially strict regime in Chistopol.

After work, Valery and I would practice our English. He would tell me rapturously about the West in general and about America in particular. As a computer specialist, he had been especially taken with the microchip revolution and the development of the personal computer, and he told me in great detail about the machines made by a new California company called Apple.

Valery was particularly impressed by the respect and consideration Americans showed for the handicapped. In the Soviet Union handicapped people were objects of shame, but this wasn't the case in America, he explained. Here there were interpreters for the deaf, special access to buildings, and even a separate category for wheelchair participants in prestigious marathons. Valery was also a great fan of Disneyland, and he explained how the long lines in front of each exhibit and ride were designed with so many twists and turns, and so much to see, that people didn't mind the long waits.

Everything would have been fine had it not been for the fact that my correspondence with home had once *again* been completely broken off. Every letter that arrived for me in March or April of 1985 was confiscated, as were all my letters to Moscow and Jerusalem. I wanted to write at least a few lines so that my family would know I was in the camp prison and could write only once every two months. But now I couldn't even do that.

Could I reconcile myself to this situation after so many years of struggling to correspond with my family? Could I sit and twiddle my thumbs while Mama and Avital were eating their hearts out with anguish and agitation? Of course not!

At the end of April, having waited three months since Mama received my last letter, I wrote a desperate note and began another hunger strike:

My dear ones,

Except for facts I can write nothing. The facts are: Don't come to see me—all meetings for 1985 have been canceled, all letters I've written to you in March and April confiscated, and all letters you sent me in the last two months also confiscated.

From now on I'll be able to write only once in two months, so you will probably receive the next letter in August.

I ask Avital and Mama to remain calm as I do.

Regards to everyone,

Yours,
Tolya

"You won't get anywhere that way," said Osin, who ran over immediately after my announcement. "You're better off writing the kind of letters we can let through!"

"What kind is that?"

"You know perfectly well."

Now, finally, it was my turn to experience the effects of the new rule "on the struggle against illegal refusals to take food." I was immediately transferred to the punishment cell, and, as always, my warm clothing was taken away. For someone already on a hunger strike the reduced dietary regime made no difference, of course, but the cold was another matter. As the wooden plank was locked up during the day, I was forced to stay on my feet and walk a lot. Perhaps this was an advantage, as I was forced not to repeat the mistake of my long hunger strike in Chistopol, when I had spent too much time lying down.

Three or four days passed without much hardship, but suddenly the weather changed abruptly and it started snowing—in May!— with a strong wind that blew through the cracks in the cell. I couldn't see the snow through the shutters on the window, but I noticed it on the guards when they came inside. I didn't have the strength to warm up by running, and the three mugs of hot water a day were of little help.

I lay on the floor, exhausted and trembling from the cold, and tried to concentrate on chess. Suddenly I saw snow whirling around me. Had they removed the shutters from the window? No, I was hallucinating.

At night I scrambled up to the top bunk. This was an important "improvement" in the punishment cell since my last time here. The cell of three square meters was equipped for two, as they had added a second bunk above the first. Both, of course, were locked up against the wall during the day, and the zeks bumped into each other below, trying not to disturb each other. Because I was alone, I had the privilege of choosing a bunk. It took energy to climb to the top one, and it grew harder by the day, but on top it was just a little warmer. If you were lucky, the guard would not switch from the daytime light to the night one. During the day the cell was lit by a lamp that hung from the middle of the ceiling, and when you lay on the upper bunk, you were only half a meter away. You were drawn to that lamp, and your thoughts circled around it. The night light burned near the entrance to the cell, far from the cold bunk.

I was lucky for several nights in a row, as the guard left on the day light. On one of those nights, as I was desperately trying to move my body as close as possible to the lamp without falling off the bunk, I had a brilliantly simple idea: I quickly removed the lampshade, burning my fingers in the process, and thrust it against my chest. This was a real hot-water bottle! It's true that in another twenty minutes it would be cold, but this gave me enough time to fall asleep sweetly. In another hour, when I woke up again, I would fasten it onto the lamp once more, and after a few minutes I could again relax in its warmth.

On the tenth day of my hunger strike they brought me a telegram from Mama: "We received your letter." They also handed me several of her recent letters, including one with a postcard from Avital. I was ecstatic: if a message from Avital could reach me even here, in the punishment cell, then surely victory was near. But I still had another five days in the punishment cell, and was forced to end my hunger strike on a punishment-cell diet.

When I returned to the camp prison, Valery eagerly gave me the food he had saved up. For some time the hunger strike had its effect, and I continued to receive mail from home and from friends. But gradually the confiscations became more frequent, and the number of letters I received started dwindling. With my next letter, it was the same old story—they didn't let it go through.

Three months passed, and in August I declared a new hunger strike. Again they put me in the punishment cell, where I tried to keep warm with the lampshade, and again I was beset by hallucinations. During these two hunger strikes, in the spring and summer of 1985, I began to have a recurring dream: I was flying to Israel, sometimes from Vienna, sometimes directly from Moscow. When the plane landed, all the passengers stepped aside so that I could be the first one off. I leaped out to the stairway. At the other end of the airport I saw the enormous figure of Misha, Avital's brother. And there she was, standing beside him, her head reaching his shoulder. We slowly moved toward each other as in a spell. At this point in the dream I would always wake up from the cold.

During this second hunger strike they added on a new punishment for every day of the strike. Before a week had gone by I had already lost the right to a meeting until the end of the following year, and my stay in the punishment cell was extended to forty days.

"Stop killing yourself," Osin advised me. "The sooner you stop the hunger strike, the better it will be for you."

After ten days they began to give me letters from home. One letter contained a postcard with a picture of the *kotel*, the surviving western wall of the ancient temple in Jerusalem. Next to it an old man was blowing an enormous shofar, a ram's horn. On the other side Avital wrote, "Tolik darling, Shalom. What shofar must I blow for you to hear me? Or should I say quietly to myself: I am with you all the time, when there are letters from you and when there aren't. . . ."

"Are you stopping the hunger strike?" they asked me.

"What about my letter home?"

The hunger strike continued, but now in my cell I distinctly heard the triumphant sounds of the shofar. On the fifteenth day they gave me a telegram from home: Mama had received my last letter. I stopped my hunger strike, but I still had to spend another twenty-five days in the punishment cell for my "illegal refusal to take food."

What was I fighting for? A principle? The right to send letters home and receive replies? So my family would not be tortured by uncertainty? For all these reasons, but most of all so that nobody could drown out the shofar signals that Avital was sending me.

During one of these summer nights I dreamed that I was sitting on a carpet with two young women, talking and drinking tea from Oriental bowls. We were joking, but also sadly recalling something. The feeling was mostly pleasant, but also a little strange and even frightening, because it felt so unnatural. I woke up quickly, but lay on the cot, trying to understand the dream. Who were these women? One was Natasha from the period of our "carpet life," when we lived together on Kaliaevsky Street. (We called it that because we had a large, cheap carpet and virtually no furniture. Avital liked to sit on the carpet and drink tea Eastern style, while I always needed a wall at my back.) But who was the other woman? I suddenly realized that she, too, was Natasha, but a different Natasha, the one in my latest picture from a year ago, with shorter hair than in Moscow, which was hidden under a kerchief, her eyes showing not expectation but resolve and decisiveness. The years had been mingled together; that's the power of a dream. In our carpet life we were asking questions about our future, and now we were already part of that future, and were answering those same questions with our lives.

For some time after the punishment cell I remained alone in the camp prison. Then they put me in the work cell, alternating shifts with Valery Smirnov. After the hunger strike I had grown considerably weaker, and the lowest food norm, 9B, was of little help in regaining my strength. Valery, who was receiving norm 9A, would leave me some of his bread, hiding it from the guards so that they wouldn't take it away. This extra bread extended my diet considerably. But this "violation of Soviet legality" was discovered in about ten days.

"Why did you engage in intercell contact with Sharansky?" shouted the indignant Osin as he showed Valery the material evidence of his "crime."

The polite, correct Smirnov, who usually avoided direct confrontation with the authorities, exploded: "You consider it your duty to starve people, but I consider it my duty to feed them. I did it and I will continue to do it."

"If you're such a good guy," snickered Osin, "let's see how much *you* enjoy going hungry." Smirnov was given fifteen days of punishment cell for "illegal transfer of his bread to Sharansky." A few weeks later he was sentenced to Chistopol.

Soon after this, I, too, was caught in a bread transfer, this time to Vazif Meilanov, who had again returned from Chistopol to the camp. They didn't even bring him into the zone, however, but took him straight to the punishment cell. As before, he refused to participate in slave labor. The years of constant maintenance on a low food norm had destroyed his body more than any hunger strike.

On our weekly bath day, I secretly stuffed my pants with dry bread, which I intended to leave for Meilanov in the so-called shower room, a tiny, cramped place for residents of the camp prison and punishment cells with hot and cold water and a little washbasin. In previous years we had often managed to hide food for each other there.

Two guards were on duty. Alik Ataev, the oldest guard in the camp, loved to scream and curse, but he was also tired of working and was too interested in an imminent pension to be truly demanding. He did, however, love his work. His partner, Zaitsev, was a nature lover who was willing to talk about all kinds of birds and animals, although his main passion was discipline. He was proud of the fact that he stood "on the front line of the struggle against ideological enemies"—he actually talked like this—and he treated every search as if he were carrying out a particularly important assignment behind enemy lines.

For some reason, Zaitsev decided to frisk me when I entered the shower room.

"What's the matter, Sharansky," he said cheerfully as he fished one piece of bread after another out of my clothing, "your provocation didn't work?" His partner was trying to return to their interrupted breakfast, which he and Zaitsev were eating in the guardroom. I could smell the strong odors of lard with onion, roast potatoes and tea, for a hungry man is always sensitive to such smells.

"Okay, let's lock up quickly and go," he said to Zaitsev, and grabbing the bread from the floor, he added, "I'll throw this stuff away."

"What? You're throwing away bread?!" Zaitsev cried out. "What did your non-Russian mother teach you? You must give it to the birds!"

Grabbing the bread out of the hands of the indifferent Ataev, he stepped outside and scattered the bread for the little birds. And why not? The birds were so beautiful in the Urals and they sang so delightfully.

During my early years of imprisonment I had observed the guards with interest and sometimes called them over to talk. But my interest waned over time, and I began to regard them simply as part of the landscape. Meilanov was different: as a nonsensologist, he was forever conducting experiments to see if it was possible to penetrate the rock-hard consciousness of the loyal Soviet citizen and to break through to the real person inside. "Kashin," he once shouted from the punishment cell to one of the noncoms, "I can smell the lard. How about some for me?"

Kashin laughed. "It's forbidden. You know what I'd get for doing that?"

"But are you really allowed to torture a man with starvation?"

"I don't torture anybody. I wasn't the one who put you here."

"Yeah, well, I didn't come on my own! Some noncom just like you brought me to prison. Do you know what I'm in for?"

"I don't know. I'm not allowed to know!"

"That's what they all say, 'It's forbidden, I didn't do it, I'm not responsible.' Therefore I, Meilanov, have to decide for everyone, including you. *I am responsible* for everything that's happening in this country, and I'll fight so that people won't starve for their views. Do you understand?"

But this reasoning was too complex for Kashin, who soon lost interest in the conversation.

"Stop your talking," he yelled.

"That's all that's left for you to do, just shut people up!" Meilanov wouldn't give up. Soon he started in from another angle: "Do you have a cow?"

"Yes," replied Kashin, who was happy to be discussing something closer to home.

"You feed her and she gives you milk in return, right?"

"Yes."

"And if you don't feed her, then she moos?"

"Yes."

"Well, the Soviet regime wants to turn me into a cow: it doesn't give me anything to eat because it wants me to moo and to think about nothing but how to get a larger portion. Look, they've already turned *you* into a cow. They've attached your head to your stomach! You don't enjoy starving me, and you'd like to feed me, but your stomach says, 'No, if you feed him you'll lose your job and your salary and then it will be worse for me, the stomach.' Your stomach makes all the decisions for you, which makes you a cow."

This Kashin understood. Offended, he screamed, "*You* are a cow! Stop talking! I will write a report immediately."

Meilanov, of course, was not intimidated, and would continue these didactic conversations for days on end.

There were all kinds of noncoms: cheerful and sullen, blond and brown-haired, old and young, sociable and taciturn, but they all acted more or less the same way and they all sang the same tune: "It's forbidden; you mustn't violate the law; I'm not responsible for this."

Meilanov once asked the almost illiterate Ataev: "Why did Lenin violate the law?"

"What do you mean? Lenin didn't violate the law."

"What are you talking about? He spent time in jail, and a noncom just like you guarded him."

"Lenin . . . in jail?" Ataev seemed to be choking from indignation.

At this point even I couldn't restrain myself. "Alik! Why is

Meilanov saying such things to you? Lenin in jail? Make a note of this slander right away or they'll accuse you of not reporting it!"

"Yes, of course! I'll call someone now and he'll write it for me." The barely educated Alik tried not to write anything himself. "And you're a witness. How do you like that? Yeah, for such slander he ought to get another ten years."

Vazif and I had a good laugh. Alik must have been a poor student if he had forgotten that Lenin had spent time in a czarist prison. But for all his attempts to overthrow the regime, Lenin spent only a few months in prison. He was then exiled, where he continued his political work, wrote books, hunted, fished, and even received a stipend from the government. Meilanov, by contrast, had merely protested Sakharov's exile, but his punishment was far more severe than Lenin's.

Although all the noncoms talked alike, there were many ways you could distinguish a bad one from a good one. Possibly the most striking was the way they gave out toilet paper in the punishment cell. Of course there was no real toilet paper in the prison; this was a problem even in the large zone. When I asked for "paper for my needs," they usually gave me scraps of old newspapers, but when I sat for weeks and months in the punishment cell, cut off from all news, from the radio, and from books, even a simple scrap of printed text was a real find. Occasionally I'd get an interesting article from a newspaper that was only a week old. A "good" noncom would tear a piece of newspaper and give it to you without looking. A "bad" one would always tear it straight down the middle, keeping the other half for somebody else so that you couldn't read a single line.

The hot summer passed. My correspondence with home stabilized and the repressions stopped, at least temporarily. As my term in the camp prison came to an end in October, I was expecting another speedy departure back to Chistopol. Instead, they extended my time in the camp prison by another six months.

During this period, one of the guards brought me a new anti-Zionist book with articles about "subversive" Jewish activities in the Soviet Union and abroad, and about attacks on me and other Jewish activists. I read it because even from propaganda you can learn something. The book included various documents that were meant to demonstrate the links between world Zionism and American imperialism, but because some of this material was in English, the authorities had overlooked that among the documents in this book was a letter of support to Avital from President Reagan. The letter was from 1983, shortly after my hunger strike, but even now, two years later, I felt as if the President himself had written to me in the prison of Perm 35. It was hard to say which I enjoyed more—that Reagan had written me this letter or that the prison authorities had unknowingly delivered it.

Although they temporarily left me alone, my neighbors Vazif Meilanov and Leonid Lubman, another imprisoned Jew, were picked on at every opportunity and literally never left the punishment cell. Therefore, on the three traditional zek holidays in October and December, I participated in one-day hunger strikes in solidarity with my friends. For this, naturally, I myself wound up in the punishment cell, each time for fifteen days. The third time, however, they suddenly took me right from the punishment cell to the hospital.

What kind of thaw is this? I wondered. Meanwhile, I enjoyed the beautiful wintry forest scenery through the spacious hospital window with the large checkered grating that had suddenly replaced the shutters of my punishment cell.

IN the hospital everything was repeated with amazing precision, like the second showing of a movie: the same two-hour walks through the winter forest, the same abundance of food, and the very same doctor prescribing the very same medicines, vitamins, and shots. Once again my chest pains gradually diminished and my strength improved by the day. In a month I gained nine kilos.

The identical scenario had unfolded in the fall of 1984, and was followed by a meeting with my family. But they had already deprived me of all meetings for this year, and for 1986, and even for the first half of 1987! Still, I thought, the Soviet Union is a land of unlimited possibilities, where anything can happen. Perhaps Mama had been able to arrange a meeting, after all?

And why not hypothesize about something bigger? What if they were preparing me not for a meeting but for export? Perhaps the additional weight they were packing onto me was part of the traditional Soviet packaging of goods before shipping them abroad? These thoughts glimmered briefly in my mind, but, as always, I quickly retreated from the dangerous world of illusions.

On January 22, almost a month after I entered the hospital, the duty officer led me in the direction of the guardhouse. So there would be a meeting, after all? But then why did they bring me a new outfit? Wouldn't they search me before the meeting? Or were they taking me back to the zone? And yet they hadn't let me bring my things, not even my Psalm book.

During the short walk to the guardhouse, I began reciting my prayer. For no matter what awaited me—a meeting with my family, a talk with some important KGB officer, or a sudden transport—I had to prepare for it.

At the guardhouse the corridor to the right led to the meeting room, while straight ahead was a heavy iron door and bars—the exit from the zone. They led me straight ahead. Before I knew it, the door had shut behind me, and I found myself in the custody of four men in civilian dress. For the first time since my arrest there was nobody in uniform around me. Although I knew perfectly well who these men were, I yelled back to the duty officer: "Into whose hands have you entrusted me? Don't you know that I won't have anything to do with the KGB?"

I wanted to shout something else in the hope that one of the zeks in the zone or in the meeting room would hear me, and would know that the KGB had taken Sharansky out of the zone. But just as nine years ago in Moscow, I was grabbed by strong hands and thrown into a car. This time, too, I was blocked on all sides.

"Take it easy, you don't need to shout!" somebody said.

It wasn't fear but curiosity that was devouring me. Why was I suddenly traveling in a civilian vehicle with a civilian escort? Maybe they were taking me to speak to their director in Perm? One of the men had radioed to his boss, and recalling my arrest and the drive to Lefortovo, I said, "Hurry up and report that the operation for the release of Sharansky from camp has taken place successfully."

My companions failed to react to this little joke; they just sat there and stared straight ahead. I enjoyed the view. The last time I rode in such a car the streets of Moscow had sped past me. Now it was forest scenery.

We soon came to a village and stopped near the police station. Parked in front of us were three vehicles—a police car followed by two black Volgas. When they told me to take a seat in the first Volga, I assumed we were driving to Perm, four hours away.

"What about my things?"

"Don't worry, they'll be coming."

I stopped short: possessions were possessions, but what about my Psalm book? Who knew what lay ahead? There might be new interrogations in Perm, new threats, new pressures. My Psalm book had to be with me. "This is robbery!" I said. "You were supposed to give me all my things. At least let me have my Psalm book!"

When they tried to lead me to the car by force, I sat down in the snow and started shouting. I knew there were dwellings nearby and that the KGB wouldn't want to attract any attention. After a brief conference, the leader of the group asked me, "What kind of Psalm book? Where is it?"

I explained, and the car that had brought me to this spot tore off. I stood among the KGB men, deeply breathing in the frosty air.

The car returned, the driver handed me the Psalm book, and I quickly took my place in the Volga. In addition to the driver, there was a tail on each side of me, just like those who used to follow me in Moscow. In front, next to the driver, was an "intellectual" with a thin face and inquisitive eyes who spoke politely and firmly: "Anatoly Borisovich, let's not argue along the way. It's time you learned how to live in peace with us." Then he took some kind of gadget in his hand and stuck it into a box in front of him; a moment later the car was filled with music. So this is a car tape deck, I thought. I had seen such a thing only once before, in the car of an American diplomat. (It was soon stolen in Moscow.) I wondered: Did everyone now have tape decks in their cars, or only the KGB?

Although the road was wide, we soon ended up in a traffic jam: a huge dump truck had swerved on a turn and cars were having trouble getting around it. Suddenly the police car in front of us turned on its siren. The light on its roof began to rotate and the sounds of a command came out of the speaker. The other cars quickly pulled over and our three vehicles rushed ahead. Fields, forests, and villages flickered past.

We sped past a police post. Did the officer actually salute, or did I imagine it? Did he mistake me for some big shot? Who else would travel in such company, with his own police car and an escort vehicle? I kept watching for the next police post. Yes, here, too, the officer saluted. Great! If he only knew whom he was honoring! I couldn't help laughing, but from the somber faces of my traveling companions it was clear that they didn't appreciate the humor of the situation. At the entrance to the next village, when a third policeman snapped to attention, I suddenly leaned over my companion, stuck my hand out the window, and gave a friendly wave. The cop, having noticed my zek's jacket and cap, stared at me and lowered his hand. My escort angrily threw me back in my seat and quickly closed the car window.

"What's going on in there?" the boss in the third car radioed to the intellectual.

"Sharansky is carrying on. He tried to yell something to the policeman."

"Close the windows."

"We already did." For a long time nobody spoke as we sped past the snow-covered expanse. I wondered whether I was being taken to some kind of meeting with my family.

A little later, I told my escorts I needed a bathroom. After conferring with the driver, the intellectual said, "Soon we'll reach a gas station."

But when we arrived they wouldn't let me out. Apparently the boss didn't like the fact that there were people around, for what if I suddenly yelled out to them? We kept driving and stopped at an empty strip along the highway. There was a thick forest on both sides, but that was considered dangerous, so they suggested that I relieve myself right on the highway. The two Volgas fenced me in while our police escort waved on the passing cars. My bodyguards stood on each side of me, and when they saw that I was going about my business and not attempting to flee, they followed my example. Having begun earlier, I finished earlier. Glancing left and right, I took a sudden step toward the forest. They followed automatically, wetting their hands and their pants. I smirked at my victory. Let them know what it is not to take me to a real toilet.

While I sat in the car my companions took a long time washing their hands, pouring water for each other from a can. We continued driving amid a tense silence. Although I tried to enjoy this latest production of the KGB theater of the absurd, where the stage had suddenly expanded from the punishment cell and the hospital ward to the infinite expanses of the Soviet Union, I couldn't stop wondering, *What does this all mean? Where are they taking me?* Nothing like this had happened in nine years. Could it really be? No, don't fall for illusions. Then, what was it? Of course—they were taking me for a talk with some KGB boss and they wanted to keep it secret even from the Interior Ministry.

While this theory had a number of flaws—it didn't explain this special car, for example—I clung to it like an anchor and tried to stop guessing. But although I managed to force the question out of my conscious thoughts, it continued to tug at me. I watched the endless snowy fields and the austere, picturesque birches and pines, but instead of bringing me peace and calm they led to anxiety and agitation, reminding me over and over that something highly unusual was going on.

I naturally tried to hide my anxiety from the KGB men, but it came out in the form of a sharp pain in my chest and a severe headache. The pain was so intense that it filled my entire head and closed my left eye. I kept my right eye half open until I could no longer bear it.

"I need a pill for a headache," I said. "Where is the first-aid kit you're obliged to carry when transporting a zek?"

But these people were clearly unaccustomed to transporting zeks. After conferring over the radio, the intellectual said, "We'll arrive soon and then you'll get a pill."

We had been on the road for four hours and seemed to be approaching a large city. There was a huge sign saying PERM—but what was this? Did we really turn by the arrow marked AIRPORT, or did it only seem that way? There's probably a prison down this road, I told myself, but at that moment we were driving up to the airport.

Suddenly we were in the midst of the long-forgotten bustle of passengers, taxis, buses, and waiting rooms. My headache prevented me from grasping whatever was going on, but I could see that we drove straight onto the field at the farthest end from the terminal, where they suddenly told me to get out of the car and sit in the plane. It was a TU-114, yet another harbinger of civilization. The plane was empty, so they had obviously boarded me first; the other hundred or so passengers would probably come on shortly. I took a window seat in the front, and the three men from the car surrounded me. The fourth disappeared into the cockpit.

"Ask the stewardess for a pill before the passengers arrive," I told the intellectual.

"Right away, right away," he replied, but just then the plane took off—with no other passengers! They brought me pills for the headache, and I took two and quickly regained my spirits.

So a special plane was sent for me. Why? Perhaps the highest ranks of the KGB wanted to talk with me. Or for some political reason they urgently had to give me a meeting with relatives in Moscow, as they had once given Edik Kuznetsov a meeting with his wife. Enough guessing, I told myself, afraid of letting hope enter my heart. We'll see soon enough.

The world, which had so suddenly burst out of the embrace of bars and barbed wire, rushed to show me its beauty. Below me were winter forests, fields, and frozen rivers. What was that—a camp watchtower in the forest? No, it must have been an illusion, I thought, as the realization that I was out of the Gulag suddenly sank in. The prison, the zone, the police van, the transport, the camp punishment cell, the hospital—in all these places I was a resident of the Gulag, fenced off from the rest of the world by machine-gunners, dogs, forbidden zones, and shutters. Now, however, I was actually *above* this world.

When I probed my feelings, I found to my astonishment that my dominant emotion was sorrow. Below me was a world I knew so well, where I was familiar with every detail, every sound, where they couldn't pull any dirty tricks on me, where I knew how to help a friend and deal with an enemy. Down there was a stern world that accepted and acknowledged me, and where I was secure, the master of my own fate. Now, lost in speculation and apprehension, driving away the hope that was now becoming impossible to dismiss, I lost my self-confidence. Suddenly I no longer felt in control.

I recited the prayer I had composed so long ago in Lefortovo. I said it over and over, five, ten, twenty times. Then, having calmed down, I began to demand an accounting of my possessions from the KGB. Where were they? Why didn't I have them?

"Everything will be returned to you, Anatoly Borisovich."

A couple of hours passed. They brought me a meal—eggs, cheese, and bread—a real feast after what I was used to. My agitation returned when we prepared to land. It appeared to be Moscow. And here I saw another miracle of technology as we came out of the clouds and landed immediately. Nine years ago the airport would have been closed with such a low cloud cover. Were we the only ones landing? No, I could see other planes, too. "A system of blind landing," the KGB man explained.

Suddenly I was in Moscow, close to Mama, Lenya, and all my

friends. Perhaps I would see them even today? So many extraordinary things had already happened; why not one more miracle?

We left the airport—I could see it was Vnukovo—and drove to Moscow, once again led by a police car with a siren, followed by two Volgas. Heads of state arrived at Vnukovo, and the prearranged crowds would greet them along this very highway. I chuckled cheerfully as, again, the police along the ceremonial route saluted me as I rode by with my honor guard and bodyguards. Wasn't this reason enough to be happy and to laugh at this idiotic Soviet world? But I was quickly losing my sense of humor, which was replaced by exhaustion and a growing sense of disappointment, for we were approaching Lefortovo.

Slowly, just as nine years ago, the double iron doors opened. Inside, they frisked me, although I had only the personal items they had given me this morning in the camp hospital. Slowly, just as last time, I walked along the corridor of the old Katherine prison, dragging a mattress, pillow, and blanket. I was greeted by my new cell mate, an elderly, solidly built man with an intelligent face and the frightened look of a new zek. This time, however, I had the confidence of a proprietor and the sentimental response of a man returning to his alma mater.

But my deep disillusionment prevailed over everything else. No matter how hard I had tried to push out of my consciousness the hope for a miracle, it had been with me all day. What, specifically, was I expecting? A meeting with my family at the airport? Immediate release? A flight to Israel? I don't know, but after being so suddenly torn away from incarceration, once the plane lifted me above the world of the Gulag everything had seemed possible. After my intoxication with the pure air of the heavens, landing back in this world was a real letdown. Now I could imagine all kinds of mundane explanations for these fantastic developments.

Maybe they had brought me here for interrogations on some other case. But why the big rush? Just look at the money they had spent on plane fuel alone! Perhaps some highly placed officer had said, "When will it be possible to start interrogating Sharansky?" and some zealous subordinate had answered, "Tomorrow, if you like." Then he had asked himself: What if the boss really *does* summon him tomorrow? I had better get him to Moscow right away.

My cell mate, a government official convicted of taking bribes, didn't believe my amazing tale about the trip from the zone to Moscow. Three cars escorting a zek, policemen saluting him—what kind of delirium was this? But my hypothesis about an invisible bureaucrat who had urgently summoned me from the zone to demonstrate his efficiency to the boss—this struck him as completely reasonable.

During the first two or three days some hope still crept in, but when five days passed, and then ten, with no interrogations and no explanations, I was soon drawn back into the normal Lefortovo routine. After all these years I could finally appreciate the truth of Chernysh's statement that Lefortovo was a resort compared with other prisons, and the food, when supplemented with the ten rubles' worth of purchasing privileges at the prison store, was no worse than the camp's hospital regime. They continued giving me vitamins, although the air I breathed during the exercise period (the yards had been moved to the roof of the prison) was noticeably inferior in purity and freshness to the crisp air in the camp.

The important thing was that I was once again able to spend time with the friends of my youthful zek years—the heroes of the Lefortovo library books. But now they no longer had to reassure me, console me, or convince me that there was a world of higher values worth dying for. These days, when they described their life experiences I listened as one war veteran listens to another, engrossed in reminiscences of common battles.

On the morning of February 10 I was reading a volume of Schiller's plays and Goethe's novel *Wilhelm Meister* when the food trap opened: "To a summons."

So they had remembered me, after all! But instead of leading me to the investigative section on the second floor, they took me instead to the buffer cell. What was this, another transport?

They undressed me, took away everything I had acquired in camp, and gave me civilian clothes. This was *really* something new. I tried to hide my excitement as I put on the fine underwear, blue shirt, and a gray suit whose pants were enormous.

"Give me a belt; the pants won't stay up."

"Belts are forbidden."

After a brief consultation, one of the guards brought me a short piece of string, and I somehow managed to tie my pants. Even so, I had to hold them up all the time. They also gave me socks, shoes, a scarf, a long blue coat, and a typical Russian winter hat. There was even a tie, but one of the guards snatched it away and said, "You'll get it later."

All of these items, which had just come from the store, seemed to signal a return to life in the large zone. They left me alone for about an hour with a copy of *Pravda*. At any other time I would have pounced on it immediately, but now as I scanned the lines nothing registered. What did all this mean? Maybe they were taking me to some public place and didn't want me in zek's clothing? But it was becoming harder and harder to restrain myself.

When they led me to the exit of the prison, I saw the same four KGB men who had taken me from the camp to Moscow. I stopped abruptly. "What about my things, both in camp and here in prison?"

"You'll soon get your things."

"I want my Psalm book with me."

They tried to take me out by force, but I raised my voice, which echoed sharply in the deathly silence of Lefortovo. The prison chief gave some kind of signal, and one of the officers left and returned with the Psalm book.

"You'll receive it on the spot," the chief said as we left the prison.

My two bodyguards took me by the arms and led me to a car. But what was this? We were being photographed by still and movie cameras. The last time I saw cameras was at my trial. Why were they here now? I didn't know, and I tried not to guess.

Again we were in a three-car convoy, speeding through the Moscow streets. Where to this time? I wondered. No, not the center of town, so that rules out a meeting with a bigwig. No, not to Vnukovo, so they're not sending me back to camp. We rode on the highway, passing through Lyubertsy. Here, just a few hundred meters to the right, was Lenya's apartment! Could it be? No, we were entering Bykovo airport, and we drove up to a plane at the far end of the field. Before they let me out of the car, the photographers took up positions. I got out.

"Where's my Psalm book?"

"You received everything that was permitted," answered the intellectual in an unexpectedly rough tone. He signaled to the tails to take me away.

I quickly dropped to the snow. "I won't move until you give me back my Psalm book." When nothing happened, I lay down in the snow and started shouting, *"Give me back my Psalm book!"*

The photographers were aghast, and pointed their cameras toward the sky.

After a brief consultation the boss gave me the Psalm book. I got up and quickly mounted the ramp. In the airplane the photographers continued to work for another ten minutes.

"Don't forget to send pictures!" I called out as they left the plane.

Once again my four traveling companions and I were alone in a huge plane. Two of the tails sat behind me, while the intellectual and the boss went into the rear section.

"Where are we going?"

"I don't know," replied one of the tails.

Take off and ascent. Where's the sun? Almost behind and to the side. So we're flying west? I squeezed my Psalm book and recited my prayer several times. For the next two hours I tried to quash my excitement by talking to the tails.

"How does it happen that in the camp the KGB's most loyal servants are those who once faithfully served the Germans?" I asked.

My companions listened carefully and remained silent, but the intellectual joined them and even allowed himself to ask a few questions. More than two hours had passed and we were still flying west. We must be abroad, I decided.

"What's going on?" I demanded again.

The boss appeared from behind a curtain. In a solemn voice he announced, "Sharansky, Anatoly Borisovich. I am authorized to declare to you that by order of the Presidium of the Supreme Soviet of the USSR, for conduct unworthy of a Soviet citizen, you have been stripped of Soviet citizenship and as an American spy you are being expelled from the Soviet Union."

It was over.

I had waited years for this moment, and now there was no longer any need to deceive myself. I stood and announced, in an equally solemn voice, "I want to make a written statement. Give me a piece of paper."

"You are not permitted to make written statements," he said in a typical guard's tone. I broke into a nervous laugh. "In that case I shall say it orally. First, I am pleased that thirteen years after I asked to be deprived of Soviet citizenship, my wish has finally been granted. Second, I shall use this occasion to declare once again: my activities as a Jewish activist and as a member of the Helsinki Group had nothing to do with espionage or treason. This work was not only in the interests of those people whose rights I defended, but also in the interests of the entire society in which I was forced to live. I wish for you that such harassments will soon come to an end in your country, and that those who organize them will be punished."

I sat down with the sound of fanfare in my ears. I knew all along that this day had to come. And now I took the Psalm book and turned to Psalm 30, which I had long ago decided to recite at the moment of my release. "A song of David at the dedication of a house," it began. Now I was reading these words en route to my own house in Jerusalem!

I extol You, O Lord, for You have lifted me up,
And not let my enemies rejoice over me.
O Lord, my God, I cried out to You,
And you healed me.
O Lord, You brought me up from Sheol,
preserved me from going down into the Pit.
O You faithful of the Lord, sing to Him
And praise His holy name
For He is angry but a moment,
And when He is pleased, there is life.
Weeping may linger for the night,
But at dawn there are shouts of joy.
When I was untroubled,
I thought, "I shall never be shaken."
For You, O Lord, when You were pleased
Made me firm as a mighty mountain.
When You hid Your face,
I was terrified.
I called to You, O Lord;

To my Lord I made appeal,
"What is to be gained from my death,
From my descent into the Pit?
Can dust praise You?
Can it declare Your faithfulness?
Hear, O Lord, and have mercy on me;
O Lord, be my help!"
You turned my lament into dancing
You undid my sackcloth and girded me with joy
That my whole being may sing hymns to You endlessly;
O Lord my God, I will praise you forever.

I continued reading one triumphant psalm after another: "A song of dreamers. When the Lord brought back the exiles who returned to Zion, we were like dreamers."

Yes, exactly like dreamers. But wasn't *this* one more dream? How many times during these years had I flown to Israel and, instead of reaching Avital, had awakened in a cold punishment cell! I was frightened, and suddenly no trace remained of the victorious self-confidence that had flooded me only a moment ago. Just then thick white clouds enveloped the plane. Yes, I thought, this really is a dream. The snowy shroud will tear open, I'll wake up, and the yellow light of the punishment-cell lamp will hit my eyes. My heart sank and a cold shiver passed over my body. Now I'll open my eyes, take the shade off the lamp, and try to warm up.

The plane burst out of the white shroud. The land was rushing toward me. Neat little homes with long slanting roofs. Hadn't I seen something like this in pictures? No, it was in Tallinn, in Estonia, where Avital and I once took a brief vacation. Where were we? Finland? No, not likely, as we were flying west the whole time. It must be Holland or Switzerland. Switzerland—of course! They had exchanged Bukovsky in Zurich!

And then the thought sank in: No matter where they release me, Avital will probably fly there. That means I'll see her soon.

I stared at the approaching airport, trying to catch sight of her. We landed. The planes we passed were marked "Interflug." The word meant nothing to me, but next to it were the letters DDR. My God, East Germany? Then Avital won't be here. The plane was surrounded by cameramen, uniformed policemen, and a contingent of men in civilian clothes. Looking at them, I was struck by how closely the German secret police resembled their Soviet counterparts.

The stairs were lowered and the door opened. The boss left first and walked over to their boss. They conferred about something, and then he signaled with his hand, waving me from the plane in the direction of a car about twenty meters away. Apparently my tails did not plan to accompany me. The intellectual said, "You see that car, Anatoly Borisovich? Go straight to it and don't make any turns. Is it agreed?"

Overwhelmed as I was by all that was happening, the word "agreed" still grated on my ears. "Since when have I started making agreements with the KGB? You know that I never agree with the KGB about anything. If you tell me to go straight, I'll go crooked."

The intellectual snorted and said something to the tails. Then he and one of the tails left the plane and stood on opposite sides of the steps. As I walked down, the movie cameras started rolling. I turned sharply to the left.

"There, *there!*" The intellectual and several of his German colleagues pointed out where I should be walking.

I turned sharply to the right, and again they started waving. Through a series of zigzags I finally reached the car. The movie cameras followed me and literally bumped into the glass of the windshield. A woman sat next to me and said in Russian, "I'll be your translator."

In front, next to the driver, sat a man who said nothing more than "*Guten Tag.*" We drove off.

"Where are we?" I asked the translator.

"In Berlin."

"East Berlin?"

"Yes, in the capital of the DDR!" she added hastily. "Now we're going to your lawyer, and he'll explain everything."

"Ooh-ah! I already have my own lawyer here!"

A tense silence set in. In order to break the tension, I started talking: "As a Jew, the word 'Berlin' evokes mixed feelings in me. But today it sounds to me like a synonym for the word 'freedom.' Just this morning I was reading the works of Schiller and Goethe without imagining that in a few hours I would be in their country. Perhaps you'll tell me about the places we are passing?"

My traveling companions immediately livened up and gave me a tour of Berlin. I took in practically nothing of what they said, although I seem to remember the word "zoo." By now I was in a state of euphoria, like a child in a fairy-tale world. I was no longer tormented by the thought that I might wake up; it was as if my sleep had become deeper.

It was dusk when we drove up to a house where a man greeted me with a handshake and introduced himself in English: "Lawyer Wolfgang Vogel."

After he escorted me inside, leaving my companions in the car, the atmosphere immediately became less official. I was greeted by Vogel's wife and the American ambassador to East Germany and his wife. By now nothing could surprise me, so I listened calmly to the ambassador's explanation that tomorrow there would be an exchange of spies on the Glienicke Bridge between East and West Berlin, and that before the exchange I would be led across the bridge and released. The Americans had insisted that I be separated from the others, since I wasn't a spy. The ambassador took a long time explaining the procedure, but I had only one question: "Where is my wife? Will she be on the other side of the bridge?"

"No, there will be too much press and police there. Apparently she'll meet you in Frankfurt."

Yet another delay before we could be together.

We all drank a toast. Before I returned to the car, the ambassador explained that I would spend the night under the supervision of the East German authorities.

They drove me to a villa in the woods near Berlin where I was immediately overwhelmed by an intoxicating aroma. Yes, I thought, it's the forgotten fragrance of freshly ground coffee. This couldn't be a dream, because during all those years I had never smelled coffee in my dreams. The translator and I and the two security men from the car sat at a luxurious table with hors d'oeuvres, meat, wine, and coffee. I declined the wine, for my head was already spinning. I tasted everything else in tiny bits, slowly, almost as if performing a sacred rite. I was afraid to be too assertive now, for fear of breaking the spell.

"You may go upstairs to your room and sleep," said the translator, "or you may want to watch television in the living room."

Sleep? No! Who knows what could happen in my sleep? What if all this disappeared? Like a sleepwalker, I went to the living room, where several men and the lady of the house were watching some kind of festive broadcast. The translator explained that certain parts of Germany were celebrating a traditional holiday with carnivals and concerts.

The vivid colors of the television only added to the fairy-tale effect. The screen was filled with topless women, singers and dancers, but I was in my own world, detached from all this.

Finally I went upstairs and took a bath. Shampoo and toothpaste—the return to civilization continued. I looked out the window; the car with a guard was standing below. It's just as it was before my arrest, I thought, with the KGB car outside my window.

The bed was not just a mattress but a fluffy feather bed, and I seemed to sink down about a meter. I felt helpless without a firm support under me. One hour passed and then another. Waiting for the time to pass, I kept calculating: How many hours before I see Avital? How many hours before we arrive in Israel?

It was clear that I couldn't sleep—at least not in this bed. If only I had the punishment-cell board under me, then perhaps . . . I got up and didn't lie down again, but paced back and forth as the minutes dragged on. Tomorrow—no, today!—I'll be free. Today I'll meet Avital. Today we'll fly to Israel. I turned on the light and started reading the Psalms.

In the morning, after a breakfast of coffee and cake, I was led into the front seat of a minibus. Behind me were a Czech and two Germans who were also being exchanged today. When we reached the bridge, I saw the Soviet flag up ahead. "How symbolic," I said. "This isn't really the border of East Germany but the boundary of the Soviet empire."

On our side it was quiet and deserted, but a dull roar could be heard from the other end of the bridge. The American ambassador to East Germany introduced me to the American ambassador to West Germany, who took me by the hand. We slowly walked over the bridge.

"Where's the border?" I asked.

"Right there, that thick line."

I joyfully leaped across it. At that moment my pants jerked down, reminding me of the thin string I was given in Lefortovo. Supporting my pants with one hand, and knowing I'd soon see Avital, I crossed to the other side.

In front of me stood a crowd of people in a blur. Smiling to everyone, I took refuge in the ambassador's car. He picked up the telephone and called directly to Washington—but nothing could surprise me now. He gave me the receiver and I mumbled some nonsense about the taste of the air of freedom. I had no idea whom I was talking to.

We drove to the American base, where American soldiers saluted us. As we sat in a small plane the soldiers gave me the ambassador's gifts—flowers, fruit, a picture of the Glienicke Bridge, and cuff links with President Reagan's signature. The plane started moving and then stopped; the brakes weren't working properly and we had to switch to another plane.

"I thought we were already in the West," I exclaimed to the ambassador, "but it seems we're still in the Soviet Union, where something always doesn't work." I was laughing happily now, for this was one of those details that distinguish real life from dreams.

Finally we left for Frankfurt, where Avital was waiting. I divided my attention between looking out the window and carrying on an urbane conversation with the American ambassador. But the only thing on my mind was that soon I'd see Avital.

All I remember from my talk with the ambassador is how astonished I was that he was only thirty-nine. "You made your career so quickly," I said.

"Well," he replied, "you're also very young and made a career quickly."

"Yes, but in my case the KGB helped. I trust that your achievement had nothing to do with them."

In the midst of this friendly banter, the picture in front of my eyes begins to twitch, as if from a nervous tic. The world seems to lose its continuity, moving jerkily from one frozen frame to another.

We land in Frankfurt.

"Where's Avital?"

We go from a military base to a civilian airport.

"Where's Avital?"

Someone greets me in Hebrew—the Israeli consul. We hug. "Shalom! Where's Avital?"

We walk quickly. A corridor, elevator, corridor. Faces appear and disappear. "Hello, hello." Then, "Shalom!" "Shalom!" "Shalom!" A bearded young man with a *kippah* on his head smiles at me, "Shalom!" and points to a door. Another bearded man with a *kippah* comes out: "Shalom!"

I fly into the room—it's empty. I turn—Avital is sitting in the corner, wearing a kerchief and a dark suit. She whispers something, but I can't hear. I take a step toward her, and another, and a third. She stands up. Her lips are trembling and her eyes are filled with tears. Yes, it's really she, my Natasha—the same girl I had promised twelve years ago, at the Moscow airport, that our separation would be brief. In a desperate attempt to swallow the lump in my throat and to wipe the tears from our faces with a smile, I tell her in Hebrew: *Silchi li she'icharti k'zat* (Sorry I'm a little late).

I hold Avital's hand just as twelve years ago I had held Natasha's hand on our way to the airport. Through twelve years of struggle, longing, and suffering, twelve years of desperate attempts not to lose hold of each other, I had been obsessed by the thought of how it would be when we finally met. Our separation lasted well over four thousand days, and when I concentrate I can still recall every significant moment during those years. I remember how it was when I first met Natasha outside the synagogue, and what it was like to take her to the airport and leave her there on the morning after our wedding. I recall the pain and abandonment I felt when they confiscated her photograph in Lefortovo, and the joy I experienced when they finally gave it back.

But this precious and amazing moment of our reunion is somehow sealed off from me, like a black hole that pulls in the light and gives nothing back. What was I thinking when we finally saw each other? What did I say, and what did Avital whisper to me? Strange as it may seem, I do not know. I recall only that my head was dizzy and my knees grew weak, as it seemed that at any moment the two of us would leave the ground and start floating up into the air.

. . .

My mind now retains rapidly changing images from the next hours—how we flew over the Mediterranean on a small plane that was sent by our government; how we landed in Israel and were greeted by so many friends; how I spoke almost without understanding my own words; how we sang "Hinei mah tov u'mah na'im shevet achim gam yachad" (How good and pleasant it is for brothers to be together)—I had sung that song so often while I was alone in punishment cells, and now I sang it with thousands of my brothers and sisters who had gathered at the airport; how I squeezed Avital's hand tightly for fear she would slip away and the dream would end. Only at night, in the Old City of Jerusalem, did I let go of her hand when the crowd carried us to different sides and I swam on people's shoulders to the *kotel,* the western wall.

Holding our Psalm book in my hand, I kissed the wall and said, "*Baruch matir asirim.*" Blessed is He who liberates the imprisoned.

Epilogue: Home

ARLY in the morning after one more sleepless night, I rise
quietly so as not to awaken Avital, and slip outside to our huge
terrace. After ten frenzied days we left Jerusalem for a long-
delayed honeymoon in the Galilee, and our hotel balcony in Safed
is the size of ten punishment cells. Off in the distance, like some
spectacular movie set, are tree-covered mountains and the rising
sun. To the side and almost within reach is a fantastic tree with
delicate white blossoms—like something out of paradise, which Avital refers to tenderly as *shkediah* (almond tree). I'll do my morning
exercises out here, and later they'll bring us breakfast, room service
as in Chistopol.

This isn't the first night I haven't slept, but that's not surprising,
as sleep returns me to the black-and-white world of the Gulag, a
stark contrast to this amazing new universe where colors, people,
and emotions keep pouring over me in waves. I prefer to avoid
sleeping, in contrast to my first days in Lefortovo when I buried
myself in sleep.

Although we escaped here in a desperate attempt to find some
privacy, we are virtually trapped on this balcony. Even in Safed,
people want to invite us everywhere. My old friend Sasha Lunts
comes to drive us to some of the most remote places in northern
Israel. At last we find a desolate spot with nobody around—only one
lonely Druze wandering along the narrow mountain path. Suddenly he stops, looks at me, and with a joyous cry runs to greet us.

But even without the seclusion we yearn for, Israel is still over-
whelmingly wonderful. As I travel around this land, which I saw

for years in my dreams and prayers, its striking beauty and magnetic power are somehow more compelling than I expected. I find it impossible to comprehend how the variety of the entire world could be compressed into this tiny wedge of earth, with its hills and forests, its plains and deserts, its roaring waterfalls in the north down to the motionless surface of the Dead Sea. And in the center of all this stands Jerusalem, the pinnacle of beauty and spirit, the city of King David, which has united our people through these thousands of years.

Every day I wait for the shock of my arrival to dissipate, but it will be weeks, months, even a year, before it ultimately begins to fade. I feel like a meteorite that finally fell to earth, and is cooling, cooling, cooling, but is still frightfully hot.

For the first week we lived under siege as I gave one interview after another—to old accomplices like Robert Toth, David Shipler, and Granada Television, and to new ones as well. For the first time in years I was no longer under surveillance, but from the moment I opened the door I saw that the prospects for privacy were no better than in prison, as people in Jerusalem almost choked me with their love.

There are two sides to all of this: the marvelous sensation of being part of one family, of being home, but also the invaded feeling that everybody knows our business. People care about us and wish us well, but each word and gesture is noticed no less than in Moscow. I say something to Avital, and I read about it in tomorrow's newspaper. Before my arrest it was the press that helped me stay free, and I was in contact with the correspondents every day. But now that the first round of interviews is over, I find myself avoiding them. Several newspapers report that the difference in religious observance between Avital and me is already threatening our marriage. But as soon as we stop reading the papers these problems no longer exist.

Everywhere I go people express their love and wish me well. How can I not respond to kind words with kind words, to greetings with greetings, to smiles with smiles? But before long my facial muscles grow sore from all the smiling and my expression becomes increasingly mechanical.

From an ocean of hatred I find myself in an ocean of love. Having left a country where only the government knows what must be done, I arrive in a society where everybody *but* the government knows what must be done. Here every taxi driver, every kibbutznik, every shopkeeper is, if not prime minister, then at least foreign and defense ministers combined. Having left a country in which criticizing the government can land you in prison, I now live in a society where the easiest thing in the world is to criticize the government, and the louder your criticisms the more popular you are.

When it comes to disagreeing with governments I have plenty of experience, but what about all these friends and supporters? People who were struggling for me, suffering with me, and who rejoiced when I came home—now each of them hopes to push me in the direction of his agenda, his party, his organization. To say no to these people can be far more difficult than saying no to the KGB, and I soon learned that defending one's freedom in the ocean of love can be no less challenging than defending it in the sea of hatred.

In prison I maintained my freedom by trying not to take the KGB too seriously. Now I must do the same—not take all the compliments too seriously, not take *myself* too seriously, and try to see the absurd side of life in the ocean of love.

And so to America, the land of individualism, the bastion of free speech. And yet almost everyone I meet—or so it seems—repeats the same three phrases: Nice to see you; You are an inspiration to me; Have a nice day. To ensure that I really do have a nice day, the mayors of Washington and New York give me a special honor: a limousine the size of two punishment cells. Moreover, I'm followed by two police cars—just as in the good old days in Moscow.

Things are simpler in Israel. Here, pedestrians don't push their children up to you for a quick photo, and don't ask for autographs. They're just happy you're here, making do with a friendly smile and a brief greeting, *Tihyeh bari,* Stay well. But by now I fear that my smile has turned into a mask, and I hear myself responding—in Hebrew!—with the stock phrases of a politician.

Walking through the streets, I notice that everyone is staring at my head: Is he wearing a *kippah* yet? Which will happen first, they want to know, will he put on a *kippah* or will she remove her kerchief? Apparently the speculation began even before we arrived—just like the assumption that I would be manipulated by

Avital's religious friends, who became her main supporters even before I was arrested. In the end they were virtually the only ones who made no attempt to use me.

Did I come home to Israel, to Avital, in order to change from a human being into a symbol? But wait—there are encouraging signs. Just yesterday I was criticized in the press, one more step toward becoming a normal Israeli. And today several people in the street failed to recognize me. In a hotel elevator a tourist from Brazil greeted me in the usual manner: "Oh, you're that man on television!" Incapable of containing his excitement, he asked permission to shake my hand, then to embrace me, and finally to kiss me. Before I could respond, he jumped on me and took me in his arms. Then, looking at me proudly, he said, "Now I'll go home and tell everyone that I met Sakharov!"

I pass by the kindergarten near our apartment. Only a few days ago these same children spotted me and greeted me with such enthusiasm that I had no choice but to come in and talk to them. Today they were all poking their fingers through the fence, pointing in my direction and calling out. I straightened up with a proud look, and gave them a kindly smile—like a hero. But why were they pronouncing my name so strangely? What were they shouting— *Sus?* Horse? I turned around and discovered the true object of the children's attention—a man riding a handsome horse. *Sic transit gloria mundi.*

There are so many trips to make, so many people to thank. On a visit to France I meet with Prime Minister Mitterrand. "That chair you're sitting in," he says, "Avital sat there often when she came to ask for my assistance. I always wanted to help her, but the truth is that I never believed she had a chance. I thought she was naive, and that they'd never let you out. But your wife was right and I was wrong."

It will take me years to absorb the full story of Avital's enormous struggle. So many people helped her, but from the very beginning, when the *Izvestia* article appeared, it was Rav Tzvi, her teacher, who understood the imminent danger and took Avital with a group of his closest students to see *his* teacher, Rav Kook. Rav Kook was very ill, but when he heard about the article he called his disciples together. "How can you sleep?" he asked. "How can you study when this woman's husband is threatened, and when the entire Jewish people is under attack?"

A week later, two days before I was arrested, I called Avital and was bitterly disappointed that she had already left Jerusalem for Geneva. Her supporters assured me they were working in my behalf, but I was so upset that I neither understood nor appreciated what they were telling me. Little did I know that an international movement working for my release had already begun, a movement that ultimately involved tens of thousands of people around the world, including students and housewives, of course, but also lawyers, scientists, politicians, and many more. It would take another book just to thank them all.

The day after my release, while flying from Berlin to Frankfurt, I learned from a West German official that an agreement had been signed stating that my family in Moscow could follow me to Israel. But it took half a year to get them out; the Soviets tried to blackmail me, letting it be known that if I didn't behave, if I didn't stop my public activity on behalf of Soviet Jews, my family would not be released. But I knew from experience that the moment the authorities believed this kind of pressure was working, my family would never be free. I continued speaking out, and as always, the combination of open pressure and quiet diplomacy brought results. Mama and Lenya's family arrived in Israel during the summer.

Lenya told me that after I was expelled he had gone to Lefortovo to collect my few belongings. "I'm sorry," he was told, "but we don't know this name 'Sharansky.' " When he returned a few days later, they gave him my things, along with the money in my prison account. They also handed him a receipt stating that one ruble and thirty kopeks had been deducted to pay for my meal during the flight from Moscow to Berlin!

Of my fellow zeks, Victoras Piatkus, is in internal exile, as is Meilanov, who still refuses to make any concessions to the KGB. Arkasha Tsurkov is back in Leningrad with his wife and child, and Poresh, too, is there—working at a menial job, but at least out of prison. In addition to their two daughters, Poresh and his wife now have a little boy. But Smirnov is still in Chistopol, and Klymchak, Kazachkov, Lubman, and many others are still in camp.

And those who betrayed us? I'm told that Tsypin now works as a police investigator, and that Lipavsky lives in a special apartment building for KGB workers. People say he changed his name to Popov, and was rewarded with a new fifth line in his passport, making him a Russian by nationality.

Sitting in Jerusalem, I remember how I felt when I first arrived in Perm 35: how could I be happy here, knowing that just a few meters away my fellow zeks were sitting in the camp prison and punishment cells? And now, in freedom, I feel the same way. In one respect prison was easier: in the punishment cell I was inwardly a free man, and I knew I was doing everything I could. Here things are far more complicated: there are thousands of opportunities to act, and who's to say what constitutes enough? In a sense I am no longer free, for I can become free only together with those I left behind.

I understand that when Reagan and Gorbachev met in Geneva in November 1985 the President told the Chairman, "You can say again and again that Sharansky's a spy, but the world believes this lady, and you won't be able to change your image until you let him go." I'd like to think that, the next time they meet, Western leaders will tell their Soviet counterparts, "You can say anything you want, but until you release all the Jews who want to emigrate, and all your political prisoners, you won't be able to change your image in the West." We must work to ensure that Soviet leaders will have good reason to take these words as seriously as Gorbachev took Reagan's comments about me in Geneva.

The night I arrived in Israel I spoke with President Reagan on the telephone. When reporters asked me why I was so calm at that moment, I told them the truth: "What could possibly add to my excitement on the day I left prison, saw Avital, and flew with her to Israel?"

I felt that way for months—that never again could I experience that marvelous sense of excitement. But then I became a father. When they brought me our baby, the first girl to be born to the Sharansky family in four generations, I was thrilled beyond words. As I tried not to cry my daughter looked up at me with an ironic smile, as if to say, "Don't be too serious, Papa." She's my daughter, after all. She's also the most beautiful girl I've ever seen.

I ran home to call my friends with the good news. But even before I picked up the phone, I heard on the radio that Avital and Natan Sharansky had a baby girl. When I returned to the hospital I was besieged by correspondents, all of whom wanted a photo of our baby, which I would not permit. The following day I attended a *brit milah,* a circumcision ceremony for the eight-day-old son of my friend Mark Nashpitz, and the next morning the papers ran pictures of me holding the baby, as if he were my own.

We called our daughter Rachel. I chose the name because the biblical Jacob worked fourteen years for his Rachel, while Avital and I had waited almost as long for ours. Avital liked the name because in Jewish tradition the matriarch Rachel symbolizes the ingathering of the exiles.

In freedom, I am lost in a myriad of choices. When I walk on the street, dozens of cheeses, fruits, and juices stare at me from store windows. There are vegetables here I'd never seen or heard of, and an endless series of decisions that must be made: What to drink in the morning, coffee or tea? What newspaper to read? What to do in the evening? Where to go for the Sabbath? Which friends to visit?

In the punishment cell, life was much simpler. Every day brought only one choice: good or evil, white or black, saying yes or no to the KGB. Moreover, I had all the time I needed to think about these choices, to concentrate on the most fundamental problems of existence, to test myself in fear, in hope, in belief, in love. And now, lost in thousands of mundane choices, I suddenly realize that there's no time to reflect on the bigger questions. How to enjoy the vivid colors of freedom without losing the existential depth I felt in prison? How to absorb the many sounds of freedom without allowing them to jam the stirring call of the shofar that I heard so clearly in the punishment cell? And, most important, how, in all these thousands of meetings, handshakes, interviews, and speeches, to retain that unique feeling of the interconnection of human souls which I discovered in the Gulag? These are the questions I must answer in my new life, which is only beginning.

Now, sitting on our balcony with Avital and Rachel, enjoying the beauty of Jerusalem and the warmth of an Israeli winter, I'm thinking about the past and wondering about the future as I ponder the many choices in this new life. Mama is nearby with her own decisions to make. Sasha Lunts has been coming to us every two weeks to take pictures of Rachel, and Mama is busy sorting through hundreds of photographs, trying to select one to send to Major Osin, the head of Perm 35. This is how she settles her account with the past.

Acknowledgments

You can't write memoirs in a Soviet prison, so for this book to be written I first had to be released. But to acknowledge by name everyone who helped me win my freedom is clearly impossible. They know who they are, and the gratitude I owe them.

I wrote this book while settling into a new life, learning how to be a husband and father, and continuing my struggle for those I left behind. It took considerable effort and time to relive my years of imprisonment, and I required a great deal of assistance.

In 1976, in Moscow, I met Robert Bernstein, chairman of the board of Random House, on a trip that led to his deep involvement in human rights. He became the founder of the Helsinki Watch in America, so it was only natural that Bernstein should be the publisher of this book.

Peter Osnos, my old-time accomplice in Moscow, turned from the job of correspondent of the *Washington Post* to that of associate publisher of Random House in order to continue our criminal collaboration, which in the past was so much appreciated by the KGB. His enthusiasm from the very beginning was the driving force of the project, so all its failures are his.

My literary agent is Marvin Josephson, head of International Creative Management, who shares with me a love for Israel and its people, and who guided me through the realities of capitalism while becoming my good friend.

Stefani Hoffman managed to efficiently translate my text almost faster than I wrote it; such devotion made it feasible to speed this complicated project along.

William Novak, who worked closely with me on later drafts, nearly convinced me that it was possible to say as much in six hundred pages of manuscript as in a thousand. His intelligent and sympathetic questions helped close the gap between the culture I came from and the one in which my book was written.

A special thanks for Ari Weiss, who for many years of Avital's struggle was anchor and coordinator of her efforts on Capitol Hill in Washington. He moved to Jerusalem and became my close friend, my counselor, and my lawyer.

Esther Lomovsky had the extraordinarily difficult task, after first grappling with my handwriting and dictation, of typing the manuscript in Russian. She performed with skill, speed, and cheerfulness.

A number of people read part or all of the manuscript along the way, and I am grateful for their advice, as well as for the excellent work of the staff of Random House.

But most of all, my thanks to Avital, who, after all those years of life as the wife of a prisoner, had to endure another two years as the wife of an author.

Index